CLASSICAL BUDDHISM, NEO-BUDDHISM AND THE QUESTION OF CASTE

This book examines the interface between Buddhism and the caste system in India. It discusses how Buddhism in different stages, from its early period to contemporary forms—Theravāda, Mahāyāna, Tantrayāna and Navayāna—dealt with the question of caste. It also traces the intersections between the problem of caste with those of class and gender. The volume reflects on the interaction between Hinduism and Buddhism: it looks at critiques of caste in the classical Buddhist tradition while simultaneously drawing attention to the radical challenge posed by Dr B. R. Ambedkar's Navayāna Buddhism or neo-Buddhism. The essays in the book further compare approaches to varṇa and caste developed by modern thinkers such as M. K. Gandhi and S. Radhakrishnan with Ambedkar's criticisms and his departures from mainstream appraisals.

With its interdisciplinary methodology, combining insights from literature, philosophy, political science and sociology, the volume explores contemporary critiques of caste from the perspective of Buddhism and its historical context. By analyzing religion through the lens of caste and gender, it also forays into the complex relationship between religion and politics, while offering a rigorous study of the textual tradition of Buddhism in India. This book will be useful to scholars and researchers of Indian philosophy, Buddhist studies, Indology, literature (especially Sanskrit and Pāli), exclusion and discrimination studies, history, political studies, women studies, sociology, and South Asian studies.

Pradeep P. Gokhale is Honorary Adjunct Professor at the Department of Pali, Savitribai Phule Pune University, Pune, India. He has 31 years of postgraduate teaching and research experience in Philosophy at Savitribai Phule Pune University, and was the Dr B. R. Ambedkar Research Professor at the Central Institute of Higher Tibetan Studies, Sarnath (Varanasi) for six years. He has written in diverse areas such as Indian epistemology and logic; the schools of classical Indian philosophy such as Buddhism, Lokāyata, Yoga and Jainism; Indian moral and social philosophy; Indian philosophy of religion; contemporary Buddhism and Ambedkar studies. His research interests have focused on the interface between orthodox and heterodox Indian thought, including between Nyāya and Buddhist logical thought. His published works include *Inference and Fallacies Discussed in Ancient Indian Logic with Special Reference to Nyāya and Buddhism* (1992) and *Lokāyata/Cārvāka: A Philosophical Inquiry* (2015), apart from six books in Marathi and the edited volume *The Philosophy of Dr. B. R. Ambedkar* (2008).

CLASSICAL BUDDHISM, NEO-BUDDHISM AND THE QUESTION OF CASTE

Edited by
Pradeep P. Gokhale

Routledge
Taylor & Francis Group
LONDON AND NEW YORK

First published 2021
by Routledge
2 Park Square, Milton Park, Abingdon, Oxon OX14 4RN

and by Routledge
52 Vanderbilt Avenue, New York, NY 10017

Routledge is an imprint of the Taylor & Francis Group, an informa business

British Library Cataloguing-in-Publication Data
A catalogue record for this book is available from the British Library

Library of Congress Cataloging-in-Publication Data
A catalog record has been requested for this book

ISBN: 978-0-8153-8167-9 (hbk)
ISBN: 978-1-003-04509-0 (ebk)

Typeset in Sabon
by codeMantra

CONTENTS

List of contributors ix
Note on transliteration xiii
Foreword: Caste in classical and contemporary Buddhism xv
GAIL OMVEDT

Acknowledgements xix

Introduction 1
PRADEEP P. GOKHALE

PART I
Classical Buddhism and caste 27

1 **Buddha's attitude towards the caste system as available in Pāli texts** 29
BIMALENDRA KUMAR

2 **Caste in classical Indian philosophy: some ontological problems** 40
PRABAL KUMAR SEN

3 **Epistemological foundations of caste identities: a review of Buddhist critique of classical orthodox Indian realism** 65
AJAY VERMA

4 **Casting away the caste: a Buddhist standpoint in the *Vimalaprabhā* commentary on the *Kālacakra* tantra** 77
SHRIKANT BAHULKAR

CONTENTS

PART II
Neo-Buddhism: Ambedkar on caste, class and gender 85

5 Buddha and Ambedkar on caste: a comparative overview 87
MAHESH A. DEOKAR

6 Neo-Buddhism, Marxism and the caste question in India 111
GOPAL GURU

7 Ambedkar's critique of patriarchy: interrogating at intersection of caste and gender 127
PRATIMA PARDESHI

PART III
Hinduism and Buddhism: interaction, conflict and beyond 149

8 Buddhism and Hindu society: some observations from medieval Marathi literature 151
SHRIKANT BAHULKAR

9 The Buddhist past as a cultural conflict: Ambedkar's exhumation of Indian history 161
UMESH BAGADE

10 Gandhi and Ambedkar on caste 178
VALERIAN RODRIGUES

PART IV
Religion, modernity and Navayāna Buddhism 209

11 Social solidarity or individual perfection: conceptions of religion in Ambedkar and Radhakrishnan 211
KANCHANA MAHADEVAN

12 Religion, caste and modernity: Ambedkar's reconstruction of Buddhism 233
P. KESAVA KUMAR

13 **Ambedkar and modern Buddhism: continuity and discontinuity** 257
PRADEEP P. GOKHALE

Appendix I: Vajrasūci 275
SANGHASEN SINGH

Appendix II: Vajrasūci *and its reverberations* 287
R. C. DHERE

Index 295

CONTRIBUTORS

Umesh Bagade is a professor in the Department of History and Ancient Indian Culture, Dr Babasaheb Ambedkar Marathwada University, Aurangabad, India. His authored books include *Reform Movement of Maharashtra and Caste-Class Hegemony* (Marathi) (2006) and *Dr. Ambedkar's Historical Method* (2015). The areas of his research and teaching interest are the history of anti-caste movements, the intellectual and social history of modern Maharashtra, historiography, studies of caste economy and the history of caste and gender.

Shrikant Bahulkar is the Director of Academic Development Programme at the Bhandarkar Oriental Research Institute, Pune, and Adjunct Professor at the Savitribai Phule Pune University, India. He has authored *Medical Ritual in the Atharvaveda Tradition* (1994) and has critically edited Sanskrit and Tibetan Buddhist Tantra works. He has held visiting academic positions in universities in Toronto, Kanazawa, Tel Aviv, Oxford and Harvard. His research areas include Vedic studies, the Atharvaveda ritual, Buddhist Studies, Buddhist Hybrid Sanskrit, Buddhist Tantric language and literature, Ayurveda and classical Sanskrit literature.

Mahesh A. Deokar is Professor and Head of the Departments of Pāli and of Buddhist Studies and the Dr Ambedkar Thoughts of the Savitribai Phule Pune University, India. He is an Editor with *Studia Indo-Buddhica* and the Chief Editor of Pune Indological Series. He is the author of *Technical Terms and Technique of the Pāli and the Sanskrit Grammars* (2008) and many research articles. The areas of his research interest include Pāli literature, grammar and different dimensions of Buddhist Studies.

R. C. Dhere (Ramchandra Chintaman Dhere: 1930–2016), holder of a PhD and two D.Lit degrees and the recipient of many other honours and awards including the Sahitya Academy Award, was an independent researcher in the areas of social history, sacred geography, theogony, saint literature, folklore, folk culture, Indology and archaeology. His scholarly works are in Marathi and include 'History of Nath cult' (*Nath*

Sampradayacha Itihaas), 'History of Dutta Cult' (*Dutta Sampradayacha Itihaas*), *Lajjagauri*, *Khandoba*, and 'In Search of Indian Theatre' (*Bharatiya Rangbhoomichya Shodhat*).

Gopal Guru, formerly Professor of Social and Political Theory at Jawaharlal Nehru University, New Delhi, India, has been the Editor of *Economic and Political Weekly* since January 2018. He co-authored with Sundar Sarukkai *The Cracked Mirror: An Indian Debate on Experience and Theory* (2012) and *Experience, Caste and Everyday Social* (2019). He edited *Humiliation Claims and Context* (2011) and authored *Varchasva Ani Samajik Chikitsa* (Marathi) (2015). His areas of research interest are Indian political thought, humiliation and social movements.

Bimalendra Kumar is Professor and Head of the Department of Pāli & Buddhist Studies, Banaras Hindu University, Varanasi, India. He has been Editor of *Mahabodhi* and *Dharmadoot,* the Mahabodhi Society journals published from Kolkata and Sarnath, respectively. Classical works critically edited by him include *Meghadūta (Tibetan and Sanskrit)* (2011) and *Bhesajjamañjūsā* 1–18 *Paddhati* (Devanagari Edition) (2015). He has edited several anthologies and contributed to many research articles. His areas of research interest are Pāli, Theravada Buddhism, Buddhist philosophy (Abhidhamma philosophy) and Tibetan Buddhism.

P. Kesava Kumar is a professor in the Department of Philosophy, University of Delhi, India. Books authored by him include *Political Philosophy of Ambedkar: An Inquiry into the Theoretical Foundations of the Dalit Movement* (2014) and *Jiddu Krishnamurti: A Critical Study of Tradition and Revolution* (2015). The areas of his research interest are social and political philosophy, critical philosophical traditions of India, contemporary Indian philosophy, continental philosophy and Dalit studies.

Kanchana Mahadevan is a professor at the Department of Philosophy, University of Mumbai, India. She teaches and researches in feminist philosophy, decolonization, critical theory, political thought, aesthetics and film. Her book *Between Femininity and Feminism: Colonial and Postcolonial Perspectives on Care* (2014) examines the relevance of Western feminist philosophy in the Indian context. She is currently working on the relationship between the secular and the post-secular with reference to gender.

Gail Omvedt is the former Chair Professor for the Dr B.R. Ambedkar Chair of Social Change and Development at Indira Gandhi National Open University, Delhi, India. Books authored by her include *Cultural Revolt in a Colonial Society: The Non-Brahman Movement in Western India* (1976); *Buddhism in India: Challenging Brahmanism and Caste* (2003); and *Understanding Caste: From Buddha to Ambedkar and Beyond* (2011). Currently, she holds an ICSSR National Fellowship on the *bhakti* movement. She has been a consultant for UN agencies and NGOs, and has served as a visiting faculty and fellow in various universities and research institutes.

Pratima Pardeshi teaches Political Science in Jedhe College of Arts and Commerce, Pune, India. She is the author of *Dr. Ambedkar aani Streemukti* (Marathi), the translation of which was subsequently published as *Dr. Babasaheb Ambedkar and the Question of Women's Liberation in India* (1998). She is the editor of *Prabuddha Bharat*. She is engaged in academic and political interventions in Dalit Adivasi movements in Maharashtra.

Valerian Rodrigues is a former professor of Political Science, Mangalore University and then Jawaharlal Nehru University, New Delhi, India. He has held positions such as ICCR Chair, Erfurt University (Germany), Ambedkar Chair, Ambedkar University (Delhi) and Visiting Professor, Simon Fraser Vancouver, Canada. He has edited *B.R. Ambedkar: Essential Writings*, (2002) and *Conversations with Ambedkar: 10 Ambedkar Memorial Lectures* (2019). His research interests include political philosophy, political ideas and institutions in India, disadvantage, marginality and preferential public policies.

Prabal Kumar Sen is a former professor of Philosophy at Calcutta University and is an Honorary Research Professor at the Centre for Ideological Studies and Research, Ramakrishna Mission Institute of Culture, Kolkata, India. His research publications include a translation of a part of the *Nyāyamañjarī* by Jayanta Bhatta, the first editions of three Nyāya texts as well as numerous articles in anthologies and national and international journals of philosophy. His research interests comprise different schools in Indian philosophy.

Sanghasen Singh is a former professor of Sanskrit and Pāli at the Department of Buddhist Studies, University of Delhi, Delhi, India. Books authored by him include *A Study of the Sphuṭārthā Śrīghanācārasaṅgrahaṭīkā* (1983). His edited works include *Ambedkar on Buddhist Conversion and Its Impact*; *Buddhism in Comparative Light* and *Aśokābhyudayakāvyam*. He is a recipient of the Certificate of Honour awarded by the President of India (2001). His major area of research interest has been Buddhist Studies.

Ajay Verma is an associate professor at the Centre for Philosophy, Jawaharlal Nehru University, New Delhi, India. His areas of interest include classical Indian philosophy, continental philosophy, comparative philosophy, Ambedkar studies and philosophy of religion. He is the co-editor of *Dr. Ambedkar's Buddha and His Dhamma: A Critical Edition* (2011). His current interests include rereading the question of identity while taking perspectives from classical Indian philosophy.

NOTE ON TRANSLITERATION

Many terms and expressions in Sanskrit and Pāli are used in the Introduction and Chapters 1–5 and 8, as well as in Appendices I and II. Sanskrit and Pāli expressions are presented in Roman script with diacritical marks. The following table can be used for reading Romanized Sanskrit or Pāli expressions:

Aids to Reading Romanised Sanskrit or Pāli

Roman letters (with diacritical marks) standing for Devanāgarī letters

Romanisation	*Devanāgarī*	*Romanisation*	*Devanāgarī*	*Romanisation*	*Devanāgarī*
A, a	अ	Ḥ, ḥ	ः	P, p	प
Ā, ā	आ	I, i	इ	Ph, ph	फ
Ai, ai	ऐ	Ī, ī	ई	R, r	र
Au, au	औ	J, j	ज	Ṛ, ṛ	ऋ
B, b	ब	Jh, jh	झ	Ṝ, ṝ	ॠ
Bh, bh	भ	K, k	क	S, s	स
C, c	च	Kh, kh	ख	Ś, ś	श
Ch, ch	छ	L, l	ल	Ṣ, ṣ	ष
D, d	द	ḷ	ऌ	T, t	त
Dh, dh	ध	M, m	म	Th, th	थ
ḍ	ड	Ṃ, ṃ	ं	ṭ	ट
ḍh	ढ	N, n	न	ṭh	ठ
E, e	ए	Ṅ, ṅ	ङ	U, u	उ
G, g	ग	Ṇ, ṇ	ण	Ū ū	ऊ
Gh, gh	घ	Ñ, ñ	ञ	V, v	व
H, h	ह	O, o	ओ	Y, y	य

In other chapters, words such as the following are used without diacritical marks and are spelt differently: varna, jati, brahmana, kshatriya, vaishya, shudra, atishudra and chandala.

NOTE ON TRANSLITERATION

Sanskrit and Pāli words and quotations are generally italicised except in the following cases:

1 Proper names of persons (e.g., Śaṅkara, Dharmakīrti), religious cults (e.g., Theravāda, Mahāyāna) and philosophical systems (e.g., Sāṅkhya, Yogācāra) are not italicised.
2 The following words are not italicised in this book because of their frequent usage: varṇa, brāhmaṇa, kṣtriya, vaiśya, śūdra, atiśūdra and caṇḍāla

FOREWORD

Caste in classical and contemporary Buddhism

Gail Omvedt

Classical Buddhism

In classical Buddhism there is a fairly clear denial of caste. We can give one example from the *Sutta Nipāta*, in *Sutta 9*, on "What is a brahmin?" It starts when two young brahmins, Vasettha and Bharadvaja, were having a dispute over what makes a brahmin—was it purity of descent for seven generations on both sides, as Bharadvaja contended, or virtue and moral conduct, as Vasettha said?

The Buddha responds by saying that "diverse breeds" exist among grass, tress, insects, various creatures and birds, but among "men alone" this is not true.

> They differ not in hair, head, ears, or eyes,
> in mouth or nostrils, not in eyebrows, lips,
> throat, shoulders, belly, buttocks, back, or chest,
> nor in the parts of shame, female or male,
> nor yet in hands or feet, in fingers, nails,
> in calves or thighs; in hue, or sound of voice; –
> naught shows men stamped by nature diverse breeds.
>
> (606–10)

He then goes on to say that a person is what he/she does.

> "The man that lives by keeping herds of cows –
> know him as farmer, not as Brahmin true.
> The man that lives by diverse handicrafts –
> know him as tradesman, not as Brahmin true.
> The man that lives by selling merchandise –
> know him as merchant, not as Brahmin true.
>
> (613–6)

And so on: the man living by arms is a soldier, the man living by sacrificial rites is a priest, the man supported by realms is a monarch. "Not birth, nor parentage a Brahmin makes....True Brahmin call I him, who shackle-free, by bonds and ties untroubled, lives his life" (621). Gotama goes on to describe almost lyrically the nonviolence, calmness, gentleness, lack of lustfulness of the brahmin, who is free from sorrow, has no longings left, has "passed away" and will face no further rebirth: the brahmin is the true Arahat. The Sutta ends with both Bharadvaja and Vasettha asking to become disciples.

This text shows the classical Buddhist strategy towards Brahmanism—redefine it. Accept the superiority of brahmins, but define them so that whoever shows such traits is a "brahmin"; the criterion of birth is removed. As a strategy, it was long lasting but in the end seems to have been ineffective. Brahmins kept their superiority and the "birth brahmin" remained the archetype.

The other classical text of Buddhist anti-caste sentiment is the *Vajrasūci* of Ashvaghosh. This also focused on the theme of "what is a brahmin?" It was scornful about brahmins in many ways, and rejects the idea that brahmin-hood comes through birth or knowledge. It denies the claim that the only duty of shudras is to serve brahmins. Instead, avoidance of sin, purity of life is what makes a brahmin. Birth is not the cause of brahmin-hood; people born of different castes like Vyasa and Vasishtha have become brahmins. There are no basic distinctions among human beings; there is only one caste, not four (Brahmin, kshatriya, vaishya, shudra). "The caste is not seen. It is good qualities that are the source of good. It is he whose life is for the Law, whose life is for others, who practices tolerance day and night, is recognized as brahmin by the gods.....Nonviolence, selflessness, abstinence from actions that are not approved, and detachment from lust and hatred are the characteristics of a brahmin" (45–7).

The *Vajrasūci* survived through the ages; there is a story that Tukaram, the great Marathi saint-poet of the 17th century, asked his disciple Bahenabai to translate it into Marathi, which she did. Regarding Bahenabai's *Vajrasuci*, the following comments can be made (references are to Abbott 1985):

Bahenabai's *Vajrasūci* is also centred on the theme of "What makes a brahmin?" However, it is prefaced by several stanzas on the superiority of brahmin, which were not seen in the original. Then she asks, "But who in reality is to be called a brahmin?" Birth does not determine brahmin-hood, neither does bodily form, nor colour, nor caste. Mere learning does not count, nor do "mere duties," nor "religious duties" (413–20, p. 126–9). Then she goes into the familiar themes that a brahmin is freed from illusion, grief, hunger, thirst, decay and death. Here there is something very Brahmanical in Bahenabai's version. "One who knows Brahma is called a Brāhmaṇa," who has experienced "Brahma," "made one the individual and the universal soul" (435, p. 134). But this is contrary to Buddhism, which holds to *anattā*, the denial of the "*ātman*." We should conclude that if the original *Vajrasūci* survived, it was heavily contaminated by Brahmanical ideas by the time of Bahenabai! This can be considered a paradigm for the "survival" of Buddhism in India—co-opted by Brahmanism, transformed and distorted.

Contemporary Buddhism

A new era of contemporary Buddhism begins with Dr. Babasaheb Ambedkar. "Classical" Buddhism of course still exists in most countries with large Buddhist populations. But in India, where Buddhism had almost completely disappeared, it was revived but in a new form with Ambedkar's "Navayana" Buddhism.

Navayana gave a new meaning to Buddhism. In his introduction to *The Buddha and His Dhamma*, Ambedkar makes it clear that he rejects four crucial elements of classical Buddhism. One is the idea of *sabbam dukkham*, "all is sorrow." "If this is true there is no way out." In fact, Buddhism does not really say that "all is sorrow," only that there is *dukkha*, and it can be overcome. Second, he rejects the notion of *karma* and transmigration or rebirth; he prefers to reinterpret *karma* to have the meaning of social causation and also perhaps genetical inheritance (in this he follows the earlier re-interpreter and reviver of Buddhism, Pandit Iyothee Thass). Third, he refutes the idea that Buddha renounced the world after seeing an old man, a sick man and a dead man, instead arguing that he was trying to avoid a conflict over water between the Koliya and Śākya clans. Finally, he rejects the notion of the Sangha as a society of world renouncers; he would prefer to have it as a kind of social service league.

This leads to the development of a rationalistic, even "materialistic," form of Buddhism. Contemporary Buddhism, Ambedkar's Navayana Buddhism, is resolutely anti-caste. His theme is the annihilation of caste; he does not want simply to analyse it but to destroy it. Caste, according to Ambedkar, is the bane of Indian society: it erects barriers between human beings, weakens solidarity and any ability to resist oppression; it is anti-national. Destroying caste must be done, first of all, by attacking its foundations—and these, Ambedkar believed, were found in Brahminic Hinduism. Thus destruction and renunciation of the sacred scriptures was a crucial task. Just as the Buddhist revolution and the revolution led by Guru Nanak had made possible political revolutions, so too a new anti-caste revolution must be found in the renunciation of Brahmanical Hinduism. Intermarriage was a factor, but it would follow most naturally on this foundation of a profound moral transformation.

He believed that Buddhism was, generally speaking, a materialistic philosophy; he saw it as helpful to abolition of exploitation. Conflicts today are because of caste and capitalist exploitation. In *Revolution and Counter-Revolution* he stressed a profound ongoing conflict between Brahmanism and Buddhism. He did not deal with the philosophy developed by later Buddhist scholars like Ashvaghosha. This is because contemporary neo-Buddhists are oriented in diverse directions such as meditation and philosophies for achieving nirvana. There are also differences among them regarding what Buddhist ideology means in practice. Thus, there is no foundation from what Babasaheb said; he did not have time to do this. Thus there is a great confusion in contemporary Navayana Buddhists in regard to the ideological aspects of Buddhism and practices to be followed. Babasaheb did not give concrete alternatives for the life ceremonies of birth, marriage, etc. Hence, for example, Buddhist marriages occurred on an ad hoc basis.

Annihilation of caste, then, was Babasaheb's goal. This also implies its possibility. The fact that caste can be overcome is founded in the historical reality that caste in India is not eternal nor even all that long lasting. Through all the millennia that Buddhism was hegemonic, the caste system was not a social reality in India. Instead, social organization was based on gahapatis, gaṇa sanghas, dāsa-kammakaras and so forth. True, the *Manusmriti* and *Arthashastra* were written during this period. But these were not descriptions of society; rather, they were prescriptions of what their Brahmanical authors saw as an ideal society. Caste itself was only firmly established at the social level after the defeat of Buddhism around the 6th century. After that, gradually the *jajmani* system came into existence and village-level social organization was solidified. But this makes caste, relatively, a recent historical phenomenon. Its different forms during modern times notwithstanding, it remains a strong factor.

Thus, the annihilation of caste is a real historical possibility, one that becomes more telling during our time. It requires, as Babasaheb emphasized in his *Annihilation of Caste*, a rejection of the Brahmanic Hindu scriptures; intermarriage taking place also helps weaken caste. Once we break the link between caste and occupation, caste is further weakened.

References

Abbott, Justine E. (1985): *Bahinabai: a translation of her autobiography and verses*, (Poona, 1929), Delhi: Motilal Banarsidass.

Ambedkar, B. R. (2014): "Annihilation of Caste," in Dr. *Babasaheb Ambedkar Writings and Speeches*, (BAWS), Vol.1, New Delhi: Dr. Ambedkar Foundation, Ministry of Social Justice and Empowerment, GOI.

Ambedkar, B. R. (2014): "Revolution and Counter-Revolution in Ancient India," in Dr. *Babasaheb Ambedkar Writings and Speeches*, (BAWS), Vol. 3, New Delhi: Dr. Ambedkar Foundation, Ministry of Social Justice and Empowerment, GOI.

Chalmers, Lord (Tr.). (2000): *Buddha's Teachings: Being the Sutta-Nipata or Discourse-Collection*, Vol. 37 of Harvard Oriental Series, Delhi: Motilal Banarsidass.

Mukhopadhyaya, Sujitkumar. (1950): *The Vajrasūcī of Aśvaghoṣa*, Sanskrit Text, (Sino-Indian Studies), Shantiniketan: Vishva-Bharati.

ACKNOWLEDGEMENTS

In 2013, while working as Dr. B. R. Ambedkar Research Professor at the Central Institute of Higher Tibetan Studies (CIHTS), Sarnath, I was also a member of the Indian Council of Philosophical Research (between 2012 and 2015). On the suggestion of a sub-committee of ICPR, which consisted of Professor Rakesh Chandra and Professor Gopal Guru, the Council assigned to me the task of organising a national seminar on a theme related to Buddhism and the question of caste. Hence an ICPR-sponsored seminar on "Classical Buddhism, Neo-Buddhism and the Question of Caste" was organised in association with CIHTS, Sarnath from October 3 to 5, 2013. I am grateful to both institutes for the help and cooperation I got from them in organising the seminar. I would like to specifically mention Prof. Mrinal Miri, Prof. Nirmalya Narayan Chakravarti and Dr. Mercy Helen from ICPR, and Prof. Ven. Ngawang Samten, Dr. Deoraj Singh and Dr. Penpa Dorjee from CIHTS, Sarnath, for their encouragement and help in conducting the seminar. The academic and social importance of the theme and contributions made by scholars stimulated me to take up the project of publishing this anthology based on the papers presented in the seminar. The paper presenters responded to my appeal positively and most of them also took pains to revise their papers in the light of the comments from the discussants, recent data and debates in the area. I am grateful to all the paper presenters whose contributions are included in this anthology. Professor Gail Omvedt had presented keynote in the seminar. I requested Prof. Omvedt to allow me to include her address as the Foreword of the anthology. I am grateful to her for her kind permission.

New essays on some topics needed to be invited in order to make the anthology comprehensive. Hence, I appealed to some scholars, who kindly came to my rescue. Professor Sanghasen Singh made his Hindi article on Vajrasūci available for translation. Dr. Aruna Dhere summarised her father's (Dr. R. C. Dhere's) work on Vajrasūci. I specially thank Professor Shrikant Bahulkar for his initiative in the latter. I am grateful to Dr. Pratima Pardeshi for contributing her paper on Ambedkar's analysis of gender and caste, and to Dr. Anagha Tambe and Dr. Swati Dehadrai for making it practically feasible.

I specially thank Prof. Kanchana Mahadevan for her advice and help in the task of editing. I always felt confident and comfortable in my work because of her initiative and participation.

Special mention should be made of Dr. Madhavi Narsale and Shri Prashant Talnikar for their translation work, as well as of Prof. Rucha Pawar for her valuable help by way of copy-editing and proof-reading.

Transcending caste identity and becoming a true human being has been the aspiration that has guided my life. This led to my participation in anti-caste and inter-caste activities in association with friends like Vilas Wagh, Tej Nivalikar, Pandit Vidyasagar, Sanjay Pawar and many others. On a personal note I should also mention Nandini, who, by marrying me, helped me become "inter-caste." These activities also had an intellectual dimension, which led to my interaction with Com. Sharad Patil, whose whole intellectual and socio-political life was aimed at abolishing varṇa, caste, class and subordination of women. In the early phase of his intellectual pursuits, Com. Patil called his position "Marx-Phule-Ambedkarism"; in the later phase he called it "Sautrāntika-Marxism." Both these phases were inspiring to me, though I differed with him on some points. All this is the background of my humble efforts of organising the above-mentioned seminar and editing this anthology.

Shashank Sinha of Routledge asked me to pursue the possibility of publishing the anthology through Routledge. Rimina Mohapatra of the Routledge team took special care in making the path smooth and easy. Special thanks are due to them.

Pradeep P. Gokhale

INTRODUCTION

Pradeep P. Gokhale[1]

It is generally admitted that Hindu society is "essentially" characterised by the stratification of its members on the basis of caste identification. There are hundreds of castes that are broadly grouped into five categories: the four varṇas, namely brāhmaṇa (priests), kṣatriya (warriors), vaiśya (farmers and business-persons) and śūdra (manual workers and scavengers), and atiśūdra (outcastes). The fifth class of atiśūdra was not given official status in the system of varṇas, and hence it was called the system of four varṇas (Cāturvarṇya). The division of Hindu society into the four varṇas gives a broad, rather simplistic formal framework, the contents of which were filled by hundreds of castes in reality. All these varṇas and castes played their role in the working of Hindu society.[2]

The varṇa-caste system was a system of distributing occupations among different strata of traditional society. It was a productive system because each caste was associated with some occupation related to maintaining traditional society. But the system also carried with it certain elements that rendered it an unjust, irrational and exploitative system. Some of these elements were as follows:

1 The varṇa-caste system divides society into groups of families. Such a society does not experience solidarity.
2 The varṇa-caste system creates a hierarchical division in which brāhmaṇas are at the top, while the atiśūdras such as caṇḍālas are at the bottom. Each intermediate varṇa/caste is inferior to some and superior to others. This inequality is supposed to be inborn and inviolable. Hence the principle of equality of humans qua humans is violated.[3]
3 The inequality among varṇas/castes is associated with the particular occupations assigned to them. There are prohibitions on leaving the occupation assigned to one's caste and adopting someone else's occupation, particularly that of a higher caste. Occupations were also ordered in terms of purity and impurity and respectability and otherwise. Hence certain castes were permanently condemned as impure and despicable, and certain castes were permanently honoured as pure

and respectable. The extreme purity and impurity attached to some castes led to the practice of untouchability, which is a great social evil. Untouchability was observed at two levels. Brahmins were untouchable to the "lower" castes for the former's alleged extreme purity. Śūdras and atiśūdras were untouchable to the "higher" castes for their alleged extreme impurity.

4 The varṇa-caste system puts restrictions on free association between members of different castes. Persons from lower caste positions were not even allowed to share seats in public places with those who occupied higher caste status. There was no permission to socialise, in either formal or informal ways, across caste hierarchy. Further, those from the lower tiers were not allowed to speak Sanskrit, as it was the prerogative of the higher castes. These restrictions were partly governed by ideas of purity and impurity that were highly irrational.

5 A basic form of prohibition on inter-caste association was that of inter-caste marriages. A general rule of marriage made by *Dharmaśāstra* was that one should marry within one's own varṇa and caste. Those who married outside the caste could not enjoy a respectable status in their own caste. Moreover, their children had to face serious social disadvantages. A child born from an inter-caste marriage was deprived of the caste status of both its father and mother. The situation was made more complicated and severe due to patriarchy. If in an inter-caste marriage the groom belonged to the higher caste, it was a lesser evil than if it were the other way around. The former type of marriage was called *anuloma* (along the stream) because it did not hamper the superiority of man, while the latter type was called *pratiloma* (against the stream) because it challenged the superiority of man. So the child born from *anuloma* marriage enjoyed an intermediate caste status, but the child born from *pratiloma* marriage was assigned a caste lower than that of both mother and father.

6 The so-called higher varṇas/castes were granted the possession of all types of wealth and powers.[4] The so-called lower varṇas/castes, particularly śūdras and atiśūdras, were supposedly born to serve other varṇas/castes and were deprived of possession of wealth and powers.[5] This led to different types of exploitation of the lower varṇas/castes by the upper varṇas/castes. This is how the system becomes essentially exploitative.

In spite of being an unjust and exploitative system, the varṇa-caste system was not felt to be so. This was for many reasons. One reason was that the inequality involved in the varṇa-caste system was not inequality pure and simple, but was what Ambedkar aptly described as "graded inequality."[6] Every caste fit somewhere in the scale of inequality such that even someone in a "lower" caste was superior to someone else in some respects (except the supposed "lowest" caste, namely the Caṇḍāla). Every caste has been associated with its distinctive customs, deities, forms of worship and lifestyle. Hence members, instead of feeling humiliated and isolated, take pride in their caste identities. Caste identity gives a certain status and stability to the members of the respective caste, insofar as they do not violate the rules imposed on the castes. Hence the traditional-minded members of Hindu society are not ready to leave their caste identity even if it is graded as "low." They believe that the caste identity is an inalienable part of their own identity. The rigidity of this is captured in the Marathi proverb, "*Jee jaat naahee tee jaat,*" translated as, "Caste is that which does not go."

The Hindu mind is closely attached to the caste system also because the latter has been justified in the religious faith of Hindus, particularly the faith in God and karma. The *Puruṣasūkta* of *Ṛgveda* describes the four varṇas as originating from different limbs of the grand Puruṣa (the Lord). The *Manusmṛti* associated the higher and lower status of varṇas with the higher and lower limbs of the Lord from which the respective varṇas originated and also with the order in which they were produced. Hence, in this view, the Brāhmaṇa caste is the highest because it is born from the uppermost part of the Lord's body and because it was born first (MS 1.92–3). The Śūdra caste is regarded as the lowest because it originated from the lowest part of the Lord's body and at the very end.[7] The divine origination of the unequal order of castes became a deep-rooted faith of the Hindus. This faith, because of its irrational character, was the target of the critical arguments made by rational- and egalitarian-minded Buddhists and other reformers.

The *Bhagavadgītā* too advocates the divine origin of the four varṇa system. There, Lord Krishna says that he created the system of four varṇas according to the division of qualities and actions.[8] This means that he created a system according to which a person born in a particular varṇa is naturally endowed with certain qualities (*guṇa*) suitable for the actions assigned to that specific varṇa. (It does not mean as is supposed sometimes, that humans are free to determine varṇas of individuals according to qualities and actions.) The term *guṇa* here could mean strands of Prakṛti as the Sāñkhya system understands it, and the term karma could mean the actions performed in past lives. In this sense brāhmaṇas are supposed to be born with *sattvaguṇa*, kṣatriyas and vaiśyas with *rajoguṇa* and śūdras with *tamoguṇa* as a result of their past karma.[9] Through this, Krishna in the *Gītā* introduces the notion of *sahaja-karma* (the action that gets assigned to one with one's birth) and says,

"Oh the son of Kuntī, one should not leave an action assigned by birth, even if it is defective. All activities are in fact surrounded by defects, like fire surrounded by smoke."[10]

The action assigned by birth is also supposed to be determined by one's essential nature (*svabhāva-niyataṁ karma*[11]). The idea that one's nature that is suitable for varṇa-specific actions is determined by birth is neither rationally nor historically acceptable. But this is a deep-rooted belief, often given in support of the birth-based varṇa-caste system.

The other religious faith given in support of this system is the doctrine of karma. The point may be made as follows: If God is the creator of the system of the four varṇas, then he can be blamed for being the creator of an unequal, unjust social order. This would imply that God is an evil-doer. To get rid of this problematic suggestion, Indian theists claim that caste-based inequalities are not caused by God, but by the actions performed by individuals in their past lives.[12] Hence, the unequal social order, which is apparently unjust and exploitative, becomes regarded as a just order because one's birth in a particular caste—which determines status in society— is regarded as the result of one's own past action. The doctrine of karma was in fact regarded as the stronger justification of the varṇa-caste order as it was accepted by the theist as well as atheist Brahmanical systems. Hierarchical social order is maintained through the mechanism of karma according to an orthodox Hindu, whether or not he or she believes in God. Birth in a particular varṇa was regarded as a "*gati*" (the species-status in which one is born) and the hierarchical order of the *gatis* was determined by using the parameters of the *Sāṅkhya* categories, *sattva*, *rajas* and *tamas*. Hence, we find the *Manusmṛti* suggesting a scale of nine categories, consisting of three major categories (Sāttvika, Rājasa and Tāmasa), each of which are further divided in to three subcategories: highest, middle and lowest.

If we designate the three major categories as S, R and T and the subcategories as 1, 2 and 3, then Manu's categorisation of different "species" including the varṇas can be given in tabular form as shown in Table 1.[13]

According to Manu's categorisation, the species-status of brāhmaṇas is S3 (lowest in Sāttvika category, but at par with ascetics, hermits, celestial troops, constellations and *daityas*[14]). The species status of śūdras on the other hand is T2 (the middle of the Tāmasa category, which is on par with animals, beasts, despicable persons and *mlecchas*). The status of kṣatriyas is R2 or the middle of the Rājasa category. Vaiśyas are missing in this categorisation, which could be Manu's oversight. But we can imagine that the species status of the vaiśyas must be T1 or R3. Each of these is a "*gati,*" or a position determined by past karma.

One claimed defence of the Brahmanical view of caste is that the latter does not support the superiority of brāhmaṇas purely on the basis of birth: If a person born as a brāhmaṇa does not perform the ascribed duties and maintain moral character, then he or she is only a "brāhmaṇa by birth" and not a real brāhmaṇa. A twofold answer can be given to this defence. One, there are statements available in *Dharmaśāstra* literature which say that a brāhmaṇa becomes superior to others by his birth itself.[15] Second, even if a person born brāhmaṇa is expected to perform

Table 1 Species status determined by past karma

*The species-status (*gati*) determined by birth*	*Species born with the respective status*
S1	Brahmā, Dharma of the creator, *Mahat* and *Avyakta* (*Prakṛti*)
S2	Brāhmaṇas who perform sacrifice, sages, gods, the Vedas, stars, years, ancestors and *sādhya*-deities
S3	Ascetics, hermits, **brāhmaṇas**, celestial troops, constellations and *daityas*
R1	Semi-gods like Gandharva, *guhyaka*, *yakṣa*, attendants of Gods and the celestial damsels
R2	Kings, **kṣatriyas**, royal priests and professional debaters
R3	Jhalla, Malla (mixed castes lower than kṣatriya), actors, weapon-sellers, gamblers and drunkards
T1	Wanderers (*cāraṇa*), eagles (*suparṇa*), hypocrites, demons (*rakṣas*) and ghosts
T2	Elephants, horses, **śūdras**, *mlecchhas*, despicable persons, lions, tigers and pigs
T3	Plants, germs, insects, fish, reptiles, tortoises, (other) animals and beasts

Source: Manusmṛti, 12.42–50.

the requisite duties (rendering his birth insufficient), birth still remains generally regarded as a necessary (though not sufficient) condition for being a true brāhmaṇa.[16]

Hence Hindu society—variously called Vedic, orthodox, Brahmanical and so on—advocated the hierarchical varṇa-caste system, supposedly created by God, based on birth and regulated by the past karma of the respective beings. Non-Vedic strands in Indian society were critical of caste-based division of society from the beginning. Hence, we find critical arguments against varṇa and caste among the three non-Vedic philosophical traditions: Lokāyata, Jainism and Buddhism. Lokāyata is opposed to caste because it accepts neither God nor karma. It is strongly critical of Brahmanical ritualism. But its criticism of caste is rather sketchy. The other two non-Vedic traditions, Jainism and Buddhism, are opposed to caste discrimination partly on similar grounds. Both are atheistic systems and hence oppose the divine origin explanation of the varṇa-caste system. Both are critical of birth-based discrimination and support the idea of superiority or inferiority based on actions and moral character. Both reject *Brāhmaṇatva-jāti* as an ontological entity.[17] Such similarities aside, Buddhism is more radical and elaborate than Jainism in its criticism of caste. For example, Jainism seems to accept the caste differences through its formulation of the doctrine of karma, as it acknowledges *gotrakarma* as a specific karma that determines one's birth in a particular caste. Though Buddhism too advocates the karma doctrine, it does not explain or justify caste differences in terms of it. Moreover, Jainism advocates non-violence in all realms including intellectual realm; because of this it sometimes has a relationship of compromising with Hinduism. On the other hand, because of its negation of soul and eternality, Buddhism stands in diametrical opposition to Hinduism.

This is not to say that Hinduism advocated the varṇa-caste system uncritically at all levels. Broadly speaking we can identify two distinct trends in Hinduism as religion. *Dharma*-oriented and liberation-oriented. By *dharma*, I mean the various socio-religious obligations prescribed in the *Dharmaśāstra* texts. These texts prescribe obligations specific to varṇa, caste, stage in life (*āśrama*), gender and so on. This gives us the structure of "specific obligations" (*viśeṣa-dharmas*). Apart from them, some common obligations (*sādhāraṇa-dharmas*), such as truthfulness, non-violence and non-stealing, applicable to all human beings qua human beings, are also prescribed. Though both these types of obligations are prescribed in these texts, specific obligations set the framework in which common obligations are followed. This gives subordinate status to common obligations as compared to specific obligations. And since the framework of specific obligations essentially involves the hierarchy among castes, domination and exploitation of the "lower castes" by the "upper castes," and also control over women by men, the *dharma*-oriented trend in Hinduism becomes essentially unjust and exploitative. In contrast, the liberation-oriented trend emphasises common obligations and at least temporarily releases the burden of specific obligations. For example, in the context of *jñānayoga* (the path of knowledge leading to liberation), it is held that since all *ātman*s are equal, they are identical with Brahman, and hence there is no inequality. Or in the context of *bhaktiyoga* (the path of devotion to God leading to liberation) it is held that, like upper-caste men, even vaiśyas, śūdras and women can attain liberation through devotion.[18] Hence, we have a tradition of saints in Hinduism who emphasise moral conduct and an egalitarian approach to all living beings, and who do not attach importance to inequalities related to caste and gender. The saint tradition has points of overlap, interaction and mutual influence with the Śramaṇa tradition, which mainly consisted of Buddhism and Jainism, whereas the ritualistic and non-egalitarian Brahmanical tradition was their common object of criticism.

However, due to the simultaneous presence of these two trends, the essence of the common Hindu psyche gets divided into the two influences: one non-egalitarian and the other egalitarian. This gives rise to a paradoxical situation. The god who has created the non-egalitarian framework of caste and gender is the same god who asks the Hindus to treat all living beings as equal in order to attain liberation. The paradox is sometimes resolved by accepting two levels of existence: ultimate or transcendental level on the one hand and practical-empirical level on the other. Equality or unity is accepted at the ultimate level, but denied at an empirical-practical level. Hence Śaṅkara in his commentary on *Brahmasūtra* describes the ultimate reality *Brahman* as devoid of the distinctions like brāhmaṇa and kṣatriya, but at the level of *vyavahāra* accepts Manu as authority and denies śūdras the right to study the Vedas.[19] Similarly, devotees belonging to a cult such as the Bhāgavata may temporarily forget caste discriminations in their devotional stance, but come back to their unequal status in their daily, practical life. Some saints tried to transcend the inequality even in practice. This led to the formation of new religious communities. The few examples of the latter include Guru Nanak, Basaveshvar and Narayanaguru. Their religious movements tended to create egalitarian alternatives to Brahmanical Hinduism, but their relation with Hinduism remained ambiguous, because they shared a common metaphysical foundation in Saguṇa or Nirguṇa Brahman with only a change in terminology.[20]

As compared to the above trends, Buddhism differs from Brahmanical Hinduism in both its metaphysics and its social-practical approach. Buddhism denies Brahman, God and *ātman*, which are core doctrines of Brahmanical Hinduism. Like in Advaita-Vedānta, we find a distinction between ultimate truth (*paramārtha*) and practical/conventional truth (*saṁvṛti-satya* or *vyavahāra*) in Buddhism also. But through this distinction Advaita-Vedānta tried to preserve the caste system at practical level. Buddhism, on the other hand, was also critical about birth-based inequalities of caste at practical/conventional level. This sharp contrast between Hinduism and Buddhism was probably one of the reasons why Babasaheb Ambedkar chose Buddhism when he was in search of an alternative to Hinduism within the Indian tradition—an alternative that could emancipate his "untouchable" followers from the clutches of caste.

Development of the theme

This anthology addresses the problem of the caste system as it was dealt with by Buddhism during its different stages, from Early Buddhism to Neo-Buddhism. "Neo-Buddhism," also termed "Navayāna Buddhism," refers to the Buddhist way of life as it was interpreted and professed by Dr. B. R. Ambedkar. The anthology focuses mainly on the stages and phases of Buddhism in India, occasionally referring to the modern multinational phenomenon called Engaged Buddhism in whose framework Neo-Buddhism can be situated.

Schools of Buddhism on caste

The term "Buddhism" itself has diverse interpretations. Though literally it refers to the way of life introduced and advocated by the Buddha, it is understood here that the Buddha's message and the way of life he advocated itself underwent different interpretations and formulations through the course of history, leading to diverse sects in Buddhism as a religion and diverse schools in Buddhism as a philosophy. In the ancient and medieval period, Buddhism as religion—as long as it was alive and influential in India—took three broad forms: Śrāvakayāna, Bodhisattvayāna and Tantrayāna.[21] Śrāvakayāna, also called Hīnayāna, includes Theravāda (whose literature is in the Pāli language) and the philosophical schools Vaibhāṣika and Sautrāntika. Bodhisattvayāna, called Mahāyāna, includes the philosophical schools Yogācāra and Madhyamaka. Tantrayāna, while regarded as a part of Mahāyāna, differs from mainstream Mahāyāna due to the former's special ritualistic practices and the method of transformation of passions into the Path. Though the three sects differ in their metaphysical views and spiritual practices, they share some common views. They believe in the impermanence and soullessness of all phenomena and are critical of the Brahmanical tradition, which supports sacrificial rituals and a hierarchical social structure based on the four varṇas and the caste system, governed by birth.

This anthology contains chapters pertaining to all the three forms of classical Buddhism. Bimalendra Kumar in Chapter 1 discusses the Buddha's attitude towards the caste system as found in Pāli texts. He brings out the Buddha's observation that the way there are different species among animals and plants with different bodily features, different varṇas and castes among humans cannot be called different species of human beings. He refers to the Buddha's declaration that "it is merely the empty sound that the brāhmaṇas are superior, others are inferior; Brāhamaṇas are of high caste, others are low caste." Actually speaking, "the people of all the four castes are equal and I see no difference in them." In fact the Buddha's mission, which results from his radical criticism of the caste system, was two-fold. He was a reformer of the society governed by Brahmanical religion, as well as the founder of a new religion in which caste had no place. Through constant dialogues with brāhmaṇas, he criticised the Vedic ritualism of sacrifices, challenged the claim of Upaniṣadic thinkers about realisation of ultimate reality (Brahman) and questioned the hierarchical social order governed by varṇa/caste, determined by birth and given divine sanction. Simultaneously he developed a theory and discipline of an alternative form of religious life and formed the religious organisation called Saṅgha, which provided for the moral-psychological and spiritual development of human beings. The Saṅgha was framed in such a way that it was a society of members free from caste identity. As Bimalendra Kumar refers to the Buddha's statement recorded in *Cullavagga:*

> Just as the great rivers, such as, the Gaṅgā, the Yamunā, the Acirāvatī, the Sarabhū and the Mahī, when they pour their waters into the Great Ocean, lose their names and origins and become the Great Ocean precisely so, you monks, do. These four castes—the

> Khattiya, the Brāhmaṇa, the Vessa and the Sudda—when they pass, according to the doctrine and discipline of the Tathāgata, from home to homelessness, lose their names and origins.

The above passage indicates how the Buddha, through Saṅgha, tried to establish an alternative culture of moral-seekers, based on egalitarian and democratic values. (Mahesh A. Deokar in Chapter 5 explains how the Buddha adopted certain safeguards and healthy practices to ensure that there was no discrimination against any member of his Saṅgha, and the feeling of solidarity and fraternity developed amongst them.)

After the Buddha, Buddhism underwent a schism and different stages of philosophical development and diversification. But the anti-caste spirit was maintained among the different sects and schools of Buddhism. Sometime around the beginning of the common era, we come across the formation of philosophical schools (*darśana*). Hence, the debate on caste is raised to ontological and epistemological level. *Vaiśeṣikasūtra* of Kaṇāda accepted *jāti* or *sāmānya* (universal) as a *padārtha* (ontological category). Nyāya-Vaiśeṣika philosophers accepted *brāhmaṇatva* etc. as kinds of *jātis*, thereby suggesting that the castes such as brāhmaṇa and kṣatriya have a well-defined and permanent ontological status. Kumārila-Bhaṭṭa, a Mīmāṁsā philosopher, joins Vaiśeṣikas in accepting *brāhmaṇatva*, etc. as eternal universals. In opposition to the Vaiśeṣīka and Bhāṭṭa-Mīmāṁsā view, which gives a permanent ontological status to universals (*sāmānya* or *jāti*) in general and the caste determining universals in particular, we have the Buddhist view developed by Diṅnāga and Dharmakīrti, according to which there are no eternal ontological entities called *sāmānya* or *jāti*. Prabal Kumar Sen discusses in Chapter 2, with many technical details, how different orthodox schools explained and defended brāhmaṇa-hood and other varṇa-identities by giving them the ontological status of universals (*sāmānya* or *jāti*). It also shows how Mahāyāna Buddhist philosophers like Dharmakīrti and Jaina philosophers like Prabhācandrasūri questioned this status given to caste-identities. Sen also refers to the egalitarian thoughts found in orthodox texts that deny rigid varṇa-identities based on birth.

Dharmakīrti's philosophical position has two faces: Sautrāntika and Yogācāra. Hence, he can be described as belonging to both the Śrāvakayāna and Mahāyāna Buddhist traditions. Ajay Verma in Chapter 3 regards Dharmakīrti as a Mahāyāna philosopher. But Verma's main point is not that Dharmakīrti was a Mahāyānist, but that he was anti-essentialist. Hence Verma focuses on the debate between Mahāyāna Buddhism and Nyāya as that between essentialism and anti-essentialism. Nyāya adherence to *jāti* at ontological level and the caste system at social level was a mark of its essentialism—which Mahāyāna Buddhism was fundamentally opposed to.

The third form of Buddhism that is important in the context of its criticism of caste is Tantrayāna. Shrikant Bahulkar in Chapter 4 discusses the anti-caste views expressed in *Vimalaprabhā*, a commentary on *Kālacakratantra*. He brings out how the *Vimalaprabhā* ridicules the religious explanation of the caste system and exposes its irrationality. He also refers to *Vimalaprabhā*'s criticism of the sacredness of the Sanskrit language.

In fact the justification of caste in the Brahmanical Hindu tradition does not come alone, it comes as a part of a package: the Vedas (either as eternal or as God's creation), God, karma (as the determiner of caste), the Smṛtis and the purity of Sanskrit language, the superiority of brāhmaṇas and the caste determined by birth—all these doctrines are interconnected and Buddhist thinkers criticise them all. This is true in both classical Buddhism and Neo-Buddhism.

Neo-Buddhism: Ambedkar on caste, class and gender

The anti-caste egalitarian thought of B. R. Ambedkar had a complex lineage: that of the thoughts of saints like Kabir, non-Brahmanical social reformers like Jotiba Phule and also the Buddha's life and mission, which was introduced to Ambedkar in his teenage years through a book gifted to him by his teacher, Mr. Keluskar.

Ambedkar's criticism of caste, however, was not just "religiously" oriented, but more so scientifically and philosophically. Mahesh A. Deokar, in Chapter 5, presents a comparative analysis of early-Buddhist and Ambedkarian approaches to the issue of caste. He points out that the Pāli *suttas* mention peculiar characteristics of the caste system such as endogamy, caste-based division of labour, graded inequality and the denial of the right to education to "lower" castes, but none of them attempt a formal definition of caste nor discuss its genesis and mechanism. Deokar discusses Ambedkar's treatment of caste as it has evolved from his three works, *Castes in India*, *Annihilation of Caste* and *The Buddha and His Dhamma*. He finds a strong connection between the Buddha and Ambedkar on the matter of refuting castes and on the remedy for overcoming it. He also points out an important difference between the two—while the Buddha's safeguards against inequality were only operational within the limits of his Saṅgha, Ambedkar extends them to all Indians by incorporating them into the Indian constitution.

Like caste, class too has been used to explain the stratification and hierarchical order in society. However, the two concepts are different. Though Ambedkar defined caste in terms of class, he also distinguished between them. As Gopal Guru clarifies in Chapter 6, India according to Ambedkar had a two-fold challenge before her: capitalism and Brahmanism. Naturally, the final goal was to create a classless and casteless society. Both these elements were relevant to Buddhism, according to him. The Buddha as depicted by Ambedkar was not only a critic of the caste system, but was also concerned with the problem of class conflict causing social suffering. Gopal Guru points out that the alienation of the proletariat and of untouchables are categorically of different natures. Ambedkar articulated a form of Buddhism that could combat both types of alienation. The Buddha of Ambedkar had an answer to Karl Marx in this sense.

Caste and gender are also closely connected issues. The status of a woman in Hindu society was regulated by her caste, and caste status of a child born from an inter-caste marriage was regulated by the relative caste-status of its mother in the family. Ambedkar in his writings brought out the relationship between caste and gender. As Pratima Pardeshi explores in Chapter 7, Ambedkar, through his anthropological study of caste, maintained that the basis of the caste system is "endogamy," which gives rise to the problems of surplus man and surplus woman within an endogamous group. Practices like *sati*, enforced widowhood, enforced celibacy and child marriage are attempted remedies to perpetuate endogamy and the caste system. Ambedkar, in this way, maintained that women are the gateways to the caste system. As Pardeshi argues, according to Ambedkar, though all women are exploited due by the patriarchy, they are not all exploited to the same degree. Dalit women are doubly exploited—both by the patriarchy as well as by caste. Ambedkar held that the Buddha paved the way for granting women status equivalent to that of men.

The impact of Buddhism on medieval India and the role of the Vajrasūci

On the way from Classical Buddhism to Neo-Buddhism, we come across an intermediate phenomenon, represented by the works like *Vajrasūci* and *Vajrasūci-upaniṣad*, as well other signs of the influence of Buddhism on Hinduism. *Vajrasūci* is an important text as it aims at refuting the caste ideology by advancing logical as well as scripture-based arguments. The author of the text is Aśvaghoṣa, which is the popular name of the 1st century author of poetic works such as *Buddhacarita* and *Saundarananda*. Hence, Sujitkumar Mukhopadhyay (who edited the text in 1949) argued that *Vajrasūci* must be from the same Aśvaghoṣa who authored *Buddhacarita*. This claim is debatable as, although the author of *Vajrasūci* starts by saluting Mañjughoṣa (a mark of the influence of Mahāyāna Buddhism), he starts his argument by accepting the authority of the Vedas and the Smṛtis, which is quite unlike a typical Buddhist author. So Sanghasen Singh argues in Appendix I (entitled "*Vajrasūci*") that the Aśvaghoṣa who authored *Vajrasūci* is not the same one who wrote *Buddhacarita*, but some later author named Siddhācārya Aśvaghoṣa, who probably lived in the 8th or 9th century. This Aśvaghoṣa must have been a spiritual master but not a thorough scholar of the Vedas, the Smṛtis and the *Mahābhārata*, which he regards as authorities. He must have had affinity for Buddhism, but must not have been a staunch Buddhist.

Whether *Vajrasūci* can be regarded as a purely Buddhist text or not, it can be said to reflect the overlap between the egalitarian trend in Hinduism, represented by saints and spiritual masters on one hand and the Buddhist tradition on the other. Even a Buddhist can appreciate the text, although it apparently accepts the Vedas and the Smṛtis as authority. He or she could say that the text in fact brings out the inconsistency in the Hindu tradition by showing that "authoritative scriptures" like the Vedas and the Smṛtis, which are supposed to strongly support the caste system, in fact contain many counter evidences. Morally and spiritually oriented members of Hinduism would also appreciate the text like this, as it supports an egalitarian approach within the framework of the Vedas and the Smṛtis. Hence, we find that an abridged and "edited" version of *Vajrasūci* acquired the status of an Upaniṣad and continued to inspire some Hindu saints and reformers in the medieval and modern periods. We get a picture of the impact of *Vajrasūci* on saints like Bahenabai and reformer-thinkers like Raja Rammohan Rai, Tukaram Tatya Padwal and V. D. Savarkar in Appendix II of this anthology, which is based on the study conducted by the late Marathi Indologist Ramchandra Chintaman Dhere.

Chapter 8 by Shrikant Bahulkar too records the influence of Buddhism on Hindu society. Hindu society considered the Buddha the ninth incarnation of Viṣṇu. The chapter indicates that in the Bhakti literature of medieval Maharashtra, this notion is reflected in two ways: first, the saint poets considered their God, Viṭṭhal or Viṭhobā, the Buddha—the ninth incarnation of Viṣṇu; and second, their teachings bear close similarity to the teachings of the Buddha and are said to have been influenced by Buddhist philosophy. The chapter observes that like the Bhakti movement in other parts of India, the Bhakti movement in Maharashtra was also anti-caste and anti-orthodox and opposed the authority of the Vedas, the sacrificial religion advocated by the Vedas and the ancient system of the *Varṇāśramadharma*.

After 12th century, India saw a decline in Buddhism. In this period that lasted about seven centuries, the egalitarian approach transcending caste discriminations in the spiritual realm was advocated by saints of different cults, in whose literature the indirect influence of Buddhism can be traced, through occasional references to Buddhist ideas and to the Buddha. Of course Buddhism must have formed a very small part of the source of egalitarian ideas available to Hindu saints in medieval India. Many Hindu saints came in contact with Islam and must have seen the possibility of religious life without a caste system, as available in Islamic culture. This gave rise to an equality between Hinduism and Islam at a spiritual level, reflected in the literature of the saints like Ekanath, Nanak and Kabir.

On the conflict between Brahmanism and Buddhism

Ambedkar situated his critique of caste as a part of the cultural history of India. As Umesh Bagade explains in Chapter 9, Ambedkar presented Indian history as that of cultural conflict between two forces: Brahmanical and Buddhist. According to Ambedkar, Brahmanism represented the coercive and hegemonic force of varṇa, caste and gender subordination, whereas Buddhism represented egalitarian spirit of liberty, equality and fraternity, incessantly acting as an ideological powerhouse of anti-caste rebellions. Revolution and counter-revolution are important categories in Ambedkar's articulation of Indian history. In his view, the condition of Brahmanism before the Buddha was that of utmost moral degradation. Against this, the Buddha's teaching proved to be a religious revolution, which posed a challenge to the infallibility of the Vedas, the Creator God and the eternal soul and the revision of regnant conceptions of *kamma*. It was also a social and political revolution exemplified by equal opportunity for low-caste individuals and women, as well as equal access to education. As a reaction to the Buddha's revolution, there was a counter-revolution launched by Brahmanism, marked by social processes turning varṇa into caste; indiscriminate coercion against Buddhism under the reign of Puṣyamitra Śunga; the channelization of rituals, beliefs and laws elevating the status of brahmins and prohibiting inter-dining and inter-caste marriages and the construction of an ideology that subordinated women.

Ambedkar's act of reviving Buddhism in India through mass conversion and his reinterpretation of the life and teachings of the Buddha can be deemed his attempt to revive the Buddha's revolution under modern conditions. Buddhism as adopted by Ambedkar does not remain Hīnayāna or Mahāyāna as understood by tradition, but becomes a part of "modern Buddhism." In order to distinguish the form of Buddhism he adopted from traditional Buddhism, Ambedkar agreed to the nomenclature "Navayāna," which is popularly translated as "Neo-Buddhism."

Critique of caste by saints, reformers and by Ambedkar

In the 19th and 20th centuries, India saw a period of revival, reformation and enlightenment influenced by the Enlightenment in Europe. In this spirit, there were attempts to interrogate and critique the caste system. Broadly speaking, we come across two types of reformist thinkers at this stage: Vedic and non-Vedic. Vedic reformer thinkers tried to trace anti-caste thinking in sources like the Vedas, Upaniṣads, the *Gītā*, Vedāntic philosophies and the literature of saints. However, critiques of caste based on Vedic tradition could not radically challenge the caste system, either because, by making a slippery distinction between varṇa and caste, it allowed caste to prevail through the back door; or because by restricting the scope of equality to the spiritual realm, it permitted inequalities to prevail in the social realm.

Some non-Brahmin reformer thinkers questioned the authority of the Vedas and the Smṛtis and traced egalitarian thoughts to non-Vedic sources. P. Kesav Kumar in Chapter 12 refers to non-Brahmin thinkers such as Jothibha Phule and Periyar, and also to Iyothee Thassar and Lakhmi Narasu of Madras presidency. Phule took inspiration for his anti-caste thinking from the views of Bṛhaspati (Cārvāka), the Buddha and also deism (as presented by Thomas Paine). He proposed the religion of Universal Truth (*sārvajanik satya dharma*). Periyar attacked Hinduism from an atheistic point by arguing the distinctiveness of Dravidian culture from the Brahmanical Aryan religion. Iyothee Thassar and Lakhmi Narasu invoked Buddhism against Hinduism.

A modern world view and modern values have posed a challenge for all religions. Naturally Buddhism, too, has to face this. Buddhist thinkers seem to have found this challenge comparatively easy because many core features of the religion were already modern in character. And though it did have some other-worldly and dogmatic features, they could be got rid of, or at least bracketed. The Buddha's own statements in *Kālāmasutta* reveal his insistence of not accepting anything on the basis of the so-called authority of a text or a person, but accepting or rejecting a view only on the basis of one's own experience and reason. Hence, we have secular forms of the Buddhist way of life advocated by some contemporary Buddhist thinkers and spiritual masters.[22]

However, it was not equally possible for reformers of other religions to secularise their religions. Here, however we are mainly concerned with the reformation of Hinduism vis-à-vis caste. We find that though 19th- and 20th-century Hindu thinkers and reformers do not advocate the traditional caste system in its rigid form, they did try to defend it in some way or the other. Some of them were radically critical of caste, but they were not influential enough to generate an anti-caste turn in Hinduism. A few models can be considered in this context:

A Vedāntic/spiritual/saintly model

According to this model, all living beings are of ātman-Brahman-nature and are, therefore, equal. Hence there were Hindu saints who were egalitarian at a spiritual level, though at a material and social level they generally compromised with caste. It is accepted under this model that one's spiritual point of view can have an impact on one's material life also. Hence, we have radical examples like Basaveshvar and Nanak whose egalitarian spiritual movements resulted in the formation of sects on the border of Hinduism or outside it. Narayanaguru was another example of someone opposed to caste in a spiritual as well as social, practical realm. Another example is Swami Vivekananda, who is known for his Practical Vedānta. Vivekananda was against untouchability but he was not opposed to the caste system as such. He believed that caste had a historical role to play and a historical purpose to serve: to transform all into brāhmaṇas.[23] Gandhi's critique of caste falls, to some extent, in the category advanced by saintly thinkers. Like them, Gandhi believed in the equality of all beings; so even if he accepted the varṇa system, he denied the hierarchy among varṇas. This brings him close to Ambedkar in terms of regarding equality a basic human value. Valerian Rodrigues, while giving a comparative account of the views of Gandhi and Ambedkar on caste in Chapter 10, refers to this similarity in terms of "equality as a value," while immediately pointing out the difference between the two figures in terms of "freedom as a value." Gandhi believed that the profession of a Hindu person may be determined by his varṇa, that is, by his birth, whereas Ambedkar believed that this takes away the freedom of a Hindu to choose their own profession. Rodrigues makes a significant observation:

> .... what Gandhi considered as the degeneration of Hinduism is seen by Ambedkar as its essential characteristics. For Ambedkar there cannot be an impulse for equality from within the central tenets and institutions of Hinduism. It can come only from a radical reorganisation of Hinduism or from outside it. To the contrary, Gandhi argued that the central tenets of Hinduism and its institutions uphold equality. Reforms are required to shed the dross, rather than reinvent Hinduism.

Rodrigues gives his comparative account impartially. He seems to leave the reader to make his or her own judgement.

B The model of distinguishing between varṇa and caste

Some Hindu reformer thinkers based their critiques of the caste system on the distinction between varṇa and caste. They held that the caste system, which originally had the nature of varṇa, was fine and just. It degenerated as caste system with untouchability as its extreme form, in later centuries. So Dayananda, the founder of Aryasamaj, held that, as the Vedas are the authority, varṇas are assigned according to qualities and actions, not birth. So he denied the caste system as it was practiced and tried to reduce it to a system of four varṇas. He accepted the hierarchy among varṇas but denied its birth-based character. As Deokar in chapter 5 points out, Ambedkar, in *Annihilation of Caste*, argues that organising a caste-ridden society into four varṇas is impractical.

Dayananda's approach can be compared with that of Gandhi, which are prima facie similar but fundamentally different. According to Gandhi, as Rodrigues points out, the law of varṇa means that everyone shall follow as a matter of *dharma*—duty—the hereditary calling of their forefathers insofar as it is consistent with fundamental ethics. Accordingly, a person earns his livelihood by following that calling. Hence, one's varṇa is determined by birth. But Gandhi did not accept hierarchy among varṇas as Dayananda did. Gandhi thought that the varṇa system itself does not contain the sense of "high" and "low," the caste system does.

It is important to note in this context that both Gandhi's and Ambedkar's approaches to the caste system underwent changes and development. Initially, Ambedkar tried to run the anti-caste movement as a Hindu reformer. He led movements like drinking water at Chavdar Lake and temple entry. When he realised futility of these, he argued that the caste system should be combatted with stronger remedies, like propagating inter-caste marriages and, more importantly, the rejection of *Dharmaśāstra* texts. Finally, since Hinduism was unable to implement such radical means to annihilate caste, Ambedkar left Hinduism and embraced Buddhism, which was essentially a casteless religion.

Gandhi was supporter of Hinduism (as he interpreted it), though he would treat it and other religions as equal. He was vehemently opposed to untouchability in all stages of his social career, though not equally opposed to caste. As Rodrigues records, Gandhi initially—that is, in 1922—defended the caste system. However, by the second half of that decade he had come to criticise caste. His initial acceptance of caste was based on his view that Hindu society was sustained by caste. His subsequent criticism of caste was based on his view that caste fundamentally involves the idea of "higher" and "lower." At the latter stage he accepted varṇa instead of caste. The four varṇas according to him were not hierarchical, but implied a division of labour determined by ancestral calling, that is, by birth. Varṇa in this sense carried at least one character of caste. Since the birth-based character of varṇa implied that marriages should take place within the same varṇa/caste, Gandhi regarded restricting marital relation to one's own caste to be naturally consistent with *varṇāśrama*.[24] His views on inter-caste marriage seem to have undergone a drastic change by 1946, when he appealed to all boys and girls seeking to get married and who belonged to the Congress party, not to get married in Sevagram Ashram unless one of the parties was a Harijan. He added, "I am convinced that there is no real difficulty in this. All that is needed is a change of outlook" (Bose 1972, 268). What change of outlook was Gandhi talking about? Does this imply that Gandhi's own outlook had changed? Had he left the position that marrying in one's own caste is naturally consistent with *varṇāśrama*?

Gandhi's new outlook seemed to bring him closer to Ambedkar's position in *Annihilation of Caste*. Ambedkar in this text proposed two means to annihilate caste: intermarriages and criticising religious texts. Gandhi at this late stage seems to have agreed to the first means, but seems to have remained as dogmatic as before with respect to the authority of religious texts. Of course, Gandhi was not of the view that religious scriptures should be followed blindly. He believed that the core teaching of all religious texts is truth and non-violence. And if there are statements inconsistent with this core then they should be treated as interpolations.

It is doubtful whether this hermeneutical approach of Gandhi is defensible. The authors of religious texts are, after all, human beings susceptible to error; it is not necessary to believe that they must be fully consistent in their views. To believe that religious texts/scriptures are fully consistent and authentic is a dogma—the dogma of authenticity (*prāmāṇya*). Gandhi first projects the doctrines of truth and non-violence as the core of given religious texts and then treats the statements in them inconsistent with the core as interpolations. This is just a case of the dogma of authenticity. Secondly, even if a given religious text contains principles like truth and non-violence, it is doubtful whether this is sufficient to regard the text as authentic. The question is about what place is given to the principles in the total scheme of the text. For example, in *Manusmṛti* these principles are included in the list of abridged obligations (*sāmāsika-dharma*).[25] But, as I have stated before, they are given subordinate status in the framework of the hierarchical system of specific obligations (*viśeṣadharma*) of varṇa, caste and gender. If one were to follow Gandhi's policy of interpretation, a major part of *Manusmṛti* would have to be discarded as interpolation in order to retain the authoritative character of the text. Instead, Ambedkar's policy was to dethrone such a text from its authentic status. This policy seems to be more reasonable.

Hence Ambedkar, in *Annihilation of Caste*, appealed to Hindus to make a radical decision to get rid of their anti-egalitarian *Dharmaśāstra* and adopt those texts that propagate values such as liberty, equality and fraternity. He also suggested that perhaps the Upaniṣads could be such a text.[26]

C Religion as personal and caste as social: the model of S. Radhakrishnan

S. Radhakrishnan was an important scholar of Indian philosophy, and a spokesman for Hinduism and Vedānta. His approach to caste was influenced by both the above models. As Mahadevan points out in Chapter 11, Radhakrishnan rejected the notion of caste determined by birth, and justified it as varṇa forming the basis of a graded social order united through a harmonious performance of diverse functions. This view is similar to that of Dayananda, who accepts hierarchy as natural diversity. On the other hand, Radhakrisnan upheld religion as an individual's inclination towards the spiritual, which is realized through human perfection. He seems to reconcile spirituality with caste through the Advaitic notion of "a common clay of human nature" that is nevertheless differentiated as "wise" and "foolish" or "high" and "low". Radhakrishnan's approach to religion and caste can be contrasted with that of Ambedkar. Ambedkar distinguished between religion and Dhamma (TBHD, IV.I.2), which was virtually the distinction between theistic religion and Dhamma (religion based on morality). In theistic religion, one's relationship with God is central and morality is secondary. In Dhamma, on the other hand, the egalitarian moral relationship of humans with other humans is essential. Religion as understood by Radhakrishnan was based on the God-human relation or *jīva*-Brahman relation, which can accommodate caste and inequality at a practical-social level.

D Rational critique of caste in the service of Hindu nationalism: V. D. Savarkar's model

V. D. Savarkar, a freedom fighter whose freedom movement aimed at a free Hindu Nation, believed that Hindus cannot be one nation unless they are free from caste division. In 1924, he was confined by the British government in Ratnagiri and, prohibited from performing political activities, he focused on social activities aimed at consolidating Hindu society by eradicating caste divisions among them. He was in Ratnagiri until 1937. During this period Savarkar wrote a number of essays he called "*Jatyucchedaka Nibandha*" (*Caste-eradicating Essays*).[27] In these, he criticised different prohibitive rules (Bandī) that banned the study of the Vedas by lower castes, touching other castes, accepting professions of other castes, co-dining and intermarriages. Interestingly, in one of his articles, he endorsed the position of Aśvaghoṣa's *Vajrasūci* by including his Marathi translation of the text in it (Savarkar 1964, 532–42).[28] At practical level he focused on arranging co-dining programs where all castes were involved. His approach was more rational as compared to the saintly/spiritualist approach of the first model and the traditionalist approach of the second model. Hence, we find Savarkar criticising traditionalism symbolised by the expression "*Śrutismṛtipurāṇokta*" (the authority of the Vedas, Smṛtis and Purāṇas) and propagating modernism symbolised by the expression "*adya-yāvat*" (up-to-date).[29] However, the limitation of Savarkar's anti-caste approach and modernism was that it was subservient to his main mission of making India an independent Hindu nation. It consisted of uniting Hindus by undermining their internal differences. His definition of Hindu neither implied freedom from the caste system nor an emphasis on rationality.[30]

Ambedkar's critique of caste stands out in comparison to all the above models. Unlike the first model, he was not criticising caste from a theist or idealistic point of view, but from a humanist perspective. Caste, according to him, was opposed to human integrity and dignity. Unlike the second model, he did not want to replace the caste system with a varṇa system, which too carried evil elements in his estimation. Unlike the third model, he did not regard religion as a personal affair, which would imply compromise with caste distinctions. And unlike the fourth model, his rational critique of caste was not aimed at the narrow goal of organising Hindus, but at reconstructing society on a foundation of universal values. The latter comprises liberty, equality, fraternity and justice.

Though Ambedkar did not rule out the theoretical possibility of Hindu society being reorganised on the basis of these universal values and becoming free from caste divisions, such a reorganisation involved drastic steps including abandoning the traditional rule-bound *Dharmaśāstra*. Such a step was empirically impossible for Hindu society in near future. Hence, abandoning their Hindu religious identity was inevitable for the downtrodden masses according to him. A study of religions informed Ambedkar's view that the Buddha's Dhamma was the best choice as it had universal morality and rationality at its core. It was the best religion not only for downtrodden Hindus but for humanity.

As mentioned before, Ambedkar's approach to the caste system underwent stages of change and development. He started as a Hindu reformer, but after realising the futility of the reform movement, declared that he would not remain a Hindu and finally embraced Buddhism, which he himself reinterpreted into a modern form. But in these phases of change there is also continuity. Even after he decided to abandon his Hindu identity, he did not cease to be a reformer of Hinduism. This is visible in his creation of the Hindu Code Bill, aimed at a progressive transformation of Hindu society. Ambedkar in this way played a dual role. As a reformer, he tried to free Hindu society from evils like the subordination of depressed castes and women; and, as the leader of Navayāna Buddhism, he tried to create an alternative to the caste-ridden Hinduism.

This duality resonates with the dual role played by the Buddha. A question is often asked about the Buddha as to whether he was a founder of a new religion or just a reformer of the existing Brahmanical religion. I have tried to argue elsewhere that the Buddha played a dual role. On one hand, he raised conflict with Brahmanical religion and suggested ways to reform it. On the other hand, he presented a picture of an alternative form of religious life that, according to him, was the ideal form.[31] Ambedkar, in this way, followed the legacy of the Buddha.

Neo-Buddhism as a form of modern Buddhism

As Kanchana Mahadevan highlights in Chapter 11, a modern advocate of religion and Vedāntic spirituality such as S. Radhakrishnan emphasises the need for religion and spirituality in the modern world against rival forces such as naturalistic atheism, agnosticism, scepticism, humanism, pragmatism and modernism. Radhakrishnan's conception of Hinduism was based on this model. Ambedkar's concept of ideal religion was based on his understanding of Buddhism, which in his view was consistent with modernity. As Mahadevan remarks (p. X), "Unlike Hinduism, Buddhism had the potential to be social and foreground the principles of liberty, equality and democracy, which were central to modernity." In this context, she brings out Ambedkar's resonance with Kant, who reconciled religious faith with reason and morality.

P. Kesava Kumar in Chapter 12 talks about multiple modernities. He distinguishes Dalit modernity from colonial modernity and Brahmanical modernity. Colonial modernity is an immediate reference point for other modernities. Exponents of Brahmanical modernity professed equality in the spiritual realm but did not extend it to the material realm. Dalit modernity professes equality based on human dignity and self-respect. Kesava Kumar argues that Ambedkar, like Dewey, looked for reasoned religion and in this way overcame the tradition-modernity dichotomy. For Ambedkar, Buddhism is not a religion of rituals but rather is rationalistic. Its morality is not derived from a supernatural source; it is "this-worldly." This is how Ambedkar constructs modern or Navayāna Buddhism.

Orthodox Buddhist critics of Ambedkar sometimes regard his reinterpretation of Buddhism—as a religion characterised by scientific rationality, secular morality, democracy, socialism and gender equality—as inauthentic or non-Buddhist. I have argued in Chapter 13 that Buddhism already had these progressive elements and Ambedkar was not the only one to notice this. I have tried to show that many Buddhist thinkers and spiritual leaders of the 19th and 20th centuries have underlined the above elements in Buddhism and Ambedkar continues this prevailing trend. Where Ambedkar becomes distinct from other modern, engaged Buddhists is in his emphasis of the anti-caste approach of Buddhism. In Ambedkar's image, the Buddha was essentially a critic of Brahmanism in general and of the caste system in particular.

Chapter scheme: a sketch

This work is a multidisciplinary anthology on Buddhism and caste. The contributors belong to different disciplines: literature (Sanskrit, Pāli), philosophy, Indology, Buddhist studies, history, political science, women studies and sociology. They throw light on different aspects of the central theme by relating it to their own discipline. The chapters are arranged in a sequence broadly taking into account the logical development of the theme. Chapters were divided into four parts followed by appendices for the convenience of readers and keeping each chapter's dominant sub-themes in mind. Of course, there cannot be a strict logical order among the chapters and sections, as the treatment of many sub-themes overlaps or criss-crosses on a multidisciplinary platform.

The first part entitled "Classical Buddhism and Caste" contains four chapters that deal with the Buddhist approach to caste in the classical context. To recount this briefly, in the first chapter Bimalendra Kumar discusses the approach to the caste system found in Pāli Buddhism. In the second chapter Prabal Kumar Sen discusses how the caste system was dealt with in different schools of Classical Indian philosophy. In the third chapter, Shrikant Bahulkar discusses the Buddhist criticism of caste found in a Buddhist Tantra text called *Vimalaprabhā*, a commentary on *Kālacakratantra*. In the fourth chapter, Ajay Verma discusses the Mahāyāna Buddhist criticism of essentialism inherent in the Nyāya justification of *jāti*.

The second part, entitled "Neo-Buddhism: Ambedkar on Caste, Class and Gender," contains three chapters dealing with the important concepts of caste, class and gender expounded by Ambedkar in his formulation of Neo-Buddhism. In the fifth chapter, Mahesh A. Deokar shows how Ambedkar's analysis of caste contains many elements already present in classical Buddhist literature and, at the same time, differs due to his use of history, sociology and anthropology in understanding caste and his application of Buddhist insights to reforming Indian society at large. In Chapter 6, Gopal Guru brings out the relevance of Ambedkar's perspective to Marx and Marxism, and shows that Ambedkar, in his formulation of Buddhism, was concerned with the exploitation and alienation caused by both class and caste. In the seventh chapter, Pratima Pardeshi brings out Ambedkar's anti-patriarchal perspective, which is inseparable from his anti-caste approach.

The third part, entitled "Hinduism and Buddhism: Interaction, Conflict and Beyond," contains three chapters that deal with the interface between Buddhism and Hinduism in India. In the eighth chapter Shrikant Bahulkar deals with the impact of Buddhism on Hinduism, particularly in medieval Maharashtra with reference to the appropriation of the Buddha in the form of Viṭṭhala and the Bhakti movement, which undermined caste discrimination. In the ninth chapter, Umesh Bagade discusses Ambedkar's interpretation of Indian history as that of the conflict between Brahmanism and Buddhism. In tenth chapter, Valerian Rodrigues juxtaposes Ambedkar's approach to varṇa, caste and untouchability with that of Gandhi.

The fourth part—"Religion, Modernity and Navayāna Buddhism"—contains three chapters throwing light on Ambedkar's approach to religion in general and Buddhism in particular. In eleventh chapter, Kanchana Mahadevan argues that Ambedkar's conception of religion is compatible with rationality and science, and that he goes beyond Radhakrishnan's understanding of the modern. P. Kesava Kumar argues in the twelfth chapter that Ambedkar's reconstruction of Buddhism transcends the dichotomy of religion and modernity. In the thirteenth chapter, I have discussed how Ambedkar's interpretation of Buddhism was continuous with many modern Buddhist thinkers in different parts of the world, but becomes different because of his emphasis on the Buddha's role as a critic of caste.

The two appendices deal with the nature and historical role of *Vajrasūci*, the anti-caste text attributed to Aśvaghoṣa. In Appendix I, Sanghasen Singh presents the contents of the text and examines the identity of its author. In Appendix II, R. C. Dhere expounds the impact of *Vajrasūci* and *Vajrasūcikopaniṣat* on saint cults such as Mahānubhāva, Vārakarī and Nātha and also on some of the social reformers of the 19th and 20th centuries.

This is a rough outline of the chapters in the anthology; the authors present many more arguments that cannot be spelt out in this short introduction. In fact, I learnt many things from these authors and also that there awaits even further learning from their work. I am sure that the volume will help readers in enriching their understanding of the social role of classical Buddhism and Neo-Buddhism.

I close with a customary disclaimer. I do not necessarily agree with the contributors in all respects. While editing the volume I found myself in tune with all the authors in a broad way but not necessarily in all details. Similarly, I do not expect that they agree with what I have said here. I can claim, however, that the chapters have made me think more seriously about the problems and their possible solutions, and I suppose that the reader will have the same experience when he or she goes through the anthology.

Notes

1 I am grateful to Prabal Kumar Sen for his valuable suggestions on the earlier draft of the Introduction.

2 Here we are using the word "Hindu," for the sake of convenience, to refer to the society of the Indian subcontinent that accepted texts such as the Vedas, the Smṛtis and the *Gītā* as authoritative, along with the varṇa-caste identity of its members.

3 Sometimes it is claimed that there is a basic difference between varṇa and caste. Castes are determined by birth, but varṇas are determined by "qualities and actions" (*guṇakarmavibhāgaśaḥ*). This claim does not seem to be warranted. The main difference between the two is that varṇa refers to a broad classification, whereas caste (*jāti*) refers to further diversification. It will be argued that according to the Hindu *śāstra* texts like *Manusmṛti* and the *Gītā*, both are supposed to be determined by birth.

4 "*sarvaṃ svaṃ brāhmaṇasyedaṃ yat kiñcij jagatīgatam| śraiṣṭhyenābhijanenenedaṃ sarvaṃ vai brāhmaṇo'rhati||*" MS 1.100 [All the wealth, whatever exists in the world, belongs to Brahmins. A Brahmin deserves everything because of his superiority and his lineage.] Here and elsewhere I have referred to *Manusmṛti* as the representative of the *Dharmaśāstra* of Brahmanical religion. Similar references can be found in other *Dharmaśāstra* texts such as *Yājñavalkyasmṛti* and *Nāradasmṛti*. For an exposition of the views in different *Dharmaāstra* texts on the varṇa-caste inequality, see Chapter 3: "The Duties, Disabilities and Privileges of the Varṇas," Kane (1997, 105–64)

5 "visrabdhaṃ brāhmaṇaḥ śūdrād dravyopādānam ācaret| na hi tasyāsti kiñcit svaṃ bhartṛhāryadhano he saḥ||" MS 8.417 [A Brahmin may take possession of money from a śūdra unhesitatingly. For, no wealth belongs to the latter, as his money is worth being taken away by his master.]

6 "Caste system has two aspects. In one of its aspects it divides men into separate communities. In its second aspect, it places these communities in a graded order one above the other in social status." Ambedkar (2010, 72).

7 'At the end' means temporally after other varṇas were created.

8 "*cāturvarṇyaṁ mayā sṛṣṭaṁ guṇakarmavibhāgaśaḥ*", BG 4.13ab [I have created the system of four varṇas according to qualities (or strands of *Prakṛti*) and actions.]
9 It will be seen that *Manusmṛti* also classifies varṇas in terms of the *guṇas* of *Prakṛti*.
10 "*sahajaṁ karma kaunteya sadoṣam api na tyajet| sarvārambhā hi doṣeṇa dhūmenāgnir ivāvṛtāḥ||*", BG 18.48 [One should not shun the action assigned to one by birth, even if the action is defective. For all activities are covered by defects like the fire covered by smoke.]
11 "*śreyān svadharmo viguṇah paradharmāt svanuṣṭhitāt| svabhāvaniyataṁ karma, kurvan nāpnoti kilbiṣam||*", BG 18.47 [It is better to perform one's own duty even if it is defective, rather than performing someone else's duty well. One who performs an action determined by one's own nature, does not acquire sin.]
12 In this context Prabal Kumar Sen drew my attention to the statements from *Chāndogya Upaniṣad* 5.10.7 and *Kausitaki-Brahmana-Upanisad* 1.2 where it is claimed that the birth of a person in a particular caste is determined by past karma.
13 "sthāvarāḥ kṛmikīṭāś ca matsyāḥ sarpāḥ sakacchapāḥ| paśavaś ca mṛgāś caiva jaghanyā tāmasī gatiḥ|| hastinaś ca turaṅgāś ca śūdrā mlecchāś ca garhitāḥ| siṁhā vyāghrā varāhāś ca madhyamā tāmasī gatiḥ|| cāraṇāś ca suparṇāś ca puruṣāś caiva dāmbhikāḥ| rakṣāṁsi ca piśācāś ca tāmasīṣūttamā gatiḥ|| jhallā mallā naṭāś caiva puruṣāḥ śastravṛttayaḥ| dyūtapānaprasaktāś ca jaghanyā rājasī gatiḥ|| rājānaḥ kṣtriyāś caiva rājñāṁ caiva purohitāḥ | vādayuddhapradhānāś ca madhyamā rājasī gatiḥ|| gandharvā guhyakā yakṣā vibudhānucarāś ca ye| tathaivāpsarasaḥ sarvā rājasīṣūttamā gatiḥ|| tāpasā yatayo viprā ye ca vaimānikā gaṇāḥ| nakṣatrāṇi ca daityāś ca prathamā sāttvikī gatiḥ|| yajvānaḥ ṛṣayo devā vedā jyotīṁṣi vatsarāḥ| pitaraś caiva sādhyāś ca dvitīyā sāttvikī gatiḥ || brahma viṣvasṛjo dharmo mahān avyaktam eva ca| uttamāṁ sāttvikīm etāṁ gatim āhur manīṣiṇaḥ||" MS 12.42–50.
14 Though *daityas* are generally counted as demons, in Manu's categorization there is a distinction between *daitya* and *rakṣas*. *Daityas* are far superior to *rakṣas*. The former are Sāttvika whereas the latter are Tāmasa.
15 "*brāhmaṇaḥ sambhavenaiva devānāmapi daivatam| pramāṇaṁ caiva lokasya brahmātraiva hi kāraṇam||*"MS 11.84 (A brāhmaṇa becomes a god of gods by his very birth. He becomes an authority of the world. Here his spiritual power is the only reason.). Also see MS 1.98–9; 2.135, 8.20.
16 A radical view that it is not even a necessary condition, expressed exceptionally in some texts and expressed by some saints and reformers, has been considered separately.
17 For Buddhist criticism of *jāti* in general and the Jaina arguments against *brāhmaṇatva-jāti*, see Chapter 2.
18 "*māṁ hi pārtha vyapāśritya ye'pi syuḥ pāpayonayaḥ| striyo vaiśyās tathā śūdrās te'pi yānti parāṁ gatim||*", BG 9.32 [Oh the son of *Pṛthā*! Whosoever are born from sin, women, vaiśyas as well as śūdras, they too attain the highest position by taking refuge in me.]
19 *Apaśūdrādhikaraṇam*, BSSB 1.3.34–8, In this context Prabal Kumar Sen drew my attention to the fact that there is also an *Apasudradhikarana* in the *Mīmāṃsasūtra* (6.1.25–38), where the ineligibility of śūdras for studying the Vedas and participating in Vedic sacrifices has been sought to be established. However, this would not amount to the paradoxical relation between empirical and transcendental which it does in Advaita-Vedānta, as the Mīmāṃsa system is not known for accepting equality at metaphysical level.

20 The God of Guru Nanak is called Akāla (The Timeless One), Basaveshvar accepted Śiva as God and Narayanaguru upheld the *Advaita Brahman*.
21 Technically, one should also include *pratyekabuddhayāna*, that is, the path of an individual Buddha. I have not included it as a sect of Buddhism because it cannot be called an organised form of Buddhism, whereas the other three forms are organised forms.
22 For my discussion of the possibility of secular Buddhism, see Gokhale (2017, 2018).
23 "I do not propose any levelling of castes. Caste is a very good thing. Caste is the plan we want to follow......In India from caste we reach the point where there is no caste. Caste is based throughout on that principle. The plan in India is to make everybody a Brahmin, the Brahmin being the ideal of humanity" (Vivekananda 1989, 214).
24 This is derived from *Harijan*, 16-11-35 as quoted in Bose (1972, 774). Gandhi held that "self-imposed restriction against inter-marriage and interdining is essential for rapid evolution of soul." See *Harijan* 29-4-33, quoted in Bose (1972, 267 fn.)
25 "*ahiṃsā satyam asteyaṃ śaucam indriyanigrahaḥ| etaṃ sāmāsikaṃ dharmaṃ cāturvarṇye'bravīn manuḥ||*" MS 10.63 [Non-violence, truth, non-stealing, purity and control over senses: Manu has stated this consolidated obligation applicable to all the four varṇas.] However, Manu's non-egalitarian framework does not allow equal pursuit of these values by all the varṇas. Manu allows compulsory servitude imposed on śūdras, which is systemic violence committed on lower castes by upper castes. Equal pursuit of truth by all presupposes equal access to the knowledge of truth for all. But Manu deprived śūdras of the right to study the Vedas. Purity could not be practiced equally by all because Manu assigned impure professions to śūdras and pure professions to Brahmins. In this way caste rules which Manu made mandatory for all made the equal pursuit of the "consolidated obligations" impossible.
26 "Whether you do that or you do not, you must give a new doctrinal basis to your religion—a basis that will be in consonance with Liberty, Equality and fraternity, in short, with Democracy.........But I am told that .....you could draw for such principles on the Upanishads" (Ambedkar 2010, 77–8).
27 See for example Savarkar (1964, 433–90).
28 Also see Appendix II in this volume.
29 "*Dona śabdāṃta dona saṃskṛti*" (Two Cultures in Two Words), in Savarkar (1964, 354–63).
30 "*āsindhu-sindhu-paryantā yasya bhāratabhūmikā| pitṛbhūḥ puṇyabhūś caiva sa vai hindur iti smṛtaḥ||*" [He is known as a Hindu who regards the land of Bhārata, from Sindhu river to the ocean, as the ancestral land as well as the pious land.] (Savarkar 1964, 1).
31 For my discussion of this theme see Gokhale (2014).

References

Ambedkar, D. Babasaheb, (2010) *Dr. Babasaheb Ambedkar Writings and Speeches*, Vol. 1, Mumbai: Dr. Babasaheb Ambedkar Source Material Publication Committee, Government of Maharashtra, (Second Edition).

BG: Śrīmadbhagavadgītā, Pune: Datta Lakshmi Trust, 1976.

Bose, Nirmal Kumar, (1972) *Selections from Gandhi*, Ahmedabad: Navajivan Press, (Second enlarged edition, Reprint.

BSSB: *Brahmasūtraśāṅkarabhāṣya*, Madras: Shri Kamakoti Koshasthanam, 1954.

Gokhale, Pradeep P., (2018) "Can One be a Buddhist without Believing in Rebirth? A Question before Engaged Buddhist Thought," *Madhya Bhāratī*, July–December 2018 (Platinum Edition), Saugar: Dr. Harisingh Gaur Vishvavidyalay, pp. 314–20.

Gokhale, Pradeep P., (2017) "The Possibility of Secular Buddhism," in Shaumyan Tatyana Lvovna, Kuzmin Sergey Lvovich (Eds): *Proceedings of the Institute of Oriental Studies, RAS. Issue. 1: Tibetology and Buddhology at the Crossroads of Science and Religion*. Moscow: Institute of Oriental Studies, pp. 160–72.

Gokhale, Pradeep P., (2014) "Buddhism and Interculturality: Understanding the Buddha's Dual Approach," *Sandhan*, Journal of Centre for Studies in Civilizations, Vol. XI, Number II, July–December 2011 (Published in 2014), pp. 29–37.

Kane, Pandurang, Vaman, (1997) History of Dharmaśāstra. (Ancient and Medieval Religious and Civil Law), Vol. II, Part I, Pune: Bhandarkar Oriental Research Institute (Third Edition).

MS: *Manusmṛti with Manvarthamuktāvali of Kullūkabhaṭṭa*, Mumbai: Nirnaya Sagar Press, 1915.

Savarkar, Vinayak Damodar (1964), *Samagra Savarkar Vangmay*, Vol. 3 (*Nibandhakhanda*) (Marathi), Date Shamkar Ramchandra (Ed), Pune: Kal Prakashan.

TBHD: Ambedkar, B. R., (1974) *The Buddha and His Dhamma*, Bombay: Siddharth Publication.

Vivekananda, (1989) *The Complete Works of Swami Vivekananda*, Vol. V, Calcutta: Advaita Ashram, (Second Reprint of Subsidised Edition).

Part I

CLASSICAL BUDDHISM AND CASTE

1

BUDDHA'S ATTITUDE TOWARDS THE CASTE SYSTEM AS AVAILABLE IN PĀLI TEXTS

Bimalendra Kumar

The Pāli texts of the *Tipiṭaka* of Theravāda Buddhists do not agree with the Brahmanic order of the varṇas,[1] i.e., Brāhmaṇa, Kṣatriya, Vaiśya and Sūdra. Instead they change the order to the effect—Kṣatriya, Brāhmaṇa, Vaiśya and Sūdra (Khattiya, Brāhmaṇa, Vessa and Sudda). Buddhism considers the view that one caste is superior to another false and evil—"*pāpakaṃ diṭṭhigataṃ*."[2] All the four so-called castes, it says, are exactly the same, equally pure and none of them is superior to the others.[3] But the Buddha's attitude towards the division of society on the basis of caste was antagonistic all along. He denounced the idea that Brāhmaṇas are superior on the grounds of birth. During his lifetime, society developed into a new structure of social order, generally known as "Four-Fold Assembly" or "*Catu-parisā*." It is the assembly of monks (*Bhikkhu-parisā*), assembly of nuns (*Bhikkūni-parisā*), assembly of lay devotees (*Upāsaka-parisā*) and assembly of lay female devotees (*Upāsikā-parisā*). The Buddha often talks about many things common to all of them. In the *Mahāparinibbānasutta*, the Buddha says to the Māra, who asked him to attain *parinibbāna*, that he will not do so until all members of all four groups become well versed in his teaching. There are also occasional references to another four-fold classification as the assembly of Khattiyas (*Khattiya-parisā),* assembly of Brāhmanas (*Brāhmaṇa-parisā*), assembly of Gahapatis (*Gahapati-parisā*) and the assembly of recluses (*Samaṇa-parisā*)[4] but the former is seen as more inclusive and popular than the latter. It is interesting to note that there is a reference to eight assemblies (*aṭṭha parisā*) in the *Dīghanikāya*.[5] The *Vasala Sutta* and *Vaseṭṭha Sutta* of the *Suttanipāta, Madhura Sutta, Assalāyana Sutta* and *Caṅki Sutta* of the *Majjhima Nikāya*, the *Ambaṭṭha Sutta* of the *Dīgha Nikāya*, etc., prove the worthlessness of the castes. In fact, the Buddha did away with all sorts of social distinctions between man and thus pleaded for social justice. He is reported to have said in the *Cullavagga*:

> Just as the great rivers, such as, the Gaṅgā, the Yamunā, the Acirāvatī, the Sarabhū and the Mahī, when they pour their waters into the Great Ocean, lose their names and origins and become the

> Great Ocean precisely so, you monks, do These four castes—the Khattiya, the Brāhmaṇa, the Vessa and the Sudda—when they pass, according to the doctrine and discipline of the Tathāgata, from home to homelessness, lose their names and origins.[6]

Buddha's attitude towards the caste system

The Buddha thus stood for the equality of man and the negation of the caste system. He maintained that it was *kamma* (deed, action) that determined the high and low state of a being. By birth one does not become an outcaste, by birth one does not become a Brāhmaṇa.[7] Every living being has *kamma* as its master, its kinsman, its refuge.[8] According to Pāli texts, there was no distinction of caste in the Buddha's order of monks and nuns. The Buddha's chief disciples even belonged to the so-called lower castes, such as barbers, sweepers and Caṇḍālas. Upāli, the most prominent Vinaya teacher after the Buddha, was from a barber family. He occupied a very high position in the Buddhist fraternity (Saṅgha).

There is no discrimination at all in terms of being low or high, well-born or ill-born, big or small etc. The discriminating order (Brāhmaṇa, Kṣatriya, Vaiśya and Sūdra existing immediately before the advent of the Buddha and the slightly changed order of Khattiya, Brāhmaṇa, Vessa and Sudda at his time[9]) had no valid ground for existence so far as the nature of human beings is concerned. "It is merely the empty sound, says the Buddha, that the Brāhmaṇas are superior, others are inferior; Brāhamaṇas are of high caste, others are low caste,"[10] which can be translated to mean: "The people of all the four castes are equal and I see no difference in them."[11] Distinctions, however, may be seen in various species because of their observable distinguishing marks:

> "You know the worms, and the moths, and the different sorts of ants, the marks that constitute species are for them and their species are manifold." "Know you also the birds that are born along on wings and move through the air, the marks that constitute are for them, and their species are manifold." "But as in these species, the marks constitute species are abundant, so in men the marks that constitute species are not abundant." "There is no difference as regards head, ears, eyes, mouth, nose, tongue, etc., difference there may be, if any, of their bodies, and that is also nominal."

This can be seen among humans as professional names—"One, who lives by different mechanical arts, is an artisan, and so also whoever amongst men lives by serving, is a servant. One is named so because he lives on archery; one is merchant because lives by trade etc."[12] According to this, one is named because of one's deeds. The reality is that – "not by birth does one become an outcaste, by deeds one becomes a Brāhmaṇa."

> "A Brāhmaṇa, born in a preceptor family, friend of the hymns of the Vedas, when continually indulge in sinful deeds, is blamed in this world, and goes to the hell after death; his birth neither save him from birth in hell nor from the blame in the world." On the other hand, Sopāka, born in a low caste family, did virtuous deeds and attained the status of a sage Mātaṅga by name, reached the highest fame, such as was very difficult to obtain, as well as many Khattiyas and Brahmaṇas went to serve him. Further, being free from the dust, having abandoned sensual pleasures went to the Brahma-world after expiry of his life. His birth neither prevented him in getting highest fame nor in entering into the Brahma-divine world after death.[13]

In the *Vāseṭṭha sutta* of the *Sutta Nipāta*, the Buddha proves scientifically that there are no distinguishing marks in men, whether they are black or yellow, as are found in different species of animals and plants. Beetles, ants, moths and termites are different because each species is distinguished by different marks. Quadrupeds both small and large, snakes, fish and birds are different from one another because of different marks found in them. So is the case with different kinds of plants. But where are such distinguishing marks in men?

> Not by hair, nor head, nor ears, nor eyes, nor nose, nor mouth, nor lips, nor eyebrows, nor neck, nor shoulder, nor belly, nor back, nor buttock, nor chest… nor fingers, nor nails, nor calves, nor thighs, nor colour, nor voice is there a distinguishing mark arising from their species as in other species.[14]

All *Homo sapiens* constitute one species. According to the Buddha, *jāti* is primarily a biological term that means "species." The biological test of distinction between two species is that a male of one and female of the other are unable to mate for the purpose of procreation. It is to this sense the Buddha asserted, "*Aññamaññā hi jātiyo*." The social division among men cannot be treated as *jātis* in the above sense. These divisions are occupational and congenital. The Buddha's view of caste is different. According to him, a man is high or low by virtue of his action.[15] *Kamma* is to be understood in its widest possible sense as occupation of all kinds, including traditional culture.

Thus, becoming low or high socially depends on immoral and moral deeds. One can be a Vasala because of immoral deeds and a Brāhmaṇa because of moral ones.[16] Expressions like Mahāsammata, Khattiya, Brāhmaṇa, Jhāyaka, Ajjhāyaka, Vessa, Sudda, etc. came to be accidently by way of conventional communications and not based on some basic principle of inheritance of a lineage or birth in a particular family. There is no solid ground of truth conveying the sense of superiority or inferiority in them. "*Dhamma* or righteousness alone is the Superior here in this world and hereafter."[17] What is *Dhamma*? It is the *Vijjā* and *Caraṇa*. One, who is endowed with them is superior to men and gods alike—"*Vijjā-caraṇa-sampanno, so seṭṭho devamānuseti.*"[18]

In the *Assalāyanasutta* of the *Majjhimanikāya,*[19] the Buddha discusses Brāhmaṇas' claims of being superior and the best varṇa, of being as white in colour, as pure, and the real sons of Brahmā, born from his mouth. The Buddha challenges the claim that they are birthed from the mouth of Brahmā by pointing out that they are born from the wombs of Brāhmaṇa women who conceive them, deliver them and feed them in the natural course of things. The Buddha also exploded the claims by Brahmins of inherent superiority with reference to several points. Brahmins were believers in the law of *kamma*. The Buddha pointed out to them that, like others, they have to suffer the consequences of their misdeeds. If there is any inherent superiority in Brahmins neither would they commit such deeds nor would they suffer for them. But Brahmins do commit them and suffer the consequences thereof.

With reference to this point, Mahākaccāna, one of the chief disciples of the Buddha, says to Avantiputta, King of Madhura, "If a noble kills, robs, fornicates, lies, slanders, a bitter of tongue, tattles, covets, harbours ill-will, and has a wrong outlook, will he, after death at the body's dissolution, pass to a state of misery and woe?"

"Such a noble will pass to a state of misery and woe, this is my view, and this is what I have heard from sages."

"Would the like doom await a Brahmin, or a middleclass man, or a working class man of like disposition?"

"Yes, it would."

"If this be so, do you think all classes are on precisely the same footing herein or not?"

"Undoubtedly, if this be so, all four classes are on precisely the same footing, and I see no difference between them."[20]

The same holds good with reference to their righteous conduct. This very argument has been used by the Buddha to convince Assalāyana and other Brahmins of the emptiness of their pretensions. Equality before moral law belies the claim by the Brahmins of inherent superiority.

In addition, the penal code of the country made no distinction with regard to different castes. For the same offence, members of different castes underwent the same punishment. This is again evident from the discussion between Mahākaccāna and Avantiputta. The former says to the king, "If a noble is a burglar; thief, house breaker, footpad or adulterer, and if your people catch him and haul the malefactor before you for sentence, what would you do to him?"

"I should put him to death or confiscate his goods or banish him or otherwise deal with him as circumstances required, for the noble is now a malefactor."

"Would the same apply to the malefactor from any of the other three classes?"

"Yes, it would."

"If this be so, are all four classes on precisely the same footing herein or not?"

"Undoubtedly, all four classes are on precisely the same footing, and I see no difference between them."[21]

So this point also disproves the superiority of Brahmins.

Mahākaccāna, after advancing many points in refutation of the supremacy of the Brahmins, points out to the king that a wealthy man of one caste could employ the service of a man of any other caste. Thus he says, "If a noble grows rich and wealthy, can he have as his servant another noble, or a Brahmin or a middle-class man, or a working-class man to get up early, to go late to bed, to serve him diligently and to carry out his orders?"

"Yes, he could."

"And if it were a Brahmin who had thriven, could he likewise have as his servant a Brahmin, a middle-class man, a working-class man, or a noble?"

"Yes, he could."

"And if it were either a middle-class man or a working-class man who had thriven, could he likewise have his servant someone of the three other classes?"

"Of course, he could."

"If this be so, do you think all four classes are on precisely the same footing?"

"Undoubtedly, if this be so, all four classes are precisely on the same footing, and I see no difference at all between them."[22]

So a poor Brahmin could wait upon a rich Shudra to earn his bread. This point too proved false the claim of inborn superiority on the part of Brahmins. Winternitz calls the *Assalāyana sutta* "excellent" because of this reasoning and further remarks that "such dialogues about that problem of caste as the between the young Brahmin Assalāyana and Gotama Buddha must frequently have occurred in real life."[23]

The Buddha points out that in Yona, Kamboja and other frontier countries there are only two varṇas – *ārya* and *dāsa*, and a person can change from one to the other. He brings out the similarity in the four varṇas by pointing out that all can progress morally and that a Brāhmaṇa who has good conduct and does good to all is respected. Buddhism recognized that the caste system arose historically due to racial prejudice and socioeconomic conditions. It was indeed a revolution in social thought when the Buddha proclaimed that caste and class prejudices are obstacles to higher morality and knowledge and, therefore, to salvation.[24]

Some discrepancies and later degenerations

The Buddha is very much explicit in stating that in the Buddhist order all castes lose their distinctions and become one. With regard to lay people, there was no preaching against caste or observance of caste regulations. In fact, in the *Mahāpadāna sutta*, it is said that the Buddha could be born only in the two higher castes, Brahmins and Kshatriya.[25] The commentator of the *Suttanipāta* says that a Buddha is born either in a Kshatriya or Brahmin family and a Paccekabuddha can be born even in the Gahapati family in addition to the two mentioned above.[26] This view of caste where even spiritual hierarchy based on caste is inbuilt makes the caste system look fundamental and eternal, and regards it a basic factor to make a distinction between the high and the low. In the *Apadāna* text, it is stated that Bhagwan Kassapa and other Buddhas are shown to have been always born in Brahmin families. The intention here is to perpetuate the caste system and say that it is not a structure made by man to smoothly and efficiently organize society, as claimed by people who are not conservative. There is definitely some kind of vested interest from which such theories are propounded.[27] In some dialogues like *Ambaṭṭha sutta*, the Buddha even takes pride in being a Kshatriya. This does not appear consistent with his alleged "no caste" teaching. According to the *Jātaka* commentary, the Bodhisatta is said to have surveyed the world prior to conception, considering a few factors including the caste recognised as the highest at the time. This is significant. It is also important that, according to the Buddhist tradition, Buddhas are born as Brahmins when that caste is considered the highest, and as Khattiyas when they are the highest. It was in keeping with this traditional law that Gotama Buddha selected the Khattiya caste.[28]

There was also no distinction of caste in the Buddha's orders of monks and nuns. The Buddha's chief disciples belonged to even the so-called lower castes, such as barbers, sweepers and Caṇḍālas, who attained *arhathood* and became the teachers of people at large.[29] But in the later Pāli commentarial texts, Caṇḍālas were treated in a different manner. In one of the *Jātakas*, a Caṇḍāla is mentioned as a mongoose-trainer (*koṇḍa-damaka*)[30] and in another, Caṇḍālas learn *caṇḍālavaṃsadhopana*.[31] One *Jātaka* calls a person an "odious Caṇḍāla" (*mahācaṇḍāla*).[32] Originally, the Caṇḍālas seem to have been an aboriginal tribe. This is clear from the use of their own argot.[33] Gradually, they came to be looked upon as "untouchables." One *Jātaka* describes the Caṇḍālas as the vilest people on the earth.[34] In one *Jātaka* story, when a Caṇḍāla enters a town, people pound him with blows and render him unconscious.[35] The extent to which the Caṇḍālas were abhorred could be deduced from the various mentions of them in some of the Jātakas.[36] Contact with air that touched a Caṇḍāla's body was regarded as contamination. Even the sight of the Caṇḍālas from a distance was enough for high caste people, especially women, to wash their eyes with scented water (*gandhodaka*) to remove the contamination, as narrated in the *Citta-Sambhūta Jātaka*.[37] Same sort of incident is related in the *Mātaṅga Jātaka*[38] when the daughter of a Seṭṭhi of Vāranasi upon seeing a Caṇḍala washed her eyes with perfumed water, as she had been contaminated by a mere glance at that despised person.

Upāli, who was the most prominent teacher of Vinaya, belonged to a barber family and occupied a very high position in the Buddhist Saṅgha. But Dharmananda Koshambi, quoting from the *Majjhima-Nikāya*, has tried to prove that caste discrimination occurred in the Saṅgha.[39] The scholastics among the monks, who formed a very powerful group in the order under the leadership of Brahmin converts to Buddhism (of them only a fraction was genuine) during the life time of the Buddha, had acquired prominent positions by the dint of their proximity to the Buddha. After the passing of the Buddha, that same group became more powerful. They made the exegetical study of the teachings of the Buddha and formulated the Abhiddhammic terms and consequent details.[40]

Concluding remarks

These discrepancies and degenerate views were inconsistent with the Buddha's original message. His attitude towards the caste system was concerned with the welfare of all human beings without any discrimination. Many Indian and western scholars have discussed the social aspects of Buddhism. Swami Vivekananda was the first Indian to recognize the "social element" of Buddhism as its "unique element."—"The Buddha was the first to preach universal brotherhood of man"; he was "the only great Indian philosopher who would not recognize caste;" he was "the great preacher of the equality of man."[41] The second Indian to recognize this aspect of the Buddha's teachings was P. L. Narasu, whose writings had an impact on B. R. Ambedkar. Narasu (1912, 7) says that the "spirit of Buddhism is essentially socialistic." Anagarika Dharmapala, one of the great revivalists of Buddhism in India, was one of the first to speak about "the social gospel of the Buddha." In a lecture at Shanghai in 1913, Dharmapala declared: "A progressive evolution with a definite ideal, its realization here and now, making life cheerful, energetic, serene, worth living for the sake of doing good for the welfare of others, this the Tathāgata proclaimed."[42] Modern scholar Richard F. Gombrich (1988, 81) says that the Buddha was not concerned with politics, but Trevor Ling (1973, 418) assesses that the Buddha may justly be described as a social and political theorist. The Buddha's approach follows from his concentration on the problem of suffering at an individual level. His concern was neither political nor social, but purely salvific.[43] Several studies have contributed to social aspects of Buddhism, especially those of R. S. Sharma (1958), G. C. Pande (1984, 4–8), Uma Chakravarty (1987), Vijay Kumar Thakur (2001) and K. T. S. Sarao (2002), who do discuss some Buddhist arguments concerned with the social and historical data found in Pāli literature.

Notes

1 The two terms *jāti* and varṇa must be distinguished, even if the Sanskrit term *Jāti* is used in both cases. It should be noted the Tibetans used the word *rigs* to render alternatively *jāti* and varṇa, but also *kula* (which can in fact have the same meaning as varṇa), or even *gotra* (also often translated by the Tib. *Rus*). When the Sanskrit is lacking, the Tibetan term *rigs* remains ambiguous. Cf. Eltschinger (2012, xvii–xviii).

2 *Majjhima Nikāya* II, pp. 155–6.

3 '*Ime cattāro vaṇṇā samasamā honti. Samaṇo Gotamo cātuvaṇṇiṃ suddhiṃ paññāpeti*"- ibid., p. 89.

4 "*Svāyaṁ evaṁ bhāvanāsampanno ......-yadi khattiyaparisaṁ yadi brāhmaṇa-parisaṁ yadi gahapatiparisaṁ yadi samaṇaparisaṁ –visārado upasaṅkamati amaṅkubhūto*"-*Paṭisambhidāmagga*, p. 511. "It has been argued that the four varṇa scheme, consisting of Khattiyas, Brāhmaṇas, Vaiśyas are theoretical, and that the Buddha talks about it only during his conversations with the Brahamaṇs and the kings. However, when he talks with the laity, the expressions such as Khattiya, Brāhmaṇa and Gahapati are used"- See Chakravarti (1987, 104–5).

5 *Aṭṭha parisā-khattiyaparisā, brāhmaṇaparisā, gahapatiparisā, samaṇaparisā, catumahārājikaparisā, tāvatiṁsaparisā, māraparisā, brāhmaṇaparisā*"- *Dīghanikāya*, Vol. II, (Nalanda) p. 86. Vol. III, p. 200.

6 Cf. "*Seyyathāpi, Bhikkhave, yā kāci mahānadiyo seyyathīdaṁ-, Gaṅgā, Yamunā, Aciravatī, Sarabhū, Mahī, tā Mahāsamuddaṃ pattā jahanti purimā nāmagot-tāni, Mahāsamuddo tvaveva Saṅkhaṁ gacchanti. Evameva kho, Bhikkhave, Cattāro me vaṇṇā — Khattiyā, Brāhmaṇā, Vessā, Suddā. Te Tathāgatappave-dite dhammavinaye agārasmā anagāriyaṁ pabbajitvā jahanti purimamāni...*" - *Cullavagga*, p. 356.

7 *Cf. Vasala Sutta, Suttanipāta*, in *Khuddaka Nikāya* I, p. 290.
"*Na jaccā vasalo hoti, na jaccā hoti brāhmaṇo*
Kammunā vasalo hoti, kammunā hoti brāhmaṇo."

8 *Kammassakā, Kammadāyādo, Kammayoni, Kammabandhu, Kammapaṭisaraṇo.*

9 *Majjhima Nikāya* II, 310–16.

10 Ibid., p. 110.

11 *Dīgha Nikāya* I, p. 80.

12 "*kassako kammunā hoti, sippiko hoti pi kammunā/*
vānijjo kammunā hoti, pessiko hoti kammunā"//
na jaccā brāhmaṇo hoti, na jaccā hoti abrāhmaṇo/
kammunā brāhmaṇo hoti, kammunā hoti abrāhmaṇo" - *Khuddaka Nikaya* I, p. 368.

13 "*Tadaminā pi jānātha, yathāmedaṁ nidassanaṁ/*
caṇḍālaputto sopāko, mātaṅgo iti vissuto//

so yasaṁ paramaṁ patto, mātaṅgo yaṁ sudullabhaṁ/
āgacchuṁ tassupaṭṭhānam, khattiyā brāhmaṇā bahu//
devayānaṁ abhirūyha, virajaṁ so mahāpathaṁ/
kāmarāgaṁ virājetvā, brahmalokūpago ahuṁ/
na naṁ jāti nivāresi, brahmalokūpapattiyā" - ibid, pp. 289–90.

14 Ibid., pp. 364–55.

15 "*na jaccā bhāhmaṇo hoti, na jaccā hoti abrahmaṇo/*
kammunā brāhmano hoti abrāhmaṇo//" ibid., pp. 289–90.

16 "*na jaccā vasalo hoti, na jaccā hoti brāhmaṇo/*
kammunā vasalo hoti, kammunā hoti brāhmaṇo" // ibid., p. 290.

17 *Dīgha Nikāya* III, pp. 72–75.

18 *Dīgha Nikāya* I, pp. 86–91.

19 *Majjhima Nikāya* II, p. 88.

20 *Majjhima Nikaya* II, p. 44.

21 Ibid., p. 45.

22 Ibid., p. 44.

23 Winternitz (1933, 50).

24 "*Ye hi keci jātivādavinibaddhā vā gottavādavinibaddhā vā...ārakā te anuttarāya vijjācaraṇasampadāya. Pahāya kho, jātivādavinibaddhā cā gottavādavinibaddhā cā...anuttaāya, vijjācaraṇasampadāya sacchikiriyā hotī ti*"-*Dīghanikāya*, I, p. 87.

25 "*Vipassi, Bhikkhave, Bhagavā arahaṃ sammāsambuddho khattiyo jātiyā ahosi, khattiykule udapādi. Sikhī, Bhikkhave, Bhagavā arahaṃ sammāsambuddho khattiyo jātiyā ahosi, khattiyakule udapādi.... Kassapo, bhikkhave, Bhagavā arahaṃ sammāsambuddho brāhmaṇo jātiyā ahosi, brāhamaṇakule udapādi. Ahaṃ, bhikkhave, etarahi arahaṃ sammāsambuddho khattiyo jātiyā ahosi, khattiykule uppanno.*" - *Dīghanikāya*, Vol. II, pp. 3–4.

26 "*Evaṃ imāya patthanāya iminā ca abhinihārena yathāvuttappabhedaṃ kālaṃ pāramiyā puretvā Buddha loke uppajjanta khattiyakūle va brāhmaṇakūle vā uppajjanti, paccekabudha khattiyabrāhmaṇagahapati- kūlānaṃ aññatarasmiṃ, aggasāvakā pana khattiyabrāhmaṇakulesseva Buddha iva vivattamāne kappe uppajjanti*"- *Sutta Nipāta Aṭṭhakathā*, Vol. I, p. 64.

27 Chaudhary (2009, 117).

28 *Jātaka (with commentary)*, (1962), p. 46.

29 For reference to the outcastes admitted into the Buddhist order, See Dhammaratana, (1969, 20–30).

30 *Jātaka*, (1877–1897) Vol. IV, p. 389.

31 Ibid., p. 390.

32 Ibid., p. 200.

33 Ibid., p. 391f.

34 Ibid., p. 397.

35 Ibid., pp. 376, 391.

36 "Staying to the Windward and Washing Eyes with Perfumed Water: An Examination of the Brahmanical Attitude Towards Caṇḍāḷas and Other Outcastes as Reflected in the Pali Literature" - (Sarao 2009, 24).

37 *Jātaka*, (1877–1897) Vol. IV, pp. 390–401.

38 Ibid., pp. 375–90.

39 Cf. Koshambi (2009, 166–81).

40 Cf. Singh (1984, 110).

41 Cf. Vivekananda (1963, Vol. V, p. 309; Vol. II, p. 486; Vol. VIII, p. 98).

42 Quoted in Murty (1984, viii); Cf. Thakur (2008, 107).

43 Mudagamuwe (2005, 29–30).

References

Pāli sources

Cullavagga, Kashyap, Bhikkhu J. (Ed.), Nālandā: Pali Publication Board, (1956).
Dīghanikāya vol. I, II. & III, Kashyap, Bhikkhu J. (Ed.), Nālandā: Pali Publication Board, (1958).
Jātaka (with commentary) vol. I–VI, V. Fausboll (Ed.), London: Pali Text Society (1877–1897), (1962).
Khuddakanikāya vol. I (Suttanipāta), Kashyap, Bhikkhu J. (Ed.), Nālandā: Pali Publication Board, (1959).
Majjhimanikāya vol. I, II. & III, Kashyap, Bhikkhu J. (Ed.), Nālandā: Pali Publication Board, (1958).
Paṭisambhidāmagga, Kashyap, Bhikkhu J. (Ed.), Nālandā: Pali Publication Board, (1960).
Sutta Nipāta Aṭṭhakathā vol. I, Chaudhary, Angraj (Ed.), Nalanda: Nava Nalanda Mahavihara, (1974).

Secondary sources

Chakravarti, Uma (1987) *Social Dimensions of Early Buddhism*, Delhi: Oxford University Press.
Chaudhary, Angaraj (2009) "Buddha's View of Caste and Social Harmony" in Shukla, H. S. and Kumar, Bimalendra (Eds.) *Buddhism and Social Ideals*, Varanasi: Banaras Hindu University.
Dhammaratana, Bhikkhu U. (1969) Buddha and Caste System, Sarnath: Secretary, Buddhist Education Society of India, Shravasti (Bahraich), 117–126.
Eltschinger, Vincent (2012) *Caste and Buddhist Philosophy*, (tr. From French to English by Raynald Prevereau), Delhi: Motilal Banarasidass Publishers Private Limited.
Gombrich, Richard F. (1988) *Theravada Buddhism: A Social History from Benares to Colombo*, London: Routledge.
Koshambi, Dharmanand (2009) *Bhagawan Buddha: Jīvana Aur Darśana*, Allahabad Lokabharati Prakashan, (On behalf Sahitya Akademi, New Delhi), (Second Paperback Publication).
Ling, Trevor (1973) *The Buddha: Buddhist Civilization in India and Ceylon*, New York: Penguin.
Mudagamuwe, Mathrimurthi (2005) "The Buddha's Attitude to Social Concerns as Depicted in Pali Canon" in the *Buddhist Studies Review* Volume 22, Part I (The Journal of the UK Association for Buddhist Studies).
Murty, K. Satchidananda (1984) "Foreword" in Tiwary, Mahesh (Ed.) *Bodhi-Raśmi*, New Delhi: First International Conference on Buddhism and National Cultures, vii–xi (foreword).
Narasu, P.L. (1912) *The Essence of Buddhism*, London: Asian Education Services, New Delhi (Second AES Reprint) (1993).
Pande, G.C. (1984) "On the Question of Social Origins of Buddhism" in Tiwary, Mahesh (Ed.) *Bodhi-Raśmi*, New Delhi: First International Conference on Buddhism and National Cultures, 5–18.

Sarao, K.T.S. (2002) *Origin and Nature of Ancient Indian Buddhism*, Delhi: Department of Buddhist Studies, University of Delhi, (Reprint).

Sarao, K.T.S. (2009) "Staying to the Windward and Washing Eyes with Perfumed Water: An Examination of the Brahmanical Attitude Towards Caṇḍālas and Other Outcastes as Reflected in the Pali Literature" in Shukla, H. S. and Kumar Bimalendra (Eds.) *Buddhism and Social Ideals*, Varanasi: Banaras Hindu University, 19–38.

Sharma, Ram Sharan (1958) *Śudras in Ancient India: A Survey of the Position of the Lower Orders Down to the Circa A.D. 500*, Delhi: Motilal Banarsidass.

Singh, Sanghasen (1984) "Dogmatism and Revisionism in Early Buddhism" in Tiwary, Mahesh, (Ed.) *Bodhi-Raśmi*, New Delhi: First International Conference on Buddhism and National Cultures, 109–119.

Thakur, Vijay Kumar (2001) *Social Dimensions of Buddhism*, Patna: Janaki Prakashaṇ.

Thakur, Vijay Kumar (2008) "Perspectivising the Universality of Buddhism: A Note on Its Socio-Economic Constructs" in *Dhammadesanā: A Buddhist* Perspective *(Prof. Mahesh Tiwary Commemoration Volume)*, Varanasi: Publication Cell, Banaras Hindu University.

Vivekananda (1963) *Complete Works*, (Vols II, V and VIII), Calcutta: Swami Vivekananda Centenary.

Winternitz (1933) *A History of Indian Literature*, (Vol. II), Calcutta: Calcutta University.

2

CASTE IN CLASSICAL INDIAN PHILOSOPHY

Some ontological problems

Prabal Kumar Sen[1]

The system of Cāturvarṇya, according to which Indian society was divided and arranged hierarchically into four groups (viz. brāhmaṇa, kṣatriya, vaiśya and śūdra), has been one of the most obnoxious and baneful features of the latter. Despite the rule of foreigners who did not observe the system, and the emergence of some indigenous reformist religions like Buddhism and Jainism that flourished in the pre-Christian era and later social phenomena like Sikhism and the Arya Samaj and Brahmo Samaj movement that challenged this system; the grip of this oppressive system—in which some people known as *nirvasita śūdras* in Indian society were once considered to be untouchable (*aspṛśya*) and even more impure than some sub-human creatures—is still intact. The accounts of the emergence of this classification as given in the *Puruṣasūkta* of *Ṛgveda* (10/90/12), *Taittirīya Āraṇyaka* (3/12/13), *Taittīrīya Saṃhitā* (7/1/1) or *Bhagavadgītā* (4/3) are too well known to be recounted here. Among the Brahminical schools, Nyāya, Vaiśeṣika and Bhāṭṭa Mīmāṃsā maintain the view that properties like brahminhood, kṣatriyahood, etc. are natural and mutually incompatible characteristics like "cow-ness," "horse-ness," etc., and hence, one has to accept this four-fold classification of human beings as given fact and not subject to any change that may be brought about by human effort. A similar view is found also in some grammatical works like the commentaries and sub-commentaries on the *Aṣṭādhyāyī* of Pāṇini. Just as one cannot obliterate or deny the 'property' of "cow-ness" that all cows possess and that also distinguishes cows from other animals like horses, buffalos, dogs, cats, etc., one has also to admit brahminhood as the natural "property" that exists in all brahmins, whether present, past or future, and that is also absent in all non-brahmins. Similar is the case with properties like kṣatriyahood, etc. Each such property is one, eternal and located in a number of individuals (*vyaktis*) that exemplify it. Such natural properties that help us classify objects are admitted as "universals" (*sāmānya/jāti*) in many philosophical systems. In this chapter we will briefly survey accounts of the concept of universal (*sāmānya/jāti*) and universal properties like brahminhood, etc. in the philosophical systems such as Grammar, Pūrvamīmāṃsā, Nyāya-Vaiśeṣika, Buddhism and Jainism.

Discussion of Brahminhood in grammar texts

The Aṣṭādhyāyī *aphorism* "nañ"

Our discussion of the grammatical texts begins with the *Aṣṭādhyāyī* Aphorism "*nañ*" (2/2/6), which expresses similarity, negation, difference, etc. and, along with another word, can form nominal compounds (*samāsa*s) known as "*nañ-tatpuruṣa*" (i.e., a determinative compound with a negative component). In *tatpuruṣa samāsa*, usually the meaning of the second term becomes predominant. When *nañ* occurs as the first component of such a compound, the question arises—which of these two terms would have the dominant meaning? Patañjali has chosen the word "*abrāhmaṇa*," which has been formed with the first component *nañ* and the second component "brāhmaṇa," which means a brahmin. The compound word "*abrāhmaṇa*" means someone who is not a brahmin but resembles one, e.g., a kṣatriya; who, like the brahmin, studies the Vedas, wears the sacred thread and performs sacrifices; but unlike a brahmin, cannot act as a priest or a teacher of the scriptures. In this case, the word "brāhmaṇa" is employed as praise, which indicates the presence of some good qualities or virtues in that person. While discussing such issues, the meaning of the term "brāhmaṇa" has come up and one response is that it stands for "universal brahminhood" (*brāhmaṇatva/brāhmaṇya*). Then the issue arises—is brahminhood dependent on birth alone, or also on some other factors such as good conduct, knowledge of scriptures, etc.? Physical attributes like having fair complexion, tawny eyes and reddish brown hair, along with pure conduct, are also sometimes considered to be factors that identify a person as a brahmin. Patañjali has said also here that a person who is as dark-complexioned as a heap of black beans and who is sitting in a shop is not ascertained by any one as a Brahmin. Patañjali has also quoted a verse that says the brahminhood of a person depends on (i) practice of austerities, (ii) learning and (iii) birth from a brahmin couple. One who lacks the first two factors is said to be a brahmin by birth alone (*jātibrāhmaṇa*, i.e., one who is born of brahmin parents).[2] Patañjali has said that sometimes, when the usage of a term depends on a member of certain conditions, one observes the term being used even when it satisfies only some of those conditions. For example, one says, "oil has been consumed," "clarified butter has been consumed," even though what has been consumed is only a portion and not the whole quantity. Likewise, the term "brāhmaṇa" is used even when the person is a brahmin by birth alone. But there are also cases where in the absence of conduct, etc., or in the absence of being born of brahmin parents, a person is said to be an "*abrāhmaṇa*" (which may mean either someone who resembles a brahmin or one who is different from a brahmin). Thus, a brahmin whose conduct is not pure (i.e., in accordance with the rules laid down in scriptures), e.g., a brahmin who urinates or eats while standing, is castigated as "*abrāhmaṇa*," i.e., one who is not a brahmin proper (and hence, does not deserve the respect that is shown to a brahmin), since his conduct is contrary to scriptural injunctions. But in some cases, due to resemblances in terms of physical characteristics or conduct, one may mistake a non-brahmin for a brahmin. Likewise, due to wrong instructions, e.g., "a brahmin resides in such and such place, go and bring him," one may bring a resident of that place who is actually not a brahmin. In both these cases, one comes to know subsequently that the person concerned is *abrāhmaṇa*, since he is not born of parents who are both brahmins. Once brahminhood is thus primarily decided on the basis of birth, it is but natural to think that it is a universal like "cow-ness," "horse-ness," etc., the presence of which in some individual is determined solely by birth. No wonder, that Kaiyaṭa considered the possibility of treating brāhmaṇa as a *jātiśabda*, i.e., a word that has some universal as its referent, and that Nāgeśa also supported this view.

The Aṣṭādhyāyī *aphorism* "alpāctaram"

We now consider Pāṇini's aphorism "*alpāctaram*" (2/2/34). Aphorism 2/2/32 is "*dvandve ghi*," and as per the rule of *anuvṛtti*, the word "*dvandve*" has to be understood to be repeated in this aphorism as well. The meaning of aphorism 2/2/34 has to be that while forming nominal compounds (*samāsas*) known as *dvandva samāsas* (i.e., copulative compounds) by joining together two or more words, the word that contains the lesser number of vowels must occur as the first member of the compound. This phenomenon is known as "*pūrvanipāta*." For example, if a *dvandva* compound is formed by joining the words, "*plakṣa*" (the Sanskrit name of the Indian holy fig tree) and "*nyagrodha*" (the Sanskrit name of the Indian fig tree), then the resultant form would be "*plakṣa-nyagrodhau*;" which is in dual number since it is formed out of two words—the word "*plakṣa*" occurs first as it has fewer vowels than the word "*nyagrodha*." Similarly, the *dvandva* compound formed by combining the words "*dhava*," "*khadira*" and "*palāśa*" (all three being names of different trees) would be "*dhava-khadira-palāśāḥ*," which is in plural number since it contains more than two components—the word "*dhava*" occurs first, since it has fewer vowels than the other two words. However, the seventh supplementary rule (*vārttika*) of Kātyāyana (viz. "*varṇānām ānupūrvyena pūrvanipātaḥ*) points out that an exception has to be made in the case of a *dvandva* compound formed by putting together the names of the four castes, viz. "brāhmaṇa," "kṣatriya'," "viś" and "śūdra," because in the resultant form, these names have to be arranged in accordance with the superiority and inferiority of these castes as indicated by the places of their origin.[3] It has been stated in the Vedas that Prajāpati created brāhmaṇa from his mouth, kṣatriya from his arms, vaiśya from his thighs and śūdra from his feet. Accordingly, the copulative compound formed by these four names would be "*brāhmaṇa-kṣatriya-viṭ-śūdrāḥ*," even though the number of vowels present in "brāhmaṇa" and "kṣatriya" is greater than the number of vowels present in "viś" and "śūdra." Since the supposed place of origin determines the hierarchy of the four-fold classification of men according to their castes, the names of these castes are likely to be treated as examples of *jātiśabda*, i.e., a word that has some universal as its referent.

The Aṣṭādhyāyī aphorism "puṃyogād ākhyāyām"

The aphorism of *Aṣṭādhyāyī* to be discussed next is "*puṃyogād ākhyāyām*" (4/1/48) along with the vārttika no. 10 (*avadātāyaṃ ñīpprasaṅgaḥ*) on it. The aphorism no. 4/1/48 states that the suffix "*ñīṣ*" has to be added to words for males in order to form the words that denote their wives. Thus, by adding the suffix *ñīṣ* to the word "*gaṇaka*" (meaning an astrologer), we derive the word "*gaṇakī*" (meaning the wife of an astrologer). Vārttika no. 10 (*avadātāyāṃ ñīpprasaṅgaḥ*) points out that the expression "*avadātā brāhmaṇī*" is grammatically correct. The problem here is that as per the aphorism "*varṇādanudāttāttopadhātto naḥ*" (4/1/39), which states that each of the words like "*eta*," "*śveta*," etc. that (i) are the names of colours, (ii) have an unaccented letter at the end, and (iii) have "t" as their penultimate letter, can have two alternative forms in their corresponding feminine gender, i.e., it can be (i) "*etā*" or "*enī*," (ii) "*śvetā*" or "*svenī*" and so on. Since the word "*avadāta*," meaning the colour white, also satisfies the two other conditions mentioned above, along with '*avadātā*', we should also have the alternative form "*avadānī*" that would be the adjective of the substantive "*brāhmaṇī*," which is in the feminine gender and means "the wife of a brahmin." In defence of the usage of "*avadātā brahmaṇī*," Patañjali has said here that here the word "*avadāta*" means "pure" and not "white." In support of this claim, Patañjali quoted a verse that said a brahmin whose learning, birth and conduct are pure can be treated as a respectable brahmin.[4] In this verse, the word "*avadāta*" has been used to mean "pure." In *Pradīpa* and *Uddyota*, it was said that the word "*avadātā brāhmaṇī*" is correct, irrespective of whether the brahmin woman concerned has a fair or dark complexion, provided her birth and conduct are pure, i.e., free from any blemish. Here it is also said that purity of birth is an essential condition for being a brahmin, which in turn suggests that for the authors, brahminhood is a universal.

The Aṣṭādhyāyī aphorism "jāterastrīviṣayād ayopadhāt"

Finally, while commenting on the aphorism "*jāterastrīviṣayād ayopadhāt*" (4/1/63), Patañjali gave a definition of "*jāti*," i.e., universal. This aphorism means that if a word (i) expresses some universal, (ii) is not invariably in the feminine gender, and (iii) does not have "y" as its penultimate letter, then by adding the suffix "*ñīṣ*" to it, we can derive the corresponding word in feminine gender. Thus, from the word "*sūkara*" (hog) one can derive the word "*sūkarī*" (sow), and likewise, from the words "*kukkuṭa*" (cock), "*mayūra*" (peacock), "*brāhmaṇa*" (brahmin), "*vṛṣala*" (śūdra), etc., we can derive corresponding words in the feminine gender like "*kukkutī*" (hen), "*mayurī*" (peahen), "*brāhmaṇī*" (a woman who is brahmin by caste), "*vṛṣalī*" (a woman who is śūdra by caste), and so on. These illustrations have been taken from *Kāśikā*; while the examples given in *Māhābhāṣya* of such words in the feminine gender are "*kākī*" (a female crow), "*pikī*" (a female cuckoo), "*śukī*" (a female parrot), "*ulūkī*" (a female owl) and so on. With the inclusion of words like '*brāhmaṇī*' and '*vṛṣalī*' in this list, it becomes clear that for these grammarians, words like "brāhmaṇa," "śūdra," etc. are *jātiśabdas*, i.e., words that have universals as their referents. Words like "kṣatriya" and "vaiśya" are counter-examples in explanations of this aphorism, not because they are not *jātiśabdas*, but because they have 'y' as the penultimate letter.

Patañjali has also provided here a definition of *jāti* (i.e., universal) in a versified form. This verse has four parts, viz. (i) "*ākṛtigrahaṇā jātiḥ*," (ii) "*liṅgānāñca na sarvabhāk*," (iii) "*sakṛdākhyātanirgrāhyā*" and (iv) "*gotrañca caraṇaiḥ saha*."[5] The first quarter of this verse states that *jāti* is something that can be known through *ākṛti* (i.e., some specific configuration or arrangement of component parts). While this definition is applicable to universals like "cow-ness," "horse-ness," etc. that are instantiated by individuals having specific configuration, it is not applicable to universals like brahminhood, since it is not grasped through the presence of any specific configuration. That is why the second quarter of this verse provides another criterion for identifying *jātiśabda*. It has been said here that such words cannot be associated with all three genders (viz. masculine, feminine and neuter). The words "*brāhmaṇaḥ*" and "*brāhmaṇī*" are respectively in the masculine gender and feminine gender and they mean a male brahmin person and a female brahmin person respectively. But the word "brāhmaṇa" cannot be associated with the neuter gender (*klīvaliṅga*). Accordingly, brahminhood, which cannot also be associated with *all* three genders, satisfies the second definition provided in this verse. The same is true for properties like kṣatriyahood, vaiśyahood and śūdrahood. This conclusively shows that for these grammarians, properties like brahminhood are genuine universals and not complex properties (*sakhaṇḍa dharma*) that are constituted of a number of simpler properties.

The views of Kumārila Bhaṭṭa on universals and brahminhood

Let us now note the view of Kumārila Bhaṭṭa on the issue under consideration as expressed in his two main works, *Ślokavārttika* and *Tantravārttika*. In the *Pratyakṣasūtra* section of *Ślokavārttika*, Kumārila Bhaṭṭa admitted the perceptibility of universals like "cow-ness," while commenting on some sentences of Śabarasvāmin's *Bhāṣya* on *Mīmāṃsāsūtra* 1/1/5, which states (i) the nature of perception and (ii) the reasons for *not* treating perception as a source of knowledge through which *dharma* and *adharma* can be known. While discussing the nature of perception, this aphorism stated that perception occurs due to a specific connection (*samprayoga*) between a sense-organ (*indriya*) with some existent object (*sat*) that can be grasped by that sense-organ. Not all entities can, however, be perceived by us; hence, a proper account of perception should also state the types of the entities that may be perceived and also the relations obtained in such cases between the sense-organ and the objects perceivable through them. In the *Pratyakṣasūtra* section, Kumārila Bhaṭṭa clearly stated that in a determinate perception, which occurs after an inderterminate perception, the perceived object can be cognized as characterized by features like universals, etc.[6] In this connection, Kumārila Bhaṭṭa also stated in the section *Vanavāda* of *Ślokavārttika,* that universals like brahminhood can be perceived by us, since otherwise we would not be able to explain why, after seeing a person, we sometimes have a doubt of the form, "Is this person a brahmin or not?"[7] In the context of this doubt, brahminhood and its absence are the two mutually incompatible alternatives that are presented to us, just as in the case of, "Is that a man or a tree trunk?" which sometimes occurs after seeing a distant object, the alternatives (called *koṭi*), are (i) the property of being a man and (ii) the property of being a tree-trunk. Now, one who has never perceived these two last mentioned properties cannot have a doubt in the form, "Is this a man or a tree trunk?" Likewise, unless one has previously perceived brahminhood and its absence, one cannot also have a perceptual doubt such as, "Is this man a brahmin or not?"

Here, one may legitimately raise the question that supposing brahminhood *is* a universal, like the property of being a man or "cow-ness" or "horseness," why does not one immediately perceive brahminhood in a person who actually *is* a brahmin? In that case, just as the thing seen is known with certitude as a man, the fact that the man concerned is a brahmin would also be known with certainty and there would be no scope for doubt in the form, "Is this person a brahmin or not?" The very fact that unlike the property of being a man, the brahminhood of that man is not grasped immediately, proves conclusively that brahminhood *cannot* be perceived.

In the verses nos. 26–29 of *Vanavāda*, Kumārila Bhaṭṭa tried to show that in certain cases, universals can be perceived only when the sense-organ concerned is associated with some other factor. In many cases, awareness of properties like colour, taste, smell, touch and spatial and temporal features as well often help us in comprehending universals present in the things we perceive. Thus, the property of gold (*suvarṇatva*) in a piece of metal can be ascertained through its colour, weight, etc. Molten butter, which resembles oil, can be identified by its specific smell and taste. The presence of fire covered by ash can be ascertained by touch. That an animal at a distance is a horse (i.e., characterised by "horse-ness") can be ascertained by the neighing sound it makes. The presence of pot-hood in a utensil can be ascertained by its configuration. Likewise, brahminhood located in a person can be ascertained when it is known that both his parents are brahmins; and in certain countries, where the king compels each of his subjects to observe the rituals and customs specific to the caste he/she belongs to, one can ascertain brahminhood from the conduct of that person concerned.[8] This knowledge comes from spatial factors. Likewise, from seeing someone perform the *agnyādhāna* ritual in the spring, it can be ascertained that this person is a brahmin. This is due to temporal factors.

In *Tantravārttika* connected with Śabarasvāmin's *Bhāṣya* on the *Mīmāṃsāsūtra* 1/2/2 (*śāstradṛṣṭavirodhācca*)—which discusses how one can establish the authority of the vedic sentence "*na caitad vidmo vayaṃ brāhmaṇā vā abrāhmaṇā vā*" [*Taittirīya Brāhmaṇa* 2/1/2 (i.e., "we do not know whether we are brahmins or not")] and which, according to Śabarasvāmin, is contradicted by perception since the brahminhood of a person can be known perceptually—Kumārila Bhaṭṭa reiterated most of the claims stated above. But he denied that brahminhood can be determined merely from the conduct of a person because, under such a condition, when a person behaves like a brahmin he would be ascertained a brahmin and if the same person behaved like a śūdra, he would be ascertained a śūdra, which would result in the absence of caste distinctions.[9] He has also tried to meet the criticism that when our sense-organs need to be assisted by other factors for knowing something, that knowledge ceases to be perceptual. Even when we visually perceive things placed before us, our visual organ requires the assistance of light, a centain proximity to the object, contact of sense-organ with mind and so on. In order to see something situated on top of a mountain, we have to climb the mountain. Does that render the knowledge of that thing non-perceptual? But there are passages also in *Tantravārttika* on *Śābarabhāṣya* 1/2/2 that mention some scriptural passages that do not seem to be consistent with the view that brahminhood is a universal. One of them is from *Yājñavalkya Smṛti*[10] and a half-verse from an unknown source.[11]

Kumārila has quoted only the initial parts of these verses. The verse from *Yājñavalkya Smṛti* means that if a kṣatriya is married to a man who is brahmin by caste and if a daughter is born to them, then the daughter would be treated as *mūrdhāvasikta*, someone superior to kṣatriyas in caste, but inferior to brahmins. If she is married in turn to a brahmin and a daughter is born to them, then that daughter would be superior in caste to *mūrdhāvasiktas*. If this process goes on for four generations, then the daughter born in the fifth generation would attain brahminhood. In the case of women who are vaiśyas, this change would occur in the sixth generation, and in the case of a śūdra woman, this change would occur in the seventh generation. Contrarily, if a son who is *mūrdhāvasikta* marries a kṣatriya woman, then any son born to them would be inferior in caste to *mūrdhāvasiktas*. If such a son again marries a kṣatriya woman and a son is born to them, then the caste of such a son would be even more inferior. If this process continues for four generations, then the son born in the fifth generation would be treated as a kṣatriya. (This is how Someśvara Bhaṭṭa explained this verse in his *Nyāyasudhā*.[12]) But such an increase or decrease in status cannot hold in the case of universals, which are considered eternal and immutable. The second half-verse quoted above means that if a brahmin continues to sell milk for one month, then he becomes a śūdra in this very birth. This, too, is inconsistent with the claim that brahminhood, etc. are universals—because an individual instantiating a universal U_1 cannot, all of a sudden, become bereft of U_1 and become an instance of another universal U_2. According to Kumārila, however, this second half-verse merely means that selling milk is unbecoming on the part of a brahmin.

It may, however, be noted here that Kumārila Bhaṭṭa has *not* taken into account a few scriptural passages, some of which maintain that brahminhood depends primarily on specific good qualities and the practice of virtues, and not on birth. There are also some other passagess that specifically maintain that through the practice of *dharma*, a person born in a lower caste can be elevated to a higher caste, while through the practice of *adharma*, a person born in a higher caste can be downgraded to a lower caste.

Some examples of these are found in the *Mahābhārata*, *Bhāgavata Purāṇa* and *Āpastambadharmasūtra*. For instance:

1 "Oh Devī, by performing these actions in this way, a śūdra attains brāhmaṇa-hood and a vaiśya attains kṣatriya-hood."[13]

2 "All these brāhmaṇas are made so by conduct. A śūdra established in conduct attains brāhmaṇa-hood."[14]

3 "He is known as a brāhmaṇa, in whom are seen truthfulness, charity, absence of hatred, kindness, humility, compassion and austerity."[15]

4 "If this (list of virtues) is seen in śūdra and it is not there in a twice-born one, then the śūdra will not be a śūdra and the brāhmaṇa will not be a brāhmaṇa."[16]

5 "Whichever varṇa-indicating sign has been stated in the case of a person, if it is seen in another person, then one should designate that person by that respective varṇa."[17] (Śrīdharasvāmin, while explaining this

verse says, "The primary usage of the word brāhmaṇa is in respect of calmness, etc. and not just in respect of birth."[18])

6 "By meritorious behaviour a lower varṇa reduces to prior and prior varṇa in the next birth."[19]

7 "By bad behaviour a prior (that is, higher) varṇa reduces to lower and lower varṇa in the next birth."[20]

Jayanta Bhaṭṭa on brahminhood as a universal

Jayanta Bhaṭṭa defended the perceptuality of brahminhood on two occasions. In *Āhnika* III of his *Nyāyamañjarī*, he stated and rejected the view of Prābhākara Mīmāṃsakas, who maintain that the property of being sound (*śabdatva*) that is present in all sounds is not *jāti*, i.e., a universal proper—it is nothing but the property of being audible, i.e., being perceptible by the auditing sense-organ (*śrotrendriyagrāhyatva*), which is only an imposed property (*upādhi*). In this connection, he has said that just as brahminhood is a perceptible property, so too is the property of being a sound.[21]

Again, in *Āhnika* VI of *Nyāyamañjarī*, in regards to the question of whether grammatical correctness (*sādhutva*) and grammatical incorrectness (*asādhutva*) can be known perceptually, Jayanta Bhaṭṭa has said that these properties too can be perceived by a person who has received proper training in grammar—just as one can perceive the brahminhood in a brahmin when one is told that the person has been born of brahmin parents. His arguments very much resemble the arguments given by Kumārila Bhaṭṭa and he also quoted from *Ślokavārttika* and *Tantravārttika* in defence of his views. He also noted the view of some unidentified thinkers who maintain that one may perceptually know the brahminhood present in a person simply after seeing his/her pleasant and placid appearance.[22]

The opposition between Nyāya-Vaiśeṣika and Buddhist views on universals and brahminhood

According to the Nyāya and Vaiśeṣika schools, the relation through which a universal is situated in the individual instantiating it is known as "inherence" (*samavāya*), which is also one and eternal and which occurs between two relata that are "inseparable" (*ayutasiddha*). Five pairs of relata are regarded as inseparable: (i) a composite substance (*avayavin*, e.g., an earthen pot) and its component parts (*avayava*s); (ii) a substance (*dravya*) and its qualities (*guṇa*s, e.g., colour, touch, smell, etc.), (iii) a substance (*dravya*) and the movements (*kriyā*s) characterising it, (iv) a universal (*jāti/sāmānya*) and an individual (*vyakti*) that instantiates it and (v) an eternal substance (*nitya-dravya*) and the "differentiator" or "particularity" (*viśeṣa*) that differentiates each such substance from other eternal substances. The Bhāṭṭa

Mīmāṃsā school does not admit the existence of inherence—instead, they admit the relation of *tādātmya*, which is identity that is compatible with difference (*bheda-sahiṣṇu-abheda*). They also do not admit the existence of particularities. According to the Nyāya, Vaiśeṣika and Bhāṭṭa Mīmāṃsā schools, if an individual is perceptible, then the universal present in such an individual is also perceptible. In accordance with this view, these three schools maintain that common properties like brahminhood, which are universals, are also perceptible, just as universals like "pot-hood" are. In this way, these three schools try to show that the system of varṇas is natural and not man-made.

Such a view has been severely criticised by Buddhists who belong to the Svatantra-Yogācāra school developed by Diṅnāga, Dharmakīrti and their followers. According to these Buddhists, all real entities are momentary, and hence the reality of universals, which are supposed to be eternal, cannot also be admitted. The same opinion is expressed about inherence, which is also supposed to be eternal. As to the reality of the relation known as *tādātmya* admitted in Bhāṭṭa Mīmāṃsā, they point out that the very notion of identity-in-difference involves a logical contradiction; and hence, the question of admitting its reality does not arise. Thus, neither the universals nor their alleged relation to individuals can be treated as real. The individuals, who are devoid of any common character and who are also unrelated due to their momentariness, happen to be unique particulars (*svalakṣaṇas*). Some of them have the capacity of producing similar effects and accordingly are grouped together and given a common name on that basis. There is no eternal and identical property known as "cow-ness" that is present in all cows in an identical manner, though all cows are capable of yielding milk and carrying loads.

Those who admit universals as real entities point out that unless we admit universals, we cannot satisfactorily explain why the same expression is employed while describing a certain group of individuals, nor can we explain why those individuals, despite their mutual differences, are perceived in the same manner with respect to a certain aspect. Thus, the twin phenomena of uniform cognition (*anugatapratīti*) and uniform usage (*anugataśabdaprayoga*) that are not sublated by subsequent cognitions cannot be due to those individuals alone, which, according to the Buddhists, are unique particulars. If things which are totally different from each other are capable of producing such uniform cognition or uniform usage, then the latter could also happen in the case of a non-homogenous collection consisting of a man, a triangle, a table and a mosquito. But this never happens. Hence, only some identical thing that (i) is different from those individuals and (ii) is at the same time related to those individuals, can cause such uniform cognition and uniform usage. The possibility of such cognitions and usages cannot be restricted only to the present. Accordingly, such properties should be treated as eternal. In this way, the admission of universals as real and eternal entities becomes unavoidable. It should, however, be kept in mind that even though all universals are abstract and common properties, all common or abstract properties are not universals. Thus, a common property cannot be treated as a universal under the following conditions:

- i If an abstract property, due to its abstractness, seems to be a common property and yet resides in only *one* locus;
- ii If admitting a common property as a universal leads to a vicious infinite regress;
- iii If admitting a common property as universal results in denying the very nature of the loci in which it is located;
- iv If a common property fails to be related to its loci through the relation of inherence;
- v Again, if two common properties p_1 and p_2 are such that both of them are instantiated by exactly the same set of individuals, we cannot treat both of them as separate universals—only one of them may be admitted as a universal.
- vi Besides, if two common properties p_1 and p_2 are such that p_1 is present with the absence of p_2 in a locus L_1; p_2 is present with the absence of p_1 in another locus L_2; and yet, both p_1 and p_2 are co-present in a third locus L_3; then they are said to be vitiated by the defect called "cross-division" (*sāṅkarya*) and none of them can be treated as a universal. Such conditions, under which some abstract or common properties fail to become a universal, are known as *jātibādhaka*s.[23]

Two conditions that a common property must satisfy if it has to qualify as a universal are that (i) it should be simple or unanalyzable (*akhaṇḍa*), i.e.. it should not be a composite (*sakhaṇḍa*) property that is analyzable into simpler component properties (*ghaṭaka-dharmas*) and (ii) it should not also vitiated by any of the six *jātibādhakas*. The common properties that cannot be regarded as universals are known as "imposed properties" (*upādhi*s), which may be again of two types—viz. analyzable (*sakhaṇḍa*) and unanalyzable (*akhaṇḍa*). Such stipulations are admitted for the sake of parsimony (*lāghava*), so that there is no unnecessary multiplication of entities.

Buddhists are not, however, impressed by these arguments. They try to point out that one cannot explain how the relation supposed to connect a universal with the individuals instantiating it can obtain in the first place. Take, for instance, the property of being a pot, i.e., "pot-ness" (*ghaṭatva*) that is regarded by the Naiyāyikas and others as a universal. This property is supposed to be present uniformly in all the pots that exist at present. But how would it be related to a pot that is not existent as yet but is going to be produced in the near future? An earthern pot is made from two pot halves, viz. the lower one called "*kapāla*" and the upper one called "*kapālikā*." Now, "pot-ness" is not present in any one pot half; because had it been present in any one, then that pot half would have to be treated as a pot. Yet, when the two pot halves are joined together, they produce a pot, where "pot-ness" is present in a pervasive manner. Now, how can this fact be explained, since "pot-ness" was previously absent in the places occupied by those two pot halves? Has it come from some other location or has it been produced there? Neither of these two alternatives can be admitted, since an abstract entity like "pot-ness" cannot have any movement and, being eternal, it cannot also be produced. Moreover, movement on its part is also ruled out by the fact that it does not abandon its earlier substrata, which continue to be pots even when a new pot is produced. Nor can it be said that it exists in its earlier substrata through some parts and becomes related to the new pot by virtue of some other part, because "pot-ness" does not have any such component parts. Besides, if "pot-ness" is absent in both the constituent parts of a pot, then how can it be pervasively present in that very pot? Can it be the case that each thread of a cloth is black while the cloth as a whole is white?

Again, if this earthen pot happens to be broken, then "pot-ness" does not reside in any of the shards that are left behind. How can this be explained? Does "pot-ness" go away somewhere or is it destroyed? Once again, none of these alternatives is admissible, since universals are supposed to be immobile and eternal things cannot be destroyed. Thus, the admission of universals as distinct entities over and above individuals creates more problem than it solves. Dharmakīrti, a famous Buddhist thinker, summed up these arguments in four verses of his *Pramāṇavārttika*.[24]

Moreover, as the Naiyāyikas themselves have admitted in many cases, uniform cognition and uniform usage can also be explained with the help of "imposed properties" (*upādhis*) like the property of being a cook (*pācakatva*) that can be analysed into some other entities [e.g., (i) agency (*kartṛtva*), (ii) the relation of being conducive (*anukūlatva*) and (iii) the act of cooking (*pākakriyā*)] that one must admit (*avaśyakḷpta*) under all circumstances, and so admitting a large set of eternal and additional entities called universals for explaining these two phenomena goes against the principle of parsimony (*lāghavatarka*). Buddhists maintain that the functions of classification, uniform cognition and uniform usage can be explained in terms of *anyāpoha*, i.e., difference from other entities.[25] If universals are rejected in this manner, then the claim that properties like brahminhood, etc. are universals and, hence, natural principles of classification becomes totally untenable. Accordingly, Dharmakīrti has included pride due to belonging to a particular caste among the five things that, in his opinion, are five inferential marks of stupidity, the other four such marks being (i) admitting that the Vedas are authoritative, (ii) admitting that there is a creator of this world, (iii) treating ritual bath as a means of attaining purity and (iv) undergoing mortification of the body to get rid of sin.[26]

Jaina critique of brahminhood as a universal

Another critique of treating brahminhood, etc. as examples of universals is found in some Jaina texts like *Prameyakamalamārtaṇḍa* of Prabhācandra, which is a commentary on the *Parīkṣāmukhasūtra* of Māṇikyanandī. Unlike Buddhists, Jainas admit the existence of universals, even though they do not share all the views of the Nyāya-Vaiśeṣika school regarding these universals. To start with, the Jainas do not maintain that universals and particulars are totally distinct and independent things that are somehow connected through some relation. Every entity has a dual nature—one aspect of it is universal while the other is particular. This Jaina view is somewhat similar to the Bhāṭṭa view that a particular without universals or a universal that is unrelated to a particular is as unreal as the horn of a hare.[27] Jainas maintain that even if causal efficacy is admitted as a mark of reality, one has to admit that an entity having both common and uncommon features can produce some effect and, hence, both these aspects have to be accepted as real. Universals are, again, of two types—(i) "horizontal universal" (*tiryak-sāmānya*) and (ii) "vertical universal" (*ūrdhva-sāmānya*).[28] But even while conceding universals, Jainas point out that properties like brahminhood (*brāhmaṇya/brāhmaṇatva*) cannot be treated as universals, since there is no evidence in favour of such a claim. Those who admit that brahminhood, etc. are universals, claim that such properties can be established by perception, inference and verbal testimony. That brahminhood is a common property can be claimed on the basis of uniform cognitions like "this person is a brahmin," "this person is also a brahmin" and so on, which are perceptual in nature. In such cases, the fact that such persons are known as brahmins also depends on the knowledge that their parents are brahmins. Such perceptions are not illusory as they are not sublated. Nor are they cases of doubt, since they do not ascribe incompatible properties to the same entity. Hence, just as veridical and certain uniform perceptual cognitions like "this is a cow," "this is also a cow," etc. establish universal "cow-ness" (*gotva*), uniform perceptions like "this is a brahmin," "this is also a brahmin," etc. establish that brahminhood is a universal.[29]

The inference employed for establishing brahminhood as a distinct entity is of the following form:

i The term "brahmin" is related to a single property that is different from individuals, and is also the ground of application of that word to those individuals,
ii because it is a word,
iii for example, the word "cloth."[30]

Scriptural statements like "a brahmin should perform sacrifices" (*brāhmaṇena yaṣṭavyam*), "brahmins should be fed" (*brāhmaṇo bhojayitavyaḥ*), etc., also show that brahminhood is a common property like "cow-ness" and hence should be admitted as a universal.[31]

Jainas, however, reject such claims. Contradicting the claim that brahminhood can be established through perception, they ask—"Is this perception indeterminate/non-qualificative (*nirvikalpaka*) or determinte/qualificative (*savikalpaka*)?" The first alternative is not admissible, because in an indeterminate perception non-attributive in nature and also ineffable, one cannot apprehend universal and particular features *as* universal and particular respectively. This has been admitted by Kumārila Bhaṭṭa, the founder of Bhāṭṭa Mīmāṃsā, in his well-known work *Ślokavārttika*.[32]

The second alternative is also not acceptable, because even in a qualificative perception, persons who are said to belong to groups of brahmins like Kaṭha, Kalāpa, etc. are perceived and identified as human beings and not as brahmins, unless the person perceiving them is told by somebody else that they are brahmins. But one does not need such a statement from some other person to apprehend "cow-ness" in a cow. Nor can it be said that once we know that the parents of a person are brahmins we can ascertain that the person concerned is also a brahmin, because on what basis can someone tell us that the parents of a person are brahmins? It cannot be said that the basis of such a statement is perception because in that case, it would be a clear instance of mutual dependence (*anyonyāśraya*), since perception of brahminhood would be dependent on such an utterance and such an utterance would be, in its turn, dependent on perception.[33] Moreover, ascertainment of brahminhood on the basis of parentage is not always possible, because sometimes brahmin women who are unfaithful may enter into adulterous relations with non-brahmin men, and the children born from such unions are not in any way distinguishable from children whose parents are both undoubtedly brahmins. When there is a union between a mare and a stallion, the offspring is a horse; and in the case of a union between a mare and a male donkey, the offspring is a mule. But such is not the case in the issue under condition.[34] Moreover, sages like Vyāsa, Viśvāmitra, etc. were said to be brahmins, although it cannot be said that both the parents of such sages were brahmins. Hence, brahminhood cannot be decided on the basis of the parentage of a person.[35]

Moreover, a property that is supposed to be a universal is always present in the individual that instantiates it. It cannot be the case that an animal that was a cow at the time of its birth suddenly becomes a horse under certain circumstances. But a brahmin ceases to be a brahmin and becomes a śūdra if he ingests food prepared by a śūdra, establishes familial ties with a śūdra and so on, as has been stated in some brahminical scriptures. This clearly shows that brahminhood is not an unchanging property like "cow-ness" and hence it is not a universal.[36]

Likewise, brahmin women who enter brothels and become prostitutes are considered impure and unfit for marriage to brahmin grooms. If brahminhood is a universal, then that property, being eternal, would be very much present even in those women; and since brahminhood is supposed to be the grounds for the purity and respectability of brahmins, such women also should be considered pure and respectable. If it is said that they lose their purity and become outcastes since they have ceased to observe the rituals and customs of brahmins, then the same condition should apply to a *vrātya*, i.e., a brahmin who has not received initiation and sacred thread within the stipulated period and who has also not studied the Vedas. It is, however, maintained that the universal called "brahminhood" is present in the *vrātya*.[37]

In this way, Jainas attempt to show that brahminhood is nothing but a non-natural and composite property ascribed to a certain group of human beings on the basis of the performance of certain rituals, like officiating as priests at religious functions, recitation of the Vedas, offering sacrifices, etc., and also some distinguishing marks like the sacred thread (*upavīta*). The conclusion drawn by them on the basis of the arguments stated so far is that brahminhood is not a natural, eternal and unanalyzable property like "cow-ness" and hence, it is not also a universal. It is, on the other hand, an "imposed property" (*upādhi*), i.e., a property that has been artificially constructed out of simpler elements. Accordingly, Prabhācandra stated that the usage of the property brahminhood (*brāhmaṇatva*) is *aupādhika*.[38]

Prābhākara Mīmāṃsakas on brahminhood

Finally, we may note here the views of Prābhākara Mīmāṃsakas regarding the ontological status of properties like brahminhood. Unlike Buddhists and Jainas, Prābhākara Mīmāṃsakas are staunch supporters of the caste system, just as Nyāya-Vaiśeṣika and Bhāṭṭa Mīmāṃsaka thinkers are. Like these three group of thinkers, they also admit the existence of universals; and in agreement with the Nyāya-Vaiśeṣika school, they also admit that universals are located in their respective substrata through the relation of inherence. They, however, reject some Nyāya-Vaiśeṣika views regarding universals and inherence. According to the Nyāya-Vaiśeṣika school, all substances, qualities and actions/motions are characterised by universals, which can be arranged hierarchically in accordance with their pervasiveness (*vyāpakatva*). The universal called "*sattā*," which resides in every substance, quality and motion is the most pervasive among all universals, and, accordingly, it is called "*parasāmānya*" or "*parājāti*." Next in order of pervasiveness are the three universals substancehood (*dravyatva*), qualityhood (*guṇatva*) and motionhood (*karmatva*), which are present in all substances, all qualities and all motions respectively. At the lowest rung of this hierarchy are universals like "pot-hood" (*ghaṭatva*), which do not pervade any other universal. (It may be noted that for the Nyāya-Vaiśeṣika school the two universals *sattā* and *dravyatva* are related as pervader [*vyāpaka*] and pervaded [*vyāpya*]; while the two universals *dravyatva* and *guṇatva* are opposed [*viruddha*] to each other, since they can never be present in the same locus. Hence, if two properties P^1 and P^2 are such that neither of them is pervaded by the other and that both of them have at least one common locus, then they cannot be universals. This explains why the defect known as "*sāṅkarya*" is treated as one of the *jātibādhakas*.) Inherence, the relation through which these universals reside in their respective substrata, is one and eternal.

But for Prābhākara Mīmāṃsakas, a property cannot be admitted as a universal unless it is perceptible, and such perceptible universals are manifested (*abhivyakta*) only by the perceptible configuration (*ākṛti*) of the individual where that universal is located. Such a "configuration" is nothing but "the arrangement of component parts" (*avayavasanniveśa*), which can be present only in composite (and hence, non-eternal) substances. Eternal substances like atoms, the self, etc. are devoid of component parts, and so are all the qualities and movements. For Prābhākara Mīmāṃsakas, common properties like *sattā*, *dravyatva*, *guṇatva*, etc. are only "imposed properties" (*upādhis*) constructed out of simpler properties. Thus, in their opinion, *sattā* is nothing but the property of being the object of some veridical cognition (*pramāṇaviṣayatva*), substance-hood (*dravyatva*) is nothing but the property of being the locus of some quality (*guṇāśrayatva*) and so on.[39] Inherence, the relation through which universals are located in their substrata is also not one, but many; since it is (a) eternal only if *both* its relata are eternal and (b) non-eternal in other cases. Now, once we admit this doctrine, it becomes clear that brahminhood cannot be a universal; since there is no specific configuration that is peculiar to brahmins alone—the configuration of their limbs is also present in persons who are non-brahmins. According to Prābhākara Mīmāṃsakas, from time immemorial certain people, who perform certain acts and observe certain rituals, were known as brahmins. A child born from a brahmin couple is also known as a brahmin. In cases where it has been ascertained that there has been no mixture of castes, one can know with certainty that the child is also a brahmin. Thus, for Prābhākara Mīmāṃsakas, properties like brahminhood, kṣatriyahood, etc. are nothing but "imposed properties" (*upādhis*).[40] This Prābhākara view is presented in the *Jātinirṇaya* section of *Prakaraṇapañcikā* by Śālikanātha Miśra. Subsequent Nyāya, Vaiśeṣika and Bhāṭṭa works like *Nyāyasāra* of Bhāsarvajña with (i) the auto commentary *Nyāyabhūṣaṇa* and (ii) the commentary *Nyāyamuktāvalī* by Aparārkadeva; *Nyāyakandalī* of Śrīdhara Bhaṭṭa, *Nyāyakusumāñjali* of Udayana, *Nyāyalīlāvatī* of Śrivallabhācārya and *Mānameyodaya* of Nārāyaṇa have either stated the Nyāya-Vaiśeṣika view about *brāhmaṇatva* or tried to reject the Prābhākara view regarding the nature of universals, and also to re-establish the claim that brahminhood is a universal.[41] Several copies of unpublished manuscripts of later Nyāya works by unknown authors, all of which are entitled *Brāhmaṇatvajātivicāra* and that are deposited in various manuscript libraries, also try to justify the claim that brahminhood is a universal. The space at our disposal here does not allow a discussion of these additional arguments.

Criticism of caste in the Avadāna texts[42]

Criticism of caste in Śārdūlakarṇāvadāna

The question about the alleged superiority or inferiority between different castes has also been discussed at length in *Śārdūlakarṇāvadāna*, one of the longest stories included in *Divyāvadāna* (pp. 314–425). It narrates the dispute between Triśaṅku, a Caṇḍāla chieftain, and Puṣkarasārin, a Brahmin learned in the three Vedas. Triśaṅku had proposed the marriage of his son Śārdūlakarṇa to Prakṛti, the daughter of Puṣkarasārin. Puṣkarasārin was enraged, since he considered this proposal a grave insult, and rejected it outright as something as impossible as placing a mustard seed on the tip of a hair or as binding air in a trap. He pointed out that just as one can never equate gold with ash or obliterate the distinction between light and darkness, one cannot also treat a Caṇḍāla, (who is the lowest even among untouchables) as equal to a Brahmin, who belongs to the highest caste and who is honoured by all the other castes. Marriage can take place only between equals, and hence, the proposal of Triśaṅku was preposterous and not worth considering.[43]

After listening to the enraged brahmin's tirade, Triśaṅku answered that a brahmin does not differ from a non-brahmin in the same manner in which gold differs from ash, or light differs from darkness. He further pointed out that unlike fire that is generated by the rubbing of two sticks known as "*araṇi*," brahmins are not born from elements like earth, air, or *Ākāśa*—brahmins are born from the wombs of their mothers, just as non-brahmins are also born from the wombs of their mothers. Hence, there is no reason to claim that brahmins are superior to non-brahmins like Cāṇḍāla-s because of their birth. Again, after the death of a brahmin, his corpse is considered as impure and defiled as the corpse of a non-brahmin. What, then, are the grounds for treating a brahmin as intrinsically superior to a non-brahmin?[44]

Thereafter, Triśaṅku pointed out that brahmins have promulgated many cruel and sinful acts like killing animals in sacrifices on the pretext that animals thus killed go to heaven. But in that case, why do they not kill themselves, or their near and dear ones, to ensure their safe passage to heaven? Even after performing such cruel and sinful acts merely to satisfy their craving for meat, brahmins claim that they are pure by birth. Moreover, a brahmin can be expelled from his rank for committing grave offences like stealing gold, drinking wine, committing adultery with the wife of his preceptor, and killing another brahmin. Any brahmin guilty of such an offence becomes a non-brahmin and must practice severe penances for 12 years before such a "fallen" person can again be treated as a brahmin. This obviously shows that brahmins are not intrinsically superior to others. Hence, all human beings should be treated as equals.[45]

With the help of a suitable example, Triśaṅku explained here that expressions like "brāhmaṇa," "kṣatriya," etc. are purely arbitrary and are not based on any objective factors. Children playing on the street often make heaps of dust and then attach different names to them, e.g., "this is condensed milk," "this is yoghurt," "this is meat," "this is clarified butter" and so on; but by assigning such nomenclature, dust does not actually turn into things that can be eaten. Human beings are indistinguishable in respect of their anatomical details and, hence, no distinction can be drawn between them on account of their birth; especially in comparison to the distinctions that can be drawn between different non-human creatures in terms of their different modes of birth, food habits, (e.g., some are oviparous and others are viviparous; some are graminivorous, while others are carnivorous); and different physical features. Moreover, if all human beings are offsprings of Prajāpati, as is claimed by Puṣkarasārin, then all of them should be of the same type.[46]

Criticism of caste in Aśokāvadāna

It seems to me that in some instances, the attitude of Buddhists towards the question of caste was somewhat ambivalent. We may recount here one story of Emperor Aśoka found in *Aśokāvadāna* [which is actually a collection of four legends: viz. (a) *Pāṃśupradānāvadāna*, (b) *Kuṇālāvadāna*, (c) *Vītaśokāvadāna* and (d) *Aśokāvadāna*; all of which deal with the different phases of the life of the famous Emperor Aśoka] and that is also included in *Divyāvadāna*, a larger collection, where they have been assigned the numbers 26, 27, 28 and 29 respectively. As is well known, people from all strata of society were admitted as monks and nuns in the Buddhist Saṅgha, irrespective of their castes and provided they were found otherwise fit for ordination. Whenever Emperor Aśoka met a Buddhist monk, he used to bow down to them. This was disliked by Yaśa, the emperor's trusted minister. He pointed out that since Aśoka was a kṣatriya by caste, it was improper for him to bow to monks who were members of lower castes earlier. Emperor Aśoka used a clever strategy to convince Yaśa about the propriety of his own acts. He ordered that the heads of different birds and beasts be brought to him, while Yaśa was asked to bring a human head. Once they were brought, Aśoka ordered them to be sold in the market. All these heads except the human head were sold. When this was reported to Aśoka, he ordered that the human head be given to someone free of cost. But nobody agreed to accept it because of its repulsiveness (*aprāśastya*). Then Aśoka asked whether only that human head was repulsive or whether all human heads, irrespective of their owners, were repulsive. When Yaśa admitted the second alternative, Aśoka asked: "Is my head also repulsive?" When Yaśa was forced to give an affirmative answer, Aśoka said, "What is the harm if this repulsive head is lowered before persons who are spiritually superior?" Then he told Yaśa that one should consider the issue of caste only in matters of marriage, not in matters pertaining to religion.[47]

Aśoka indicates that he respects the Buddhist monks because of their virtues and good qualities that are not in any way related to their castes. In the next three verses, Aśoka points out to his minister that the defects or bad qualities of people are censured, even if they are of a higher caste. In that case, why should we not appreciate the good qualities of people even if they belong to a lower caste? The body of a person is dependent on birth in a certain family and is either praised or censured according to the mental states associated with it. Since the mental states of the Buddhist monks are pure, they deserve the respect of others. People born in higher castes are declared as "fallen" or excommunicated from society if they are devoid of good qualities. In that case, people born in lower caste should also be honoured by bowing down to them if they are endowed with good qualities.[48]

The story from *Aśokāvadāna* shows that even for people who had a lot of respect for Buddhism, the issue regarding castes could not be ignored in social matters like marriage, though it was not a significant factor in matters of religion. In his *Nyāyamañjarī*, Jayanta Bhaṭṭa also criticised Buddhists for adopting a double standard regarding the issue of caste, since they decry the caste system on one hand and avoid touching caṇḍālas on the other—which is certainly a glaring inconsistency.[49]

Notes

1 I express my gratitude to Dr. Nrisingha Prasad Bhaduri for giving me the exact references of some quotations.

2 "*atha vā sarva ete śabdā guṇasamudāyeṣu vartante—'brāhmaṇaḥ', 'kṣatriyaḥ', 'vaiśyaḥ', 'śūdra' iti—*

tapaḥ śrutaṃ ca yoniścety etadbrāhmaṇakārakam|

tapaḥśrutabhyām yo hīno jātibrāhmaṇa eva saḥ ||

tathā—'gauraḥ śucyācāraḥ piṅgalākṣaḥ kapilakeśa' ityetān apy abhyantarān brāhmaṇye guṇān kurvanti." [*Aṣṭādhyāyī* (2006), Vol. III, pp. 175–76].

3 "*varṇānāñ cānupūrvyena pūrvanipāto bhavatīti vaktavyam. brāhmaṇakṣatriyaviṭśūdrāḥ.*"

(*Māhābhāṣya* as in *Aṣṭādhyāyī* (2006), Vol. III, p. 243). Also see Pradīpa and Udyota on the same. Also see *Kāśikā with Nyāsa, Padamañajarī* and *Bhāvabodhinī as in Aṣṭādhyāyī* (1987), Vol. II, p. 390.

4 "*avadātāyāntū ṅīpprāpnoti —'avadātā brāhmaṇī'. 'varṇādanudāttāttopadhātto naḥ' iti. naiṣa varṇavācī. kiṃ tarhi? viśuddhavācī. ātaśca viśuddhavācī—evam hyāha:*

trīṇi yasyāvadātāni vidyā yoniś ca karma ca| etac chive! vijānīhi brāhmaṇāgryasya lakṣaṇam||" (*Māhābhāṣya*: as in *Aṣṭādhyāyī* (2006), Vol. V, p. 73).

5 " '*jāter'ity ucyate, kā jātir nāma?*
ākṛtigrahaṇā jātir liṅgānāñca na sarvabhāk/
sakṛdākhyātanirgrāhyā gotrañca caraṇaiḥ saha//"
(*Māhābhāṣya* as in *Aṣṭādhyāyī* (2006), Vol. V, pp. 86–87).

6 "*tataḥ paraṃ punar vastu dharmair jātyādibhir yayā| buddhyā'vasīyate sā'pi pratyakṣatvena sammatā||*" *Ślokavārttika, Pratyakṣasūtra*, 120.

7 "*arād dṛṣṭe ca puruṣe sandeho brāhmaṇādiṣu| na syād yadi na gṛhyeta sāmānyaṃ cakṣurādinā* ||" ŚV, *Vanavāda*, 25.

8 "*tasyopalakṣaṇam cāpi kvacit kenacid iṣyate| rūpādīnāṃ viśeṣeṇa deśakālādyapekṣayā||.*
suvarṇaṃ bhidyate rūpāt tāmratvāder asaṃśayaḥ| tailād ghṛtaṃ vilīnaṃ ca gandhena ca rasena ca || *bhasmapracchādito vahniḥ sparśanenopalabhyate| aśvatvādau ca dūrasthe niścayo jāyate svanaiḥ* || *saṃsthānena ghaṭatvādi brāhmaṇatvādi yonitaḥ| kvacid ācārarataścāpi samyag rājānupālitāt* ||" [ŚV, *Vanavāda*, verses 26–29. Also see *Nyāyaratnākara*, as in ŚV pp. 439–40].

9 "*yeṣām apy ācāranimittā brāhmaṇatvādayas teṣām api dṛṣṭavirodhas tāvad asty eva, na tv ācāranimittavarṇavibhāge pramāṇaṃ kiñcit. siddhānāṃ hi brāhmaṇādīnām ācārā vidhīyante, tatretaretarāśrayatā bhavet— brāhmaṇādīnām ācāraḥ, tadvaśena brāhmaṇādaya iti. sa eva śubhācārakāle brāhmaṇaḥ, punar aśubhācārakāle śūdra ity anavasthitam. tathā ekenaiva prayatnena parapīḍānugrahādi kurvatāṃ yugapad brāhmaṇatvābrāhmaṇatva-virodhaḥ*" [TV, p. 22].

10 "*jātyutkarṣo yuge jñeyaḥ pañcame saptame'pi vā| vyatyaye karmaṇām sāmyaṃ pūrvavaccādharottaram||*" [*Yājñavalkyasmṛti*, 1.96].

11 "*māsena śūdrībhavati brāhmaṇaḥ kṣīravikrayāt*" | [Source Unknown].

12 "*asyārthaḥ—kṣatriyāyāṃ brāhmaṇād utpannā kanyā mūrdhāvasiktā brāhmaṇāya dīyamānā mūrdhāvasiktajāter utkṛaṣṭāṃ kanyāṃ janayati, sā'pi brāhmaṇāya dīyamānā kanyāntaram evety evaṃ pañcame yuge puruṣāntare brāhmaṇyotpattyā jātyutkarṣaḥ. evaṃ 'vā' śabdāt ṣaṣṭhe vaiśyāyāṃ saptame śūdrāyām iti. mūrdhāvasiktaputraparamparāyāstu kṣatriyādistrīṇāṃ tathaiva pañcamādiṣu kṣatriyādijātīyāpatter apakarṣa iti pūrvavaccādharottaram ityuttaratrātideśāt*" [*Nyāyasudhā*, p. 27].

13 "*ebhistu karmabhir devi subhair ācaritais tathā| śūdro brahmaṇatāṃ yāti vaiśyaḥ kṣatriyatāṃ vrajet||*" (MB, *Anuśāsana Parvan*, 146.26).

14 "*sarvo'yaṃ brāhmaṇo loke vṛttena tu vidhīyate| vṛtte sthitastu śūdro'pi brāhmaṇatvaṃ niyacchati* ||" (MB, *Anusāsana Parvan* 146.51).

15 "*satyaṃ dānamathādroha ānṛśaṃsyaṃ trapā ghṛṇā| tapaśca dṛśyate yatra saḥ brāhmaṇa iti smṛtaḥ||*" (MB, *Śāntiparvan*, 189.4).

16 "*śūdre caitad bhavel lakṣyaṃ dvije tac ca na vidyate| na vai śūdro bhavecchūdro brāhmaṇo brāhmaṇo na ca||*" (MB, *Śāntiparvan*, 189/8).

17 "*yasya yallakṣaṇaṃ proktaṃ puṃso varṇābhivyañjakam| yadanyatrāpi dṛśyeta tattenaiva vinirdiśet||*" (BP, 7.11.32).

18 "*śamādibhir eva brāhmaṇādivyavahāro mukhyaḥ, na jātimātrād*" (*Śrīdharasvāmin* on BP, 7.11.32).

19 "*dharmacaryayā jaghanyaḥ varṇaḥ pūrvaṃ pūrvaṃ varṇam āpadyate jātiparivṛttau*" (ĀDS, 2.5.11.10).

20 *adharmacaryayā pūrvo varṇaḥ jaghanyaṃ varṇam āpadyate jātiparivṛttau.* (ĀDS, 2.5.11.11) (All the above passages have been quoted in Viśvarūpānanda (1988) pp. 776–7.)

21 NM, Vol. I, pp. 550–2.

22 NM, Vol.II, pp. 253–4.

23 The six conditions, each of which prevents an abstract property from being a universal proper, and are known as *jātibādhakas*, have been enumerated in the following verse by Udayana in his *Kiraṇāvalī*, "*vyakter abhedas tulyaṃ saṅkaro'thānavasthitiḥ| rūpahānir asambandho jātibādhakasaṃgrahaḥ||*" (*Kiraṇāvalī*, p. 23).

24 "*nāyāti na ca tatrāsīd asti paścān na cāṃśavat| jahāti pūrvaṃ nādhāram aho vyasanasantatiḥ||152|| anyatra vartamānasya tato'nyasathānajanmani| svasmād acalataḥ sthānād vṛttir ity atiyuktikam||153|| yatrāsau vartate bhāvaḥ tena sambadhyate na hi| taddeśinaṃ ca vyāpnoti kim apyetan mahādbhūtam ||154|| vyaktyaivaikatra sā vyaktyā bhedāt sarvatragā yadi| jātir dṛśyeta sarvatra na ca sā vyaktyapekṣiṇī||155||*" (*Pramāṇavārttika*, Chapter on *Svārthānumāna*, pp. 77–78).

25 For a detailed discussion regarding the doctrine of *Apoha*, see Siderits et al. (2011).

26 Dharmakīrti has stated these "five inferential marks of stupidity" in the following verse of *Pramāṇavārttika*: "*vedaprāmāṇyaṃ kasyacit kartṛvādaḥ, snāne dharmecchā jātivādāvalepaḥ| santāpārambhaḥ pāpahānāya ceti, dhvastaprajñānāṃ pañca liṅgāni jāḍye||340||*" (*Pramāṇavārttika*, Chapter on *Svārthānumāna*, auto-commentary, p. 176).

27 "*nirviśeṣañca sāmānyaṃ bhavec chaśaviṣāṇavat| sāmānyena rahitāś ca viśeṣās tadvad eva hi||*" [ŚV, *Ākṛtivāda*, verse no. 10].

28 The following aphorisms of PMS state these views:

(a) "*sāmānyaṃ dvedhā*" (4.3); (b) "*tiryagūrdhvatābhedāt*" (4.4); (c) "*sadṛśapariṇāmas tiryak khaṇḍamuṇḍādiṣu gotvavat*" 4/5; (d) "*parāparavivartavyāpi dravyam ūrdhvatā mṛdiva sthāsādiṣu*" 4/6 [PMS, pp. 466–88].

29 "*nanu ca 'brāhmaṇo'yaṃ' 'brāhmaṇo'yam' iti pratyakṣata evāsya pratipattiḥ. na cedaṃ viparyayajñānam, bādhakābhāvāt. nāpi saṃśayajñānam, ubhayāṃśānālambitvāt. pitrādibrāhmaṇayajñānapūrvakopadeśasahāyā cāsya vyaktir vyañjikā, tatrāpi tatsahāyeti...*" [PKM, p. 482].

30 "'*brāhmaṇa'-padaṃ vyaktivyatiriktaikanimittābhidheyasambaddhaṃ, padatvāt, paṭādipadavat*" (PKM, p. 482).

31 "*tathā 'brāhmaṇena yaṣṭavyam', 'brāhmaṇo bhojayitavyaḥ' ityādyāgamāc ceti*" (PKM, p. 482).

32 "*atrocyate—yat tāvat uktaṃ 'pratyakṣata evāsya pratipattiḥ', tatra kiṃ nirvikalpakāt, savikalpakād vā tatas tatpratipattiḥ syāt? na tāvan nirvikalpakāt, tatra jātyādiparāmarśābhāvāt, bhāve vā savikalpakānuṣaṅgaḥ.*

"*asti hyālocanājñānaṃ prathamaṃ nirvikalpakam|bālamūkādisadṛśaṃ vijñānaṃ śuddhavastujam|| na viśeṣo na sāmānyaṃ tadānīmavasīyate|tayorādhārabhūtā tu vyaktir evāvasīyate||*"; "*tataḥ paraṃ punar vastu dharmair jātyādibhir yayā|buddhyā'vasīyate sāpi' pratyakṣatvena sammatā||*" *iti vaco viruddhyeta*" (PKM, p. 482) (Here, Prabhācandrasūri is referring to ŚV, *Pratyakṣasūtra*, verse nos.112–3, p. 120).

33 "*nāpi savikalpakāt, kaṭha-kalāpādivyaktīnāṃ manuṣyatvaviśiṣṭatayeva brāhmaṇyaviśiṣṭatayāpi pratipattyasambhavāt. 'pitrādi-brāhmaṇyajñānapūrvakopadeśa-sahāyā vyaktir vyañjikā'sya—ity'apy asāram.....' brāhmaṇatvajāteḥ pratyakṣatāsiddhau yathoktopadeśasya pratyakṣahetutāsiddhiḥ, tatsiddhau ca tatpratyaksatāsiddhiḥ' — ity anyonyāśrayaḥ*" (PKM, p. 482).

34 "*prāyeṇa pramadānām kāmāturatayeha janmany api vyabhicāropalambhāc ca kuto yoninibandhano brāhmaṇyaniścayaḥ? na ca viplutetarapitrapatyeṣu vailakṣaṇyaṃ lakṣyate. na khalu vaḍavāyāṃ gardabhāś'vaprabhavāpatyeṣv iva brāhmaṇyāṃ brāhmaṇaśūdraprabhavāpatyeṣv api vaīlakṣaṇyam lakṣyate*" (PKM, p. 483).

35 "*kathaṃ caivaṃvādinaḥ Brahma-Vyāsa-Viśvāmitra prabhṛtīnāṃ brāhmaṇyas-iddhiḥ, teṣāṃ tajjanyatvāsambhavāt. tan na pitror aviplutatvaṃ tanimittam*" (PKM, p. 484).

36 "*kriyāvilopāt śūdrānnādeś ca jātilopaḥ svayam evābhyupagataḥ--.śūdrānnāc chūdrasamparkāc chūdreṇa saha bhāṣaṇāt| iha janmani śūdratvaṃ mṛtaḥ śvā cābhijāyate||*" (PKM, p. 483).

37 "*...tan na paraparikalpitāyāṃ [brāhmaṇatva] jātau pramāṇam asti yato'syāḥ sadbhāvaḥ syāt. sadbhāve vā veśyā-pāṭakādi-praviṣṭānāṃ brāhmaṇīnāṃ brāhmaṇyābhāvo nīndā ca na syāt, jātir yataḥ pavitratāhetuḥ; sā ca bhavanmate tadavasthaiva, anyathā gotvād api brāhmaṇyam nikṛṣṭaṃ syāt. gavādīnām hi cāṇḍālādigṛhe ciroṣitānām api śiṣṭair ādānaṃ, na tu brāhmaṇyādīnām. atha kriyābhraṃśāt tatra brāhmaṇyādīnāṃ nindyatā; na... kriyābhraṃśe tajjātinivṛttau ca vrātye'py asya nivṛttiḥ syād bhraṃśāviśeṣāt*" (PKM, p. 486).

38 (a) "*kiñca—aupādhiko'yaṃ brāhmaṇaśabdaḥ, tasya ca nimittaṃ vācyam....*" (PKM, p. 483); (b) "*tataḥ kriyāviśeṣādinibandhana evāyaṃ brāhmaṇādivyavahāraḥ*" (PKM, p. 486).; (c) "*tataḥ sadṛśakriyāpariṇāmādinibandhanaiveyaṃ brāhmaṇakṣatriyādivyavasthā.....*" (PKM, p. 487).

39 "*atra kecid gavāditulyatayā dravyaguṇakarmaṣvapi sattājātim aṅgīkurvanti, bhavati hi sarveṣv eva 'sat', 'sad' iti pratyayanuvṛttir iti saṃvatantaḥ. tad idam aparāmṛṣṭajāti- tattvānām uparyupari jalpitam. pūrvarūpanukāriṇi yadi dhīr udīyate, tato'bhyupeyetaiva jātiḥ. na ca nānājātīyeṣu dravyeṣu sarṣapa-mahīdharādiṣu, guṇeṣu gandharasādiṣu vā samānākārānubhāvo bhavati. kevalaṃ tu 'sat', 'sad'iti śabdamātram eva prayujyate. bhavati ca vināpi jātyā-'pācaka' 'mīṃāmsakā'diśabdapravṛttiḥ. nanv evaṃ śabdapravṛttir api naikanibandhanam antareṇopapadyate. satyam, asty evopādhir ekah pramāṇasambandhayogyatā nāma*" (*Prakaraṇapañcikā*, p. 97).

40 *Prakaraṇapañcikā*, pp. 100–2.

41 (a) *Nyāyabhūṣaṇa* (as in Nyāyasāra (1968)), pp. 336–7; (b) *Nyāyamuktāvalī* (as in Nyāyasāra (1961)), pp. 251–2; (c) *Nyāyakusumāñjalī*, pp. 285–6; (d) *Nyāyakandalī*, pp. 34–35; (e) *Nyāyalīlāvatī.*, pp. 226–9.

42 In many places of the Pāli Tripiṭaka, Buddha has discussed the issue of caste with various persons; and in all such cases, he has rejected the claim of some *brāhmaṇa*-s that by virtue of their birth, they are superior to non-brahmins. The suttas like *Ambaṭṭha Sutta* and *Soṇadaṇḍa Sutta* of *Dīgha Nikāya*, *Vasala Sutta* and *Vāseṭṭha Sutta* of the *Sutta Nipāta* and *Brāhmanavagga* of *Dhammapada* are relevant in this context. I am not discussing the Buddha's critique of caste expressed in these canonical texts here to avoid repetition as it has been dealt with elsewhere in this book, for example by Bimalendra Kumar (Chapter 1) and by Mahesh Deokar (Chapter 5).

43 Some of the verses containing the statement of Puṣkarasārin are to be found in *Divyāvadāna*. See DA pp. 320–1.

44 See the verses 15–19, DA, p. 323.

45 See verses 20–23, 29, 30, 36 and 37, DA p. 323. Verse 37 is followed by the sentence, "*tad idaṃ brāhmaṇa te bravīmi—saṃjñāmātram idaṃ lokasya yadidam ucyate 'brāhmaṇa' iti vā 'kṣatriya' iti vā, 'vaiśya' iti vā, 'śūdra' iti vā. sarvam idam ekam eva...*"

46 DA, pp. 324–5.

47 "*āvāhakāle'tha vivāhakāle, jāteḥ parikṣā na tu dharmakāle| dharmakriyāyāṃ hi guṇā nimittā, guṇāś ca jātiṃ na vicārayanti ||4||*", DA, p. 242.

48 For these verses, see DA, pp. 242–3.

49 Jayanta Bhaṭṭa has castigated Buddhists for denying caste distinctions on one hand and avoiding the touch of people like Cāṇḍālas, who were treated as

untouchable by vedic society, on the other. Buddhists, he alleges, also prohibit the admission of such "untouchables" as monks in the Buddhist Saṅgha:

i "*yathā caite bauddhādayo'pi durātmānaḥ vedaprāmāṇyaniyamitā eva caṇḍālādisparśaṃ pariharanti. niraste hi jātivādāvalepe kaḥ caṇḍālādisparśe doṣaḥ*"? NM, Vol. I, p. 638.

ii "*yad api bauddhāgame jātivādanirākaraṇam, tad api sarvānugrahaprav aṇa-karuṇātiśaya-praśaṃsāparaṃ na yathāśrutam avagantavyam. tathā ca tatraitat paṭhyate—'na jātikāryaduṣṭān pravrājayet'iti,*" NM, Vol. I, p. 643.

In this connection, my Pāli scholar friends pointed out that Vinaya texts do not make any such rule recommending avoidance of touching Caṇḍālas (or persons belonging to any specific castes for that matter). The Buddha regarded persons belonging to the lowest castes, such as Caṇḍāla and Pukkasa, equally eligible for the life of self-control and attainment of Nibbāṇa as persons from high castes. In many dialogues in the Pāli Tripiṭaka, the Buddha rejected the claim of some Brāhmaṇas that by virtue of their birth, they are superior to non-brahmins. *Ambaṭṭhasutta* and *Soṇadaṇḍa Sutta* of *Dīgha Nikāya* and also *Dhammapada* (*Brāhmanavagga*) may be referred to in this context. The *Sutta Nipāta*, (e.g., *Vasala Sutta*, verses 137–42, *Vāseṭṭha Sutta*, verses no 600–11, 620–50) states that while there are physical distinctions in terms of specific configuration, colour, food, etc. among different types of non-human creatures, the same is not true of human beings belonging to different castes. "Brāhmaṇa," "Kṣatriya," "Vaiśya" and "śūdra" are mere names. One is treated as a brahmin due to moral excellence, and not due to birth. Prof. Bimalendra Kumar suggests that originally the Caṇḍālas seem to have been an aboriginal tribe. This is clear from the use of their own argot (*Jātaka*, Vol. IV, 391f). Gradually, they came to be looked upon as untouchables. One *Jātaka* describes the caṇḍāla as the vilest people on the earth (ibid, 397). In a *Jātaka* story, when a caṇḍāla enters a town, people pound him with blows and render him unconscious (ibid, 376, 391). The extent to which the caṇḍālas were abhorred can be seen in various mentions in some of the *Jātakas*. Contact with air that touched a caṇḍāla from a distance was enough for high caste people, especially women, to wash their eyes with scented water (*gandhodaka*) to remove the contamination, as told in the *Citta-Sambhūta-Jātaka* (ibid, 390–401). A similar incident is related in the *Mātaṅga Jātaka* (ibid, 375–90) when the daughter of a Seṭṭi of Varanasi, seeing a caṇḍāla, washed her eyes with perfumed water, as she was considered to have been contaminated by a mere glance at that despised person. Jayanta Bhaṭṭa's comment could be based on such references which are contrary to the Buddha's own intentions.

References

Primary sources

ĀDS: *Āpastambadharmasūtram with Haradatta's Ujjvala*, edited by A. Mahādevaśāstrī and K. Rangācārya, Governement of His Highnessthe Maharaja of Mysore, Mysore, 1898.

Aṣṭādhyāyī: *Aṣṭādhyāyī* of Pāṇini with *Kāśikā* by Jayāditya and Vāmana, *Nyāsa* of Jinendrabuddhi and Padamañjarī of Haradatta, edited by J.L. Tripathi and S. Malaviya, Tara Printing Works, Varanasi, Vol. IV, 1987.

Aṣṭādhyāyī: *Aṣṭādhyāyī* of Pāṇini with *Māhābhāṣya*, of Patañjali, *Pradīpa* of Kaiyaṭa, *Uddyota* of Nāgeśa, *Śabdakaustubha* of Bhaṭṭoji Dīkṣita, etc. edited by G. P. Shastri, Rastriya Sanskrit Sansthana, New Delhi, Vol. I–IX, (Reprint) 2006.

Bhagavadgītā.

BP: *Śrīmad-Bhāgavata-Mahāurāṇa* (Vols. I and II), Gita Press, Gorakhpur, 2018.

DA: *Divyāvadāna*, edited by P.L. Vaidya, Mithila Institute for Post Graduate Research in Sanskrit, Darbhanga, 1959.

Jātaka (with commentary), Vol. I–VI Ed. V. Fausboll, Pali Text Society, London, 1962.

Kiraṇāvalī of Udayana on *Padārthadharmasaṁgraha* of Praśastapāda, edited by Jitendra Jetley, Oriental Institute, Baroda, 1971.

MB: *Mahābhārata* (Vulgate edition) with the commentary *Bhāratabhāvadīpa* of *Nīlakaṇṭha*, edited by R.S. Kinjwadekar, Second Reprint, Vol. I–VI, Oriental Books Reprint Corporation, New Delhi, 1997.

Nyāyabhūṣaṇa: *Nyāyabhūṣaṇa* of Bhāsarvajña as included in *Nyāyasāra*, 1968.

Nyāyakandalī of Śridhara Bhaṭṭa on *Padārthadharmasaṁgraha* of Praśastapāda, edited with Hindi translation by Durgādhara Jhā, Sampurnananda Sanskrit Visvavidyalaya, Varanasi, 1977.

Nyāyakusumāñjalī of Udayana with *Bodhanī* of Varadarāja, *Prakāśa* of Vardhamāna Upādhyāya and, *Prakāśikā* of Ruchidatta Upādhyāya, edited by Padmaprasāda Upādhyāya and Dhuṇḍirāja Śāstrī, Chowkhamba Sanskrit Series, Varanasi, 1957.

Nyāyalīlāvatī of Śrivallabha with *Kaṇṭhābharana* of Śaṇkara Miśra, *Prakāśa* of Vardhamāna Upādhyāya and *Vivṛti* of Bhagīratha Ṭhakkura, edited by Harihara Śāstrī and Dhuṇḍirāja Śāstrī, Chowkhamba Sanskrit Series, Varanasi, 1927.

NM: *Nyāyamañjari* of Jayantabhaṭta, with the gloss *Nyāyasaurabha*, edited by K.S. Vardacharya, Oriental Institute, Mysore, Vol. I, 1970, Vol. II, 1983.

Nyāyamuktāvalī: Nyāyamuktāvalī of Aparārkadeva as included in *Nyāyasāra*, 1961.

Nyāyaratnākara: *Nyāyaratnākara* of Pārthasārathi Miśra as included in ŚV.

Nyāyasāra (1961): *Nyāyasāra* of Bhāsarvajña with *Nyāyamuktāvalī* of Aparārkadeva and *Nyāyakalānidhi* of Ānanadānubhāvācārya, edited by S.S. Śāstrī and V.S. Śāstrī, Government Oriental Manuscripts Library, Madras, 1961.

Nyāyasāra (1968): *Nyāyasāra* of Bhāsarvajña with auto commentary *Nyāyabhūṣaṇa*, edited by Swāmī Yogīndrānanda, Ṣaḍadarśana Prakāśana Pratiṣṭhāna, Varanasi, 1968.

Nyāyasudhā: *Nyāyasudhā* of Someśvara Bhaṭṭa as included in TV.

PKM: *Prameyakamalamārtaṇḍa* of Prabhācandra, edited by Mahendra Kumar Jain, Nirnaya Sagar Press, Bombay, 1941.

PMS: *Parikṣāmukhasūtram* by Māṇikyanandī as included in PKM.

Prakaraṇapañcikā of Śālikanātha Miśra with *Nyāyasiddhi* of Jayapurī Nārāyaṇa, edited by A. SubrahmaṇyaŚāstrī, Benaras Hindu University, Varanasi, 1961.

Pramāṇavārttika of Ācārya Dharmakīrti, with *Svopajñavṛtti* of the author, edited by R. Gnoli, Instituto itatiano per il mealo ed extreme oriente, Roma, 1960.

Ṛg-Veda Saṃhitā (*Sanskrit Text, English Translation, Notes and Index of Verses*), edited by Raviprakash Arya and K. L. Joshi, translated by H. H. Wilson with Bhāṣya of Sāyaṇācārya, Parimal Publications Pvt. Ltd., Delhi, 2016.

Sutta Nipāta—Bengali translation by Bhikṣu Śīlabhadra, Mahabodhi Book Agency, (Reprint) 1998.

ŚV: *Ślokavārttika* of Kumārilabhaṭṭa with *Nyāyaratnākara* of Pārthasārathi Miśra, edited by DvārikādāsaŚāstrī, Tara Publications, Varanasi, 1976.

Taittirīya Āraṇyaka. (Kṛṣṇa Yajurveda), Text in Devanāgarī, edited by R. L. Kashyap, translated by Shrikant Jamadagni, Vols. I and II, Shri Aurobindo Kapali Shatry Institute of Vedic Culture, Bengaluru, 2016.

Taittirīya Brāhmaṇa of Black Yajurvedawith the Commentary of Sāyaṇa Ācārya, edited by Rājendra Lāla Mitra, Asiatic Society of India, Calcutta, 1862.

Taittirīya Saṃhitā. (*Kṛṣṇayajurvedīyā*) Sanskrit Text with Indexes, Meharchand Lakshmandas Publications, New Delhi, 2018.

TV: *Tantravārttika* of Kumārila Bhaṭṭa in *Mīmāṃasādarśana* with *Bhāṣya* of Śabarasvāmin, *Bhāṣyavivaraṇa* of Govindāmṛta Muni, *Tantravārttika* of Kumārila Bhaṭṭa and *Nyāyasudhā* of Someśvara Bhaṭṭa, edited by M.L. Goswami, Tara Printing Works, Varanasi, Vol. I, Vikram Samvat 2041 (=1984 CE).

Yājñavalkya-smṛti along with commentary of Aparārkadeva, edited by H.N. Apte, Anandasrama, Poona, Vol. I (*Ācārādhyāya*), 1903.

Secondary sources

Siderits, M., Tillemans, T., and Chakrabarti, A. (Eds.) (2011): *Apoha: Buddhist Nominalism and Human Cognition.* New York: Columbia University Press.

Viśvarūpānanda, S. (1988): *Vedāntadarśana* [containing *Brahmasūtra-śāṅkarabhāṣya* along with (i) the gloss *Bhāṣyaratnaprabhā* by Rāmānanda Sarasvatī, (ii) Bengali translation and (iii) *Bhāvadīpikā*, an exposition in Bengali)] Vol. I. Calcutta: Udbodhana Karyalaya.

3

EPISTEMOLOGICAL FOUNDATIONS OF CASTE IDENTITIES

A review of Buddhist critique of classical orthodox Indian realism

Ajay Verma

One of the foremost tasks of philosophers is to look for order in the way things are or to suggest ways that may make a better order possible among things. But the question, "How are things ordered?" is secondary to the question, "What is the actual nature of things?" In general, "what" questions come before "how" questions since order of things (how) cannot be studied in isolation from our ontological presumptions regarding those things (what). Similarly, it is important to first study the ontological nature of society in order to theorize about the order of society. Further, the reasons for what we do are invariably ingrained in what we believe to be fact. Thus, there are reasons to believe that there is an inextricable link between epistemology and ethics. In recent years Habermas (1998: 228) has explicated this link more explicitly than ever before. He maintains that a correct understanding of the meaning of an action is tantamount to correctly grasping the reasons for which it is performed. Further, he argues that these reasons are embedded in the linguistic character of our being. Since language is a shared phenomenon, the action, its meaning and the reasons for which it is performed should, in principle, be accessible both to the interpreter and the agent, rather than being in the domain of the agent alone. One could take this a step further and argue that how the meaning-generating process becomes possible in language has an intimate connection with how knowledge becomes possible in language. Further fallout of this conception would be that our ideas regarding knowledge and language have an important bearing upon how we act and how we understand actions. If understanding actions rests upon problems of meaning and language, then the arena of our inquiry into meaning of actions becomes much wider. In this chapter, I attempt to examine Nyāya epistemology and Buddhist Mahāyāna criticism with these assumptions regarding the interrelationship of epistemology and (social) action in mind.

Mahāyāna Buddhism against essentialism and realism

When it comes to examining Buddhism as a philosophy and religion challenging Brahmanical oppression against the lower castes, scholars have generally paid more attention to Pāli canon than Sanskrit Mahāyāna texts. It has even been argued by some that Sanskrit Mahāyāna texts, instead of challenging Brahmanical Hindu notions of castes, etc., were influenced by some orthodox systems of the time, resulting in religious practices that were marred by the same practices that the Buddha was always against. I argue in this chapter that some of the foundational texts of Mahāyāna philosophy do pose implicit challenges to orthodox classical thought systems in India.[1] These texts represent a fundamental challenge against the orthodoxy of the day by confronting their epistemic tenets. Since orthodoxy and orthopraxy (knowledge and practice) have an ineluctable connection, Buddhist Mahāyāna critique of orthodox schools also clear the ground for alternate *epistemes* to emerge which could be more conducive to *praxis* devoid of any kind of essentialism or logo-centricism.

Before we examine how some of the basic Mahāyāna texts challenge epistemic and ontological foundations of essentialism we must look at the popular definition of essentialism:

> **Essentialism** is the view that, for any specific entity (such as an animal, a group of people, a physical object, a concept), there is a set of attributes which are necessary to its identity and function... An *essence* characterizes a substance or a form, in the sense of the Forms or Ideas in Platonic idealism. It is permanent, unalterable, and eternal; and present in every possible world.[2]

With this understanding in mind, let us examine some of the fundamental tenets of different brands of Indian Realism. The Nyāya school is probably the best representative of realism amongst Indian schools of philosophy. Naiyāyikas believe that the world is objectively real, that is to say that world exists independently of our mind. Secondly, they believe that objects in the world represent themselves in their entirety, as they actually are and are knowable in their entirety as such. This means that the representation of objects is always total in terms of its universality, particularity and its relationship with its own parts and other entities and that linguistic understanding fully captures it. This understanding of the world makes it look like a tightly woven fabric/matrix of objects and their interconnections at the micro as well as macro level. Furthermore, the categories that put this matrix together as it appears to us are not transcendental categories to enable our judgments but are rather viewed as natural entities existing out there, always available for cognition. Thus, by providing us a metaphysical framework of objectively real categories, Nyāya philosophy achieves a huge philosophical feat. In doing this, Naiyāyikas naturalize our subjective ways of looking at things and foreclose any hermeneutic possibility of understanding our world. One might comment at this point that there is apparently nothing wrong with this process. If there were no objective basis to our subjective modes of thinking, it would lead to loss of any commensurability principle to argue for right from wrong, which was one of the main agendas of Nyāya thinkers. The main aim of the Nyāya system, as the name itself suggests, is to investigate what constitutes right knowing and argumentation. The term "*nyāya*" in its axiological sense means fitness, propriety or justice. Justice comprises of looking at the actual state of affairs of an event and subsequently judging them in terms of normative principles with legal binding. Thus, facts are not merely epistemological entities, their importance extends to how they are subsequently viewed as a part of more overarching entities like society and state. Thus, looked at this way, general meaning and current usage of the word "*nyāya*" is indicative of the actual philosophical pursuit that these thinkers were following. Subsequently, it also makes the epistemological enterprise more amenable to analysis through methodology that is available to us after Habermas.

On language

Now to understand the challenge posed by Śūnyavāda to a realist worldview of this kind, let us imagine a world where everything is in a constant flux. It is a world absolutely indifferent to our modes of intelligibility. By the time we propose a name for it, it is already else-way. It is a world constantly poised as "yet-to-be." Can our ordinary language function in such a world? The answer, I believe, should be both yes and no, depending on what we want to achieve with language. If we suppose the main task of language is to refer to the world, then on close analysis we find that at metaphysical level there is a gap between the two. Our words seem to but do not have any real point of correspondence with the outside world. To understand this, we need to focus on the fact that we are born into a language and do not actually create one for ourselves. Language with its definite set of presuppositions is a pre-given mode of existence. One of the most fundamental features of language that is not so much the concern of linguists or philosophers of language is the fact that "names" presuppose permanent or static referents. For example: we would retain an understanding or meaning of the word "chair" even if all the chairs in the world were to disappear for a few hours. Actual so-called chairs in the world come and go, but the word "chair" in language would stay. Buddhists point out that the so-called chair is *actually* not there because it is in a state poised to disappear in the next moment. Therefore, its "chair-ness" with its implicit features of stability and permanence is only a projected imposition of something in the mind. What this means is that the source of illusion of permanence is in our minds and, further, it is in the mind because the mind feeds upon language. But the next problem this leads to is that the world is unmistakably *there*, indifferent to any language. Therefore, to say that there is something wrong with it would presuppose the aforesaid connection between the language and the world, which is precisely what Buddhists put at stake. Buddhists might further argue that the fundamental existential fact of human suffering as represented in the first Noble Truth could be viewed as an indirect consequence of this presupposed connection between the language and its referent. This point can be understood as follows: Language beguiles us into thinking that there is something permanent about the world. This happens because language proclaims its self-presence along with the claim that it has a direct correspondence with the world; that it refers to the world outside as being "so-and-so." This belief that the world is there to stay with us along with its essences is gradually reinforced in our minds. It gives birth to clinging and the desire to possess. This can lead to frustration, *dukkha*, which takes hold of us when the object of clinging—which by very nature is momentary—disappears, leaving its referents behind as apparently still meaningful. Language as a set of concepts is not under any obligation or duress to remain faithful to particulars. But our actual world is housed not with universals but particulars. Our emotions are evoked not by universals but by particulars. One does not love "womanhood" in the actual world but a particular woman. Thus, the claim that language refers to the particulars and it actually failing to do so leaves us with an unbridgeable gap. For Buddhists, a proper understanding of this gap between the universals that make language work and the particulars that expose the limitation of language in actually corresponding with the world is the first step towards a more liberal understanding of the world.

Let me rephrase the argument from the point of view of essentialism. Actual nature or *svabhāva* of an object should refer to something that would stay always, but since it is possible to imagine the object as not-to-be, how can we ever have a view of the so-called actual nature or *svabhāva* of an object? Therefore, language works with, works in and works through an implicit contradiction that Śūnyavādin sets out to explicate. This contradiction is that language apparently claims to expose an object as an actual so-and-so as if the so-and-so-ness were an essential feature of the object. However, whereas "object-ness" of the object is supposed to be universal and apodictic in nature, it claims to refer only to a particular, which lacks both these features. Śūnyavādin is more concerned about the psychological implications of this point than the epistemological ones. The implicit assumption in the function of language is that it refers to permanent definitive features of impermanent objects. The repeated use of such language function reifies this belief in us that there is something permanent about the objects being so referred. What is permanent is also considered essential to the object. This linkage lends epistemological justification to our cognition of the object as essentially so-and-so. The object thus seemingly signifying itself as so-and-so evokes a specific psychological response from us like *rāga* (attachments), *dvesa* (disinclinations) or prompts certain behaviour in us through *saṁkalpas* (ideas or determinations) thus aroused in mind.

Thus, the issue of language is affronted by Mahāyāna Buddhists on the following counts:

a Language by psychological reification of referring to permanent entities covers up the temporary nature of things.
b By offering us a linguistically conceptualized definitive worldview it prevents us from seeing the world with its alternate possibilities.

Further, one of the main ways of essentializing, objectifying and reifying the idea of *svabhāva* is to present a transcendental argument from causality. According to *Satkāryavāda*, essence may undergo modifications in manifestation but intrinsically/substantially remains immutable and same. One of the main arguments for the caste system comes from the *Puruṣa-sūkta* from *Ṛgveda*, according to which the four varṇas are manifestations of Puruṣa, the eternal cause. Since the distinctions of varṇa are inherent in the ultimate cause, they are therefore immanently inherent in its various manifestations and are all the same immutable. Similarly, though Nyaiyāyikas through their conception of *asatkāryavāda* argue for new creation of things, newness for them only means negation of its prior absence. Thus, examined closely, the Nyāya conception of the newness/novelty of an entity is essentially a temporal notion. Thus an entity is only laterally new or has a new beginning only along the horizontal axis of time, but along the vertical axis it is definitive and makes itself amenable to our understanding of it qua *sāmānya* or universal that inheres in it and marks the periphery/frontier of what it could ever be. Nāgārjuna presenting it as *pūrva-pakṣa* writes:

> An essential property is something an object cannot lose without ceasing to be that object. Nāgārjuna observes that "*svabhāva*" [in the sense of essence] cannot be removed, like the heat of fire, the fluidity of water, the openness of space.
>
> (Westerhoff, 2009: 22)

Existential and notional aspect of an object

The Mahāyāna distinction between *sāmānyalakṣaṇa* and *svalakṣaṇa*[3] is of paramount importance in this regard. According to Mahāyāna tradition, there are two main ways in which we take an object into consideration.

Svalakṣaṇa means an intrinsic feature of an object without which it cannot be the kind of object we consider it to be. We could call it the "existential aspect" of an object. As opposed to this, one could have a notional aspect of an object. Here this would mean a semantic aspect of it. The important difference between the existential and notional aspects of an object is that whereas the former refers to the ontological aspect of our understanding of an object, the latter pertains to the belief-aspect of the same. Mahāyāna Buddhist thinkers recognize these two aspects as two different epistemological realms altogether. The difference between the two for them is not one of degrees but of kind. The notional aspect according to them is imbued with linguistic categories that evolve out of countless changing contexts of our empirical lives. Accordingly, we view objects as subject to our notions regarding them. But it stands to reason that the notional aspect of objects is based solely upon how they are negotiated within our contexts of living. In other words, this view of objects is solely based upon the utility value of the object concerned. This way the ontological/existential sphere of enquiry is clearly and unequivocally delineated and distinguished from its notional/empirical sphere by Mahāyāna Buddhists. One of my aims in this chapter is to explicate that an omission to make this differentiation on the part of orthodox realists results in consequences that not only have soteriological but certain social implications as well.

For any socio-political collectivity we need to mutually recognize and respect two kinds of identities. First, we have identities that are absolutely fundamental to us as a part of that collectivity and in virtue of which we become a recognized part of that collectivity with the same rights and duties as all other members. On the other hand, we may also have some, other more temporary identities that are subservient to some shifting contexts in life. We have certain human rights ascribed to us as virtue of our being humans. This is something that we essentially are and signifies a bare minimum that we must acknowledge, recognize and respect in all human beings as much as in ourselves. On the other hand, my profession, my nationality, my religion, my gender and now even my sex provide to me temporary affiliations that may all seem important to me depending on the context but that are not definitive of me all the same. An important point I wish to bring out here is that these temporary affiliations do not in any way formalize my core identity as a human being. Epistemologically, this distinction could be viewed in several ways. Though not an exact parallel, this distinction could also be viewed in some way as similar to Locke's distinction between primary and secondary qualities. Whereas primary qualities in Locke's view reside within the object irrespective of our vantage point, secondary qualities are those ones amenable to our view of them. This notwithstanding, the overall point I am trying to make here is that how we are viewed in a social collectivity inevitably draws upon epistemological questions/inquiry and this is where an enquiry into orthodox realist schools' theory of *pramāna* and their Buddhist opponents holds a key to understanding what kind of social collectivities they envisaged. In this regard, the schools of realism in classical India propose metaphysic that is more conducive to obfuscation of such distinctions in identities rather than their explication. As Prabal Kumar Sen points out, the Nyāya-Vaiśeṣika school as well as the Pūrva-mīmāṁsā school maintain that properties like brahminhood, kṣatriyahood, etc. are *sāmānyas* like cowness, horseness etc., and hence, one has to admit this four-fold classification of human beings as a given fact, not subject to any change that may be brought about by human effort.[4] Even though Naiyāyikas make a distinction between "contingent" and "necessary" with regard to their conception of the relationship amongst objects, there is no such distinction in their metaphysics with regard to the "whatness" of objects. Furthermore, the Nyāya theory of *pramāṇa-samplava* suggests that the nature of the object of cognition remains the same irrespective of the epistemological means employed for the same. This notion is challenged by the Buddhist notion of *pramāṇa-vyavasthā.*

Thus, language is viewed as having fixed designations by most orthodox schools. One could even say that the post-Heideggerian hermeneutical turn in western European philosophy does not have any counterpart in Indian thought. There are fixed ways of knowing the Other, whether as an object or as a person, such that the Other has a fixed unalterable status in the matrix of collectivity. Dominant trends in Indian philosophy allow internal pluralism but do not give an adequate and balanced account of dynamism, growth and mobility, which are essential indices of liveliness of things.[5] Much like some early Greek ideas, Indian orthodox thought systems show one-sided emphasis on essentially defined ways of epistemological access to an object.

Identity politics: subjective and objective identity

Another important point that emerges here is that from the perspective of identity politics, there can be two types of identities, as many philosophers including Bilgrami (2007) maintain. On one hand there are "objective identities" that are affixed to an individual. The constructions of such identities draw upon certain structures of meaning that are projected upon a person in virtue of her caste, creed, nationality and other affiliations without her subjective approval. In virtue of their source in linguistic practices, these structures are often considered immutable and non-negotiable just like words are. It could be interesting to note in this regard that social practices or "*lokavyavahāra*" is considered almost on par with *pramāṇa* in Nyāya philosophy. And although Naiyāyikas regard words as non-eternal and word-meaning relations as conventional, in order to maintain the authority of the Vedas, they regard word-meaning relations concerning the Vedic literature as instituted by God (Potter, 1977: 153). Mīmāṁsakas, on the other hand, regard words as well as their relation with meanings as eternal. Universals are eternal and they are meanings of words according to both. This underscores the immutable structure of language as advocated by these realist schools. Hence the conceptions of language and reality of the realist schools in classical Indian philosophy provide the groundwork for presumably unalterable or immutable objective identity attributions.

As opposed to objective identities, subjective identities are those that have their basis in either the life-world or subjective inclinations of the concerned individual or whatever else,. but what differentiates them is that these identities are not affixed or projected upon an individual from outside of themselves; rather, they are consciously chosen by the person concerned and therefore have the personal approval and even assertion of the individual concerned. This further requires that the subject under consideration be viewed as having her own historical consciousness that projects itself as the rudiments out of which the subject constructs her identity. Needless to say, that formation of such identities may only be possible with a hermeneutical view of the subject, where the subject is reflexive and reflective at the same time and constantly emerges and constructs herself from within this dialectical tension and is therefore never complete. On examination of the above, it seems that there is a general lack of epistemological models available in classical Indian philosophical traditions that would support the notion of subjective identity. In other words, given rigid notions of "what-ness" of things as we find in the Nyāya system or in case of varṇa-based identities, there seems to be insufficient hermeneutical space for more flexible notions of identity to evolve within the epistemological and ontological fabrics of classical Indian orthodox realist worldviews.

I have attempted to argue here that as opposed to such conceptions of the world, Śūnyavāda philosophy is more akin to existentialist notion of *being*, where the "what-ness" of an object is not defined by the universal or *sāmānya* residing in it; rather, it evolves in and through our engagements and negotiations with others in specific contexts. Since the caste system builds itself upon reification of our contingent temporary affiliations, treating them as ontologically essential to our being, Mahāyānist critiques of essentialism expose and hit at the epistemological foundations of caste identities.

Furthermore, it should not be out of place to mention here that even though there is an explicit mention of different varṇas and a critique of the discrimination based on that in many early Pāli Buddhist literary sources, some scholars have pointed out that in the context of *nirvāṇa* varṇa distinctions are irrelevant as presented in early Pāli Buddhist literature (Krishnan, 1986: 71–84). But even though these distinctions are considered irrelevant once a seeker or *bhikkhu* gives himself up to the pursuit of *nirvāṇa*, these caste hierarchies are not put into question on ontological or epistemological grounds specially in the Buddhists Pāli texts. Moreover, the scholars like Y. Krishan (1986) and Bimalendra Kumar (2020) have pointed out that there are passages in Pāli Buddhist canons that can be construed as uncritically descriptive of caste hierarchies, if not outright supportive of it. Bimalendra Kumar (2020), however, counters such a position by making a distinction between the Buddha's own approach as reflected in Pāli literature and the views attributed to the Buddha or developed by Buddhists later on. He concludes, on the basis of several citations from different Pāli sources, that such misconceptions can arise only when one fails to take into consideration the distinction he amply demonstrates between the Buddha's own approach to varṇa hierarchy and later Buddhist developments on this issue.

In modern times, however, B. R. Ambedkar was of the opinion that since the varṇa system provides the main bedrock for the formation of caste hierarchies, Hindus (notably among them Gandhi), should give up the notion of varṇas if they were at all serious about upliftment of oppressed castes. Ambedkar's position in this context would be best argued if there could be a possible criticism of the philosophical ideas that lend ontological and epistemological credibility to the varṇa system. Such critiques of epistemic support to the varṇa system are conspicuously available in Mahāyāna-śūnyavādin tradition as pointed out earlier.

Possibilities beyond Śūnyavāda

Society as a form of collectivity may have only a virtual existence that has an important practical purpose but it has to also have some idea of individual units that hinges upon and is invested with some notion of reality in terms of their experiences, sheer physicality or whatever else. Critics of Śūnyavāda philosophy therefore argue that some minimal idea of reality is indispensable for the formulation of rules of collectivity. Without such rules, no credible conception of collectivity can be constructed and subsequently any idea of social reformation would be, at best, good fiction. Therefore, one could argue that a *śūnyavādin* achieves the goal of challenging varṇa hierarchies only half way through, if at all. Critics may also point out that a *śūnyavādin* does not make direct reference to the notion of varṇa. Their critique in the texts is primarily directed against the classical realist's notion of *pramāṇas* in the epistemological context and also towards their conceptualization of *sāmānya* (universal) in the ontological context.

A possible reply to such criticisms could be to bring the critic's attention to *śūnyavādin's* suggestion of a two-fold distinction between *saṃvṛti-satya* and *paramārthataḥ satya*. For *śūnyavādins* all concepts exist at the level of *saṃvṛti* or at the level of practical utility alone and their truth has only provisional value within certain contexts. In this regard, they even point out that their negation of essences is also significant within the context of their effort to destabilize any metaphysical foundations of the very notion of essence (*svabhāva*) and therefore should not be considered as a philosophical position or thesis outside that context. That being so, having presented an insurmountable challenge to realist notion of essences, a *śūnyavādin* would not close himself to suggestions regarding what would be best forms of collectivities given the practical utility value of those rules. But an important question that arises here is whether such a position is explicitly available in Mādhyamika texts. Mādhyamika tradition, originating as it does in the Buddha's silence, leaves more unsaid in terms of their actual philosophical stance—if they have any—on such issues. In the absence of the latter, no robust critique of the notion of caste, which would also lend itself to ethical and social considerations, can be developed.

This lacuna is filled by latter Buddhist logicians, notably amongst them Diṅnāga, who carries the *śūnyavādin*'s lineage in a direction that positions itself on a better epistemologically and ontologically delineated ground than Śūnyavāda itself. This in turn makes the Buddhist Mahāyāna position in its realist garb more robust in taking on the challenge posed by Naiyāyikas' brand of realism. But before we delve further into the debate, it would be worthwhile to take a closer look at the very idea of realism. In this connection, Pradeep Gokhale (1996) presented an interesting take on the issue. He points out that *śūnyavādin* is mainly concerned with the critique of *svabhāva* or the alleged essence of objects that not only lends ontological ground to their being so but also thereby makes these objects amenable to intelligibility. Gokhale asks in this connection, "But what about existence as *svabhāva*? If a thing exists by its very nature, by its essence, then it cannot cease to exist," and argues that "Advaitins and Mādhyamika Buddhists agree with this implication though they use this implication in opposite directions." He further points out that later Buddhist logicians like Diṅnāga and Dharmakīrti contend that 'existence' "as an object of inference and language has a logico-linguistic status and not the ontological status like the one alleged to be that of *sāmānya* or *jāti*." The only basis of reality of "*sat*" or "existence" is its depositional status or "*arthakriyākāritva*." On such a conception of "existence" Dharmakīrti stipulates that something that is real must have some dispositional character or functionality. But functionality as the only mark of reality is precisely what would also render the being of an object non-eternal. According to Gokhale (1996: 209):

> If productivity or functionality is the very nature of everything real, then a real must itself undergo change. The thing which does not change itself cannot produce anything. And a thing which does not produce anything cannot be real. By an argument of this kind Dharmakīrti shows that everything real must be changing. Now a

> changing thing must change immediately. If change is *svabhāva* of a thing, it cannot remain unactualized. Secondly, change being contrary to the idea of sustenance, a thing cannot change and yet retain its identity. So, a thing which is real and therefore changing by its very nature, must be momentary.

Thus, even though the Śūnyavāda doctrine of "no-essence" provides an important critique to disrobe the classical realist position—whether in its eternalistic garb in Advaita or in its common sense garb in Naiyāyikas—it leaves vacuous the space for any discourse on the collectivity that is so important to the Buddha's notion of Saṅgha. The notion of *saṁvṛti-satya* initially developed in Śūnyavāda is rather unintelligible. It provides no ground for explaining the so-called practical utility insofar as something that does not exist cannot be useful or the so-called alleged practical utility of an object is equally imaginary. As such, it could be argued that it cannot go together with Ambedkarism. According to Ambedkar, the opposite sides of the equation in his critique of Brahmanism are Brahmanical realism and some Buddhist counterpart of the same (realism), and not so much realism and anti-realism (Śūnyavāda). Ambedkar's critique of caste and its concomitant demand for deconstruction of the epistemological and ontological ground of caste therefore can better be developed on Sautrāntika lines in comparison to their Śūnyavāda counterpart.

Notes

1 Though it is true that Vajrayāna system does show dominant influence of the Hindu *Tantra* tradition, some Buddhist Tantras exhibit an explicit anti-caste approach. Shrikant Bahulkar (2020) has shown this with special reference to *Kālacakra-tantra* and its commentary *Vimalaprabhā* edited by Vrajavallabh Dvivedi and him (1994).

2 http://www.artandpopularculture.com/Essentialist.

3 This distinction was first introduced by Diṅnāga and then elaborated by Dharmakīrti. It was adopted by later Mahāyāna thinkers.

4 See "Nature of Caste: Some ontological problems," by P.K. Sen (2020). Here it can be noted that recognition of *brāhmaṇatva*, *kṣatriyatva*, etc. as *jāti*s has an interesting social implication. Naiyāyikas, while giving a special ontological status to *jāti*, also introduce the restrictions on something being regarded as *jāti* (*jātibādhaka*s). One such restriction is that any two *jāti*s should not overlap each other; that is, they should not have *saṅkara*. This gives an additional reason for Naiyāyikas to oppose the admixture of varṇas ('*varṇa-saṅkara*').

5 I believe that this trend is unfailing even up to Gandhi who, though influenced by Jaina philosophy of non-violence, was a strict adherent of *varna-ashrama* system for the large part of his life. B. R. Ambedkar realized that unless this orthodoxy in the Hindu way of life is given up, it does not have any space for consensus and dialogue—the true hallmark of any democratic setup.

References

Bahulkar, Shrikant. 2020. "Casting Away the Caste: A Buddhist Stand-point in the *Vimalaprabhā* Commentary on the *Kālacakra tantra*," included in the present volume.

Bilgrami, Akeel. 2007. *Politics and the Moral Psychology of Identity*. Cambridge, MA: Harvard University Press.

Gokhale, Pradeep. 1996. "Essentialism, Eternalism and Buddhism." In *Buddhism in India and Abroad*, edited by Kalpakam Sankarnarayan and others. 199–210. Mumbai: Somaiya Publications.

Habermas, Jürgen. 1998. *On the Pragmatics of Communication*, edited by Maeve Cooke. Cambridge: Polity Press.

Krishan, Y. 1986. "Buddhism and the Caste System." *Journal of the International Association of Buddhism Studies*, 9, no. 1. pp. 71–84.

Kumar, Bimalendra. 2020. "Buddha's Attitude Towards Caste System as Available in Pāli Texts," included in the present volume.

Potter, Karl. 1977. "Introduction to the Philosophy of Nyāya-Vaiśeṣika." In *Encyclopedia of Indian Philosophies, Indian Metaphysics and Epistemology: The Tradition of Nyāya-Vaiśeṣika up to Gaṅgeśa*, edited by Karl Potter. 1–208. Delhi: Motilal Banarsidass.

Sen, P.K. 2020. "Caste in Classical Indian Philosophy: Some Ontological Problems," included in the present volume.

Vrajavallabh, Dwivedi, S.S. Bahulkar (Eds.). 1994. *Vimalaprabhā: Vimalaprabhāṭika of Kalkin Srīpuṇḍarīka on Srīkālacakratantrarāja*, Rare Buddhist Text Series 13. Sarnath: Central Institute of Higher Tibetan Studies, 1994.

Westerhoff, Jan. 2009. *Nāgārjuna's Madhyamaka: A Philosophical Introduction*. Oxford: University Press.

4

CASTING AWAY THE CASTE

A Buddhist standpoint in the *Vimalaprabhā* commentary on the *Kālacakra* tantra

Shrikant Bahulkar

Tantric Buddhism is a branch of Mahāyāna, generally denoted by the terms "*Mantrayāna*" or "*Vajrayāna.*" The Mahāyāna tradition believes that the teachings in the *Mantrayāna* were given by the Buddha when he turned the Wheel of Law for the second time. While he gave the teachings of the *Pāramitānaya* at Gṛdhrakūṭa, he manifested himself at the same time at Śrīdhānyakaṭaka and gave the teachings of the *Mantrayāna.*[1] The tradition also believes that all the Buddhist Tantras were taught by the Buddha, who manifested himself in different forms. According to the historical view of modern scholars, one of the earliest Buddhist Tantric works, namely the *Guhyasamājatantra*, dates back to the 3rd or 4th century CE, while the last one, the *Kālacakratantra* (KC), was disseminated in the 10th or 11th century CE. Buddhist Tantric literature thus marks the last phase of Indian Buddhism and possesses some unique characteristics in relation to their contents and language. These works furnish details of Tantric ritual consisting of various rites such as the initiation of a disciple into a particular Tantric cycle, the worship of particular deities in the Maṇḍala, various consecrations or empowerments, yogic practices and so on. The path of enlightenment prescribed in the *Pāramitāyāna* would require many a lifetime to reach the goal, while the *Mantrayāna* is a quick path, through which it is possible to attain "complete enlightened Buddhahood" (*samyaksambuddhatva*) in the present lifetime and body. The language of Buddhist Tantras is supposed to be Sanskrit. However, it is not necessarily Buddhist Hybrid Sanskrit, it is much more corrupt.

While the Tantras are believed to have been taught by the Buddha himself, there are a number of secondary works evidently composed by Tantric masters, who came from different social backgrounds. They hailed from different castes and classes in Indian society and pursued different professions and lifestyles. For example, Sarahapāda, the author of the *Dohākośa*, was formerly a learned brāhmaṇa named Rāhula, master of the Vedas and the *Śāstras*. He decided to embrace Buddhism and became a monk. Some came from royal families: Indrabhūti, the author of the *Sahajasiddhi* (Toh. 2260) was a king and his sister, Lakṣmīṅkarā, who wrote a commentary on that work (Toh. 2261), was a princess. Some masters came from low classes and had low professions. Some even belonged to tribal communities. Among these, there were arrow-makers, cobblers, rag-pickers, street-sweepers, entertainers and menial labourers of all types. The caste, the class, the profession or even the gender was not an obstacle in the path of Buddhahood. In this regard, there is a verse quoted in the *Vimalaprabhā* (VP), the celebrated, encyclopaedic commentary on the KC. The verse says:

> *caṇḍālaveṇukārādyāḥ pañcānantaryakāriṇaḥ* |
> *janmanīhaiva buddhāḥ syur mantracaryānucāriṇaḥ*|| (VP I, p. 15)

"Outcastes (*caṇḍāla*), flute-makers and so forth, and those who commit the five sins of immediate retribution (*ānantarya*), may become Buddhas in this very life, by pursuing the Mantra conduct" (VP I, p. 15).

In connection with the topic of this chapter, we come across, in the VP, a forceful argumentation aimed at refuting discrimination on the basis of one's caste, class and profession. The KC available to us at present is called the Concise *Kālacakratantra* (*laghukālacakratantra*), an abridged version of the Root-tantra (*mūlatantra*) called the *Paramādibuddha*.

According to the legend narrated in the KC and the VP, the Root-tantra was taught by the Buddha to King Sucandra, an emanation (*nirmāṇakāya*) of Vajrapāṇi, the tenth-stage Bodhisattva. King Sucandra in turn composed the Abridged Tantra in 12,000 verses in the *anuṣṭubh* metre and wrote an extensive commentary consisting of 60,000 *ślokas*, i.e., a unit consisting of 32 letters each. He gave the teachings of this Tantra to the people residing in the 960 million villages of the country called Śambhala.

The VP records the prophesy of the Buddha, according to which in future there will be born, into Sucandra's lineage, a descendant called Yaśas, the emanation of Mañjuśrī. He will compose a concise version of the Root-tantra in 1,030 verses in the *Sragdharā* metre. His son Puṇḍarīka will compose a commentary consisting of 12,000 *ślokas*. King Yaśas will be called "Kalkin" as he will bring the four varṇas into a single clan (*kalka*) by means of the Vajra-family initiation. Puṇḍarīka will be the second Kalkin. The word *kalka* has a peculiar meaning in this context; it means "a mixture of all classes into one single clan." And the word *kalkin* means "one who possesses the (single) clan." *Kalkin* appears to have been borrowed from Brahmanical Purāṇic sources, according to which Kalkin is the future and tenth incarnation of Viṣṇu. The Kālacakra tradition has, however, its own context and interpretation.

The VP narrates a story how King Yaśas effected the maturation of people by teaching them this Tantra and bringing them into one clan. The story echoes the attempt of Buddhists to refute Brahmanical proponents of caste-class discrimination. According to this story, King Yaśas gave the teachings in the Concise Kālacakra Tantra to the 35 million brāhmaṇa sages, headed by Sūryaratha, residing in the 960 million villages in the country of Śambhala, at the Malaya Garden in the village Kalāpa, on the other bank of the Sītā river.

The story narrated in the VP shows how this Tantra came into being in order to convert the followers of the Vedic Dharma into Buddhism, particularly Tantric Buddhism. It also shows that it was necessary to convert first the brāhmaṇas so that those of other varṇas would follow them. It also aims at removing the ego for caste or class from the minds of the followers of the Vedic Dharma. The VP elsewhere quotes a verse that says that the Buddha gave the teaching into the Vajrayāna in order to remove one's clinging to one's family ("*kulagrahavināśāya*," VP I, p. 16).

In this connection, the VP also explains how the Tantra deliberately uses irregular or ungrammatical forms and construction in order to eliminate the ego or obsession with pure language on part of people belonging to high castes and classes. It reflects the conflict between the elites and the masses over the purity of language. Puṇḍarīka, the author of the VP, argues that King Yaśas, the composer of the Concise KC, relied on meaning and deliberately used faulty construction. The sole purpose behind that was to remove the obsession of a certain class with a grammatically correct word and its correct pronunciation. For instance, in some verses there are corrupt forms. In some verses, there is a violation of (a rule of metre named) *yatibhaṅga*. Somewhere there is a word without the case ending. In some words, letters and vowels are dropped. In some verses a long vowel is short and a short one is long. Somewhere the locative case is used for the ablative and the genitive for the dative.[2] The statement of the VP echoes the thought met with in the *Laṅkāvatārasūtra*. It says: "O one of great intelligence! a Bodhisattva, the Great Being, should rely upon the meaning and not upon the letters."[3]

This detailed explanation given by the author of the VP is aimed at attacking the followers of the Vedas and the Śāstras, the language of which is Sanskrit, prescribed by the Pāṇinian system of grammar. The Vedas have to be studied with great care and perfection so that there is no mistake in regards to the pronunciation of mantras, not even a mistake of a letter or an accent. Moreover, Patañjali, the author of the *Mahābhāṣya* on Pāṇini's *Aṣṭādhyāyī*, says at the outset that Pāṇini's work is the "instruction into the words" (*śabdānuśāsana)* that includes both Vedic words as well as those used in the language of the people. He further lays great emphasis on the importance of proper words, as there are a number of corrupt forms of one word when uttered by a variety of people.[4] The language with ungrammatical words would not be called Sanskrit. Thus, the emphasis laid on the proper language represents the ego of high-class people towards their caste, class, family and gender. This might be one of the reasons for a norm laid down in the *Nāṭyaśāstra*, according to which inferior characters and women in Sanskrit plays speak Prakrit and not Sanskrit. The Prakrit languages are supposed to be the languages of the masses and not the elites in those days. In this regard, it is interesting to note how a Prakrit poet defends his language, praising the beauty of a Prakrit composition in the following words:

"The compositions in Sanskrit sound harsh, while that in Prakrit appears delicate. Whatever is the difference between a man and a woman, the same is the difference between these (two languages)."[5]

Clinging to the standard Sanskrit language is closely related to the Dharma and the Dharmaśāstra of high-class people. Common people belonging to the class of merchants and low castes do not understand Sanskrit. This is the reason why Lord Mahāvīra and Lord Buddha began to give their teachings in the languages of laymen and laywomen, in the vernaculars of those respective provinces. The Mahāyāna tradition maintains that both the Pālī Tripiṭaka and the Mahāyāna Sūtras are the sayings of the Buddha. The VP further elaborates this point and shows how the Buddha used a variety of languages to teach the Dharma to people residing in a variety of provinces.[6] The VP further explains how the Tathāgata gave teachings in various manners and remarks with the following words: "Because if this Sanskrit speech of limited extent (*prādeśika*), without the omniscient language having the nature of the utterance of all sentient beings, the Buddha would also be one of limited extent" (VP I, p. 34).

Though the first three of the four varṇas—namely, the brāhmaṇas, the kṣatriyas and the vaiśyas—are entitled to study the Vedas and the Śāstras, it appears that this precept was no longer in practice at the time of the composition of the VP. At some point in the medieval period, a notion came into being, which stated that in the Kali age there remains only two varṇas, the brāhmaṇa and the śūdra (*kalāv ādyantayos sthitiḥ*).[7] At the time of the composition of the VP, in the 10th or 11th century CE, it was believed that the brāhmaṇas and the kṣatriyas alone were entitled to the study of the Vedas. This belief can be corroborated by a statement in the Bhagavadgītā that says: "Women, the vaiśyas and the śūdras as well— these too can attain the supreme destiny, i.e., liberation."[8]

Thus, having attacked the Sanskrit language and the scriptures of the adherents of Vedism, Vaiṣṇavas and Śaivas, that discriminate people of the four varṇas on the basis of their birth, the VP further attacks the very notion of the divine origin of the four varṇas. The oldest reference to this notion is found in the famous *Puruṣasūkta* of the Ṛgveda (X. 90.12). The verse in question mentions all four varṇas together and speaks of their origin. It is said in that hymn: "The brāhmaṇa was His mouth; the one of the royal race was made His two arms; as for the vaiśya, he was His two thighs; while the śūdra was born from His feet."[9] The KC refers to this mantra, while mentioning the doctrine of Brahmā and Viṣṇu (KC II. 166). The VP refutes this doctrine, saying:

> Here the origin of brāhmaṇas is supposed to be the mouth of Brahmā. etc. Thus there are four varṇas. Now, there is the fifth varṇa, next to the four ones, namely that of the outcastes (*caṇḍāla*). Then what is the origin of that varṇa? And moreover, if it is indeed true that the brāhmaṇas were born from the mouth of Brahmā, then I ask—'Were the brāhmaṇa women too born from the same? If they were (born from the same mouth), they become the sisters of the brāhmaṇas, for they were born from one and the same womb. Thus, is it (not true) that the marriages of kṣatriyas and so forth are arranged with their respective sisters? How? And if so, then it is the upsurge of the Mleccha Dharma. On the upsurge of the Mleccha Dharma, there takes place the decadence of castes, and as a result of the decadence of castes, one attains the hell. This is the doctrine (of the Vedists and so forth).[10]

Thus, having ridiculed the belief in the divine origin of the four varṇas as expressed in the *Puruṣasūkta*, the VP attempts to show that the concept of caste cannot be justified on the basis of logic. It says:

> Here, if there is only one creator of (his) offsprings, how could then there be four varṇas? As for example, if there are four sons of one father, each of them does not have a separate caste. The same (can be said) in relation to varṇas. If you say that the difference (can be justified) on the basis of (their origin from different parts of Brahmā's body, such as) the mouth and so forth, then it cannot be proved logically. How? As for example, there is no difference between the fruits of the fig (*udumbara*) tree; (although they) are born at the bottom, at the middle part and at the top (of the tree). Similar is the case with the offsprings of Brahmā. And also, as there is not seen any difference between men, due to the difference in their colour, namely, white, red, yellow and black, and also there is not seen the difference as regards the seven basic constituents (*dhātu*s, i. e. *rasa*, *rakta* and so on), the faculties (*indriya*), happiness, sorrow, learning, knowledge and so forth; therefore, it is established that the caste cannot be determined (on the basis of birth).[11]

The VP elsewhere refutes the doctrines of Vedas, the *Gītā*, the Purāṇas, the *Rāmāyaṇa* and the *Mahābhārata* (VP III, pp. 94–95). The Dharma centred around horse sacrifice and other sacrifices is not a real Dharma. In order to show the futility of the pursuit of the Vedic Dharma, the author quotes a verse ascribed to Śuka or Śukra, which says: "Having cut (a wood for) the sacrificial pole, having killed an animal (in the sacrifice), having created the mud of blood, if (by all these evil deeds) one attains the heaven, by what act does one attain the hell?."[12] The VP concludes—

> Therefore, the Veda is not self-born; the mouth and so forth (of Brahmā) is not the origin of people. The saying as to 'there is no Dharma other than the horse sacrifice' is all inconsistent utterance and (too) meaningless to be considered. Thus, the doctrine of Brahmā and the doctrine of Viṣṇu have to be discarded along with that of Īśvara (i.e. Śiva)[13]

The KC and its commentary VP were probably composed in the 10th or 11th century CE, against the background of the Islamic invasion. This is the only Buddhist Tantra that echoes the Islamic invasion and the advent of Islam in India. The expression "Mleccha Dharma" refers to Islam. The Tantra appears to have been composed with a view to defeating Islamic troops in battle and establishing the Dharma. This Tantra had a twofold task: On one hand, it had to refute Vedic tenets advocating the Dharma that supported the hierarchy among people on the basis of birth, caste, class and so forth. On the other, it had to confront the newly arrived Mleccha Dharma. By showing the similarities between these two Dharmas, it attempts in its unique way to refute doctrines supporting discrimination on the basis of caste, class and so forth.

Notes

1 This statement about the teaching of Mantrayāna is found in the *Sekoddeśaṭīkā*: "*gṛdhrakūṭe yathā śāstrā prajñāpāramitānaye | tathā mantranaye proktā śrīdhānye dharmadeśanā ||*" *Sekoddeśaṭīkā* (Sferra and Merzagora 2006: 66) ["As the Teacher (gave the teachings) into the way of Prajñāpāramitā on the Gṛdhrakūṭa (mountain), in the same manner, (he) gave the teaching into the Mantra way in the Śrīdhānyakaṭaka"].

2 This is a gist of the original passage, see, (VP I, pp. 29–30).

3 "*arthapratiśaraṇena mahāmate bodhisattvena mahāsattvena bhavitavyaṃ na vyañjanapratiśaraṇena* |" (Vaidya 1963: 79).

4 VB, Vol. 1, pp. 1 and 2.

5 "*parusā sakkaa-bandhā pāua-bandho-vi hoi suumāro / purisa-mahilāṇaṃ jettiam ihantaraṃ tettiam imāṇam //*" *Karpūramañjarī*, I.7.

6 For details see (VP I, p. 31).

7 This is an oft-quoted *pāda*. However, the source is not yet traced. Vaidya (1924: 312–7) discusses the dictum in detail. According to him, Kamalākarabhaṭṭa at the end of his *Śūdrakamalākara* quotes the complete verse, referring to some Purāṇa text as the source (*purāṇāntare'pi*) but does not support it. Kamalākara cites the opinion of his father, Rāmakṛṣṇabhaṭṭa, according to whom, there are kṣatriyas and vaiśyas in the Kali age though their appearance is concealed and their karma and mode of life is defiled.

Vaidya argues that the statement must have emerged sometime between 1300 and 1600, though he was unable to trace its original source (1924: 314). Vaidya quotes the relevant passage (1924: 315). The work, although known as *Śūdrakamalākara*, is titled *Śūdradharmatattva*. The edition available to me is a Litho press edition, published in Mumbai in 1861 (śake 1783), jointly printed by Ganesh Bapuji Sahstri Malvankar and Vishnu Bapuji Shastri Bapat. The text reads: *purāṇāntare' pi | brāhmaṇāḥ kṣatriyā vaiśyāḥ śūdravarṇās trayo dvijāḥ | yuge yuge sthitās sarve kalāvādyantayos sthitiḥ* || (pp. 93–94). I have also consulted another edition in Marathi edited and translated by a group of scholars and published by Nirnaya Sagar Press, Mumbai. The relevant portion is found on p. 299. I am thankful to Prof. Patrick Olivelle and Dr. Michael S. Allen for sending me the reference to Vaidya's book.

8 "*striyo vaiśyās tathā śūdrās te 'pi yānti parāṃ gatim* |" *Bhagavadgītā*, 9.32cd.

9 "*brāhmaṇo 'sya mukham āsīd bāhū rājanyaḥ kṛtaḥ* |.
ūrū tad asya yad vaiśyaḥ padbhyāṃ śūdro'ajāyata ||" *Ṛgveda* (X. 90.12).

10 "*iha kila brahmamukhaṃ brāhmaṇānāṃ yonih | tadutpannatvād iti | evaṃ bhujau kṣatriyāṇāṃ yoniḥ | ādiśabdād ūrudvayaṃ vaiśyānāṃ yoniḥ, pādadvayaṃ śūdrāṇāṃ yoniḥ, evaṃ catvāro varṇāḥ | eṣāṃ caturṇām antimo varṇaḥ pañcamaḥ caṇḍālānāṃ; teṣāṃ kā yonir na jñāyate brāhmaṇais tāvad iti | kiṃ cānyat | iha brahmamukhād brāhmaṇā jātāḥ, kila satyam? ataḥ pṛcchāmi – kiṃ brāhmaṇyo 'pi tato jātāḥ? yadi syus tadā bhaginyo bhavanti, ekayonisamutpannatvād iti | evaṃ kṣatriyādīnām api vivāho bhaginyā sārdhaṃ bhavati? katham? atha bhavati, tadā mlecchadharmapravṛttir bhavati mlecchadharmapravṛttau jātikṣayaḥ, jātikṣayān narakam iti nyāyaḥ* |" (VP I, p. 261). The passages from VP cited here and below have been slightly edited by the present author.

11 "*iha yady ekaḥ sraṣṭā prajānāṃ tadā kathaṃ caturvarṇā bhavantīti? yathā ekasya pituś catvāraḥ putrās teṣāṃ na pṛthak pṛthag jātiḥ; evaṃ varṇānām api | atha brahmaṇo mukhādibhedena bhedaḥ, tadā sa eva yuktyā na ghaṭate | katham? yathā udumbaraphalānāṃ mūlamadhyāgrajātānāṃ bhedo nāsti, tathā prajānām api | aparo'pi śvetaraktapītakṛṣṇavarṇabhedena bhedo na dṛśyate; tathā dhātvindriyasukhaduḥkhavidyāgamādibhir bhedo na dṛśyate yasmāt, tasmāj jātir aniyateti siddham* |" (VP I, p. 261).

12 "*yūpaṃ chittvā paśuṃ hattvā kṛtvā rudhirakardamam* |
yady evaṃ gamyate svargo narakaḥ kena gamyate ||" (VP I, p. 262).

13 "*tasmān na vedaḥ svayambhūḥ, na mukhādir yonir janasya, nāśvamedhāt parato dharmo'nya iti sarvapralāpaṃ nirarthakam vicāryamāṇam iti brahmamataṃ vaiṣṇavamatam īśvareṇa sārdhaṃ dūṣaṇīyam iti* |" (VP I, p. 262).

References

Bhagavadgītā with Śāṅkarabhāṣya, Works of Śaṅkarācārya in original Sanskrit, Vol. II, 1st edition, Poona, 1929, reprint, Motilal Banarsidass, Delhi, (1981).

Dwivedi, V. V. and Bahulkar, S. S. (eds.). (1994). *Vimalaprabhā of Kalkin ŚrīPuṇḍarīka on ŚrīLaghukālacakratantrarāja*, Vols. II & III, Sarnath: Central Institute of Higher Tibetan Studies.

Islampurkar, V. S. (tr.). (1928). *Śūdradharmatattva athavā Śūdrakamalākara* with Marathi translation. 4th edition. Mumbai: Nirnay Sagar. (first edition, 1910).

Jagannatha, U. (ed.). (1986). *Vimalaprabhā of KalkinŚrīPuṇḍarīka on ŚrīLaghukālacakratantrarāja*, Vol. I, Sarnath: Central Institute of Higher Tibetan Studies.

Karpūramañjarī of Rājaśekhara, ed. N. G. Suru, Bombay: N. G. Suru, (1960).
KC: *Kālacakra Tantra* as included in Dwivedi and Bahulkar (eds.) (1994) and Jagannatha Upadhyaya. (ed.), (1986).
Malvankar, G. B. S., and Bapat, V. B. S. (eds.). (1861) (śake 1783). Śūdradharmatattva. (Litho press edition), Mumbai: published by the editors.
Sferra, F., and Merzagora, S. (eds.). (2006). *The Sekoddeśaṭīkā by Nāropā*. Volume 99 of Serie orientale, Rome: Istituto Italiano per l'Africa e l'Oriente.
Vaidya, C. V. 1924. *History of Mediaeval Hindu India* (Being a History of India from 600 to 1200 A. D.), Vol. II: *Early History of Rajputs* (750 to 1000 A. D.). Poona: The Oriental Book-supplying Agency.
Vaidya, P. L. (ed.). 1963. *SaddharmaLaṅkāvatāraSūtram*. Buddhist Sanskrit Texts No. 3. Darbhanga: Mithila Institute.
VB: *The Vyākaraṇamahābhāṣya of Patañjali*. ed. by F. Kielhorn, Third Edition, revised by K. V. Abhyankar, Pune: Bhandarkar Oriental Research Institute, (1962).
VP: *Vimalaprabhā* as in Dwivedi and Bahulkar (eds.) (1994) and Upadhayay Jagannatha (ed.), (1986).

Part II

NEO-BUDDHISM

Ambedkar on caste, class and gender

5

BUDDHA AND AMBEDKAR ON CASTE

A comparative overview

Mahesh A. Deokar

This chapter compares and contrasts the discussion on caste found in early Buddhist literature with the writings of Dr B. R. Ambedkar to understand their relationship. Scholars of Buddhism, sociology and anthropology often tend to study the Buddha's and Ambedkar's treatment of caste in isolation. As a result, they fail to notice the strong connection between the Buddha and Ambedkar on the matter of the refutation of caste and the remedy for overcoming it. They also miss the evolution in Ambedkar's treatment of caste. In the following pages, I have tried to show how Ambedkar's treatment of caste evolved over a period of time and how it was considerably influenced by early Buddhist critiques of caste. I have also shown how the remedies Ambedkar proposed for the annihilation of caste are fundamentally rooted in the Buddha's teaching.

In order to understand the early Buddhist approach towards caste, I have relied on the relevant discourses of the Pāli *Tipiṭaka*. My main sources for Ambedkar's approach to caste are his writings from three different periods, marking three stages in the development of his thesis on caste. These are:

1 *Castes in India: Their Mechanism, Genesis and Development*: a paper presented before the anthropology seminar of Dr A. A. Goldenweizer at Columbia University, New York, USA on May 19, 1916.
2 *Annihilation of Caste*: an article originally prepared as a presidential address for the 1936 annual conference of the Jat-Pat-Todak Mandal of Lahore.
3 *The Buddha and His Dhamma*: posthumously published in 1957.

In addition to these, I have also consulted Ambedkar's unpublished work *Revolution and Counter-Revolution in Ancient India*, which was posthumously published in *Dr. Babasaheb Ambedkar Writings and Speeches, Vol. 3*. I will deal with the present topic in two parts, one devoted to early

Buddhism and the other to Ambedkar. Each of them will be further subdivided under the five following headings:

1 Understanding Caste
2 The Genesis, Mechanism and Spread of Caste
3 Evils of the Caste System
4 The Ground for the Refutation of Caste
5 The Remedy Adopted for the Abolition of Caste

Part 1. Early Buddhism on caste

Understanding caste

As a result of the interweaving of the two systems of varṇa and *jāti*,[1] often in older Pāli literature, the distinction in the usage of these words appears blurred. The word "varṇa" is generally used in the context of a four-fold social structure, e.g., "these are the four varṇas, namely, kṣatriyas, brāhmaṇas, vaiśyas, and śūdras."[2] However, while making an inquiry regarding one's social status, the question is always asked with the word *jāti*, which can be a reference to either the varṇa or a subdivision within it. A similar mixing of ideas is also found in the answer to such questions. For instance, while answering the question of King Bimbisāra—"Being asked, tell your *jāti*"[3]—Siddhārtha Gotama replied, "As per the *gotra*, I am *ādicca*, as per the *jāti*, I am *sākiya*,"[4] thus referring to his *jāti* as Śākya, quite fitting to the below mentioned features of *jāti*. However, answering a similar question asked by Sundarikabhāradvāja, "What is your *jāti*?"[5] the Buddha replied, "I am neither a Brahmin, nor a son of a king, i.e., kṣatriya, nor a vaiśya, nor anybody else,"[6] thus referring to the varṇas instead of their subdivision.

It is interesting to note that in the famous *Cullavagga* passage (p. 139) regarding *sakā nirutti*, the two Brahmin brothers are described as *brāhmaṇajātikā*—"belonging to the *brāhmaṇajāti*." Sometimes, the inquiry about *jāti* is even made directly with the question, "Are you not a Brahmin?"[7] The word "*gotra*," on the other hand, is generally used to refer to a family lineage or clan distinct from *jāti*, as mentioned above in the *Suttanipāta* (423ab). However, occasionally, it is also employed in a sense similar to that of *jāti*, as is found in the *Sundarikabhāradvājasutta*. Here, the Buddha, after being asked about his *jāti*, replied to the Brahmin Sundarikabhāradvāja that asking him a question regarding his *gotra* was improper.[8] In a *Cullavagga* passage (p. 139), monks going forth from different social backgrounds are described as *nānāgottā nānājaccā nānākulā pabbajitā* ("[monks of...] various clans, various social strata have gone forth from various families") (*Cullavagga* translation, p. 194). These diverse usages indicate that there was an overlap in the ideas conveyed by the words "varṇa," "*jāti*," and "*gotra*" in Pāli literature.

Even though we do not find a clear-cut understanding of these ideas, the peculiar characteristics of the caste system, such as endogamy, caste-based forced division of occupation, graded inequality among the castes, and denying lower castes the right to education are discernible in Pāli *suttas* like the *Esukārīsutta*, the *Assalāyanasutta* and the *Lohiccasutta* of the *Majjhimanikāya*, and the *Vāseṭṭhasutta* of the *Suttanipāta*. None of these *suttas*, however, attempt a formal definition of caste.

As per the early Buddhist literature, expressions like *saṃsuddhagahaṇiko* (of pure descent) and *akuṭṭho jātivādena* (not reviled on account of birth) (*Mahāvagga*, p. 115), *jātiyā suddho* (pure with respect to birth) and *ubhato sujāto mātito ca pitito ca* (well-born from both sides, i.e., from the sides of the mother and father) (*Dīghanikāya*, vol. I, pp. 113, 25) found in Pāli *suttas* point to the practice of endogamy.

The *Esukārīsutta* of the *Majjhimanikāya* informs us that Brahmins believed that they were entitled to a superior social position and to regulate the privileges, duties and occupations of the members of the four varṇas. The Brahmin Esukārī presents the position taken by the Brahmins as follows:

a Each varṇa is to be served by persons of its own varṇa and of the lower varṇas, but not by persons of higher varṇas.
b Brahmins have fixed the occupations of each varṇa. The one who does not follow that (to use Ambedkar's term) "ancestral calling" is someone who does what he ought not do (*akiccakārī*) and is like a custodian committing theft. This idea of ancestral calling, which is the main feature of the caste system, is also discernible in the *Vāseṭṭhasutta*.

The *Lohiccasutta* of the *Majjhimanikāya* brings forth another important feature of the caste system, namely the denying of the right to knowledge to members of the lower castes. The Brahmin Lohicca held the view that one should not give knowledge to people of the śūdra class. Other features of the caste system, namely the prohibition of inter-dining and intermarriage, are clearly discernible in post-canonical Pāli as well as Sanskrit literature, though not so in early Pāli literature. (CF. *Viḍūḍabha-vatthu* of the *Dhammapadaṭṭhakathā* vol. I, part 1. pp. 337–62 and *Lalitavistara*, p. 109)

The genesis, mechanism and spread of caste

It is noteworthy that questions of the genesis and mechanism of caste were not dealt with specifically in early Buddhist literature. As per the question of genesis, the *Assalāyanasutta* points to the theory of the divine origin of caste. The Brahmin Assalāyana believed that the Brahmins were born from the mouth of Brahma and, therefore, are his genuine heirs (Ambedkar 1957: 302). In a number of *suttas*, good or bad karma from the past life are said to decide the birth of a person in a high or low caste (*Majjhimanikāya*, vol. III, p. 205). The *Esukārīsutta* suggests that being inspired by scriptural statements and eulogies, Brahmins started believing in their supremacy over the people of other varṇas and being carried away by it, and took up for themselves the task of defining the privileges, duties and occupations of the four varṇas. Although this explains how the scheme of—to use Ambedkar's words—"graded inequality" (1957: 87) was introduced along with the caste-based division of occupations and how the institution of caste claimed religious sanctity, it still does not explain, in real terms, how caste groups were formed in Hindu society.

The Buddha, as presented in Pāli canon, did not attempt to give his own theory of the genesis and mechanism of caste. What we find in the Pāli *sutta*s is his refutation of Brahmins' belief in the theory of the divine origin of caste. This refutation clearly shows that for the Buddha caste was certainly a human creation and not a divine one. However, the deterministic theory of karma, used to explain and justify caste, contradicts this refutation since it makes caste unquestionable by maintaining its religious sanction. Moreover, the fact that the Buddha's entire criticism and advice over the issue of caste was directed towards Brahmins may imply that in his view they were the chief upholders and promoters of the caste system, if not the originators.

Although there is no clear mention, it can be inferred from Pāli *sutta*s that the spread and strengthening of the caste system relied on:

- a the common acceptance of the theory of divine origination of varṇas and the theory of karma and rebirth,
- b promotion of rites and rituals in the religious life,
- c promotion of the esoteric and metaphysical ideas in the spiritual domain and
- d the eulogising of Brahmins by religious scriptures.

Evils of the caste system

The discussion, in clear terms, about the evil effects of the caste system on society is altogether missing in early Buddhist literature, with the sole exception of the *Lohiccasutta*. Only there, and later in the Tantric tradition in works like the *Vimalaprabhā* commentary on *Kālacakratantra* (vol. I, pp. 40–41), it has been categorically stated that the caste system has forcibly kept lower caste ignorant by depriving them of the right to education. Besides this, the early Pāli discourses in general have been silent on the other deplorable social and ethical effects the caste system has had on society. As will be clear in the next section, these discourses simply showed that believing in caste is illogical and irrational. The *Assalāyanasutta* of the

Majjhimanikāya (vol. II, p. 155) considers the belief in caste discrimination to be an evil and false view (*pāpakam diṭṭhigatam*). Discourses such as the *Vasalasutta* of the *Suttanipāta* and the *Sunītattheragāthā* of the *Theragāthā* are, however, clear testimonies of the deplorable effects the caste system had on society at large. On one hand, it made the upper classes feel proud and arrogant while, on the other, it robbed the lower classes of their self-esteem.

Additional grounds for refutation of caste

Unlike the initial three points, early Buddhism has a whole inventory of arguments to refute caste. In order to refute the upholders of caste, the *Vāseṭṭhasutta* of the *Suttanipāta* argues that the institution of caste is unnatural, because unlike the marks of distinction that can be found in different species of animals, no such distinctions are found among human beings of different varṇas. Distinction among human beings is, however, possible only based on the work they do; for example, the man who takes care of cows can be called a cowherd, one who farms can be called a farmer and so on. Only by possessing high moral qualities and actions, not by birth, can one achieve high status in the society. Thus, according to the *Vāseṭṭhasutta*, since caste is not natural—to use Ambedkar's words—the worth of a person and not his birth alone should decide his status in society. The same is echoed in the *Vasalasutta* of the *Suttanipāta*. This basic principle advocated by the Buddha is at the core of even neo-Buddhists' argument against caste. In the *Assalāyanasutta* of the *Majjhimanikāya*, the Buddha critically evaluates and criticizes Brahmins' false claim to superiority, purity and liberation. He refutes this view with the following arguments:

1 Like persons of other varṇas, Brahmins are also born of the same biological process.
2 In countries like Kamboja and Yavana, there are only two varṇas: that of *Ārya* and *Dāsa*, and it is possible for each one of them to change their varṇa. Hence the caste system is not a universally accepted and static social order.
3 Persons of all varṇas are equal before the moral law of karma and they equally bear the fruits of their evil or good deeds.
4 Persons of any varṇa have an equal capacity for self-culture.
5 Actions performed by persons of different varṇas yield the same result.
6 Intercourse between two people of different varṇas does not result in the birth of a being of a different species.
7 Between two persons of the same varṇa, society honours and respects the person who is superior in moral virtues and knowledge.

In the *Esukārīsutta* of the *Majjhimanikāya*, the Buddha challenges the authority of the Brahmins in determining and fixing the privileges, duties and occupations of the four varṇas. He refutes this position saying:

a People of all varṇas have not given to Brahmins the right to decide their privileges, duties and occupations.
b Moreover, imposing them unilaterally on people without their consent is improper and unethical.
c Brāhmaṇa, kṣatriya, vaiśya and śūdra are mere designations obtained from being born in a particular family, since an action performed by persons of different varṇas does not yield different results.
d As per moral laws and the potential for self-culture, people of all the varṇas are equal.

The Buddha further adds that it is proper to serve a person, if through serving that person one acquires welfare and moral virtue. To follow the noble *dhamma* is the duty of all.

According to Kosambi (1989: 174–89), even after the passing away of the Buddha, his disciples continued to oppose the caste system. In support of this statement, Kosambi quotes the *Madhurasutta* of the *Majjhimanikāya*. In this *sutta*, the Buddha's disciple Mahākaccāyana declares that the brahmins' claim to superiority is mere propaganda; for, if anyone acquires wealth or power, he will be served by people of all varṇas. Besides being equal before the moral law, people of all varṇas are equal even before the law of the state. Anyone who violates the law of the state ceases to be a brāhmaṇa, kṣatriya, vaiśya or śūdra, and is simply treated as a defaulter by the law. It may be noted that the situation did not remain that way when the Smṛtis gained a stronghold on society. They prescribed differential punishment to the members of different varṇas for the same offence (cf. Kane 1941: 105–64). Thus, according to the *Madhurasutta*, the institution of caste is neither eternal nor unalterable and can be rendered meaningless by the changed economic and political status of a person. Moreover, the institution of caste cannot be justified from either a moral or legal point of view.

In the *Lohiccasutta*, the Buddha rejects the narrow outlook of the Brahmin Lohicca that only the higher varṇas should have access to knowledge. He advocates that knowledge should be freely distributed to people of all varṇas (male and female); for, those who deny the right to knowledge to the lower classes (śūdras and women), are danger-makers, unsympathetic and hostile towards those who depend on them. They are the followers of the wrong doctrine. The Buddha on the other hand admitted people of every varṇa to his Saṅgha, in order to give knowledge to all.

Thus, early Buddhist arguments refuting caste are focused on:

a Proving caste distinction to be irrational and unnatural

b Declaring it to be neither universal, eternal nor unalterable in all circumstances
c Highlighting biological equality, equality of potential, and equality with respect to the law of karma among all classes
d Showing the importance of moral virtues and knowledge as the ultimate parameters of higher social status
e Pointing out how the denial of the right to education of the lower classes, a corollary of the caste system, is unethical and unlawful

However, early Buddhist literature does not discuss in explicit terms:

a Other socially and ethically deplorable implications of the institution of caste to the society that practices it
b Its unjust and unethical nature
c Its opposition to the universal principles of liberty, equality and fraternity
d Its failure as a social order

The remedy adopted for the abolition of caste

It may be noted that the mind plays an important role in the Buddha's religion. According to him, true religion exists in cleansing the mind of wrong notions and immoral thoughts. His discourses on caste indicate that he considered caste one such wrong views (cf. the *Assalāyanasutta* of the *Majjhimanikāya*, vol. II, p. 155).

The Buddha adopted a dual policy for fighting caste: on one hand, he rejected the *śāstra*s and the divine authority behind the caste system and, on the other, he appealed to the reason of the intellectual class of society. This is exactly the line of thought adopted by Ambedkar in finding solutions to the problem of caste. The Buddha, through his teachings, refuted the theory of the divine origin of caste and challenged the authority of scriptures on rational grounds. In the *sutta*s like the *Tevijjasutta* of the *Dīghanikāya*, he questioned the infallibility of so-called religious texts. He invoked rational acumen among people through his discourses like the *Vīmaṁsakasutta* of the *Majjhimanikāya* and the *Kālāmasutta* of the *Aṅguttaranikāya*.

The Buddha gave to people—to use the expression of Ambedkar—guiding principles of life instead of behavioural rules. He gave people parameters such as purity of intention, well-being of oneself and society[9] and the principle of *ātmaupamyatā*,[10] i.e., putting oneself in others' shoes to judge one's own behaviour. It is on this solid doctrinal foundation that the Buddha could dream of building an ideal society. However, this alone was not sufficient to actualize his ideal.

The Buddha backed up his ideology with an equally effective action plan, which shows his deep understanding of the problem of caste. He kept the admission to his Saṅgha open to all, without any caste consideration. This not only opened the doors of knowledge and *saṁnyāsa* to people of all castes but also made possible the rehabilitation of all those foreign communities who otherwise did not have a place in the fixed caste framework of Hindu society.[11] It also helped people of different social backgrounds disown their past caste identity. In the *Aṭṭhakanipāta* of the *Aṅguttaranikāya*, the Buddha takes pride in declaring that varṇa and *jāti* have no place in his Saṅgha. Just as all rivers lose their individual names when they enter an ocean and are simply called an ocean, similarly all those who join his Saṅgha would lose their earlier designations of family and caste, and are simply known by the name of Buddhist monks. This apparently simple move can well be taken as suggestive of the Buddha's understanding that caste consciousness cannot be removed without discarding the designations associated with it—the same point that Ambedkar later highlighted in the Annihilation of Caste when refuting the Arya Samajists.

Besides this, the Buddha adopted certain safeguards and healthy practices to ensure that there was no discrimination against any member of his Saṅgha, and that a feeling of solidarity and fraternity developed amongst them. These include:

1 Accepting the democratic model for his Saṅgha, where each member had an equal right of opinion, irrespective of their former varṇa or caste affiliation.
2 Adopting the ideal of common ownership, giving members an equal share in requisites such as clothing, food, beds, seats and medicine.
3 Acknowledging no special privileges to monks based on their birth or any other past background. Seniority in the Saṅgha was the only criterion on which monks were expected to show reverence to their colleagues.
4 Practice of the principle of *sapadānacariyā*, i.e., begging for alms from successive houses without preference and *saṁvibhāga*, i.e., distributing the gathered alms/food equally among members of the community; encouraging members of the Saṅgha to overcome their caste-consciousness by inter-dining.

These measures seem to have helped members of the Buddhist Saṅgha get rid of their caste-consciousness and function as a community with a sense of social binding. There is, however, no need to think that the Buddha's reforms were limited to the monk community alone. He was spreading his message among lay people through his teachings and actions. Many households that came into contact with him stopped practicing caste and treated their so-called low-caste colleagues with human dignity. The stories of Sujātā and Anāthapiṇḍaka setting their maid servants free are a good testimony of this fact.

Although there is not much on the issue of inter-caste marriages in the Pāli texts, in an interesting passage occurring in the *Lalitavistara* (p. 140), Śuddhodana asks his priests to find a suitable bride for the young Siddhārtha. He says:

"Inform me about such a girl who has these qualities, no matter whether she is a Brahmin or a Kṣatriya or a Vaiśya or a Śūdra. My son is not proud of either clan or family. It is in the virtues, the truth and righteousness where his mind delights."[12]

This shows the Buddha's acceptance of inter-caste marriage.

According to Kosambi (1989: 174–89), there is no evidence that the other Śramaṇic schools and their leaders opposed the caste system as the Buddha did, even though they themselves did not observe caste discrimination in their own Saṅghas. Unlike the Jain Saṅgha, which later in its career partially accepted caste discrimination and prohibited the admission of untouchables into its Saṅgha, the Buddhist Saṅgha maintained its casteless nature until its disappearance from India. However, as can be seen in the literature, though the Buddha established a casteless community based on democratic principles, he was not able to make it the order of the day. Even though kings like Pasendi Kosala and Bimbisāra were his faithful followers, they did not adopt it as a state policy. As a result, in spite of all their efforts, *śramaṇa*s were unable to fully destroy the deep-rooted institution of caste.

Part 2. Dr. Ambedkar on caste

Understanding caste

In the paper entitled *Castes in India: Their Mechanism, Genesis and Development*, Ambedkar (1982: 7) argued that caste should be defined in the context of endogamy. He defined it as "an artificial chopping off (*sic*) the population into fixed and definite units, each one prevented from fusing into another through the custom of endogamy." In his view, "prohibition, or rather the absence of intermarriage-endogamy, to be concise is the only one that can be called the essence of Caste when rightly understood" (1982: 7). In his opinion, caste can also be described as the "parcelling into bits of a larger cultural unit" (1982: 31).

In the same article, Ambedkar held that the varṇa system was essentially a class system, in which individuals when qualified could change their class. Caste, on the other hand, is an "enclosed class" (1982: 19). He felt that the subdivision of society based on the division of labour is natural. What is unnatural is that it "lost the open door character of the class system and became self-enclosed units called castes" (1982: 24).

Ambedkar maintained a similar view regarding the distinct characteristics of varṇa and jāti in his later writings. In 1936, in his response to

M. K. Gandhi's criticism of his article *Annihilation of Caste*, Ambedkar states that the Vedic conception of varṇa as understood and preached by people like Swami Dayanand Saraswati was sublime. Its essence was "the pursuit of a calling, which is appropriate to one's natural aptitude" (1945: 22). The essence of caste on the other hand is a pursuit of an ancestral calling based on birth. Ambedkar admitted that although he opposed the varṇa system, he found the Vedic theory of varṇa to be sensible and an inoffensive thing. He held that varṇa and caste are fundamentally different. Varṇa is based on worth, whereas caste is based on birth (1945: 23). It is in the later period that the distinction between the two was lost, and varṇa too began to signify the ancestral calling.

In section IV of his article *Annihilation of Caste,* Ambedkar refuted those who try to understand and justify caste in India as a division of labour system. He pointed out that it is not merely a division of labour, but a division of labourers. It is a watertight division with graded inequality, in which the division of labourers is graded one above the other. This division of labour is neither spontaneous nor based on the natural aptitude of labourers. In this system, people neither have the choice of selecting their occupation nor is there any place for their sentiments and preferences. Rather, it is based on the dogma of predestination.

Further in the same article, Ambedkar also rejected the theory that caste is based on the principle of eugenics to maintain racial purity. He argued that Indian society is a mixture of different races and has not maintained any racial purity.

Moreover, customs like prohibition of inter-dining, which is part and parcel of the caste system, has nothing to do with racial purity. He remarked that caste has no scientific origin and those who were trying to support it through science were attempting to give a eugenic basis to what is grossly unscientific.

In Chapter 7 of *Revolution and Counter-Revolution in Ancient India*, Ambedkar underlined the similarities and differences between varṇa and *jāti*. According to him:

> [v]arna and Caste are identical in their *de jure* connotation. Both connote status and occupation. Status and occupation are the two concepts which are implied in the notion of Varna as well as in the notion of Caste. Varna and Caste however differ in one important particular. Varna is not hereditary either in status or occupation. On the other hand Caste implies a system in which status and occupation are hereditary and descend from father to son
>
> (2008: 285–6)

Following John Dewey (Democracy and Education, 99) he points out the difference between the natures of a class society and a caste society saying, "[t]he difference between a society with the class system and a society with the caste system lies just in this namely the class system is merely non-social but the caste system is positively anti-social" (2008: 306).

In Ambedkar's magnum opus, *The Buddha and His Dhamma*, which can be treated as the culmination of his search for a solution to the caste problem, he enumerated the following salient features of a caste-based society:

- a division of society into four castes,
- b unequal division of rights and privileges among the four castes based on the principle of graded inequality,
- c division of occupations,
- d denial of the right to education to śūdras and women and
- e denial of the right to *saṁnyāsa* to śūdras and women (1957: 87–88).

It is noteworthy that unlike his previous two writings, in *The Buddha and His Dhamma* Ambedkar established a direct connection between these features of the caste system and different discourses of the Pāli canon. He has interpreted the views of the Brahmin Esukārī as propagating "the permanent division of occupations" (1957: 304). Based on the arguments against caste found in *Vāseṭṭhasutta*, Ambedkar deduced that the Buddha treated the division of society based on the division of labour as natural and acceptable, where mobility across the classes is possible. The Buddha, however, did not advocate the unfair principle of ancestral calling.

The genesis, mechanism, and spread of caste

In the *Castes in India: Their Mechanism, Genesis and Development* (1982: 9), Ambedkar observed that superimposing endogamy over exogamy is the mechanism of creating caste. According to him, customs like *satī* (enforced widowhood for life) and child-marriage are the means of maintaining endogamy. He believed that "strict endogamy could not be preserved without these customs, while caste without endogamy is a fake" (1982: 18).

Ambedkar maintained that the origin of caste is the origin of the mechanism for endogamy. He argued that since the existence of a definite class in a society is a fact, the answer to the question of the genesis of caste should be sought in the answer to the question, "What was the class that first made itself into a caste?" He showed that it was the Brahmin class that first enclosed itself to form a caste.[13] In his opinion,

> the strict observance of these [above mentioned] customs and social superiority advocated by the priestly class in all ancient civilizations are sufficient to prove that they were the originators of this 'unnatural institution' founded and maintained through these unnatural means
> (1982: 19–20)

As for the question of the growth and spread of the caste system, in the same article Ambedkar maintained that the institution of caste was neither imposed upon the docile population of India nor by a law-giver like Manu as divine dispensation nor was it grown according to some law of social growth peculiar to the Indian people. He held that the varṇa system was initially a class system allowing social mobility. Later, at some stage, the priestly class socially detached itself from the rest of the people and, through a closed-door policy, became a class by itself. The other classes, being subject to the social law of division of labour, underwent differentiation. Such groups became castes through imitation and excommunication. Thus, the origin of caste is due to the conscious enclosing of class by the "superior" community and its growth and spread is due to imitation by those inferior to it on the one hand and those closed out in society because of excommunication on the other (1982: 20ff).

In Chapter 7 of *Revolution and Counter-Revolution in Ancient India*, Ambedkar clearly held Brahmins responsible for the genesis and strengthening of the caste system. Here, he explicitly states that Brahmanism converted varṇa into caste by making status and occupation hereditary. He envisaged three stages of this conversion. In the first stage, "the duration of Varna i.e., of status and occupation of a person was for a prescribed period of time only" (2008: 286). In the second stage, "the status and occupation involved the Varna of a person ensured during lifetime only" (2008: 286). In the third stage, "the status and occupation of the Varna became hereditary" (2008: 286). According to Ambedkar, in legal language, "the Estate conferred by Varna was at the beginning an Estate for a term only. Thereafter it became a life Estate and finally it became an Estate of inheritance which is tantamount to saying that Varna became Caste" (2008: 286).

In the same book, Ambedkar showed how through *Manusmṛti*'s legal code, the caste system was created and strengthened. In his view, the two laws of *Manusmṛti* against intermarriage and inter-dining created the caste system. Commenting on the close relationship between these two laws and the caste system he remarks:

> [p]rohibition of intermarriage and prohibition against interdining, are two pillars on which it rests. The caste system and the rules relating to intermarriage and interdining are related to each other as ends to means. Indeed by no other means could the end be realized (2008: 293)

According to Ambedkar, "[G]irl marriage, enforced widowhood and Sati had no other purpose than that of supporting the Caste System which Brahmanism was seeking to establish by prohibiting intermarriage" (2008: 301). He further points out that excommunication is another means used by *Manusmṛti* to maintain the caste system. In his view, "once Brahmanism was determined to create the caste system the law against the outcast was absolutely essential. For only by punishing the outcast can the caste system be maintained" (2008: 304). Here, Ambedkar clearly spells out *Manusmṛti*'s role in legalizing the conventional caste system saying, "this old Chaturvarna was conventional. It was the ideal of the Society but it was not the law of the State. Brahmanism isolated the Varnas and sowed the seed of antagonism. Brahmanism made legal what was only conventional" (2008: 328).

Evils of the caste system

In the *Annihilation of Caste*, Ambedkar presented a detailed analysis of the caste problem and suggested methods for abolishing it. While preparing ground for its abolition, he underlined the evils of the caste system from Section VI up to Section XIII of his article as follows:

a The caste system has not done any good to improve economic efficiency nor has it improved the race. On the contrary, "it has completely disorganized and demoralized the Hindus" (1945: 25).

b Although there are similarities of habits and customs, beliefs and thoughts, there is no sense of social binding among Hindus as the community is divided into castes: the "Caste-system prevents common activity, and by preventing common activity it has prevented the Hindus from becoming a society with a unified life and a consciousness of its own being" (1945: 27–28).

c An anti-social spirit is the worst feature of Hindus: "The existence of Caste and Caste Consciousness has served to keep the memory of past feuds between castes green and has prevented solidarity" (1945: 29).

d "Caste is... the real explanation as to why the Hindu has let the savage remain a savage in the midst of his civilization without blushing or without feeling any sense of remorse or repentance" (1945: 30–31), according to him. He further warned that if these savages and aboriginals have been claimed by other religions that are hostile to Hindus, these new converts could pose a big threat to the existence of Hindus. Similarly, Hindus have not made any effort to help low-caste people rise to their cultural standards.

e The Hindu religion was a missionary religion in its initial stages. However, it ceased to be so with the strengthening of the caste system. The caste system made the process of *śuddhi*, i.e., the rehabilitation of converts into the Hindu religion as well as the *saṅghaṭana* (the feeling of forming a group) impossible. He wrote, "So long as Caste remains, there will be no Sanghatan and so long as there is no Sanghatan the Hindu will remain weak and meek" (1945: 35).[14]

f “Caste in the hands of the orthodox has been a powerful weapon for persecuting the reforms and for killing all reform” (1945: 37).
g Caste has a deplorable effect on the ethics of Hindus. It killed the public spirit. It has also destroyed the sense of public charity and has made public opinion impossible.

In Chapter 7 of his *Revolution and Counter-Revolution in Ancient India*, Ambedkar claimed that *Manusmṛti* was composed to re-establish Brahmanism by destroying Buddhism. Here, he enumerated the effects of the triumph of Brahmanism over Buddhism as follows:

a It established the right for the Brahmin to rule and commit regicide.
b It made Brahmins a class of privileged persons.
c It converted varṇa into caste.
d It brought about a conflict and an antisocial feeling between the different castes.
e It degraded Shudras and women.
f It forged a system of graded inequality.
g It made a legal and rigid social system which was conventional and flexible (2008: 275).

In the same book, Ambedkar opined that *Manusmṛti*’s object of converting varṇa into caste was “to make the high status enjoyed by the Brahmins from ancient times the privilege of every Brahmin and his progeny without reference to merits or qualifications” (2008: 289). According to him, this conversion had harmful spiritual and secular consequences. From a spiritual point of view, it placed the Brahmin in sole charge of the spiritual affairs of people, even though he did not possess learning or morality. From the secular perspective, it introduced a most pernicious mentality among Hindus to disregard merit and regard only birth. He further remarks, “Brahmanism in instituting Caste system has put the greatest impediment against the growth of nationalism” (2008: 304).

While highlighting the miserable state of Shudras and women due to the caste system Ambedkar says,

> [i]t is this huge mass of people that has been doomed by Brahmanism to eternal servility and eternal degradation. It is because of the colossal scale of degradation whereby 75% of her people were deprived of their right to life. liberty and pursuit of happiness that India became a decaying if not a dead nation
>
> (2008: 317)

Ambedkar took pains to show how the principle of graded inequality runs through the whole *Manusmṛti* and its successive Smṛtis, which pervade all departments of life. According to him, because of the system of graded inequality, "Hindus have been stricken with palsy" (2008: 320). He marked the difference between inequality and graded inequality. In his opinion, the latter is far more dangerous than the former, for it does not allow the creation of the general discontent that forms the seed of revolution and does not make sufferers unite against a common foe and a common grievance, and thereby sustains the system of caste (2008: 320).

Thus, in his writings, Ambedkar enumerated a number of vices of the caste system and showed how it badly it has affected Hindu society in particular and the country in general.

In *The Buddha and His Dhamma*, in the section 'The Brahmanas' of the fifth part 'The Buddha and His Predecessors' of Book I (1957: 91), Ambedkar claimed that the Buddha did sense that graded inequality might spread in society "an ascending scale of hatred and a descending scale of contempt and might be a source of perpetual conflict." After examining the *cāturvarṇya*, the Buddha understood that it is based on a wrong philosophical foundation: "[i]t did not serve the interest of all, much less did it advance the welfare of all." It was deliberately created to serve the interest of a few "self-styled supermen." It was calculated to suppress and subjugate the weak.

It may be noted that what Ambedkar claimed was not directly stated by the Buddha in any of his discourses. It is rather a result of his own analysis and interpretation of the Buddha's opposition to the varṇa system. These claims can best be treated as possible logical conclusions of the early Buddhist approach to caste.

Additional grounds for refutation of caste

Besides the above-mentioned evils of the caste system, there are some additional grounds to call for its abolition. In Sections II and III of his deliberation in the *Annihilation of Caste*, Ambedkar highlighted that no political revolution is possible without a prior social or religious revolution. According to him, the political revolution by Chandragupta was successful as it was preceded by the religious and social revolution by the Buddha. Moreover, like political reforms, even economic reforms cannot solve social problems, for, without social reforms, no political or economic reform is sustainable. Hence, according to Ambedkar, any successful political or socialist reform in India must be preceded by social reform in the form of abolishing the menace of caste.

In Section XIV of *The Annihilation of Caste*, Ambedkar discussed an ideal form of society. According to him, a society based on liberty, equality and fraternity—just another name for democracy—is an ideal society. The institution of caste is opposed to these cardinal principles as it neither allows a person the choice of his own occupation nor does it give him equal status in society as a human being nor does it promote a sense of fraternity or democracy, which is an associated form of living among persons of different castes.

In Section XVI of the *Annihilation of Caste* Ambedkar has shown that as a system of social organization *cāturvarṇya* is not only impractical, but also harmful and has turned out to be a miserable failure. He enumerated the causes of its impracticability, harmfulness and failure in Sections XVI–XVIII of his article as follows:

A The adoption of *cāturvarṇya* to organize the society is not practical, for,

1 The reduction of 4,000 castes based on birth into four varṇas based on worth is difficult.
2 The qualities of individuals are so variable that it would not be possible to classify people accurately into four classes.
3 To maintain *cāturvarṇya* in the wake of the problem of a transgressor is not easy.

B The reorganization of Hindu society based on *cāturvarṇya* is harmful because the effect of the varṇa system is to degrade the masses by denying them opportunities to acquire knowledge and to emasculate them by denying them the right to be armed.

C *Cāturvarṇya* has consistently failed since its inception in the Vedic period.

Moreover, in Section XIX of the *Annihilation of Caste*, Ambedkar pointed out that caste in Hinduism is fundamentally different from the caste system found in other religions. Unlike other religions, caste has caused disintegration among Hindus. It has more social significance to Hindus than to non-Hindus. Caste is a sacred institution to the former, whereas it is just a practice to the latter. According to Ambedkar (1945: 53), "[r]eligion compels the Hindus to treat isolation and segregation of castes as a virtue." As a result, integrating forces, which would overcome the disintegration caused by caste, are not to be found in Hindu society. In spite of the fact that the Hindu society has survived long, the quality of its survival is deplorable owing to the evils of caste mentioned above.[15]

In Section XX (1945: 55), Ambedkar gave a clear warning that unless Hindus change their social order, they can achieve very little by way of progress. Neither can they mobilize society for offence or defence, nor can they build a society or a nation. Anything based on caste is going to crack and can never be whole. These additional grounds for the refutation of caste can be summarized as follows:

a For the success of any political or socialist reform in India, social reform in the form of abolishing the menace of caste must precede.

b As a system of social organization, *cāturvarṇya* has proved impracticable, harmful and has turned out to be a miserable failure.
c Hindus can achieve very little by way of progress unless they change their social order that is based on caste.

The remedy adopted for the abolition of caste

From Section XX onwards of *The Annihilation of Caste*, Ambedkar talked of measures to abolish caste. Refuting those who feel that the first step towards this it to abolish sub-castes, Ambedkar argued that doing so would be erroneous, for the fusion of sub-castes is impossible due to the diversity evident in them. Moreover, there is no guarantee that abolishing sub-castes would necessarily lead to the abolition of castes overall. Thus, this remedy is neither practical nor effective.

Ambedkar equally rejected the idea of Āryasamājists to reorganize the Hindu society on the principle of *cāturvarṇya* based on worth instead of birth, by doing away with the 4000 sub-castes and maintaining simply the old labels of the four varṇas. He argued that if society is to be organized not on the basis of birth but worth, then maintaining the labels of varṇas would be futile. In fact, it would not only be futile, but rather would be the opposite of the idea of equality in status, for, it is a common experience that certain names become associated with certain emotions and sentiments that in turn determine a person's attitude towards people and things. The designations brāhmaṇa, kṣatriya, vaiśya and śūdra are associated with a sense of hierarchy based on birth. Hence, if new notions are to be inculcated in the minds of people, it is necessary to give them new names. To continue with old names is to make reform futile.

Criticizing those who were in favour of inter-caste dining as the remedy for caste, Ambedkar (1945: 57) said, "It is a common experience that inter-dining has not succeeded in killing the spirit of Caste and the consciousness of Caste." According to him, the primary remedy for the problem of caste is inter-marriage. Although, this would still not be the end. One must try to find out why people do not inter-dine or inter-marry with persons of different castes. The answer to this question, according to him, is that inter-dining and inter-marriage are repugnant to the beliefs and dogmas Hinduism regards as sacred. He further said that caste is a notion; it is a state of mind. Hence, the destruction of caste would mean a notional change.

For Ambedkar, it was not the people who were wrong, but the religion that inculcated the notion of caste. Hence, in order to abolish caste, one should grapple with the *śāstra*s, which teach the religion of caste. Thus, the real remedy is to destroy the belief in the sanctity of the *śāstra*s, for, the acts of people are merely the results of the beliefs inculcated in their minds by the *śāstra*s. If people become free from the thrall of the *śāstra*s and if their minds are cleansed of the pernicious notions of castes founded on the *śāstra*s, they will naturally inter-dine or inter-marry.

In Ambedkar's opinion, one should take the stand—also taken by the Buddha and Guru Nānak—to not only discard *śāstra*s, but also deny their authority. It may be noted that this is the only place in the *Annihilation of Caste* where we can find a reference to the Buddha or his teaching. Ambedkar (1945: 60) further observed that

> [c]aste is the natural outcome of certain religious beliefs which have the sanction of the Shastras, which are believed to contain the command of divinely inspired sages who were endowed with a supernatural wisdom and, whose commands, therefore, cannot be disobeyed without committing sin.... To ask people to give up Caste is to ask them to go contrary to their fundamental religious notions.

Since castes are believed to have a divine basis, Ambedkar appealed to people to destroy the sacredness and divinity with which caste has been invested, meaning that one must destroy the authority of *śāstra*s and the Vedas. According to Ambedkar, this is a difficult task for Hindus, since Brahmins, the intellectual class of Hindus, will not take this up as it would adversely affect their own class. Secondly, the destruction of caste is not possible, for the structure is such that each caste takes pride and consolation in the fact that in the hierarchical scale, it is above some other caste. Hence, it is impossible to organize a common front against the caste system. Moreover, it is also difficult for a Hindu to discard caste as being contrary to reason, because he is not free to follow his reason. Reason and morality are the two most powerful weapons in the armoury of a reformer. To deprive him of these weapons is to disable him from acting. Ambedkar said that religion must mainly be a matter of principles and not rules. The moment it degenerates into rules, it ceases to be a religion as it kills responsibility, which is the essence of a truly religious act. In his view, the Hindu religion is not mainly governed by principles, but by rules. He said that there is nothing irreligious in working for the destruction of religion, which is a mass of different types of rules and regulations. He believed that once the people realize that religion they are following is not a religion but a law, they will be ready either to abolish it or to amend it.

As per Ambedkar, after abandoning the religion of rules, one should replace it with the religion of principles. He appealed to the Hindus that they must give a new doctrinal basis to their religion, one that is in consonance with liberty, equality and fraternity—in short, with democracy. In his reply to Gandhi's criticism of the *Annihilation of Caste* (published in *Harijan* of 11th and 18th July 1936), he cautioned that in the matter of eradicating caste, one cannot totally rely on saints, as they were concerned with the relation between man and god; they did not preach that all men were equal. Rather, they preached that all men were equal in the eyes of the gods.

When Ambedkar became convinced that the Buddha's *dhamma* is the only one that meets all the parameters of an ideal religion and the only one that can fulfil the expectation of liberating oppressed people from their suffering, he—along with his millions of followers—decided to embrace Buddhism. He wrote *The Buddha and His Dhamma* as a blueprint of his ideal religion. In this book, he tried to unearth the social message of the Buddha. He pointed out the rational and moral values embedded in the Buddha's teachings, which the Buddha had used to fight the caste system. He showed how the Buddha challenged scriptural authority and established a new religion based on principles.

In *The Buddha and His Dhamma*, Ambedkar tried to demonstrate that the Buddha cherished the democratic principles of liberty, equality, fraternity and justice and gave prominence to worth over birth. He highlighted that the Buddha founded his religion on the noble virtues of *dāna* (offering), *sīla* (morality), *khanti* (forbearance), *mettā* (loving kindness), *karuṇā* (compassion), *muditā* (altruistic joy) and *paññā* (wisdom), which are necessary to create a truly righteous and democratic society (1957: 127). He demonstrated that in the Buddha's teachings, principles are the governing factors of human life, not rules. According to him, the Buddha differentiated between what is *dhamma* (religion) and what is *saddhamma* (ideal religion). He explained *saddhamma* to be those principles that turn *dhamma* into *saddhamma* (1957: 281ff). In *The Buddha and His Dhamma*, he categorically stated that true religion should promote equality between man and man, so that the best would survive even if he was not the fittest, for society wants the best and not the fittest (1957: 308).

Without citing any particular text, Ambedkar suggested that the Buddha was in favour of conversion as the remedy for the problem of caste. He said that according to the Buddha, a religion that does not preach equality is not worth having (1957: 308). The Buddha also realized that since the caste system is believed to be a divinely ordained social system, it cannot be amended and can only be ended (1957: 92). Ambedkar is justified in inferring this implication from the Buddha's teaching, as the Buddha gave paramount importance to worth over birth. The facts that observance of varṇa and *jāti* has formed the core of Brahmanic religion and that the Buddha preached against it and was encouraged followers of that religion to abandon it in favour of equality, implies in a way that the Buddha suggested people abandon their old religion and accept a new life, by either becoming a member of the Saṅgha or a lay follower. Ambedkar asked new converts to give up their humiliating occupations and habits. In *The Buddha and His Dhamma*, he interpreted the Buddha's advice found in the *Esukārīsutta* to do only profitable service as his injunction, to refuse those services that make one bad and not good (1957: 304).

Wherever Ambedkar noticed logical inconsistencies in the presentation of traditional Buddhism, he did not shy away from removing them. He rejected the orthodox understanding of the notion of *saṁsāra* (transmigration of soul) and the doctrine of karma, since they not only contradict the basic principle of non-self, but also justify the untenable institution of caste. According to Ambedkar, the Brahmanic doctrine of karma is a part of the thesis of transmigration of the soul after death. As per their understanding, the doctrine of karma is "the determination of man's position in present life by deeds done by him in his past life" (1957: 103). We do find an echo of this traditional notion of how the law of karma works in some of Pāli *sutta*s like the *Kammavibhaṅgasutta* of the *Majjhimanikāya*. Despite this, Ambedkar held that the Buddha repudiated such a fatalistic view of life. According to him, although the Buddha accepted the great law of cause and effect with all its corollaries, he did not believe that all deeds done in some previous life "have the potency to produce suffering," thereby leaving the "present activity impotent" (1957: 104). Ambedkar (1957: 91) felt that the Buddha recognised that the Brahmanical theory of karma was designed "to sap the spirit of revolt completely," and hence replaced it with a much more scientific view of karma. Keeping in view the Buddha's theory of non-self, he proposed a new and more scientific interpretation of rebirth. He held that in order to oppose the karmic justification of caste, the Buddha replaced the notion of transmigration with "the doctrine of rebirth" (1957: 104). According to this, it is not the person who is reborn, rather the elements that dissolve into nature at the time of death are reborn.

Just like the Buddha, Ambedkar also backed up his ideological fight against caste with institutional and constitutional remedies. As suggested in the *Annihilation of Caste*, Ambedkar established a social organization called "The Buddhist Society of India" to train, examine and certify Buddhist priests with the purpose of actualizing the principle of giving prominence to worth over birth. In order to extend the benefit of the Buddha's Dhamma to the citizens of India, Ambedkar translated the Buddhist vision of an ideal society into a constitution based on the principles of liberty, equality, fraternity and justice—the Indian one. Being the chairman of the constitution drafting committee, he incorporated a number of safeguards against any possible violation of fundamental human rights. Thus, he took his discourse on caste from a theoretical plane up to the height of practical implementation.

Ambedkar's remedies to the problem of caste can be summarized as:

a Cleansing people's mind of the pernicious notions of caste.
b Giving new names to people by discarding old ones, to inculcate new ideas in their minds.

c Destroying the sanctity of caste and varṇa by grappling with *śāstra*s, which preach the religion of caste.
d Denying the divine authority of the *śāstra*s.
e Making an appeal to the reason and morality of people, to help them deny this authority.
f Making people realize that real religion lies in principles, not in rules. Hence, there is nothing irreligious in abolishing or amending the rules.
g Reorganizing society on a religious basis, which would recognize principles of liberty, equality and fraternity.
h Converting to Buddhism and practicing a life of dignity based on worth.
i Incorporating Buddhist ideals and safeguards of human rights in the Indian constitution.

To conclude, the comparison between the Buddha's and Ambedkar's approaches to caste can be summarised as follows:

In his analysis of caste, Ambedkar initially described caste from the point of the principle of endogamy. However, in *The Buddha and His Dhamma* the same is discussed in terms of its other features, such as graded inequality, division of occupation, etc., which he tried to trace back to the Buddha's discourses. His theory of the genesis, mechanism and spread of caste, as well as his detailed analysis of the negative effects of the caste system on Hindu society, has no parallel in early Buddhist literature. As for arguments refuting caste, those supporting the necessity of social reforms, and those proving the impracticability, harmful nature and failure of the *cāturvarṇya* system, are absent in early Buddhist discourse. However, other issues raised by Ambedkar in this context are present in early Buddhist discourse, at least in a nutshell. The section dealing with the refutation of caste exhibits more similarity between the two approaches than other sections. Ambedkar and the Buddha appear to have fought against caste on the same lines. Both of them challenged the authority of religious scriptures, appealed to the reason of their followers, encouraged conversion to a new life, and created safeguards against the violation of equality in their respective institutions.

The above-mentioned observations clearly show that Ambedkar's understanding of the issue of caste evolved over a period of time. His contact with Buddhism played a vital role in transforming and shaping his approach to the problem of caste and its solution. In his 1916 paper *The Caste in India* and in his 1936 address *Annihilation of Caste*, which came a year after his announcement of abandoning Hinduism, Ambedkar analysed the issue of caste as an ethnologist and a sociologist. We do not find any direct influence of Buddhism on his writing until this stage. However, when Ambedkar started studying the Buddhist religion seriously as one of the options he could convert to, he must have noticed the similarities in the Buddha's rational criticism of caste and his own doctrine of the annihilation of caste. During this period, he must have also realised that values of liberty, equality and fraternity, which are fundamental to ensure the annihilation of caste and a democratic way of life, also form the basis of the Buddha's religion.

The Buddha's treatment of caste is of a religious and ethical nature. The Buddha was neither an ethnologist nor a sociologist. He mainly fought the menace of caste on the ground of reason and morality. He strongly opposed the unscientific explanation and justification of the varṇa system found in religious scriptures and its unethical practice in society. He created a rational and ethical ideological framework in the form of Dhamma and built an ideal society called Saṅgha, which were instrumental in removing caste-consciousness from the minds of people. Although the Buddha neither openly supported inter-caste marriages nor directly asked people to abandon their earlier religions, his arguments certainly suggest that there is nothing wrong in doing so.

Although we do not find any clear influence of Buddhism on Ambedkar's early works, in *The Buddha and His Dhamma* of 1956, he showed considerable change in his approach to caste. There, it is evident that he certainly took a religious and ethical turn. As he tried to unearth the social message preached by the Buddha, Ambedkar made clear the relationship between his and the Buddha's approaches to the issue of caste. Based on the Buddha's rational arguments refuting caste and remedies he suggested thereof, Ambedkar drew implications in line with his own understanding and solution to the caste problem. The Buddha and Ambedkar shared a common point of view, which was rational and humanistic. In their philosophy, there was no place for God, scriptural authority or orthodoxy of any kind. This commonality in outlook is responsible for the similarities in their approaches to the question of caste.

Ambedkar's presentation of the Buddha's teachings, however, is creative in nature. It does not simply echo traditional Buddhist thoughts, but rather reflects his own unique understanding of caste, which was deepened by his study of history, sociology and anthropology. It would not be wrong to say that Ambedkar took the early Buddhist discourse on caste to its logical conclusion. He realised that merely refuting the divine origin of caste is not sufficient to shake the foundation of the caste system. It is also necessary to reject the traditional Buddhist notion that one's birth in a particular caste is determined by one's good or bad past karma. Based on the Buddha's doctrine of non-self, Ambedkar rejected the traditional understanding of transmigration, and thereby redefined the karma theory from a social and materialistic point of view. Thus, by destroying the karmic basis of caste, Ambedkar completed the Buddha's mission of denying caste a religious sanction.

The Buddha was a religious teacher, not a lawmaker. Hence, his safeguards against inequality were only operational within the limits of his

Saṅgha. They could not become the law of the land. Ambedkar knew that fraternity—the foundation of liberty and equality—cannot be established by sheer force or law. He, however, believed that the law was necessary to protect the interests of minorities. For this reason he made safeguards against injustice available to all citizens of India by incorporating them into the Indian constitution.

Thus, the neo-Buddhist approach to the problem of caste is not fundamentally different from the early Buddhist approach. Rather, it issues forth and develops from the former. In other words, it is an advancement or a restatement of early Buddhist thoughts, made to suit the modern times. In addition to this, the neo-Buddhist approach has been enriched by the anthropological and sociological insights of Ambedkar. As he himself said, "An Anthropologist is the best person to study religion."

Notes

1 Irawati Karve described varṇa, which she prefers to translate as "rank," as made up of a "caste cluster." According to her, "The varṇa system was modified and the varṇa and *jāti* systems were interwoven together to form a very elaborate ranking system" (1991: 47).

2 "*cattāro 'me vaṇṇā khattiyā brāhmaṇā vessā suddā*" (*Cullavagga* p. 239).

3 "*jātiṁ c' akkhāhi pucchito*" (*Suttanipāta* 421d).

4 "*ādiccā nāma gottena sākiyā nāma jātiyā*" (*Suttanipāta* 423ab).

5 "*kiṁjacco bhavam*" (*Suttanipāta* p. 80).

6 "*na brāhmaṇo no 'mhi na rājaputto na vessāyano uda koci no 'mhi* |" (*Suttanipāta* 455ab).

7 "*brāhmaṇo no bhavam*" (*Suttanipātap* p. 81).

8 "*akalla maṁbrāhmaṇa pucchasi gottapañhaṁ*" (*Suttanipāta* 456d).

9 Cf. the *Ambalaṭṭhikā-Rāhulovādasutta* of the Majjhimanikāya (vol. I, p. 414ff).

10 "*yathā ahaṃ tathā ete yathā ete tathā ahaṃ, attānaṃ upamaṃ katvāna haneyya na ghātaye.*" (*Suttanipāta*, verse 705).

11 As stated by Kosambi, both the Buddhist and Jain sects did a great job by admitting foreigners into Hindu society. Foreign communities like the Greeks, *Śaka*s, *Hūṇa*s, *Mālava*s and *Gurjara*s came to India and, through the gateway of these two religions, entered Hindu society.

12 "*brāhmaṇīṃ kṣatriyākanyāṃ vaiśyāṃ sūdrīṃtathaiva ca* |
yasyā ete guṇā santi tā me kanyāṃ pravedaya ||
na kulena na gotreṇa kumāro mama vismitaḥ |
guṇe satye ca dharme ca tatrāsya ramate manaḥ ||"

13 Here it may be noted that although Kosambi discussed the Buddhist approach to caste in the tenth chapter entitled "*Jātibheda*" of his book *Bhagavān Buddha*, he did not attempt to figure out the genesis of the caste system in India. He simply observed that the belief that the problem of caste in India has its roots in the *Puruṣasūkta* of the *Ṛgveda* is wrong; for, like *ahiṁsā*, the institution of caste was also prevalent in the Saptasindhu region even before the Vedic period. As in Sumeria, the priest usually became king—Brahmins were at the head of the society even in this region.

14 The same ideas can be found in Ambedkar's earlier article *Caste and Conversion*, published in the *Telugu Samachara* Special Number in November 1926 (1989: 422, fn. 1).

15 It may be noted that a similar comment by Ambedkar on the survival of the Hindu religion is found in his article *Caste and Conversion*, published in the Telugu Samachar Special Number of November 1926, exactly ten years before the publication of *Annihilation of Caste* (1989: 422, fn. 1).

References

Pāli sources

Dhammapadatthakathā. Vol. I, Part 1. Edited by H. C. Norman. The Pāli Text Society. Oxford. 1993. (First edition 1906, Reprint 1970).

Lalita Vistara. Leben und Lehre des Çâkya-Buddha. Textausgabe mit Varianten-, Metren-, und Worterverzeichnis. von S. Lefmann. Verlag der Buchhandlung des Waisenhauses. Halle. 1902.

The Majjhima-Nikāya. Vol. I. Edited by V. Trenckner. The Pāli Text Society. London. 1979. (First edition 1888, Reprint 1948).

The Majjhima-Nikāya. Vol. III. Edited by Robert Chalmers. The Pāli Text Society. London. 1977. (First edition 1899, Reprint 1951).

The Sutta-Nipāta. New Edition. By Dines Andersen and Helmer Smith. The Pāli Text Society. London. 1913.

The Vinaya Pitakam: Vol. II. The Cullavagga. Edited by Hermann Oldenberg. Pāli Text Society. Oxford. 1995.

Other sources

Ambedkar, B. R. (1936): *Annihilation of Caste with A Reply to Mahatma Gandhi*. Amritsar: The Ambedkar School of Thoughts. 1945. Third edition. (First edition).

Ambedkar, B. R. (1957): *The Buddha and His Dhamma*. Bombay: Siddharth College Publication: I.

Ambedkar, B. R. (1982): *Castes in India, Their Mechanism, Genesis and Development*. Jullundur: Bheem Patrika Publications.

Ambedkar, B. R. (1989): *Dr. Babasaheb Ambedkar. Writings and Speeches*. Vol. 5. Compiled by Vasant Moon. Bombay: Education Department, Government of Maharashtra.

Ambedkar, B. R. (2008): *Revolution and Counter-Revolution in Ancient India*. In: *Dr. Babasaheb Ambedkar. Writings and Speeches*. Vol. 3. Compiled by Vasant Moon. Mumbai: Education Department, Government of Maharashtra. Second Edition by Hari Narake. (First edition 1987).

Karve, Irawati (1991): *Hindu Society—An Interpretation*. Poona: Deccan College. (First edition 1961).

Kane, Pandurang Vaman (1941): *History of Dharmaśāstra (Ancient and Mediæval Religious and Civil Law)*, Vol. II, Part I. Poona: Bhandarkar Oriental Research Institute.

Kosambi, Dharmanand (1989): *Bhagavān Buddha*. Nagpur and Pune: Suvicār Prakāśan Maṇḍaḷ. (Fourth reprint). (First edition 1940).

6

NEO-BUDDHISM, MARXISM AND THE CASTE QUESTION IN INDIA

Gopal Guru

Both Buddhism and Marxism, two of the most formidable philosophies, have expanded in contemporary contexts through their emancipatory potential and theoretical rigour. The expansive nature of both these philosophical/political alternatives is indicative of their growth in in terms of location and discursive formation. In terms of location, one can see different incarnations of Marxism, such as Western Marxism, Eastern Marxism, Indian Marxism and so forth. There is a context specificity to this expansive character of Marxism. It is in the same logic one may discursively talk of Dalit Marxism. These versions of Marxism could be understood particularly in terms of the limits of the original Marxism. Hence, the re-contextualization of Marxism is prompted by the specific context-dependent need of a particular society and social groups within that society. One could claim that it is possible to develop Dalit Marxism in India. Dr B. R. Ambedkar's critical engagement with Marxism provides a necessary vantage point to envision such a project. However, the methodological and philosophical openings of Ambedkar's interpretation of Buddhism reveal that Dalit Marxism is a restricted discursive option, open only at the formative stage. Ambedkar seems to have adopted a particular version of Buddhism in order to prove that it is a far more superior alternative, not only to Hinduism but to other forms of Buddhism prevailing in residual forms during his time. Ambedkar's radical reading of Buddhism is also an attempt to offer an alternative to the hegemonies of Marxism in India. In this context, this chapter explores Ambedkar's account of the relationship between Buddhism and Marxism. As I have argued elsewhere,[1] the post-Ambedkarian reading of Buddhism has taken him away from radicalism towards a more spiritual or psychological version of Buddhism, whereas the conservative trend in the scholarship has always fanned tension between Buddhism and Marxism. At the other end of the spectrum, the rigid reduction of Buddhism to a Marxist essence has been a contentious issue within the left-leaning scholarship in contemporary India. It is in this discursive domain that an attempt will be made to locate Ambedkar's response to both Buddhism and Marxism.

In this essay, I will explore the relationship between Ambedkar's Buddhism and Marxism in three parts. The first discusses the moral and political/philosophical significance of the debate on Ambedkar's version of Buddhism and the Indian version of Marxism. It argues that in the post-Buddhism phase, Hinduism as a counter point loses its discursive capacity to engage with Dalit scholars. In fact, it is Marxism that becomes the point of attraction (*Dalit Panther Manifesto*, 1974; Kasbe, 1986), amusement and even fierce critique for Dalit, as well as, non-Dalit scholars. This chapter will confine itself to the Dalit critique of Marxism mounted from the point of view of defending Buddhism as a totally separate perspective. This in turn will suggest how to read Buddhist and Marxist texts in the light of Ambedkar.

This chapter proceeds to argue in its second part that it would also be interesting to explore the possibility of discovering the epistemic deficiencies in the Marxist understanding of social reality. What are the discursive spaces that entail the categories that provide an expansive meaning; meaning that is an enlarged version of the categories that are the part of Marxism? An attempt will be made to detect Marxism as deficient in making philosophical/theoretical sense of Indian reality, particularly in relation to caste and untouchability. The third section of this chapter will also highlight the distinct vocabulary that Ambedkar adopted to join issues with the ideologue of Indian Marxism. It will explore Ambedkar's inversion of the famous Marxist architectural metaphor of base–superstructure to unravel a conversation on the relationship between Marxism and Buddhism. The alienation of the shudra cannot be reduced to that of the proletariat for Ambedkar. It will demonstrate that one cannot reduce Marxism to Buddhism, as Indian scholars tend to do. Further, it will argue that the converse reductionism is not viable either.[2]

Ambedkar on "Buddha and Marx"

Let us then begin with a discussion on reading Ambedkar's text on Karl Marx and the Buddha. This reading becomes important in the context of the extrapolation that has been practiced in the process of reproducing Ambedkar literature.

"Or"/"And" and Ambedkar's text

This argument offered from a particular embattled[3] point of view receives its moral empowerment not merely from epistemological and hermeneutic confidence but from the passive injustice done to Ambedkar by people who failed to address their ontological wounds. Most oppressed castes in India are subject to personal, social and cultural indignity. But they are also exploited economically. Caste in India determines economic status; those at the top of the hierarchy perform non-physical labour, while those at the bottom perform menial labour that oppresses both physically and psychologically. Thus, there is a close relationship between being humiliated on caste grounds and economic vulnerability. In the last 25 years, this wound has not been addressed by commentators on Buddhism and Marxism and hence it has become a kind of ontological wound. The celebration of Ambedkar without reading him or reading him mechanically has become a common practice among Dalits. Interestingly, this common practice has become so powerful that it has begun reshaping the original writing of Ambedkar. The most prominent evidence of such regulatory power is associated with Ambedkar's writings on the Buddha and Marx. As the editorial introduction to the concerned section suggests, the title of the original writing of Babasaheb Ambedkar must have been "Buddha *and* Karl Marx"[4] but in the government version it is "Buddha *or* Karl Marx"—"and" in the original seems to have been replaced by "or." The question that one needs to ask is why are Dalit scholars interested in situating the Buddha against Marx by inserting this "or" between the two thinkers of modern times? The widely discussed essay by Ambedkar on "Marx and Buddhism" has weathered many a dispute in the course of the fracture between or/and. This is because it has been, time and time again, emphasised by translators and commentators that Marx is separated from Buddhism with "or" as dividing bar, whereas in the original text of Ambedkar it is "and." These two words are not innocent; in fact, they are loaded with their integral respective qualities and discursive power. As the efforts show, "or" has been reinforced by the textually unsustainable exclusivity that has been allegedly induced between Marx and Ambedkar by interested parties. There is definitely a certain politics behind this, which seeks to epistemologically separate Ambedkar from Marx. "Or" assumes an almost absolute degree of certainty in meaning. It does not suffer from any kind of intellectual hesitation or a discursive self-doubt. It suggests a quite straightforward expression of a thought or the system of ideas. It suggests that there is only one kind of perspective, an adequate alternative that has to be adopted by people. It does not entertain any kind of epistemic pluralism. It treats a particular thinker as a single unitary vision, thus ruling out other constitutive intellectual traditions. Insistence on "or" in fact denies any genealogical connection of a thought. It rules out being part of any possibility of a *parampara* or intellectual tradition. It claims to be incomparable and rules out any overlap. It tries to follow the Greek tradition of dissociation. It suggests the individualisation of thought. It becomes almost like patent that assigns ownership rights in physical sciences, for example. "Or" makes one thought taller than other contending thoughts.

On the other hand, the word "and," opens the possibility of both sides leaning on each other. It disrupts the binary in the exclusivism of "or." In this sense, "and" is similar to Kierkegaard's "or" (1987). For Kierkegaard "or" represents the arbitrariness of choice against the determinism of logic. In his *Either Or*, he hints that one cannot really deliberate the choice between the pursuit of aesthetic pleasure by A and that of moral responsibility by Judge Wilhelm. Arguments on both sides are ultimately random, defying the claims of logic. Hence, its choice is always a leap of faith and filled with contradictions. The latter allows for elements of one position (A and the Judge's) entering the other. Hence, it questions the law of identity by actually tacitly agreeing with Hegel (sublation). Kierkegaard's "or" is, thus, a critique of the binary version of "or" that persists in modern truth-functional logic. The latter logic has also dominated translations of Ambedkar's essay via "or". However, in the spirit of Kierkegaard's "or" or "and" there is an intertextuality between Marx and Ambedkar. These two important texts talk to each other. Ambedkar's *Annihilation of Caste* (1979), as well as, Marx and Friedrich Engels' *The Communist Manifesto* (1971) actually present two texts of resistance and emancipation. Similarly, Buddhism and Marxism begin to talk to each other at least in some major respect. This has been adequately demonstrated by Ambedkar in his "Marx and Buddhism." "And" enables the epistemic pluralism that creates the possibility of tradition.

Maharashtra has engaged scholars in building an emancipatory intellectual tradition represented by Jyotirao Phule, Ambedkar, Shahu Maharaj, V. R. Shinde and Tarabai Shinde. It has, however, not been able to build up and acknowledge the Marx-Ambedkar and Gandhi traditions. Indian Marxists do not seem to have a deep interest in building up such a tradition. Although they have been very sympathetic to Gandhi, their interest in Ambedkar has often only been rhetorical for the most part. They have been cognitively generous to Gandhi, but not as much to Ambedkar.[5] Ambedkar as a thinker never got adequate space in research journals such as the *Social Scientist* that have a leftist orientation.[6] Otherwise it's Gandhi who takes over the pages in the *Social Scientist*, which is a serious research journal indeed.[7] In this special number, scholars with leftist orientations do bring Gandhi into the textual context of Marx.[8] Ambedkar himself eased out the tension between Marxism and Buddhism. In this regard, we need to mention leftist scholars such as Sharad Patil from the Marathi universe, who has found an intertextual relationship between Marx, Jyotirao Phule and Ambedkar. Although, interestingly, he left out Gandhi from this combination.[9]

In this regard, it is important to acknowledge the efforts made particularly by Dalit literary figures from Maharashtra. The Dalit Panthers for the first time brought Ambedkar and Marx together. This is categorically recorded in the Panthers' manifesto. Their historical effort was to ease the tension between Marx and the Buddha by the restoring the emancipatory purpose that is at the core of both the philosophies.

Ambedkar seeks to compare the two by bringing to central focus dialectics as a common method between Marx and the Buddha. He acknowledges the centrality of class, which according to him has been overshadowed by caste. Ambedkar, however, suggests that the annihilation of caste is a necessary precondition for the annihilation of class. This formulation suggests insight into democratic revolution is the precondition for a socialist revolution. The Indian Left has also emphasised the importance of a democratic revolution. In this regard, it would be interesting to know what exactly the Left's conception of a democratic revolution is.

Indian Left and the caste question

Arguably, the Left suggests a stage theory for social revolution. This progressive development of revolution presupposes the role of liberalism as a mediating principle between the two positions in contention or consideration. Liberalism, I argue, would help us understand the special movement that Buddhism had made, thus escaping the power of Marxism that took root in different parts of India during the 20th century. (I am planning to defer this point to some other time.) I would, with methodological devices, explore history as a possible route to gauge the commonality between the two perspectives—Ambedkar's Buddhism and Marxism. In this particular section, we will explore whether Ambedkar prescribed to the stage theory of history or a non-linear progression of history. Here, I intend to bring in the novel insights that Ambedkar himself provided to us. In his speeches in *Janata*, Ambedkar clearly stated that for a democratic mobilization of people, addressing social issues such as caste and untouchability become unavoidable. At the same time, for him, taking up such a question is not enough to address the Dalit question, which has a bearing on the material deprivation of the masses. Ambedkar puts the social before the material or economic. Interestingly, Ambedkar uses the French Revolution as an initial political condition, while he treats the Russian Revolution as a middle condition and Buddhism as the moral ethical condition for the realization of decent society as desirable—the ought condition in the linear progression of society on a radical mode.

Ambedkar and Marx do believe in the stage theory of history. Ambedkar has categorically stated that Buddhism is a social revolution and that the Russian Revolution was a material revolution. In the historical sense, for him both revolutions were necessary. In fact, for him, a social revolution is a precondition for an economic revolution. One is impossible without the other. Ambedkar uses an apt metaphor from Marathi language—"*Purnachi Poli*"—in order to explain the logical sequence of social transformation. For him, Buddhism is the outer cover of stuffed sweet bread or chapatti and the Russian Revolution is the inner core of this bread (Kamble, 1992).

The relationship between Marxism and Buddhism has been mediated through the question of caste, which had paramount importance as far as Ambedkar's thought, action and movement are concerned. The question of caste seems to have remained undertheorized as far as Marxist scholarship in India is concerned. They have neglected how labour in India is mostly caste-based and that the caste system is one of exploitation and appropriation of the labour of the other. Although, leftist activists have been paying some attention to the question of untouchability off late. Leftist intellectuals by and large paid only rhetorical attention to the caste question. It is in this context, that the current chapter seeks to evaluate both the Ambedkar and post-Ambedkar responses to issues such as the question of caste. The response has to be evaluated at the methodological as well as conceptual levels. Let us discuss two different responses to possibility and impossibility in the textual and political relationship between Marxism and Buddhism.

I am going to argue that the Left's response to the caste question has been mainly strategic, while it is also true that the leftist historians have made a seminal contribution to the very understanding of the caste question.[10] The Left has an interest in forging a democratic opposition to the ruling classes in India. Hence, they professed to take the caste question seriously. However, the Left in India could not treat caste as a national question. Secondly, it treated caste as a question of identity and as a local issue. Third, it defined the caste question primarily in terms of the Dalit ontology. The caste question when viewed from the Left does not enjoy the same national importance as the question of communalism. Although, it must be said that the regional response to the caste question, particularly at the practical political level, has been very laudable; for example left-leaning parties at the state level in Maharashtra and in Tamil Nadu have established caste annihilation conferences, or in southern Tamil Nadu an "untouchability wing." It is because of this that rival parties in the state call leftist parties the Paraya Party (the party of the untouchables). However, this is not new in electoral politics in the country. In the early years, opponents of the communists in Bihar used to deride them as the party of Chamars. The Communist Party of India (CPI) indeed had Chamars as its major social base. Opponents seem to have used Dalits as a poison weapon against the CPI. Dalits on the other hand used Marxism as a menace to democracy.

However, in the sphere of electoral democracy, common Dalits did not consider individual communist leaders as menaces but as their true representatives.[11] But the CPI did not try and resignify this poison as a positive weapon so as to use it for building up the democratic front. Those leaders who enjoyed the support of Dalits did not fear the caste question as a divisive force. This is because working-class leaders defined working-class solidarity, which was vulnerable to division on account of the caste backgrounds of the working classes. During the last two decades, such working-class solidarity has become redundant, as the working-class movement has dissipated along with the disappearance of textile mills from Mumbai, Ahmadabad, Kanpur and Chennai. Communist leaders had no reason to fear (as they did so earlier) that caste consciousness would have a fragmentary impact on working-class or proletarian solidarity in the field of electoral politics. But the communist party did not pursue this Dalit agenda. It lacked the necessary confidence as this was because of electoral politics and not subaltern substantive politics. In fact, the fear of fragmentation resulting from the caste question, which in the Left's perception appeared as a divisive force, lacked the complete emancipatory political vision of the Indian Left. R. B. More, a prominent Dalit from Maharashtra, wrote to the central committee of the CPI requesting it to accommodate an anti-caste agenda into its manifesto, although one could consider him to be more of a Dalit Communist. The Left response's to the caste question can be understood at many levels by raising several sets of questions, necessary in this context: First, how does leftist scholarship make conceptual and theoretical sense of the caste question? What has been the basis of such theorization? Has it been theoretically adequate? Secondly, what has been the nature of this response? Is it uniform or is there variation in such response?

Having said all this, it is also necessary to admit that the Left seems to have succeeded in creating only a moderate impact on the political sensibility of those social groups that are at the receiving end of caste exploitation and oppression. Although Dalits are at the receiving end of material exploitation, their struggle seems focused on social exclusion from opportunity structures. Hence, in the Dalit universe, the language of oppression has dominated their cognitive map much more centrally than material exploitation. It has been argued by certain scholars that the efforts of the Indian Left were not adequate enough to elicit a Dalit response to the efforts they made. For the Indian Left, caste annihilation does not seem to have become core of the political agenda. Although the Indian Left made some efforts to offer a few theoretical insights in understanding the caste question, they never gave it an independent theoretical status.[12] This is not to suggest that the Indian Left had an epistemic inability to understand the caste question. The bigger question is why the Left in India has not been able to develop a theoretically convincing understanding of the caste question. One could even argue that is it correct to say that the Left in India has had a deficient understanding of the caste question. Can one understand the Left's response to the caste question in terms of the evaluative mode, or do we require a more analytical mode to historicise it? In addition to these core questions, let me also raise the following subset of questions for further clarification:

1 Has the Left's perspective been self-referential to the extent that it sought to avoid the need for a serious and honest interlocutor like Babasaheb Ambedkar or Jyotirao Phule?

2 If, arguably, both Ambedkar and Marx belong to the same logical class, then why does the former fail to receive adequate intellectual attention from the Left? This question acquires validity in the context of Ambedkar treating caste as an ideology that, according to him, seeks to diffuse class consciousness.
3 Why is that the majority of Dalits do not treat both Marx and Ambedkar as belonging to the same logical class of system builders?
4 If the Left and the Dalits share the same ground at the objective level, then can they produce a corresponding coherence at the subjective level? To what extent does liberalism as a fault line create a fragmentary impact on this cohesion at the subjective level?

These questions expose the limits of political power within a liberal framework. Leftist parties could not affect structural changes in the states they govern, as upper-caste and lower-caste localities are still separate in villages.

The element of caste sets the evaluative ground on which the relationship between the Left and Dalits can be understood. Intellectual and historical responses to the caste question singularly go to leftist historians. Whether it is understanding the epics or the origin of caste, leftist historians have made the most seminal contributions. This is, however, thanks to the ethics of following protocols, which motivates leftist historians to factor the caste question into their work. This is not to suggest that these historians have no larger emancipatory interest in attending to the caste question. In fact, they have a deep interest. On the other side of the spectrum, there are leftist scholars who prioritize ideology over protocols, and even political necessity, to give importance to the caste question.

The history of social and intellectual activism prevalent particularly among Dalits in India has produced two adversaries to Ambedkar—Marx and Gandhi. Marx stands in opposition to Ambedkar on the question of understanding caste, while Gandhi is designated as Ambedkar's opponent for the former's exclusive focus on untouchability rather than caste. The opposition is more rhetorical rather than conceptual and analytical. Caste in Ambedkar's understanding is an essence of social relation, and untouchability is an essence of caste. The essence of caste operates on the maxim that in the caste hierarchy there is an ascending sense of reverence for upper castes and a descending sense of respect for lower castes. This response is expressed through untouchability. As has been rightly argued by scholars, caste hierarchy is the system of relations rather than element.[13]

Ambedkar's critique of caste acquires significance particularly in the context of the dynamics of caste operation, which he analytically unfolds to us and which involves the subjugation of Dalits to the social dominance of the upper castes. Taking a cue from Ambedkar, it can be argued that insight into social analysis of untouchability offers a theory of the caste system. The essence of the caste structure remains the same across time and space, while forms such as untouchability may change. Buddhism in case of Ambedkar acts as a guiding principle to keep the critique of caste alive. Buddhism provides grounds for both exposing the limits of caste and its transcendence. The teleological thrust in Buddhism seeks a solution to caste beyond legality. It seeks an emancipatory promise in Buddhism as the guiding principle for untouchables, while legality operates on the legal basis of the caste question. However, Ambedkar does try to address the caste question through the intervention of liberal institutions. Hence, one has to appreciate one's instrumental focus on a set of constitutional provisions and institutional mechanisms to create conditions for changing social relations on egalitarian lines. It is also true that Ambedkar certainly realised the limits of the Constitution. It is in this context that he embraced Buddhism not just for eliminating untouchability, but more importantly for liberating the upper castes from the ideology of casteism. Ambedkar suggests the social as an initial condition and ethics as the essential condition for the annihilation of social relations based on caste-induced hierarchy. Buddhism for him provides both social as well as ethical inputs for such a project. In a Marxist scheme, however, it is the dismantling of material structures that would lead to the resultant destruction of the caste system. Marx's *The Future Results of British Rule in India* (1853) does mention caste, though a class perspective will eventually abolish caste according to him. But he does treat caste as hereditary, exploitative and based on obsolete divisions in a premodern economy. His distinction between manual and mental labour is perhaps a little helpful here.

Ambedkar is well aware that this would not happen—his own experience of suffering caste discrimination despite so-called caste mobility shows as much. Here lies the basic difference in the methods Marx and Ambedkar suggested to address the question of caste annihilation. It, in fact, is less methodological and more a question of strategy. Ambedkar's response to the annihilation of caste can be understood using the metaphor of engineering. Engineering, at least in its less advanced phase, would suggest starting the demolition of a dilapidated structure from the top floor. A simple, mechanical reading of Marx could argue that if the demolition of the structure starts from the base, then the superstructure will automatically collapse. Similarly, once the material base is changed, caste as a superstructure will consequently be evaporated. Ambedkar treats the four-varna system as the four-storeyed building whose top floor is occupied by Brahmins. Hence, he starts the demolition at the top. But he does not maintain such a mechanical understanding throughout. He argues that on every floor, there is an element of Brahminism. Ambedkar treats Brahminism as a varna ideology that operates through several thousand castes and sub-castes. In Ambedkar's conceptual scheme, caste which has been arranged on the hierarchal or relative social superiority, renders any social or political consciousness difficult.[14] Hence, he suggests a total demolition of the caste system. However, it is necessary not to lose sight of an important dimension of Ambedkar's thought— he also suggests the need to end material exploitation along with Brahminism. As he says, this can be done along with the change of property relations. So, Ambedkar attacks both capitalism and Brahmanism while Marx singularly attacks the bourgeoise. For Marxism, castes are simply feudal remnants to be annihilated along with the change in the base.

Let me put it more dramatically—in this regard, the leftist intellectual tradition invests their epistemic resources in theorising the category of class. Hence, we do have an ample degree of theoretical work available on this theme. While they adopt a rather democratic attitude that has a practical aspect to it, in the Indian context the Left can share and support the anti-caste struggle led by Dalits. Leftist theoreticians and their supporters do not have to carry an ontological burden of caste while theorising about Indian society. The ontological status of their proposition is based on a social reality that is suffused with class. Ironically, it is the theoretical aspect of modernity that comes to the rescue of the Left. After all, doing theory is an act of modernity.

Buddhism offers a metaphysical space for the transcendence of caste. Buddhism, as seen by Ambedkar, is the most egalitarian option to radically undermine caste. But leftist thinkers in India have treated themselves different from the democratic that is basically radically liberal. Secondly, leftist thinkers have not been aware of the categories that have different and much deeper meanings.

Untouchable and proletariat: two spheres of alienation

The concept of alienation that comes from Marxism, however, changes its meaning when it embarks upon Indian society. The roots of alienation arguably are in the modern form of labour and its relationship to production (Luckás, 83–222). The suggested variation in the meaning of this concept has a bearing on the traditional form of labour that continues to exist in India. These forms not only involve drudgery but defilement as well. Alienation occurring from untouchability is the result of the ideology of purity–pollution that continues to socially govern industrial relations as well as patterns and attitudes of social recognition in a hierarchal society like India. Alienation results from the loss of universal recognition, which in turn is based on the nature of work. For example, clean work has been considered the definitive source of universal recognition. In this regard, alienation when viewed in the particular Indian context acquires different meanings and essence. The nature of work such as scavenging rules out a metaphysical understanding of alienation. Put differently, it does not push the relationship beyond the realm of lived human interaction and lived social relationship. It does not treat scavenging as the rare spiritual privilege; work done in the service of God. The "touchable"—even untouchable scavengers themselves—on the contrary, practically relate obnoxious, defiling work to himself or herself. When one relates the work to self in such a self-assessment and strong self-evaluation, one develops the sense of worthlessness, which is then endorsed by the upper caste on an everyday basis. Such perpetuation of the untouchable as a moving moral menace leads to his or her alienation and ultimately becomes an ontological wound. This is a deep moral wound that causes injury into the core or the soul of a being. It is in this sense that alienation does not result from materiality but from untouchability.

Thus, recognition is based both on the nature of work and its competitive quality in attracting job-seekers. If the nature of work is defiling, even if it is well paid it would not bring recognition, as is the case with scavenging in India. It could thus be true that social recognition cannot be bought by paying more for scavenging labour, because it is considered deeply defiling and cannot be compensated on utilitarian or instrumental grounds. In the Indian context, the untouchable worker and the worker, or the proletariat, as such are two different entities facing two different kinds of alienation. The untouchable feels alienated because of his/her ontological association with the dirty work while the worker in general develops alienation on account of his/her being reduced to a thing. One is reduced to an object while the other is reduced to dirt. But the proletariat has the possibility of becoming a spectre with positive power (Marx and Engels, 1971) while an untouchable can also become a spectre but with negative power. Let us see how.

Two conceptions of spectre: proletariat and the untouchable

Like alienation, there are two conceptions of "spectre" in the form of an untouchable and the proletariat. Although these spectres do have power of their own, it differs in terms of its effect. It could be argued that the power of the proletariat as a spectre is positive, while that of untouchable's is negative. But power of both these spectres differs inasmuch as the proletariat has much more power to create a systemic crisis for capitalism, whereas an untouchable as a spectre creates crisis for the touchable individual. An untouchable's power to pollute the touchable can force the latter to remain within his boundaries. Second, the spectre of proletariat can haunt the capitalist and can overthrow a capitalist system of exploitation. A spectre in the Marxist sense, therefore, has positive power. Hence, the Brahman wants to be safe from the untouchable. In the Indian context, an untouchable can acquire the force of spectre on account of his/her possessing the power to ritually pollute a pure being such as a Brahmin. It is in this sense, an untouchable can be a poison weapon. The spectre of the untouchable as a poison weapon can be seen controlling the Brahmin as a pure being in U. R. Anantmurthy's highly acclaimed novel, *Sanskara* (1981). Alienation and spectre are arguably two concepts that bring forth the philosophical difference between Marxism and Ambedkar's Buddhism.

Alienation occurring from untouchability is the result of the feeling of repulsion that is unilaterally expressed by an upper-caste person converting a living labourer into an object of dirt. In such a symmetrical social relationship, labour is denied its universal recognition. While in case of labour that is also physical, this results from the loss of control over the product. The opposite is true in regard to a form of labour considered polluting and defiling. It is the loss of universal recognition. Labour can acquire a universal character in terms of its use value for the accumulation of profit. Capitalists across time and space use this labour without distinction. The slogan, "Workers of the World" given by Marx makes sense only in this regard. Work that is considered to be defiling cannot acquire such a universal character. Thus, the slogan, "Untouchables of the World, Unite" does not become a possibility—should it be produced at all. Similarly, an untouchable worker cannot enjoy recognition of his/her labour even if they are paid high wages, which is not the case at all. It cannot be bought by paying more labour charges. The untouchable and the worker (proletariat) are two different entities facing two different kinds of alienation. For example, in Pune, untouchables were not allowed to walk the streets in the morning and the afternoon. This was not because Brahmins tended to be outdoors at this time; rather orthodox Brahmins considered the shadow of an untouchable the source of ritual pollution, and since a shadow casts longer in the morning and afternoon, Dalits were barred from entering the streets of Pune during these times.

The act of disentangling the proletariat from the untouchable is rendered difficult not due to an acute sense of competition, but more due to the need to monopolise scarce resources to one's own caste. Hence, we had the formation of caste include modern textile industries (Guru, 1987). Untouchable workers, for example, were not allowed to work in the bobbin sections of the textile mills in Mumbai (Ibid). It is in this sense untouchability resulted in denying untouchables the power of becoming a spectre. They always remained with the tag of an untouchable worker. On another level, it could be argued that the untouchability practiced by touchable workers in the textile mills tended to produce a different kind of alienation, not from the estranged self but from the social attitudes held by other workers. The process of becoming a spectre depends on two processes: moral hegemony and working-class solidarity. Workers need to acknowledge that untouchables are superior to the former in terms of skill and efficiency. This did not happen, particularly in the case of the textile mill workers in Mumbai. Caste and untouchability did not allow untouchables to be fully formed into a proletariat.[15] This is because the workers from other caste groups were not fully formed into a proletariat as they largely remained entangled within their own caste consciousness.

This, however, was not a natural disposition so much as it was the result of tendencies to monopolise higher-paid sections like weaving in textile mills. However, during the feudal period where there was no competition, the sense of superiority and patriarchy sustained this consciousness. One could then conclude that there is an acute sense of the impossibility of becoming and individual workers sought to intensify the feeling of alienation among Dalits, while among the upper castes alienation was subsidised by the relative sense of social superiority over the untouchable. In fact, at the specific level, workers enjoyed the power to regulate the industrial relationship. Hence, the sense of alienation was diluted—thanks to the caste consciousness that intersected their class consciousness. Thus, caste denies the formation of pure alienation and hence raises a serious problem for the unitary theory of alienation. In feudal times, there was an absence of a sense of self-worth, which arguably was the result of the lack of social interaction between two persons isolated by caste and untouchability. But in modern times, the sense of self-worth that results from the efforts to attach value to oneself is defined by the type of work one is doing. The work in modern times carried a utilitarian value with it. For example, work that is competitive and much sought after is quite valuable. Thus, clean, skilled work is looked at with respect. Put differently, scavenging is considered defiling and dirty. The untouchable does not attach any value to it, neither do those who create conditions for the dirt. Dirty work, which came to be physically associated with untouchable, continued to stay with them in reflective form. For example, the shadow of the untouchable also carried the negative power of polluting the touchable who then performed elaborate rituals to make themselves pure. The untouchable faces a double challenge of separating himself or herself from the dirty labour as well as his or her associative shadow. The question was: Did becoming part of the proletariat offer the untouchable a space to seek this alienation? We do need a Marxist theory of labour that has some bearing on dirt. At the moment, we do not have one.

The untouchable's struggle is fundamentally associated with how to rid oneself of the shadow that is also defiling. This shadow is not empty. It is embedded with negative meaning. In Marathi, there is a popular saying, "*Sawalilahi Ubha Rahat Nahi*" or "one keeps away from the shadow of a morally menacing person."[16] One of the mediums that Ambedkar suggested for this was the urban conditions of industrialisation, urbanisation and education. For him modernisation did offer a bright chance to destroy this double alienation. Urbanization and clean work in the textile mills were considered enabling force, within which an untouchable could become anonymous and would not be haunted by his own shadow. On the other hand, material conditions made it difficult for the touchable worker to separate himself from caste associations. He remained caste conscious vis à vis the presence of untouchables in the textile mills of Mumbai, Ahmadabad,

Chennai, Calcutta and Kanpur. The "pure" form of alienation resulting from the loss of control over their own labour and the fruits of labour never occurred to him. This was because he remained happy with the sense of superiority that he got by treating the untouchable as defiling and dirty, even in the modern industries of textile mills. Alienation based on the ritual notion of pollution and the forcible association with dirty work has been a reality in India, Nepal and Japan (in earlier days) but not in Europe. This is simply because in the European context, there was no caste division in factories. A worker's alienation, therefore, is derivative of material conditions. It was the alienation associated with it.

Conclusion

Under the influence of traditional Buddhism, Ambedkar's conception of Buddhism is rendered as spiritual and psychological at the hands of some post-Ambedkar Buddhist scholars. Hence, the anti-caste radical character of Ambedkarite Buddhism is diluted. It neglects Ambedkar's attempt to make his Buddhism have a dialogue with Marx. On the other hand, there are Ambedkarite scholars influenced by Marx who reduce Ambedkar's interpretation of Buddhism to Marxism. Both these approaches, reductionist and exclusivist, fail to capture Ambedkar's true intentions as reflected in his writing on the Buddha and Marx. In order to understand and combat the problem of caste, the insights of Marx and Marxists can play an important role. But one has also to understand and transcend the limits of Marxism. Indian Marxist scholars have done a lot of work in theorising caste. But the Indian Left in practice (barring some exceptions) does not carry the ontological burden of caste. It has considered the caste issue not a national one, but an individual or local one.

Marx would regard class as belonging to the base and caste as belonging to the superstructure. Ambedkar, instead of applying the base–superstructure model, considers the caste system a four-storeyed building with Brahmins forming the top storey and Shudras the ground floor, but with every floor also carrying an element of Brahmanism nonetheless. According to him, the building should be demolished from the top. According to Marx, the destruction of the class structure will automatically lead to the annihilation of caste. For Ambedkar, the annihilation of caste is a pre-condition of the destruction of class.

Marx focuses on the alienation of the proletariat, whereas Ambedkar on that of the untouchables. The latter, which involves the categories of purity and pollution determined by birth, is of a very different nature than the former. It is not voluntary nor does it permit mobility. Moreover, the human being undergoes a stigmatized life of humiliation, which is not quite the same as impoverishment. Hence the problem of alienation in Indian society becomes complex. Ambedkar, through his formation of Buddhism, attacks both capitalism and Brahmanism. He, therefore, questions inequality at the levels of both class and caste. He demonstrates the economic, social, cultural and personal implications of caste as entangled. Hence, his radical interpretation of Buddhism can provide tools for combating the complex problem of alienation.

Notes

1 For a detailed discussion see Guru, 1991.
2 Chattopadhya (1976) is a case in point—he builds on affinities between Buddhism and Marxism exclusively by privileging their practical turn.
3 Any Dalit talking about the possibility of overlap between the two philosophies has become an object of hate.
4 Editors of BAWS, Vol. 3 in their introduction to the Part IV entitled "Buddha or Marx" say, "The Committee found three different typed copies of an essay on Buddha and Karl Marx in loose sheets two of which have corrections in the author's own handwriting" (p. 439). This implies that the original title of the essay must have been "Buddha and Karl Marx"or "An Essay on Buddha and Karl Marx."
5 Of course, in Marathi there are some leading scholars with leftist orientations, such as Prabhakar Sanzgiri and Prabhakar Vaidhya, who wrote about Ambedkar.
6 Ambedkar does find some mention in *Social Scientist* but this occurs in the journal only on the event of his birth anniversary in 1991.
7 The *Social Scientist* journal brought out a special number on Gandhi in 2018 (Vol. 46, numbers 11–12, November to December 2018).
8 The writings of Prabhat Patnaik (2018) and Akeel Bilgrami (2018) for example.
9 Patil founded a Marathi Journal *Satyshodhak Marxwadi* (translated as "Truth-Seeking Marxist").
10 These include Vivekananda Jha, R. S. Sharma, Irfan Habib and Romila Thapar.
11 For instance, Sudam Kaka Deshmukh form Amravati.
12 "Caste and Class," *Economic and Political Weekly*, 1979.
13 Kaviraj Sudipta, Indo-centric theories,: the Marxist Framework, in ed. RS Khare, OUP, 2006, p. 154.
14 Dumont terms this "continuous hierarchy" (1999).
15 This is ignored by Marxists such as Habib (2007), who attempt to proletarianize caste.
16 This references the 19th century Peshwai rule.

References

Ambedkar, B.R. 1979 "Annihilation of Caste" in *Babasaheb Ambedkar Writings and Speeches* (vol 1), 23–96, New Delhi: Dr. Ambedkar Foundation.

——— 1987 "Buddha or Karl Marx" in *Babasaheb Ambedkar Writings and Speeches* (vol 3), 441–62, New Delhi: Dr. Ambedkar Foundation.

Anantamurthy, U.R. 1981 *Sanskara* (Trans. by A.K. Ramanuja). New Delhi: Oxford University Press.

Bilgrami, Akeel. 2018 "Thinking Radically with Gandhi." *Social Scientist*, 46 (11–12), 3–16.

Chattopadhyaya, Debiprasad 1976 *What is Living and what is Dead in Indian Philosophy*. New Delhi: People's Book House.
Dalit Panther Manifesto, Dalit Panther Movement, Mumbai, 1974.
Dumont, Louis. 1999 *Homo Hierarchicus: The Caste System and Its Implications* (Trans. by Mark Sainsbury, Louis Dumont and Basia Gulati). New York: Oxford University Press, (Second Impression).
Guru, Gopal. 1987 "Political Economy of Segregation and Discrimination in 19th Century Mumbai." *Social Science Probings*, 36.
——— 1991"Appropriating Ambedkar." *Economic and Political Weekly*, *26* (27/28), 1697–99.
Habib, Irfan. 2007 "Caste in Indian History," reprinted digitally in *Anticaste. in* https://www.anticaste.in/irfan-habib-caste-in-indian-history/, accessed on 19/1/2020.
Kamble, Arun (ed.). 1992 *Babasaheb Ambedkaranche, Janata til Agralekh*. Mumbai: Garnthali and Marathi Department, Mumbai University.
Kasbe, Raosaheb. 1986 *Marx ani Ambedkar*. Pune: Sugawa Publication.
Kaviraj, Sudipta. 2006 "Indo-centric Theories in the Marxist Framework" in *Caste, Hierarchy, and Individualism: Indian Critiques of Louis Dumont's Contributions*, 154. New Delhi: OUP.
Kierkegaard, Soren. 1987 *Either/Or* (vol 1). Princeton, NJ: Princeton University Press.
Lukács, Georg. 1971 *History and Class Consciousness: Studies in Marxist Dialectics*. Cambridge: MIT Press.
Marx, Karl 1853 "The Future Results of British Rule in India," accessed on 5/42020 https://www.marxists.org/archive/marx/works/1853/06/25.html
Marx, Karl & Friedrich Engels 1971 *The Communist Manifesto*. New York: International Publishers.
Patnaik, Patnaik. 2018 "Gandhi, Technology and Employment." *Social Scientist*, *46* (11–12), 27–36.

7

AMBEDKAR'S CRITIQUE OF PATRIARCHY

Interrogating at intersection of caste and gender

Pratima Pardeshi[1]

An analysis of Dr. Babasaheb Ambedkar's thoughts must be located within the diverse positions on the "woman's question" that were articulated during his period in Maharashtra. While some posed the question within a Brahmanical frame, others placed it within the confines of Hinduism. Yet others sought to link this question with the non-Brahminical thought of the period. The Marxist frame of class gave voice to women of the working classes. Non-Brahmanical revolutionary streams of thought launched an attack on the three institutionalized hierarchies of caste, class and patriarchy. It is this stream that is reflected in the works of Ambedkar, who drew out the links between the subordination of women and the caste system.

Women as the gateways to the caste system

Ambedkar refers to castes as being enclosed classes and traces them to the origins of untouchability in meat eating. He concludes that the absence of intermarriage or endogamy is the one characteristic that can be called the essence of castes (Ambedkar 2019, 318–74). In his detailed analysis of the caste system, he underlines the intrinsic relation between the caste system and the subordination of women. According to Ambedkar, endogamy is the primary characteristic of the caste system, rather than merely the idea of pollution or untouchability (2014 a, b; 2019, 303; 1987). We can discover the origins of caste by looking at how endogamy comes to be maintained and perpetuated in society.

Ambedkar then raises questions about how the practice of endogamy could have been maintained in society through boundaries that could not ordinarily be transgressed by people. This is so that marriages within the caste may be ensured, however normally the sex ratio in any given group is likely to be balanced (2014a). That is to say, men and women tend to be present in equal numbers and a severe imbalance in this ratio is likely to create problems as "surplus men" or "surplus women." That is to say, if a wife dies before her husband, the man is rendered a surplus man; if the husband dies before the wife, she is rendered a surplus woman. The group then faces problems: how is this surplus woman to de disposed? According to Ambedkar, in order to maintain the sex ratio, perpetuate endogamy and thereby the caste system, four different practices are deployed. These include *sati*, enforced widowhood, enforced celibacy and the marriage of child brides with older men or widowers.[2]

1. The Practice of *Sati*: After the death of her husband, the woman is rendered surplus, affecting the balance in the group. In order to avoid this, the woman is burnt on the pyre of her deceased husband. Such a practice was adopted because if the widow lives then there are several dangers: one, she is likely to marry another man from her caste group and thereby encroach upon the reserved right of young brides from the same group. Two, if she marries a man outside her caste, the boundaries of endogamy will be broken down. Therefore, burning her live on the pyre of her deceased husband was seen as essential by the group. However, it was not always possible to keep the caste group intact by practicing *sati* and therefore other practices also came to be deployed.

2. Enforced Widowhood: Ambedkar argues that the practice of enforcing widowhood on women was a relatively milder one than *sati*. Any possibility of "immoral" behaviour from the widow was regulated through practices such as tonsure, which were considered making her undesirable. Further several restrictions came to be placed on her mobility and dietary habits, etc., so as to ensure that she did not pose a "temptation" to the males of the group.

3. Enforced Celibacy: A balanced sex ratio is a crucial issue for groups who seek to become castes. Since the balance is crucial for the possibility and perpetuation of endogamous marriages, Ambedkar argues that if the needs of the people cannot be satisfied within the caste group then they are likely to look outside the group. Further, he argues that a surplus man is not burnt in society by the sole virtue of his being a man—if the surplus man is thought to be a danger to the maintenance of the caste group, he is not burnt as the woman is. Instead, celibacy comes to be enforced upon him. Some widowers themselves chose to practice *brahmacharya* or *sanyaas*. However, these practices go against natural urges in human beings. If the surplus man continues to function within the group, he can pose a danger to the moral standards set by the caste group.

4. Marriage of Child Brides to Older Men: A man who is celibate or who renounces the world is, in a sense, useless or as good as dead for the propagation of the caste group. Every caste has to increase its numbers in the race for survival, and hence enforcing celibacy on the surplus man is an impractical practice. It would serve the interests of the caste groups better if the surplus man could remain in *grihasthashram,* that is, if a bride can be found for him within the caste group. If the surplus man is to be kept tied to the caste group, then finding a bride from the yet-to-be-marriageable age becomes the only way out. This keeps intact the rules both of endogamy and caste-based morality.

Thus, to make the emergence of caste groups possible, an imbalance in the sex ratio occurs through the practices of *sati*, enforced widowhood, enforced celibacy and age-mismatched marriages. These practices are exploitative of women and thus Ambedkar underlines the fact that castes are maintained through the sexual exploitation of women. It is only through the regulation and control of women's sexuality that the closed character of the castes can be maintained; in this sense, he argues that women are the gateways to the caste system.

Ambedkar strengthens his argument regarding the philosophy of Hinduism by quoting from *Manusmriti*. He argues that Manu had a clear design as to who could marry whom. The twice-born in his first marriage had compulsorily to marry a woman from his own caste; in his subsequent marriages he had to marry women from the lower varnas. However the shudra woman could marry only a shudra man (Ambedkar 1987a, 1987b). Thus, Manu's opposition to mixed marriage is apparent, as is the fact that in the law of Manu it became regulatory to marry a woman from one's own varna. Ambedkar once again picks up the theme of mixed marriages in his analysis of religion. To the question of defining religion, Ambedkar answers saying that it is constituted by justice and fraternity, which in turn require freedom and equality (Ambedkar 1987a; 1987c; 2014b, 57–58). He then goes on to discuss how Hinduism does not then qualify by this definition of religion and underlines the utter absence of justice in *Naradsmriti* and *Manusmriti*. For instance, in both the Shruti and Smriti, the punishments prescribed vary with the varna. While for the same crime the Brahman paid in *panas*, the prostitute had to pay more *panas*, and the shudra was publicly caned. He, thus, argues that there is no equality and justice within Hinduism and that there is no scope for social mobility, and that is precisely why mixed marriages came to be severely forbidden.

However, despite severe regulations, if mixed marriages do take place, then the law that regulates them is patriarchal (Ambedkar 1987a; 2014b). There are two kinds of mixed marriages: *pratiloma* (hypogamy) and *anuloma* (hypergamy). The latter refers to the marriage between a woman of a lower caste and a man of a higher caste, while the former refers to the marriage between a woman of a higher caste and a man of a lower caste. The *pratiloma* form of marriage is not approved because the woman has transgressed the boundaries of caste. Such transgressions on the part of women could lead to a breakdown of the caste system, and hence this form of marriage comes to be severely punished with excommunication. A religious justification came to be put forth as an ideological ground for the banning of this kind of marriage. For instance, Omvedt (2014) gives the instance of the marriage between the intelligent man of the *malla* caste and a Brahmin woman. The man in pursuit of knowledge goes to a Brahmin household and obviously fakes his caste for the same. Impressed with the brilliance of the *malla* man, the daughter of the Brahmin marries him. But on realizing that her husband is an untouchable, she commits suicide, for her marriage, being a hypogamous one, would be ostracized by society. This incident also reveals the near complete internalization of caste and of the racial and patriarchal domination by women themselves. Omvedt (2014) also brings out a very significant connection between the illegitimacy of *pratiloma* and the legitimacy of the *devdasi*[3] tradition. She argues that *muralis* and *matangis* were different from the temple dancers and did enjoy some amount of autonomy in the village. But during the feudal period, matriarchal and matrilineal remnants of the custom were used to institutionalize the sexual accessibility of Dalit women for high-caste men. This easy access to Dalit women by high castes, when juxtaposed with the proscription of the relation between women of the higher castes and men of the lower castes, reveals a significant sexual dialectic (Ambedkar 2003b). The latter informs caste interactions and behaviour in the villages of India even today.

In conclusion, it is apparent that the caste system emerged through the imposition of several religious and customary restrictions on women. It is this that leads Ambedkar to conclude that women are the gateways to the caste system. This theme appears not only in his writings on the origins of the caste system, but also in his speech at the Mahad Satyagraha Parishad (Ambedkar 1928; 2014c). Thus, his views on the liberation of women in India may be summarized as:

a Caste system exploits women
b Patriarchy exploits women

The caste system is hierarchically organized and the relation between the different strata are organized on the principle of inequality and difference. Thus, the exploitation of all women is not uniform and differs by caste. This exploitation is intensified as one moves down the caste hierarchy; the exploitation of Dalit women is of a different nature than that of high-caste women. Thus, from within a Phule-Ambedkarite position, any claims to all women being Dalit is only rhetoric. To speak on behalf of all women is to deny the very core of Phule-Ambedkarism.

The caste system and the subordination of women

The speech made by Ambedkar at the Mahad Satyagraha is important as it would not be an overstatement to say that it provides a statement of what could be called the Dalit perspective on women's liberation. In an analysis of the ways in which the caste system is responsible for the subordination of women, he argues that the subordination of women in India is intensified through the subordination of class, caste and patriarchal systems (1928, 2014a). Caste-based division of labour, caste *panchayat*, caste-based personal laws all go towards subordination of women. In matters of marriage, divorce, remarriage, inheritance, etc., caste-based laws and regulations seek to make women dependent on men and dispossessed. Within this frame of caste, the exploitation of Dalit and Adivasi women is more intense; a majority of them are landless agricultural labourers. More of these women become victims of rape and sexual assault; the number of mass rapes of Dalit women in Bihar and Uttar Pradesh are cases in point. Moreover, the state takes no notice of such sexual crimes, as it is assumed that men from privileged castes are entitled to sexually exploit women from underprivileged castes. That the women of the Atishudra castes have no honour and that they are but commodities for the pleasure of men of the higher varnas is an old injunction of the Dharmashastras. Therefore, the atrocities against Dalit and Adivasi women are to be traced to the caste system and not to the class system (Patil 1983). This analysis by Patil assumes significance in this context.

Thus, Ambedkar underlines the fact that the caste system exploits women; further, in such a hierarchical system, the lower the position of the woman in the hierarchy, the more intense her exploitation. He made Dalit women at the gathering conscious of their exploitation as women born in the lowest strata of the hierarchy. By asking them to ponder why their status is so different from that of the Brahmin women, he underlined to them the fact that the annihilation of untouchability is their cause. In this context, he called upon them to join the struggle for the annihilation of the caste system. Through his analysis Ambedkar establishes the fact that there is an intrinsic relationship between the caste system and the subordination of women.

Brahmanical culture: responsible for the subordination of women

Ambedkar, one of the key thinkers in the non-Brahman tradition, himself categorizes all Indian history, tradition, religions and culture into the Brahmanical and the non-Brahmanical. He also argues that perspectives on women's liberation can also be broadly divided into the same two categories. Brahmanical culture, which Ambedkar opposed, justifies and supports the subordination of women. In his work *The Rise and Fall of Hindu Women*, he undertakes a detailed analysis of Brahmanical culture, texts and religious injunctions which push women into the dark valleys of enslavement (2014d).

Ambedkar argues that since ancient times, the birth of a daughter has always been a matter of sorrow in Hindu families. The Buddhist tradition stood in opposition to this Brahmanical tradition. The Buddha did not think that the birth of a daughter was a sorrowful event. To substantiate his argument, Ambedkar quotes from Buddhist literature the dialogue between King Prasenajit and the Buddha. The King, disappointed on the birth of a daughter, was asked the reason for his sorrow by the Buddha. On being told the reason, the Buddha gave Prasenajit a discourse on the same. The Buddha tells the king that there is no need to grieve the birth of a daughter as she can prove to be a more effective progeny than a son. "Your daughter," he continues, "will become wise and virtuous" (Ambedkar 2014d, 117–8). Through this dialogue, Ambedkar seeks to underline the fact that the Buddha did not subscribe to gender discrimination and thought that girls too could be capable and virtuous.

Brahmanical culture denies women the right to knowledge

Ambedkar highlights the fact that the Buddha allowed the entry of women in the Sangha (2014d). Hindu religion on the other hand denied women all access to knowledge and the right of renunciation was denied to Shudras and women. The reasons for this are traced to Manu's dictum that women did not have a right to learn the Vedas and therefore even the performance of the Samskaras for them should be done without chanting the Vedic mantras. According to the Vedic religion, the chanting of the Vedic mantras absolves sin, but since women were not allowed to study these Vedic texts, Brahmanical culture deemed them to be in a perpetual state of untruth and sinfulness. Ambedkar was not in agreement with this and he argued that this dictum of Manu was in keeping with the tradition of the Brahmanical texts that came before him. This Brahmanical dictum regarding women, he argued, led to the downfall of women in India; for partaking in the process of knowledge-making is the natural right of all humans and has been withdrawn from women by the Brahmins without any logical reason. Thus, women had to forego the right to spiritual growth and knowledge. Brahmanical culture believes that a man who has no spiritual knowledge is closer to God than all others by the virtue of being a man. Why is this so? Why is this not true for women? Ambedkar posed these questions to those who championed Brahmanical thought.

According to Ambedkar, the Brahmanical ideology dominant in the sphere of knowledge caused two grave injustices to women, which were abolished by the Buddha. The Buddha allowed women the access to "Parivraja" and thus at once brought an end to two kinds of injustices:

1 Women could partake in the processes of knowledge, as could men
2 Women could experience spiritual enlightenment

Thus, Ambedkar concludes that the Buddha emancipated Indian women from their enslavement and brought about revolutionary changes in their lives. Brahmanical culture denied women the right to freedom, the Buddha, however, granted freedom to women. "All women, no matter whether they belonged to the Brahmin, Kshatriya and Vaishyas, and all Shudras, ... were prohibited from acquiring knowledge. The Buddha raised a revolt against this atrocious doctrine of the Brahmins" (1992, 287). Thus, Ambedkar argues that the Buddha, by allowing the women to enter the Sangha, propagated the cause of women's freedom (2014d). By breaking the shackles of gender discrimination, not only did the Buddha throw open the path of excellence to women but he also paved the way for granting women a status equal to that of men.

Ambedkar further argues that in ancient India, women enjoyed a high social status (2014e). Women were in the forefront of the political process and also the social and intellectual spheres. They had the right to initiation or *upanayana* and could chant Vedic mantras. Quoting from Panini, he gives instances of women who excelled in the Vedas and who could debate with men on issues of religion, philosophy, the origins of the universe and the development of knowledge. The debates of Jahaksulabha, Yajnavalkya and Gargi-Maitreyi and Shankaracharya and Maitreyi are well known (2014e). Thus, women have not always been exploited, as there were times during which it was possible for them to reach the peaks of success. Ambedkar underlines the fact that India was probably the only society in which women enjoyed such a high status.

In the first volume of *Dasa-Shudra Slavery*, Sharad Patil (1983) also notes that in ancient societies women were at the forefront of matters of political governance. He argues that simple tribal societies in ancient India were matriarchal. Patil refutes the feminist assumption that women have always and already been subordinated. To say that societies were matriarchal is not to accept the Marxist notion of primitive communism. Matriarchal societies were gendered and differentiated. Women in these societies had rights in the distribution of communal lands, in governance and priesthood. This is probably because it was women who discovered hoe agriculture. Thus, in these societies the reins of governance were in the hands of women, yet this did not mean that these societies were egalitarian. They were both gendered and politically differentiated. Patil's thesis is in keeping with Ambedkar's views on the status of women in ancient India, where he underlines the fact that this status for women was limited to the pre-Manu era.

According to Ambedkar, Manu is responsible for the downfall in the status of women. He puts forth evidence for the same in his different writings by quoting from *Manusmriti*.[4] For instance, by the rule 2–213 in *Manusmriti*, "It is the nature of women to seduce men in this (world)." The rule 2–214 says, "For women are able to lead astray in (this) world not only a fool, but even a learned man, and (to make) him a slave of desire and anger." Rule 2–215 claims, "One should not sit in a lonely place with one's mother, sister, or daughter; for the senses are powerful, and master even a learned man." Rule 9–14 claims, "Women do not care for beauty, nor is their attention fixed on age; (thinking), '(It is enough that) he is a man,' they give themselves to the handsome and to the ugly." Thus through these rules Ambedkar seeks to underline the lowly status that Manu pronounced upon women. Manu also stands in opposition to freedom for women. Rule 9.2 claims, "Day and night woman must be kept in dependence by the males of their families." While rule 9.3 underlines that "a woman is never fit for independence." Rule 9.6 claims, "Considering that the highest duty of all castes, even weak husbands (must) strive to guard their wives."

Manu further stands in opposition to granting women the right to property and divorce. He, thus, justifies atrocities on women. He codifies the law that denies women the right to separate from their husbands. Thus, he binds the woman to her husband while granting the man the freedom that he desires. Men had the right to divorce their wives under the slightest of pretexts. Similarly, he equates a woman's status to that of a slave in matters of the right to immovable property and does not recognize the widow's right to property.

Ambedkar condemns this and argues that these laws of Manu, which denied women the right to property and gave them a lowly status, was in keeping with the Brahmanical religion. According to him, by the law of Manu social practices assumed the form of religious injunction and came to be enforced by the king. Women and the Shudras were the base of the Aryan (Brahmanical) religion and therefore all kinds of laws came to be enforced upon them. The strict forbiddance of mixed marriages that Ambedkar explicates is a major case in point.

Thus, Ambedkar explains how Manu came to cause the downfall of womenkind. He underlines the misogynistic nature of Brahmanical culture and religion. On the other hand, he sees Buddhism as a champion of women's freedom, as denying gender discrimination and granting women access to knowledge and liberation. It is important to note the fact that while adopting Buddhism, its tenets that were emancipatory towards women played a significant role.

The Hindu Code Bill for the liberation of women

Ambedkar sought to change the laws of Manu that were misogynistic and reduced a woman to a commodity. Thus, in the post-independence period, as the architect of the Indian constitution he granted women the basic rights to justice, equality and security; however, it may be underlined here that he did not see this as an end in itself.

It was mainly to challenge and change the law of Manu and to grant women the basic right to property that Ambedkar drafted the Hindu Code Bill (2003a). The Hindu Code Bill in a sense marks the end of the law of Manu and brings forth a text that makes possible the liberation of women. Ambedkar in a powerful symbolic gesture publicly burnt *Manusmriti*; for within this text was the justification for the enslavement of Shudras and women. Some activists in the women's movement do not grant him this and argue that he burnt *Manusmriti* not in support of women's liberation, but rather in the context of caste. Such an unfounded statement is unjust to Ambedkar's complex thinking on the intersectionality of caste and gender; it also underlines failure of many to understand that. For him, the issue of caste and that of the subordination of women are inseparable and do not present a dichotomy. It must be underlined that he had appealed to women to join the struggle for the annihilation of caste because he saw the caste system as being exploitative of women.

Women are the central core of the Hindu Code Bill and through the laws on property, marriage and divorce; he sought to enhance their cause. For instance, he argues that under prevailing Hindu Law, men could marry as many times and that this was unjust and had to be changed to a uniform principle of monogamy for both men and women. Since according to this Hindu Law, marriage was a sacrament, a break in this or divorce was not possible. Ambedkar saw this as unjust and sought to amend it. Through the 1937 Act of Inheritance, women did not have an equal share in property. He sought to amend this and to grant daughters a share equal to that of sons. He asked the question, "What does this Bill seek to do?", which he answered saying that this bill keeps old things in their place to seek primacy for the new. It granted to every Hindu man the right to make a will of his property and therefore if the daughter gets a share of the property, conservatives could do very little against it, for if they attempted to derecognize the girl child from sharing in property, they would have to do so by making a will (Ambedkar 1983).[5]

Hence, it is apparent that Ambedkar was in opposition to the prevailing Hindu Law because it denied women the rights to property and divorce, while granting them to men as well as the right to several marriages. He condemned these laws as patriarchal and sought to amend them through the Hindu Code Bill (2003a). He stressed that in the interests of Indian women, it was important that the Bill be passed. He wrote to Nehru that the Bill had for him an extraordinary importance and appealed to him to leave no stone unturned in convincing opponents and passing the Bill. That the core of this Hindu Code Bill was the liberation of women and that the efforts of Ambedkar were to this end is apparent.

Any caste *panchayat* is a product of the caste system, an institution that regulates and exploits women. The law of the *panchayat* is an oral law; the "panch," the administrators of justice, are invariably men and justice can easily be bought and sold herein. Yet several feminist activists and scholars have supported the institution of the caste *panchayat* in the context of implementing the Hindu Code Bill for Adivasi women. They see the legal process as drain on time and money and therefore not easily accessible to women, mainly those from the Adivasi community. They argue that the bureaucracy is inhuman and corrupt and often at the end of the long wait justice may not be delivered at all. On the other hand, they see the caste *panchayat* as being less time consuming, easily accessible and as delivering "justice" in a quicker time framework. For example, Rekha Thakur, activist and researcher of the Bahujan Mahila Aaghadi, argues:

> [T]he Bahujan woman is exploited more outside the home than inside it. The mechanisms which regulate her lie outside the family. Within the family, she is relatively more free than the upper caste women. Since the burden of purity of lineage was not on her shoulders she had access to separation from the husband and to remarriage. The discord within the family could be referred by her outside the four walls of the home. The caste panchayat became the mediating institution and would administer justice. Hence the legal right to divorce has not given much; customarily this right as such had been available to her.[6]

Ambedkar's prime reason for becoming a part of the ministry was to get the Hindu Code Bill passed. On realizing that the government was postponing the issue, he resigned from the ministry. In a clarification about his resignation, he said that he joined the ministry only for the Hindu Code Bill, but that he had been harassed in this context. He firmly believed that women had to be liberated from the prevailing patriarchal Brahmanical law and the oral law of the caste *panchayat*. He saw this Bill as an important event in the life of the new nation and yet it had not been taken up in any significant conference. Probably, the Hindu Code Bill would remain the single most important law to come before parliament. He concluded that any law that does not address the hierarchy and gender discrimination prevalent in Indian society and only seeks to ameliorate economic conditions is akin to building castles in the air. In a patriarchal feudal society, women were subjugated through caste-based laws of marriage, divorce and inheritance. The colonial rule led to the emergence of new classes. Women's education, their participation in social production and their overall better status came as demands from this new society. Hence Ambedkar's historic contribution lies in his sustained efforts towards getting the Hindu Code Bill passed, as a basic requirement towards the fulfilment of these new demands. In a sense, this marked the journey of the law from a caste-based patriarchal one to an individualistic and class-based societal law (Phadke 1985).

In these writings of Ambedkar, one can trace the theme of what he conceptualized as a non-Brahmanical perspective on women's liberation. Such a perspective aims not at mere improvements in the economic status but gives primacy to a revolutionary agenda of the annihilation of caste and the subordination of women. Often Ambedkar's Hindu Code Bill (2003a) is misconceived as his manifesto on women's liberation. Though, he referred to the Bill as incomparable in its importance to any other, it was not conceived by him as an end, only a beginning. He compromised and joined the ministry because he saw the granting of freedom of property, however limited, as a beginning of women's liberation. But this does not mean that his views on this topic were limited to the issues of economic freedom only. One only has to recall here his insights into the relationship between the caste system and the subordination of women, and his sustained attacks on the patriarchy. Through Ambedkar's writings and speeches it becomes apparent that the Bill represented to him a counter-revolutionary position to the prevalent law of Manu. That he dared to resign on the question of women is an unparalleled act, even among leaders of the women's movement in India. Thus, the Hindu Code Bill was conceived by Ambedkar as a way out of the impasse that the woman question was in and he never meant it as a manifesto for the liberation of women in India. That is why even in his letter of resignation from his post of Law Minister, he underlined the fact that the Bill was significant only because it proposed a law more progressive than the two other prevalent laws.

Several positions are being put forth on the issue of the Hindu Code Bill. While some believe that through it, the manifesto of women's liberation was been put forth, others argue that it was not really drafted by Ambedkar and that it marks the codification of the colonial process of making laws based on religious texts and in consultation with the Sanskrit pundits. Madhu Kishwar's (1994) and Rekha Thakur's (1999) views would subscribe to this latter position. Omvedt (2014) argues that in noting that the Hindu Code Bill was heralded by Ambedkar, we overlook the fact that the All India Women's Conference (AIWC) had lobbied for this demand since 1925. Such a comment arises from an ill-founded comparison between the creation of the Bill and those who suggested changes therein. Moreover, there is a fundamental difference in the positions of Ambedkar and the AIWC. For Ambedkar, the Bill marked a progressive step in the larger programme of women's liberation, while for the AIWC it was a political manoeuvre. This is apparent from the fact that neither did they come out in support of the Bill when Ambedkar presented it to parliament nor did they condemn the march organized by the women of the Jan Sangha in opposition to the Bill. For what reason then should we glorify the fact that the demand had been taken up by the AIWC? It is surprising that the two issues—the contribution of Ambedkar to the Bill and that of the AIWC—should be mixed up at all! His analysis of subordination of women and the agenda charted out for liberation of women highlighted his linkage of caste and gender hierarchy. We shall explore in the next section their inevitable links, as well as their interdependence.

The perspective on and agenda for the struggle for the liberation of women

In refuting the biological explanation of caste, Ambedkar underlined the linkages between the caste system and the subordination of women. In arguing that castes were created to perpetuate inequalities, he further argued that within the hierarchy every caste expresses pride in its own identity. Every caste is therefore active in keeping its difference and maintaining its own identity. It is not only that they restrict dining and marriage to the caste circle, but even food habits, rituals of marriage and clothing have been regulated by the caste system. This readily marks the untouchable from the *savarna*. While issues of food and marriage rituals are of an intra-caste nature, the issue of clothing is treated in more detail by Ambedkar. Clothing marked untouchability and hence he appealed to the people to denounce the clothing marked for them by the caste system in order to lead a life of self-respect.

Untouchable women are marked as lowly through their dress. Brahmanical tradition has thrust upon them a costume of half (above the knees) sarees and heavy and cheap jewellery, which marks them as untouchable. These traditions were designed to keep these women enslaved. He thus appealed to women to deny these symbols of enslavement. In a speech at the Mahad Satyagraha Parishad, he said,

> You all must vow to leave behind the old and dirty customs. To state the truth there is no branding on the forehead of the untouchable which would mark him so. But it is through the customs that people are able to mark the caste of a person. I am of the opinion that these customs have in the earlier times been thrust upon us
> (Ambedkar 1928)

Thus, he underlined the need for the women of the lower castes to keep a neat and clean appearance, so as to wipe away the caste markings that are thrust upon them and is in no way asking them to beautify themselves.

In any political struggle, the issue of identity is significant. Several times, identities come to be used for political purposes. Rather than debating what really constitutes identities, it is important that we study the identities of the different politically progressive trends in contemporary politics. For instance, several movements have emerged in the recent past that put at the central position the OBC, Matang, non-Buddhist Dalit, women or Dalit identities. Identities are not created overnight nor can they be thrust upon others. The crux of identity politics must be progressive. Identities are real only if they are rooted in struggles to end vested political, social and cultural interests.

Another important issue in the context of identities is the need to ask the question: which identity is being forged? Is it Brahmanical, patriarchal, inegalitarian? If it is so or if it is only an identity of political opportunism, we have to condemn it. The Dalit identity, even in the pre-Ambedkar era, has always drawn from the non-Brahmanical tradition. From Shivram Janoba Kamble, Narayan Meghaji Lokhande and Mahatma Phule to Ambedkar, we see continuity in the non-Brahmanical roots of Dalit identity. The contemporary Dalit movement also draws upon Phule-Ambedkarism and such a Dalit identity, which has emerged from the history of a long struggle, is a revolutionary identity. This identity did not emerge overnight and the Dalit community will not be willing to easily give up this identity, for it is based on a history of mass struggles. That women were also a part of this history is apparent from the fact that due to the efforts of social reformers such as Phule, Gopalbaba Valangekar, V. R. Shinde, Kamble, Shahu Maharaj, Munpande Kalicharan, Nanda Gavali; women were always present in large numbers at the public meetings.[7]

In countering different caste-based atrocities the Dalit movement took up several struggles of identity. Ambedkar himself led the Chavdaar Lake Satyagraha and the entry into the Kalaram temple. In the Dalit Mahila Parishads, several resolutions were passed in which he called upon Dalit women to stay away from *tamashas* and to refuse to carry gas lamps on their heads, as these practices marked them as lowly and contemptuous. That is to say, Ambedkar saw the question of the Dalit women's identity of self-respect as crucial to social reform and to the revolutionary struggle. Thus, his conception of identity was broad-based and therefore Dalit women constituted an intrinsic part of his thoughts and struggles.

In any social movement, there is always a long-term programme and a short-term agenda. In the early phases of the movement, it is likely that the short-term agenda is taken up. In case of Ambedkar's revolutionary programme too, struggles such as those of the temple entry were taken up by him to enhance in the minds of Dalits the anger against the injustice done to them. It is important to note here that temple entry was for him a short-term programme and the annihilation of caste and the liberation of women were the long-term ones.

Ambedkar's programme, which appealed to Dalit women to give up their caste-based costumes, with a view towards wiping away the markers of untouchability, was no doubt a short term goal in his agenda for women's liberation. That the denial of these caste-based costumes and customs will not lead to the annihilation of caste must have been obvious to a thinker and leader of his calibre. His position should not be misconstrued as the "Brahmanisation" of Dalit women. We only need to recall that if the Brahmanisation of women had been his position, he would not have underlined the question of Dalit women as a political question. Moreover, he saw abolition of caste as primarily a women's struggle and organised conferences towards that.

Consciousness rising among untouchable women

Ambedkar time and time again underlined that the abolition of untouchability was the responsibility of women. He argued that men would take a longer time to achieve this end. To this purpose, he always organized separate political meetings of women and it is this precedent that lead to the formation of the Dalit Mahila Federation.

In Ambedkar's very important speech to the Dalit Mahila Federation in 1942 he envisioned the participation of women in a movement as a measure of its relative success or failure. In the same speech, he narrated,

> Ever since I began to work among the Depressed Classes, I made it a point to carry women along with men. That is why you will see that our Conferences are always mixed Conferences. I measure the progress of a community by the degree of progress which women have achieved, and when I see this assembly, I feel both convinced and happy that we have progressed
>
> (Ambedkar 2003a, 282)

In these speeches, the faith that Ambedkar had in the capability of exploited women is apparent. It is through the propagation of his ideas and his work that Dalit women began to awaken, organise and revolt. Women participated in large numbers in the Mahad Satyagraha in 1927. This is the first time in history that Dalit women came out in public to support their social and cultural demands. Prior to this, women had come out in public for the struggles led by Gandhi; but in what could be called "transformative" or "revolutionary" struggles, it is in the Ambedkarite movement that women first took to the streets. The credit for promoting this organization among Dalit women goes to Ambedkar.

This political conscientization that Ambedkar brought about is reflected in the programmes and the leadership of the Dalit Mahila Federation. The General Secretary of the Dalit Mahila Federation, Ayu. Indirabai Patil, noted how Dalit women should break away from Brahminical Hindu religion and its conception of feminine domesticity, since these enslave women (Ambedkar 2003c; Pawar and Moon 1989, 254–5). Similarly, under the chairpersonship of Sulochanabai Dongre, there was a demand for representation of Dalit women in all institutions, starting from the local. To quote,

> ...like female representatives taken in the Central and Provincial Legislatures from female constituencies, this Conference feels that for the general progress and advancement of the women of the Depressed Classes seats be reserved for them on all legislative and other representative bodies
>
> (Ambedkar 2003c; Pawar and Moon, 213–5)

Thus, began the journey of organizing Dalit women for their identity, existence and a humane society. Society began to recognize that in the political sphere too women could operate with courage, daring and efficiency. These women realized that their struggle was for their identity and they began to publicly react to any insulting and derogatory behaviour from *savarna* (upper caste/varna) men and women. This was a direct result of their participation in new knowledges and their political conscientisation. At the proceedings of one of the Akhil Bhartiya Mahila Parishads, *savarna* women discriminated against the two Dalit women delegates by setting plates separately for them. At this January 1938 Conference, these two Dalit women publicly condemned this act, which was called "lowly" and "mean," and Dalit women were asked to keep their self-pride and identity.

This torch of struggle was lit by Ambedkar, for he believed in the strength that lay dormant in women. The incident of April 7, 1930 at the Temple Entry is a case in point. At the time of temple entry when one of the priests pushed a young Dalit girl, she slapped him (Phadke 1987). Such incidents kindled the fire of self-respect. At the political Parishads organized by Ambedkar, not only were separate Mahila Parishads organized but also the Parishad passed several resolutions condemning atrocities against Dalit women. These were mainly resolutions against those practices that enslaved women. The Parishad, in an important resolution, condemned the practice of child marriage and discussed its biological and psychological ill effects. It was proposed that the marriageable age be fixed at a minimum of 22 for boys and 16 for girls. Considering the fact that the dowry question could be lethal for women, the Mahar Panch Committee resolved that wedding expenses should not exceed a maximum of sixteen rupees and the details of how this money should be distributed were also given. For example, five rupees were assigned for the ritual of *Sakashgandha*, nine rupees for the engagement, two rupees for the wedding and it was enjoined that parents should not give any ornaments to their daughters. This resolution is extremely significant.

All this went towards kindling tremendous self-confidence in Dalit women. They refused to compromise at all when it came to their political work. They time and again proved to the community the importance of their liberation. In Nagpur, Jaibai Chaudhari qualified as a teacher and took up a job in a school. But *savarna* and Christian students refused to be taught by a Dalit teacher. She was advised to convert to Christianity, which she courageously refused. She resigned her post, realizing that the issue at stake was not so simple that it would be resolved by her conversion. This strength came from the collective struggles of Dalit women. Probably realizing that the question was of the real struggle—the annihilation of caste—she started the Chokhamela Girls' School. She remained active in the struggles of Dalit women until the end of her life. In 1920, the Bahishkrut Samaj Parishad passed a resolution that girls be given free and compulsory primary education, and on that occasion Tulsabai Bansode and the young Rukmini Kotangale delivered effective speeches in support. Thus, it is apparent that though the programmes taken up by the Dalit women's movement were short term, their ideological position was committed to the annihilation of the caste system.

Ambedkar's opposition to atrocities against women

Ambedkar, having had a deep faith in the capabilities of women, always stood in opposition to atrocities against them. The first phase of the Ambedkarite struggle was dedicated to enkindling self-respect in the minds of Dalit men and women and ensuring for them a humanitarian treatment from society. He stood against the domination and exploitation of any one varna by the other.

In 1956, amidst a gathering of lakhs of people, he embraced Buddhism and gave to the Neo-Buddhists the gift of the 22 Vows (Ambedkar 1956). These vows deny all inegalitarian practices, customs and forms of worship. One of the vows, "I shall not take intoxicants like liquor, drugs, etc." (Vow 17) was in part to protect the women at the receiving end of the ill effects of intoxicants. In his conceptualization of "Dhamma" there is an insistence on ethics. A religion such as this, Ambedkar opined, would render more justice to women. The freedom and access to knowledge for women encoded in Buddhism played a significant role in his thoughts on Dhamma.

His opposition to the atrocities against women was also apparent in the speech he delivered to a gathering of prostitutes. At this gathering of Devadasi, Potraje, Bhute, Aradhi and Jogtini sects in 1936,[8] he said,

> I insist that if you want to be with the rest of us you must give up your disgraceful life...There are only two ways open to you: either you remain where you are and continue to be despised and shunned, or you give up your disgraceful profession and come with us
>
> (Ambedkar 2003c)

That poverty should drive women to sell their bodies is perceived by him as an atrocity against women. It is in keeping with these principles that he refused to accept the money donated by Patthe Bapurao, a Brahmin *tamasha* artist, arguing that the money was earned from making Pavalabai, a Dalit woman, dance on the *tamasha* floor. It is Dalit women who are the most exploited by caste-based prostitution, such as practice of *devadasi*, and this was strongly condemned by Ambedkar.

The preface to Ambedkar's *The Rise and Fall of Hindu Women* gives us clues about his opposition to the atrocities against women (2014d). Ambedkar narrates the story of a particular village that was notified to completely excommunicate a Buddhist monk (1992, 495–496). A Brahmin woman breaks this injunction and gives water to the thirsty monk. The men of the village beat her up to teach her a lesson. In citing this story, Ambedkar reflects his opposition to violence against women.

Ambedkar: the true heir to the legacy of Mahatma Phule

Ambedkar carried forth the legacy of the non-Brahmanical thoughts of Mahatma Phule. This is also true in the context of the liberation of women. The importance of education for girls, the prevention of infanticide, the traumas of a deserted woman were all issues that informed the work of Babasaheb Ambedkar as they did for Mahatma Phule.

Ambedkar felt deeply on the issue of orphaned children and unwed mothers and he had also proposed starting a home for them at Aurangabad. He used to say, "Bring the small children here to this home, all of them poor and the orphaned, those deserted by the destitute and unwed mothers. I will personally take care of them" (Pawar and Moon 1989). This goes to show that he did not take the traditional view on the issue of unwed mothers. He opined that deserted women are left all alone to fend for themselves in a society that stigmatizes them and that he could do his bit by taking care of the children of such mothers. It needs to be noted that he placed no stigma on unwed motherhood.

Savitribai and Jotiba Phule could not beget any progeny of their own. In those times there must have been pressures on Jotiba to remarry and beget children. Yet they resisted these pressures to adopt the child of an abused widow. In the context of Hinduism, the presence of a son as the torchbearer of the lineage is extraordinary and any woman who cannot bear a son comes to be thus humiliated. Yet Phule did not remarry. As Omvedt points out, "Instead of insisting on a heir of their own blood and lineage they adopt the child of a widow (naturally an 'illegitimate' child). Neither do they adopt the child of a close relative as was the prevalent practice" (Omvedt 2001, 15). The issue being highlighted is that they did not see the begetting of progeny as the ultimate aim of conjugal life. Ambedkar also had a similar position on the issue. In dialogue with one activist, he asked him how he would feel if his wife were to desert him on the issue of failure to produce progeny and explained to him that the child is as much the wife's need as his (Pawar and Moon 1989).

In the same vein, Ambedkar also seems to carry forward the legacy of Mahatma Phule on the issue of education for girls. Ever after returning to India he strove to throw open the doors of education for Shudras and women. Even when accepting Buddhism he emphasized that the position it accorded to women's access to knowledge played a decisive role. In his speeches, he repeatedly underlined the importance of educating women. At the Mahad Satyagraha Parishad, in a speech to the gathering of women, he advocated the importance of educating women so that the community could progress.[9] If a woman is educated, it is as if the whole family is put in touch with knowledge and education and reforming ideas and ideologies becomes possible. It is with this faith that Ambedkar called upon the women to take on the responsibility of spreading knowledge and education in society. In this way, he emerged as the true and most deserving heir to the legacy of Mahatma Phule.

The non-Brahmanical path of women's liberation

To conclude, some of the key principles of Ambedkar's non-Brahmanical conception of women's liberation were as follows:

1 Ambedkar saw the caste system and the class system as the two major enemies. He saw both as being responsible for the subordination of women. He traced linkages between caste-based exploitation and the subordination of women by pointing out how castes emerged through the regulation of women. To put it briefly, he argued that women are the gateways to the caste system.
2 The subordination of women will not automatically end with the end of capitalism. Ambedkar argues that to achieve this purpose the caste system and patriarchy will have to be attacked. The subordination of women cannot come to an end in a caste-based society and it is therefore women who must lead the struggle for the annihilation of caste. He sees organic links between the struggle against the caste system and the struggle for the liberation of women. Thus, the idea of women's liberation is intrinsic to his ideology and not a token add-on.
3 His position seems to take the same stance as the feminist commitment that "the personal is the political." He sought to bring into the public sphere, within the auspices of the legal system, the atrocities that women suffered as private within the confines of the home. Issues of bigamy, maintenance, etc., were all brought into the public debate. He wished to transform these matters of the private into political

issues and to this end drafted the Hindu Code Bill (2003a). His journey of codifying the Law is one that sought to delimit the private sphere and make more encompassing the public sphere. Share in property for women, and the rights to seek divorce and marry according to one's will were all issues that come up in the Bill. These stood in opposition to the prevalent familial abuse of women. Even within the political sphere, he was opposed to private ownership of land and stood for its socialization. Thus, his views on the public/private and on political issues kept with those on the woman question.

4 Ambedkar took an anti-patriarchal position in the creation of the Hindu Code Bill. He opposed the law of Manu because it subordinates and enslaves women. He preferred the Buddhist non-Brahmanical tradition because it grants freedom to women and gives them access to knowledge. He, thus, believed that any social transformation is incomplete until gender discrimination in that society comes to an end.

Like Phule, Ambedkar analysed the caste system as the major cause of the subordination of women and called upon people to revolt against it. To develop the non-Brahmanical principles of women's liberation that are embodied in the lives and works of Mahatma Phule and Ambedkar, we need to take up the following issues:

- Ambedkar saw Hinduism as the emerging ground of the caste system and hence argued for a countering of the philosophy and the rites and rituals of this religion. To take it a step further, we need to highlight that caste-based exploitation has a material base. Hence, resisting it assumes primacy on the agenda.
- The origins of the subordination of women has been articulated in the works of Ambedkar. The issue therein needs to be put forth as a theory. That patriarchal exploitation also has a material base needs to be underlined and this must inform any agenda and revolutionary programme.
- The programme for the liberation of women needs to be seen as an intrinsic part of the struggles against the social, religious, cultural and political exploitation of the caste system. Such a trend has failed to emerge from within the contemporary Dalit movement. Even within the Republican Party of India and the Dalit Panthers, a perspective on women's liberation has not emerged, both in theory and in their practices. Efforts to develop such perspectives will have to be undertaken.
- An Ambedkarite perspective is important to the theory of the emergence and the end of the subordination of women in India because this perspective, by conceiving women as the gateways of the caste system, draws focus to the caste-based nature of this exploitation.

This theory needs to be developed further by linking it to historical materialist analyses and to the political economy of the sexual division of labour. Developing a non-Brahmanical perspective of the liberation of women in India would entail such a task.

Notes

1 This chapter is an abridged version of the book by Pratima Pardeshi, *Dr. Babasaheb Ambedkar and the Question of Women's Liberation in India*, trans. Sharmila Rege (Pune: Krantjyoti Savitribai Phule Women's Study Centre, Savitribai Phule Pune University, 1998). The original Marathi edition was published as Pratima Pardeshi, *Dr. Ambedkar aani Streemukti* (Pune: Krantisimha Nana Patil Academy, 1996). Swati Dehadrai, Assistant Professor, Krantjyoti Savitribai Phule Women's Study Centre, has edited the English edition of the book for this volume. Used with permission.
2 This is derived from (Ambedkar 2014a, b).
3 A devdasi was a woman dedicated to worshipping god and serving a deity or a temple. The system exploited these women sexually so it was outlawed in India.
4 See (Bühler 1886).
5 Extracted from (Thakur 1999).
6 This is a citation from an unpublished text.
7 The oral narratives of women in the Ambedkarite movement have been documented in (Pawar and Moon 1989).
8 In Maharashtra there is a practice in some families, mainly amongst lower castes whose family god is Khnadoba, of offering one child to him. Traditionally the boy is called "Waghya" and girl "Murali."
9 Translated from Marathi (Ambedkar 1928).

References

Ambedkar, Babasaheb 1928 *Bahishkrut Bharat* Mumbai.

Ambedkar, B.R. 1956 Twenty Two Vows (October 15, 1956, Deeksha Bhoomi Nagpur) (accessed on February 14, 2020) https://roundtableindia.co.in/index.php?option=com_content&view=article&id=1248:22-vows-of-dr-ambedkar&catid=116&Itemid=128.

——— 1983 "Speech at the Parliament of Siddharth College" *Satyashodhak Marxwadi* (June 11, 1950).

——— 1987a "Philosophy of Hinduism" in *Dr. Babasaheb Ambedkar, Writings and Speeches* vol. 3, 3–94 New Delhi: Dr. Ambedkar Foundation, Government of India.

——— 1987b "Revolution and Counterrevolution in Ancient India" in *Dr. Babasaheb Ambedkar, Writings and Speeches* edited by Vasant Moon vol. 3, 113–390 New Delhi: Dr. Ambedkar Foundation, Government of India.

——— 1987c "Buddha or Karl Marx" in *Dr. Babasaheb Ambedkar, Writings and Speeches* edited by Vasant Moon vol. 3, 391–412 New Delhi: Dr. Ambedkar Foundation, Government of India.

——— 1992 (1957) "The Buddha and His Dhamma" in *Dr. Babasaheb Ambedkar, Writings and Speeches* vol. 11 New Delhi: Dr. Ambedkar Foundation, Government of India.

——— 2003a "The Hindu Code Bill" in *Dr. Babasaheb Ambedkar Writings and Speeches* vol. 14 (part I) New Delhi: Dr. Ambedkar Foundation, Government of India.

——— 2003b "You Must Give Up Your Disgraceful Profession" in "*Dr. Babasaheb Ambedkar: Writings and Speeches* vol. 17 (part 3), 150 New Delhi: Dr. Ambedkar Foundation, Government of India.

——— 2003c "Progress of the Community is Measured by the Progress of Women" in *Dr. Babasaheb Ambedkar: Writings and Speeches* vol. 17 (part 3), 277–83 New Delhi: Dr. Ambedkar Foundation, Government of India.

Ambedkar, B.R. 2014a (1979) "Castes in India: Their Mechanism, Genesis and Development" in *Dr. Babasaheb Ambedkar Writings and Speeches* vol. 1, 3–22 New Delhi: Dr. Ambedkar Foundation, Government of India.

——— 2014b (1979) "Annihilation of Caste" in *Dr. Babasaheb Ambedkar Writings and Speeches* vol. 1, 23–96 New Delhi: Dr. Ambedkar Foundation, Government of India.

——— 2014c (2003) "Mahad Satyagraha Not for Water but to establish Human Rights" in *Dr. Babasaheb Ambedkar Writings and Speeches* vol. 17 (part I), 3–48 New Delhi: Dr. Ambedkar Foundation, Government of India.

——— 2014d (2003) "The Rise and Fall of the Hindu Woman: Who is Responsible for It" in *Dr. Babasaheb Ambedkar Writings and Speeches* vol. 17 (part II), 109–29 New Delhi: Dr. Ambedkar Foundation, Government of India.

——— 2014e "The Position of Women in Hinduism and Buddhism" in *Dr. Babasaheb Ambedkar Writings and Speeches* vol. 17 (part II), 495–8 New Delhi: Dr. Ambedkar Foundation, Government of India.

——— 2019 (1979) "The Untouchables Who Were They and Why Did They Become Untouchables?" in *Dr. Babasaheb Ambedkar Writings and Speeches* vol. 7, 252, 398–96 New Delhi: Dr. Ambedkar Foundation, Government of India.

Bühler, Georg 1886 *The Laws of Manu (Translation with Extracts from Seven Commentaries)* Sacred Books of the East vol. 25 Oxford: Oxford University Press.

Kishwar, Madhu 1994 "Codified Hindu Law: Myth and Reality" *Economic and Political Weekly* 29 (33): 2145–61.

Omvedt, Gail 2001 *Jyotiba Phule aani Stree-Mukticha Wichar* Mumbai: Lokwangmay Griha.

——— 2014 *Dalits and the Democratic Revolution: Dr. Ambedkar and the Democratic Movement in Colonial India* New Delhi: Sage Publications India.

Patil, Sharad 1983 *Das Shudranchi Gulamgiri* Wai: Pradnya Mandal Prakashan.

Phadke, Bhalchandra 1985 *Dr. Ambedkaranche Samaj Chintan* Pune: Shri. Vidya Prakashan.

Phadke Y.D. 1987 *Dr.* Ambedkar *Aani Kalaram Satyagraha* Pune: Sugawa Prakashan.

Pawar, Urmila and Moon, Meenakshi 1989 "AmhihiItihas Ghadawala (We also made history)" in *Ambedkari Chalwaliteel Streeyancha Sahabhag* Pune: Sugava Prakashan.

Thakur, Rekha 1999 "Samaan Nagari Kayadyala Tattvata Virodh Hava" (Uniform Civil Code Should Be Principally Opposed!) (Unpublished booklet).

Part III

HINDUISM AND BUDDHISM

Interaction, conflict and beyond

8

BUDDHISM AND HINDU SOCIETY

Some observations from medieval Marathi literature

Shrikant Bahulkar

It is widely known that Buddhism began to decline from mainland India around the 12th century CE and finally disappeared during the centuries that followed. The Hindu tradition, particularly, the Vaiṣṇava sect, considered the Buddha as the ninth incarnation of Viṣṇu and in a way attempted to show that Buddhism was a part of Vaiṣṇavism. It is however noticed that the notion of the Buddha as the incarnation of Viṣṇu did not get much popularity all over India. Unlike Rāmajanma or Kṛṣṇajanma, we do not find explicit references to Buddhajanma celebrations on a mass scale in India until the second half of the 20th century, when in 1956, the 2,500th anniversary of the Mahāparinirvāṇa of the Buddha was celebrated all over India, at the insistence of the Government of India.

Archaeology and literature provide evidence of Buddhism's widespread influence in India. However, it is difficult to find how many Indians at any time actually considered themselves Buddhists. While we know from Buddhist sources of the legends of upper-class Hindus who embraced Buddhism, the percentage of such people must be very less. Also, it might not be a formal conversion into becoming a Buddhist. The late Upaniṣads, composed after the Buddha, the epics, and the classical Sanskrit and Prakrit literature do not mention the Buddha and his teaching frequently and explicitly. The two Mahākāvyas by Aśvaghoṣa, namely, the Buddhacarita and the Saundarananda are not mentioned by the later poets or the authors of the works on poetics; nor do we find verses quoted from those poems as examples of the figures of speech. Many works by Buddhist pundits were ignored and consequently were lost in their Sanskrit originals. No manuscripts of Buddhist works were preserved in India, with the exception of a few. By the 12th century, the life of the Buddhist monks, the Saṅgha, Buddhist art, the interpretation of Buddhist thought, and even the knowledge of the Buddhist period, became lost to sight.

At the beginning of the 19th century, European scholars began to study Indian Buddhism and translate from Pali, Sanskrit, and Tibetan scriptures. In 1837, James Prinsep, a British government official deciphered the Brāhmī script of the Ashokan rock and pillar edicts. Alexander Cunningham, another government official identified various Buddhist holy places, using the 7th-century Chinese pilgrim, Huen-Tsang's travel book as a guide. Many Western scholars studied Buddhism in earnest and contributed to the advancement of Buddhist studies. Henry Olcott, an American Civil War Colonel and one of the founders of the Theosophical Society, went to Ceylon in 1880 to study Buddhism. David Hewavitame, a young Sinhalese, joined the Theosophical Society there and established contacts through the Society with Western Buddhist studies and Japanese Buddhism. He became a monk and came to be known as Anāgārika Dharmapāla. He founded the Maha Bodhi Society of Calcutta. Among the scholars in the West was T. W. Rhys David who founded the Pali Text Society in1881 in London. In India scholars showed a keen interest in Buddhism and began to write books and essays and translate Buddhist scriptures into English and some vernacular languages. The Buddhist Text Society was founded in 1892 in Calcutta, and Sarat Chandra Das, a renowned Tibetologist, and Satish Chandra Vudyabhushan, the first person to obtain an MA degree in Pali in 1901, worked through that Society. Other scholars in this early period of Buddhist studies in India were Rajendralal Mitra and Hara Prasad Sastri who published many Buddhist texts. In Maharashtra, R. G. Bhandarkar included Buddhism in his Indological research. Krishnaji Arjun Keluskar wrote a popular book on the life of the Buddha in 1898. A copy of this book was later presented to Dr. Babasaheb Ambedkar when he passed the matriculation examination in 1908. Through this book he was first introduced to Buddhism. Dharmanand Kosambi made a pioneering study of Buddhism. He lived for some time both in Sri Lanka and Myanmar. P. Lakshmi Narasu, professor of physics and chemistry at Madras Christian College wrote *The Essence of Buddhism* in 1907. A number of reformers considered themselves Buddhists, although they did not reject Hinduism (Zelliot 1979: 389–99; Sadangi 2008: 321–3; Omvedt 2010: 233–6). Thus, the Indian public was informed more about the Buddha and his teachings; however, it is not clearly known to what extent they knew of Buddhism before they rediscovered it during the colonial period.

The medieval religious cults, including the Bhakti movement emerged just during the decline of Buddhism. In the case of Maharashtra, the Bhāgavata cult began to take shape during the 12th century CE. The Mahānubhāva cult too emerged around the same period. It is interesting to see what the followers of those various religious cults knew of the Buddha and his teachings; to see if Buddhism influenced the teachings of the medieval Maharashtrian saints, and if so, to what extent. Hindu society considered the Buddha as the ninth incarnation of Viṣṇu. It is also interesting to find how this notion was understood in various religious traditions in medieval India in general and in Maharashtra in particular.

In the medieval literature of Maharashtra, this notion is reflected in two ways: First, the saint poets considered their god, Viṭṭhal or Viṭhobā as the Bauddha, the ninth incarnation of Viṣṇu; and second, their teachings bear close similarity to the teachings of the Buddha and are said to have been influenced by Buddhist philosophy. It is not certain however that they had a direct knowledge of the Buddha and his teachings. In the present paper, these notions will be studied.

By the end of the Gupta period (4th–6th century CE), the Buddha came to be included among the ten incarnations of Viṣṇu, as the ninth incarnation. The accounts of the Purāṇas describing him in that form have some variations.[1] The Viṣṇu Purāṇa says that in this incarnation, he converts the demons to having heterodox views to deceive them, while the Bhāgavata Purāṇa states that Viṣṇu took this incarnation in the land of the Kīkaṭas to delude people considered inferior who perform sacrifices using Vedic mantras.[2] The land of the Kīkaṭas is identified as Bihar. The Purāṇas while describing the ninth incarnation use the term *sugata-*, and mention Sarnath and Mṛgadāva. The Viṣṇu Purāṇa states that he has a shaven head and is naked. It is also mentioned that he, becoming the sky-clad (*digambara*) taught the Jaina doctrine and wearing a red robe, taught the Buddhist doctrine (Dhere and Feldhaus 2011: 185). Jayadeva, in the Aṣṭapadī of his Gītagovinda describes the ten incarnations of Viṣṇu, where he describes the Buddha, the ninth incarnation of Viṣṇu, in the following words:

> nindasi yajñavidher ahaha śrutijātaṃ,
> sadayahṛdaya darśitapaśughātam |
> keśava dhṛtabuddhaśarīra,
> jaya jagadīśa hare||
>
> Oh! You of merciful heart, you blame the Vedic scripture related to the performance of sacrifices that has shown (i.e. prescribed) the killing of animals (in the sacrifices). Victory to you, O Hari, O lord of the world, O Keśava, in the form of the Buddha.

In Hindu rituals, there is a resolve (*saṅkalpa*) for the performance to be undertaken by the sacrificer or the worshipper (*yajamāna*), in which the region and the date of the performance are to be mentioned. In Maharashtra, the "resolve" includes, sometimes, a mention of the current period as "during (the period) of the incarnation of the Buddha" (*bauddhāvatāre*), thereby keeping the memory of the Buddha.

The oldest available Marathi poem, mixed with Kannada, is found in a 12th-century Sanskrit work, the *Mānasollāsa* of Someśvara Cālukya. This poem mentions the ninth incarnation of Viṣṇu, who, assuming the form of the Buddha, "deceives" the demons and gods: the verse begins with the words: "The one who brought the Vedas from the underworld in the form of a fish..." and continues as under:

"The one who, in the form of the Buddha, deceived the demons and gods, who found fault with the Vedas: may that God of illusion and deception bless me" (Dhere and Feldhaus 2011: 185).[3]

In this connection, Dhere states:

> The Purāṇas' description of the Buddha incarnation is depressing. It is unfair to his great teaching to call the Buddha "illusory and deceptive" and to say that his philosophy was a heterodox view that he intentionally taught in order to deflect demons from the true path. In calling the Buddha an incarnation of Viṣṇu, the Purāṇas annihilated Buddhist thought. The Purāṇas accepted the Buddha, but they completely rejected Buddhist ideas.
>
> (Dhere and Feldhaus 2011: 186)

In this connection, Dhere quotes a verse from the *Merutantra*, an English translation of which is as below:

> Brāhmaṇas enamored of the left-handed path, Kuṇḍakas, people who have fallen from caste,
> those bereft of Vedic rituals, people who have become Mlecchas through a mistake they made,
> Goḷakas, and also members of the Kāyastha and other castes
> Take refuge in the Buddha Viṣṇu and reach devotion and liberation.
>
> (Dhere and Feldhaus 2011: 186)

Although we find some references in medieval Marathi literature to the Buddha as the ninth incarnation of Viṣṇu, in contrast to Vedic sacrificial religion, there are more frequent statements addressing Viṭṭhal or Viṭhobā, the most revered deity of Maharashtra, as the Buddha, Bauddha or Baudhāvatāra, the later form of the Kṛṣṇa Avatār. Marāṭhī saints frequently call Viṭṭhal by these various names. Janābāi, Nāmdev's disciple, refers to Viṭṭhal as the Buddha after Kṛṣṇa, in the description of the ten incarnations of Viṣṇu: "Becoming Kṛṣṇa, he killed Kaṃsa; now my friend became the Buddha" (Gāthā 344). The saints considered the Buddha to be Viṣṇu's ninth incarnation and attributed the adjectives "silent" and "naked" as they did in the case of Viṭṭhal. Dhere quotes a number of references from the works of Nāmdev, Tukārām, Ekanāth and the *Puṇḍalīka Caritra* of the *Pāṇḍuranga Māhātmya*, a section of the work called "Svānubhāva Dinakara" of Dinakara Svāmī Tisgāvkar (1628–87), a disciple of Rāmdās (Dhere and Feldhaus 2011: 173–88). The saints frequently called Viṭṭhal as "silent" (*maunastha*) and "enlightened" (*bauddha*) (Dhere and Feldhaus 2011: 174). Tukārām says: "My Buddha incarnation silently fixed his attention on the invisible" (Gāthā 4083). Eknāth too spoke again and again about Viṭṭhal's silence:

> "Taking the garb of silence
> he stands on a brick" (Gāthā 585).
> "He has stood on a brick for 28 yugas.
> He does not speak, he does not sit, he does not cross the limits" (Gāthā 605).
> "Driven mad, driven mad, he stood there in silence" (Gāthā 624).

Besides Marathi saint literature, we can find corroborative evidence in paintings and sculptures in Maharashtra. The old almanacs (*pañcāṅga*), printed by the litho-press have pictures of the ten incarnations of Viṣṇu where they depict Viṭṭhal as the "Buddha or Bauddha," the ninth incarnation. A book of hymns called *Śrīrāmasahasranāma* has a picture of Viṭṭhal and Rukmiṇī, his wife, along with Garuḍa and Hanumān with Viṭṭhal's name as the "Bauddha." There are at least two sculptures in Maharashtra, where Viṭṭhal is depicted in the place of the Buddha (Dhere and Feldhaus 2011: 182).

The notion of Viṭṭhal being the Bauddha's incarnation has been prevalent in the oral as well as literary traditions of Maharashtra and was recorded by modern scholars in the first half of the 19th century, when the Western scholars began to study India as a part of Oriental studies. This particular notion appears to have led Rev. J. Stevenson, a Scottish missionary, to write an essay on this religious sect. In the essay titled "An Account of the Bauddho-Vaishnavas, or Vitthal-Bhaktas of the Dakhan" (Stevenson 1843: 64–73), Stevenson bases his arguments on the literature of the followers of the sect whom he calls "Bauddho-Vaishnavas", "a convenient descriptive name" (Stevenson 1843: 64). He summarizes the account of two sources. The first is the *Pāṇḍuraṇga Māhātmya*, where the story of Puṇḍalīk or Puṇḍarīk is narrated. Kṛṣṇa, in search of his wife, Rukmiṇī, came to Pandharpur where Puṇḍalīk was living. Puṇḍalīk, being a dutiful son, was engaged with serving his parents, holding his father's feet in his right hand and scrubbing it using a brick. Kṛṣṇa appeared before him in a luminous form (*pāṇḍuraṅga*). Recognizing the god, he bowed to him, and cast the brick to sit on it. Pleased with Puṇḍalīk's devotion to his parents, Kṛṣṇa, stationed on that brick and therefore came to be called Viṭṭhal "one standing on a brick." The god asked Puṇḍalīk to request a boon, the latter requested him to stay there permanently. On the basis of another work, Mahipati's Bhakt Vijay "The Victory of the Devotees," Stevenson points out that Viṭṭhal or Pāṇḍuraṅg is a distinct incarnation of Viṣṇu (Stevenson 1843: 66). According to Stevenson,

> Viṣṇu appeared to Puṇḍalīk as a sky-clad (*digambara*), with his hands resting on his loins, according to the idea of a perfect sage among the Jains and Esoteric Buddhists, rendering it necessary for the Hindus to furnish him with clothing. He is dressed in yellow garments and hence called Pītāmbara and in the fifth chapter of the *Mahāvaṃso*, this is pronounced to be the dress peculiar to the Buddhist priesthood.

By providing some more evidence, Stevenson tries to establish a connection between this sect and the genuine Buddhists. On narrating the story from the Bhakt Vijay, Stevenson points out some more striking similarities between this sect and the Buddhist. In that story, it is said that Viṣṇu assumes the Bauddha avatār, and his devotees, namely, Uddhava, Akrūra, Vyāsa, Vālmīki and Śuka are born as Nāmā (i.e. Nāmadeva), Rāmadās, Jayadev, Tulsidās and Kabīr respectively. Viṣṇu, in the form of the Bauddha avatār, sits still and silent and sends those followers abroad to propagate the principle of piety and morality. Stevenson thinks that this story is an exact counterpart of the account found in the first chapter of the *Mahāvaṃso* and that, "though Pāṇḍuraṅg be quite a different personage from the historical Buddha, the idea of his character has been mainly borrowed from the Buddhists." The third peculiarity Stevenson points out is that the "Bauddho-Vaishnavas," unlike the followers of the Brahmanical tradition, theoretically admit no distinction of caste among true worshippers and declare that at religious solemnities, people of all castes should eat together (Stevenson 1843: 68).

In this regard, Alexander Grant, in his essay, "Tukaram: A Study of Hinduism," (1868: 14–18), makes the following observations:

> Vithoba is said to be an incarnation of Krishna, who was an incarnation of Vishnu. But some say that Vithoba was a Buddhist saint, deified by local reverence. And Dr. Stevenson describes the worshippers of Vithoba, or Vitthal, as Baudho-Vaishnavas, that is, as mixing up Buddhism with the worship of Vishnu.
>
> Tukaram represents an eclectic form of Hinduism, into which a larger leaven of Buddhism has found its way
>
> (Grant 1868: 15; Also, Halocombe 1868: 137)

Nīlakaṇṭha or Nehemia Goreh, a Brahmin from Benares who was converted to Christianity, writes a letter to the Brahmos, where he refers to Stevenson's essay and criticizes him as under:

> It is said that Dr. Stevenson describes the worshippers of Vithoba as BauddhoVaishnawas. But this I fear is one of those bold speculations which the European learned men are ever fond of

hazarding with respect to facts of other countries and ages. The writer of the article himself says that Tukaram represents "an eclectic form of Hinduism, into which a larger leaven of Buddhism has found its way.

"I should like to know what are those things which he found in Tukaram which he could not trace to the teaching of Hindooism. It is said by some that Vithoba was a Buddhist saint. Of course, I cannot vouch for the correctness of the opinions of my countrymen. They are proverbially like sheep which, if one goes astray, all follow, without examining each for itself whither it is going. They themselves have warned us in this matter by another proverb– "The course of a river and the race of gods one ought not to endeavour to trace." Vithoba may have been originally a Buddhist or a Mahommeden, for ought any one knows; but this is certain, that those who worship him think, by whatever mistake they may have begun to think so, that he is the genuine God of the Hindoos, even Krishna, the husband of Rukmini, who has been worshipped in India for ages among the Hindoos."

(Goreh 1868: 25–26; also, Halcombe 1868: 145)

Not many scholars are aware of Stevenson's essay on the Bauddho Vaishnawas and his hypothesis on that behalf. Recently, however, John Milton Keune, in his dissertation on "Eknāth" refers to Stevenson's essay and considers Stevenson's observations as "rather idiosyncratic, particularly as he sought to situate Viṭṭhal of Pandharpur within a hypothetical, supposedly forgotten Buddhist background" (Keune 2011: 40).

Although the inferences put forth by these scholars are difficult to accept in their entirety, it may be said that their observations reflect the notions prevalent in the local traditions. The foregoing discussion can be summarized in the following manner:

In the medieval period, the Bhāgavata or Vārakarī Sampradāya became prominent and came to be known as a unique feature of the Bhakti cult of Maharashtra devoted to the deity Viṭṭhal or Viṭhoba, having his main temple at Pandharpur. This Bhakti tradition of Maharashtra considers Viṭṭhal as the Bauddhāvatara, as the ninth incarnation of Viṣṇu. Maharashtrian saints addressed Viṭṭhal with epithets such as *maunastha* "standing in silence" and "Bauddha." For them Viṭṭhal is the later manifestation of Kṛṣṇa. There are some sculptures and paintings in Maharashtra, depicting the ten incarnations of Viṣṇu, where Viṭṭhal has been shown as the ninth incarnation.

Now let us see how the philosophy of the medieval saints has been influenced by the Buddhist philosophical concepts. In her book, *Buddhism in India*, Gail Omvedt has devoted a chapter to the discussion on the Bhakti movements that spread during the period after the decline of Buddhism in various parts of India (Omvedt 2010). Maharashtrian saints addressed Viṭṭhal as "Buddha" or "Bauddha" by which they pointed to the aspect of wisdom (*prajñā*). They also called him "mother" (*māulī*), thus pointing to the aspect of compassion (*karuṇā*). Their philosophy appears to have been greatly influenced by Buddhism. We thus find that Buddhism did not vanish completely; but was absorbed in the fold of the Vaiṣṇava tradition of Maharashtra.

It is sometimes believed that one of the reasons of the decline of Buddhism in India was the spread of the Vedānta philosophy elaborated by the Śaṅkarācārya who is said to have defeated in the debate the Buddhist thinkers of his period. This popular notion has taken roots in the popular belief of Hindus probably because of the legendary biographies such as the *Śāṅkaradigvijaya* of Mādhava Vidyāraṇya (14th century CE). However, that belief can hardly be entertained for want of historical evidence. Buddhism continued to flourish after the Śaṅkarācārya and was encouraged by some kings, such as the Pāla king of Bengal. After the destruction of the Buddhist monastic universities such as Nālandā, Vikramaśīla, Odanatapuri, Jagaddala and so on in the eastern part of India, Buddhism began to disappear from India. The saints emphasized certain noble thoughts, particularly, compassion toward all sentient beings, non-violence, rejection of the Vedas as an authority, and criticized the hierarchy of castes based on the discrimination of people on the basis of birth.

Most of the saints belong to lower classes and castes of Hindu society. Both men and women have contributed to the development of the Bhakti movement in India, and particularly in Maharashtra. This movement began with Jñāneśvar in the 13th century and continued in the subsequent centuries by many saints, such as Nāmadev, Bahiṇābāi, Cokhāmeḷā, Eknāth, Tukārām and so on, most of which belonged to non-Brahmin castes, some of them to lower castes. Like the Bhakti movement in other parts of India, the Bhakti movement of Maharashtra also was anti-caste and anti-orthodox and opposed the authority of the Vedas, the sacrificial religion advocated by the Vedas and the ancient system of the *Varṇāśramadharma*.

> Many believe that there was a connection between Buddhism in Maharashtra and the Bhakti movement, but the general stance of the Dalit writers, however, is to mourn that even the compassionate saint-poets upheld social distinctions, and that their compassion had little effect.
>
> Zelliot (1978: 79–80)

There is no clear evidence to believe that the saints had a direct knowledge of the Buddha and his teaching. As we have seen, the saints regarded Viṭṭhal as the ninth incarnation of Viṣṇu and thereby, they replaced the Buddha with Viṭṭhal. Thus, there is no direct reference to the Buddha in the literature of the saints. Buddhism appears to have great impact on the Bhakti movement in Maharashtra, indirectly if not directly, and the Bhakti movement in turn has been instrumental in shaping the ways of thinking and the life of the people in Maharashtra, particularly, the people belonging to Hindu society. It is however hard to say that Hindu society in Maharashtra was familiar with the Buddha, his life and his teaching. It is possible that Hindus had some knowledge of Buddhism that had come down to them traditionally; but their knowledge was enriched in the colonial period when the books on Buddhism, written in vernacular languages and in English, became available to them. As noted by some scholars, the authors of the pioneering works written in the colonial period were Hindus who considered Buddhism as a refined and pragmatic form of Hinduism. They wanted to educate their brethren about Buddhism and were sincere in their undertaking. However, the limited impact of their works on Hindu society at large is seen. While Hindu society has become much more familiar with the words of the Buddha, it will still take a long time for that society to inculcate the spirit behind the letters.

Notes

1 *Viṣṇu Purāṇa* (3.18); *Bhāgavata Purāṇa* (1.3.24; 2.7.37; 11.4.22); *Garuḍa Purāṇa* (1.1.32); *Agni Purāṇa* (Chapter 16).

2 "*tataḥ kalau sampravṛtte sammohāya suradviṣām*।
buddho nāmnā jinasutaḥ kīkaṭeṣu bhaviṣyati ॥" *Bhāgavata Purāṇa* 1.3.24.

3 "*Jeṇe rasātalauṇu matsyarūpeṃ veda āṇiyale manuśivaka vāṇiyale...*
buddharūpeṃ jo dāṇavasurāvañcaṇi vedadūṣaṇavollauṇi
māyā mohiyā to deū mājhi pāsāu karū॥" *Mānasollāsa*, Adhyāya 16, Viṃśati 4. Apparently, the word *vedadūṣaṇavollauṇi* has a variant ^{0}volladaṇi (Deshpande 1959: 1). It might be a wrong reading or a typographical error.

References

Primary sources

Agni Mahāpurāṇam, ed. by Maitreyi Deshpande, New Bharatiya Book Corporation, Delhi, 2007.

Mānasollāsa of King Bhūlokamalla Someśvara, Vol. III, ed. by G. K. Shrigondekar, Baroda: Oriental Institute.

The Bhāgavata [*Śrīmad Bhāgavata Mahāpurāṇa*] Vol. I (Skandhas I to III), Critically Edited by H. G. Shastri, 1966; Vol. IV (Skanda XI), Critically edited by K. K. Shastree (Bambhania), 1998. Ahmedabad: B. J. Institute of Learning and Research.

The Garuḍa Mahāpurāṇa, Text with English Translation & Notes, Vol. I, Edited by S. Jain, English Translation by M. N. Dutt, New Bharatiya Book Corporation, Delhi, 2007.

Viṣṇumahāpurāṇam of Maharṣi Vedavyāsa with Sanskrit Commentary "*Ātmaprakāśa*" of Śrīdharācārya, (Aṃśas 1 to 3), Vol. I, edited by Pt. Thaneshachandra Upreti, Parimal Publications, Delhi, 2003.

Secondary sources

Deshpande, A. N. 1966. *Prācīn Marāṭhī Vāṅmayācā Itihās, Bhāg* 1: Pūrvārdh [Marathi]. (*A History of Ancient Marathi Literature*, Part I (1)). Pune: Vhīnas Prakāśan.

Deshpande, J. S. (ed.). 1959. *Naveṃ Navanīt* (*New Digest*). Mumbai: Śakuntalā Moḍak (Publisher).

Dhere, R. C. 1984. *Śrīviṭṭhal: Ek Mahāsamanvay* [Marathi]. (*Śrī Viṭṭhal: A Great Synthesis*). Pune: Śrīvidyā Prakāśan. Also see, Feldhaus.

Dhere, R. C. and Feldhaus, Anne. 2011. *The Rise of a Folk God: Viṭṭhal of Pandharpur*. (English translation of *Śrīviṭṭhal: Ek Mahāsamanvay)* by Anne Feldhaus. New York: Oxford University Press.

Goreh, Nehemiah (Nīlakaṇṭha). 1868. "A Letter to the Brahmos from a Converted Brahman of Benares." 2nd ed. Allahabad: The Allahabad Mission Press for the North India Tract Society. Also, J. Halcombe (ed.). 1868. Mission Life: The Emigrant and the Heathen (Mission Life; or Home and Foreign Church Work, Volume 5). London: William Macintosh. pp. 126–57.

Grant, Alexander. 1868. "Tukaram: A Study of Hinduism." Reproduced in: Nehemiah (Nīlakaṇṭha) Goreh 1868. *A Letter to the Brahmos from a Converted Brahman of Benares*. 2nd ed. Allahabad: The Allahabad Mission Press for the North India Tract Society, 14–18.

Keune, John Milton. 2011. *Eknāth Remembered and Reformed: Bhakti, Brahmans, and Untouchables in Marathi Historiography*. A dissertation submitted in partial fulfillment of the requirements for the degree of Doctor of Philosophy in the Graduate School of Arts and Sciences. New York: Columbia University.

Omvedt, Gail. 2010. *Buddhism in India: Challenging Brahmanism and Caste*. 7th Printing. 1st ed. 2003. New Delhi: SAGE Publications.

Sadangi, Himansu Charan. 2008. *Emancipation of Dalits and Freedom Struggle*. Delhi: Isha Books.

Stevenson, John. 1843. "An Account of the Bauddho-Vaishnavas, or Vitthal-Bhaktas of the Dakhan." *Journal of the Royal Asiatic Society of Great Britain and Ireland* 7, no. 1: 64–73.

Zelliot, Eleanor. 1978. "Dalit: New Cultural Context for an Old Maraṭhī Word." *Contributions to Asian Studies* 11: 77–97.

——— 1979. "The Indian Rediscovery of Buddhism: 1855–1956." In: A. K. Narayan (editor) and L. Zwilling (Asstt. Editor). Studies in Pali and Buddhism: A Memorial Volume in Honor of Bhikkhu Jagadish Kashyap. Delhi: B.R. Publishing Corporation. 389–406.

9

THE BUDDHIST PAST AS A CULTURAL CONFLICT

Ambedkar's exhumation of Indian history

Umesh Bagade

Although colonial and nationalist schools of historiography offer two divergent versions of Indian history, both have demonstrated a common tendency to portray a monolithic and homogeneous history of ancient India. Through the oriental trope, Buddhism is represented as a cohesive and harmonious tradition of Indian culture. In representing Buddhism, colonial historiography charts two disputing tendencies. One of these was posited by Rhys Davids, while the other by Oldenburg. Rhys Davids puts forth Buddhism as a reformist movement that aimed to abolish the caste system by overthrowing the hegemonical classes of the elite and the powerful. On the other hand, the school represented by Oldenburg, portrayed Buddhism as status quoist in nature. Through recruiting the elite within the *sangh,* it neglected the exploited and the oppressed. Consequently, Buddhism as an institution never took on the efforts to minimize the cruelties of the caste system (Patil, 1999: 4–5). However divergent these two schools may appear, both interpret Buddhism masquerading as a cultural rift within Indian history. Moreover, Rhys Davids clarified that the Buddha was not against Brahma and Brahmins. She maintained that 'Buddha never contradicted the Upanishadic doctrine of immanence of Brahma in each individual. What he denied however is the existence of material soul which certain passages of Upanishads seem to suggest' (Bapat, 1997: 297).

The nationalist school, with its passionate defence of a unified homogeneous Hindu past, absolved Buddhism of any cultural antagonism against Brahmanism. Radhakrishnan argued that 'Buddhism did not start as a new and independent religion; it was an offshoot of a more ancient faith of Hindus, as schism or heresy.' According to him, the Buddha utilized the Hindu inheritance to correct some of its expressions. He attempted to enhance the contents of this Hindu inheritance, rather than demolish it altogether. While the teaching of the Buddha assumed distinctive forms in other countries in conjunction with their own traditions, here in the home of the Buddha, it has entered into, and become an integral part of, Indian culture.

The Brahmins and the Shramanas were treated alike by the Buddha, and the two traditions gradually blended. In a sense, the Buddha is a maker of modern Hinduism (Bapat, 1997: XII).

Some mutually hostile ideologies and interests which came together under the nationalist movement presented different versions of a Buddhist past according to their respective theoretical and socio-cultural positionings. A small number of social reformers invoked Buddhism to validate their ideas; G. G. Agarkar eulogized Buddhism for its agnostic grounding (Ganachari, 2016: 253). However, nationalist reformers have never been at ease with Buddhist ideals. M. G. Ranade castigated Buddhism for breeding a reaction, leading to a downgrading of women's position (Bagade, 2006: 277–78); he categorically stated that the 'nationalist mind cannot rest on Buddhism' (Ranade, 1992: 69). Hindu nationalists like V. D. Savarkar depicted the Buddhist past as a "decay" which according to him weakened the national spirit and stripped manhood from the nation through the insistence on non-violence. He held Buddhism responsible for the historical defeat of the Indian nation (Ingale, 2006: 45–62). Sociologist of the nationalist brand S. V. Ketkar had launched a blasphemous attack on Buddhism wherein he held Buddhism responsible for every social evil that ruined India. Such a vitriolic condemnation of the Buddhist past remained an inexhaustible tendency among Hindu nationalists. Nationalists espousing social reforms like Dharmanand Kosambi passionately defended the Buddhist past from all such castigating attacks (Phadake, 1985: 98).

Amidst this clamour of two contradictory historiographies, Ambedkar inaugurated the search for the Buddhist past. He objected to this tendency of homogenization of Indian history. He categorically stated that there has never been a common Indian culture, that historically there have been three Indias: the Brahmanic India, the Buddhist India and the Hindu India. He claimed that the history of India is the history of the moral conflict between Brahmanism and Buddhism. According to him, the dominant lineage of history writing in India not only produced a political and dynastic history, but also neglected its social and spiritual significance (Ambedkar, 1987: 275). Ambedkar's attempt was to restore this social and cultural significance of Indian history.

The cultural and the material

Ambedkar's emphasis on the cultural was based on his understanding of the phenomenon of caste. The cultural and the ideological apparatus of religion remained the grounding force of caste. This privileging of the cultural in Indian history led him to combat the rigid Marxist economism.[1] He stated that unlike the other societies of the world, caste system in India is a unique phenomenon. Nowhere in the world is the economic activity informed by religion, except in India. He writes,

> The Hindus are the only people in the world whose social order—the relation of man to man is consecrated by religion and made sacred, eternal and inviolate. The Hindus are the only people in the world whose economic order—the relation of workman to workman is consecrated by religion and made sacred, eternal and inviolate.
>
> (Ambedkar, 1989: 190)

Ambedkar identified the key role of religious sanctions in the sustenance of the caste system. He stated that legal and religious sanctions were both equally powerful engines to keep the caste-system thriving. The legal penalty for the breach of caste-rules was twofold. It involved excommunication and a loss of right to inheritance. And the religious sanction is so central that the caste system has been maintained solely by it. He asserted that religious sanction was the highest sanction because the religious was the social, and the religious was sacred. Here Ambedkar quoted Durkheim in his support (Gore, 1993: 264). The Marxists regard religion, ideology and culture as products of an economic reality. Durkheim moved from this position by regarding ideas and beliefs as a derivative of social facts, suggesting that symbolic thought is a condition of a society and that it explains prevalent social structure. His ideas on the sociology of religion are relevant to the analysis of Indian society, since religion is often regarded as the crucial variable that gave a particular direction to it (Thapar, 1993: 34–35). This viewpoint on religion has acknowledged the religious grounding of caste. As a result, Ambedkar draws from Durkheim's ideas on religion like the bipolarity of purity and pollution to define the hierarchy of the caste system.

Ambedkar emphatically criticized the Marxist reading of class. He lambasted the practice of the Indian Marxist to assume that there are only two classes. He further expressed his disagreement with the liberal economist who claimed the economic essence of man. He claimed it to be wrong to hold that economic man (or a rational man or a reasonable man) is a fact (Khairmode, 1998: 92) and focused on cultural constituents of economic class.[2] Ambedkar questioned the assumption of European Marxism that class struggle is the sole determinant of history. He talked about the role of caste in the economic realm and identified the peculiarity of the caste–class mechanism in the Brahmanical and capitalist system of exploitation and domination.

Thus, by identifying the role of caste in the economic sphere, Ambedkar acknowledges non-economic spheres like religion and sociality as the structures of power. In his renowned speech, 'Annihilation of Caste,' he argued that religion, social status and property are sources of power and authority and hence must be given equal importance. If the source of power and dominion is at any given time or in any given society, social and religious, then social and religious reform must be accepted as the necessary sort of reforms' (Ambedkar, 1979: 44–47).

Ram Bapat cites parallels between Ambedkar's and Ricœur's critique of Marxism regarding economic and non-economic power plots enmeshed to form history. Ricœur writes:

> ...the error of Marxism resides not so much in its lack of political horizon as in its reduction of the critique of power to economic transfer of work to capital (that is, the critique of surplus value). Thus Marxist critique tends to ignore that there can be more pernicious form of power than capital—for example, the totalization of all the resources (the resources of work force, of the means of discussion and information, education research, etc.) by the central committee of the party or state.... May be the economic analysis of class struggle is but one of the many plots that makes of the complex history. Hence the hermeneutics of sociality that could unravel the plurality of power plots which enmesh to form our history.
>
> (Kearney, 2004: 34–35)

Amongst several power plots Ambedkar privileged the religious (socio-cultural) power plot of history. Religion has always played a dual role in world history. On one hand, by its ideological and ritualistic apparatus it served the existing system of exploitation and domination. But on the other, counter-cultural religious upsurges had provided an emancipatory space to downtrodden masses. Ambedkar cites Christianity of early era, which according to him provided this emancipatory space to toiling masses. 'The slaves of Rome, crushed under the tyranny of Patricians, roaming on the roads without bread and shelter, embraced Christianity for salvation and freedom' (Ambedkar, 2002: 436). Ambedkar envisaged this religious power plot of Indian history. He argued for the case of the egalitarian and emancipatory nature of Buddhism that represents the revolutionary era of Indian history (Ambedkar, 1987: 65–228).

The Marxist notion of religion 'as an inverted consciousness of alienated labourers' influenced the Marxist historiography of India. Marxist historians, however, condemned the progressive character of Buddhism as false consciousness.[3] In defence of Buddhism, Ambedkar refuted every charge levelled by communists against religion. According to him, the charge that religion made people otherworldly and made people suffer poverty in this world and that religion is the opium of the people are not applicable to Buddhism (Ambedkar, 2007: 21). He reversed the often-used Marxist architectural analogy of base and superstructure to unravel the necessity of cultural conflict. He emphasized that the mental hold of religious slavery has to be destroyed. He writes:

> But the base is not the building. On the basis of economic relations, a building is erected of religious, social and political institutions. The building has just as much truth (reality) as the base. If we want to change the base, then first the building that has been constructed on it has to be knocked down. In the same way, if we want to change economic relations of society, then existing social, political and other institutions will have to be destroyed.[4]

Ambedkar observed that political revolutions have always been preceded by social and religious revolutions. He cited several examples of world history and Indian history to support this view. Ambedkar advocated the socio-religious revolution as the prerequisite of socialist revolution (Ambedkar, 1979: 43–44). Moreover, he posed a noteworthy question to communists as to what happens when a revolutionary state ceases to exist. Marxists believed that after a socialist revolution, the state will wither away. He fervently argued that religion will take the place of state when the force of state will be withdrawn (Ambedkar, 2007: 21).

Prioritizing the history of cultural and moral strife

Ambedkar's privileging of cultural is strongly reflected in his unfinished work, *Revolution and Counter-revolution in Ancient India*. Through this book, his attempt was to unravel a cultural conflict through the exhumation of the debris of historical evidence. His narrative of social conflict unfolded social and cultural processes involving contradiction, violence and exploitation (Omvedt, 1994: 242). He depicted the conflict between Brahmanism and Buddhism as a central antagonism of Indian history which subsumed caste, patriarchal contradictions and shaped the ethos of Brahminic, Buddhist and Hindu periods.

Ambedkar's recovery of a Buddhist past was premised as a contrast to Brahmanism. In his scheme of history, Buddhist revolution was preceded by the Aryan decadence (?) and was followed by a Brahmanical counter-revolution. He depicted the early phase of Brahmanism where Aryan civilization comprised the worst kinds of debauchery: social, religious and spiritual. The degradation was so immense that gambling and drinking became widespread and Brahmins had fallen to the utmost depth of moral degradation (Ambedkar, 1987: 153–64). Against this was the Buddha's teaching, initially a "religious revolution," which became a social and political revolution exemplified by equal opportunity for low-caste individuals and women as well as an equal access to education. The Buddhist "revolution" was also marked by a challenge to the infallibility of the Vedas and a revision of regnant conceptions of *kamma*. Buddha criticized the notion of an omnipresent god as a creator. Further, he rejected the idea of soul and put forth the doctrine of dependent origination (Ambedkar, 1992). Ambedkar regarded Buddha as the 'first social reformer and the greatest of them all.' Buddha's first contribution was to live a moral life and to teach a new, superior morality to a corrupt society entangled in the practices of ritual and superstition. Buddha campaigned against the Yajnyas and the practice of inequality based on caste (Gore, 1993: 294). Masses suffering under the Aryan decadence flocked to the Buddha for his superior morality and inspiring personality (Ambedkar, 1987: 165–66). By rejecting the mythical account of Buddhism, Ambedkar placed Buddha's renunciation in the material milieu of tribal conflict.

The Brahmanical forces which faded and marginalized under the Buddhist era resurrected during the counter-revolution marked by the social processes turning varna into caste. Under the reign of Pushyamitra Shunga, the state used indiscriminate coercion against Buddhism. Brahminism channelized and organized rituals, beliefs, laws, ideology and culture to eliminate the forces of Buddhism. Under these conditions of counter-revolution, the caste-system came to prominence in India through a process of warfare, subversion and conflict. Ambedkar observed the social and cultural processes facilitating the triumph of Brahmanism. He graphed the structure and processes involved in counter-revolution through a critical examination of Manusmriti. According to him, a counter-revolution established the right of Brahmins to rule and commit regicide. It elevated the status and authority of Brahmins. Manusmriti put poverty and service as the ideal for Brahmins that served as a tool to mislead masses. It also resurrected the image of the Brahmin in the eyes of non-Brahmins through laying down disciplinary prescriptions. Material benefits were ensured to Brahmins through royal patronage and scheme of rituals. Brahmins were awarded several privileges which enhanced their authority. *Varna* was turned into caste by making occupation hereditary and erecting the principle of graded inequality. Brahmanism outlawed intermarriages between different varnas, prohibited inter-dining and exhibited control over women's sexuality. The system of caste initiated an autonomous mechanism of exclusiveness and isolation through the practice of excommunication. Brahmanism as a cultural and ideological apparatus carried out a total subjugation of *shudras* and women. Ambedkar marked that ideological constructs of women's subordination have not enslaved them; rather practice of caste–patriarchy has given rise to ideologies of women's subordination (Ambedkar, 1987: 266–331). As per Ambedkar, gender and kinship came to play a central role in the evolutionary narrative of caste and state formation (Rao, 2009: 152).

Ambedkar examined the role of Brahmanism in shaping and maintaining of caste hierarchy and patriarchy. It was identified as a hegemonic and coercive apparatus where any attempt of revolution against Brahmanism was met with either coercion or addressed through assimilative mechanisms. His reading of the *Gita* unfolded the complexity of social conflict explicating this assimilative mechanism and its ascendancy under the counter-revolution (Ambedkar, 1987: 332–80).

Ambedkarite historiography theorizes Brahmanism as a complex ideological and cultural system that offered material and cultural unity to a caste society (Ambedkar, 1979: 16). It governed material relations of production and its exchange as well as regulation of social and psychological relations within a caste-based society. Additionally, it played a key role in the surplus appropriation based on graded discrimination and exploitation. As an ideological and cultural apparatus it conformed to caste patriarchy by establishing endogamy as a structural basis to gender relations regulating women's sexuality and exchange within the limits of caste.

Therefore, this historiography sees the emergence of untouchability in the context of the conflict of Buddhism with Brahmanism. Ambedkar states that the broken men were a distinct group of Buddhist tribesmen, wandering defeated in a battle, degraded and homeless. Due to their condition of destitution, they were forced to accept the social servitude of *baluta-jajmani* relationship.[5] Their incessant struggle with Brahmanism resulted in a permanent infliction of impurity on them. Untouchability thus subordinated and stigmatized their labour, enchained them in social slavery, degraded and humiliated their entire existence. By placing genealogy of untouchability in the history of Buddhism–Brahmanism conflict, Ambedkar has assigned an insurgent subject position to Dalits.

For Ambedkar, while Brahmanism represented the coercive and hegemonic forces of varna, caste and gender subordination, Buddhism represented the egalitarian spirit of liberty, equality, and fraternity embodied through anti-caste rebellions. Brahmanism, through its devices like theology, mythology, ritualism, and metaphysics enslaved the minds of caste-subalterns. On the contrary, Buddhism's ideological offshoots provided a countercultural terrain to caste subaltern insurgency.

Issues were raised over Ambedkar's preference to the cultural, his emphasis on socio-cultural analysis of Buddhism and particularly his assertion that the conflict between Buddhism and Brahmanism is essential to understand the dynamics of Indian history. M. S. Gore questioned the efficacy of a socio-cultural analysis over a materialist concept of history by contrasting Ambedkar's version of Buddhism with that of D. D. Kosambi. He asked,

> Should Buddhism be seen as an effort to oppose the Aryans, a movement against the ritualism and exclusiveness of Brahmins and a movement that tried to stabilize Indian society of that period, by accommodating newer ethnic groups through the enunciation of more universal ethic? Or was it to be seen, as suggested

> by Kosambi (1956), as a religion that facilitated the political and social shift from tribal loyalties and tribal organization to a larger form of political organization?
>
> (Gore, 1993: 307)

Sharad Patil also critiqued Ambedkar for his failure in understanding the crux of Buddhist revolution. He argued that the Buddha initiated the revolution by annihilating the varna and tribal slavery in ancient India (Patil, 1993: 226).

Gail Omvedt gives a careful treatment to Ambedkar's formulation of conflict between Buddhism and Brahmanism. She comments that as a general principle of a socio-historical analysis of Indian society, it may be said to be necessary but insufficient. She further argues:

> To say that 'Buddhism' and 'Brahmanism' as frame work or ideologies or philosophies were a factor in history, in the sense that they were not simply reflections of socio-economic base but played an autonomous role, is one thing. To say they can serve as sole or major determining explanation is another. In the first sense, Ambedkar's formulations are correct, in the second sense, it is inadequate.
>
> (Omvedt, 2003: 279)

Ambedkar did acknowledge the inadequacy in relying solely on cultural analytics by stating that

> purely religious point of view would give only a superficial picture. The questions about the way the masses and classes of India live; the social and economic terms of their associated lives and the influences of the religion constituting their condition of life are very important.
>
> (Ambedkar, 1989: 129)

Since Ambedkar was well aware about the economic basis of socio-religious phenomenon, he unpacks the structure of social dependence within which untouchables as broken men were subjugated to social servitude. Omvedt rightly identified Ambedkar's formulation of the Buddhism–Brahmanism conflict as Weberian in spirit where efforts are made to add cultural–ideological factors to explanation in terms of economic factors (Omvedt, 2003: 280).

Ambedkar has advocated the formulation of the Buddhism–Brahmanism conflict as a corrective stance (Ambedkar, 1987: 275). While reconstructing the social history of India, he had given more emphasis on the moral dimension of Buddhism; his portrayal of Brahmanism is socially complex; however, his depiction of Buddhism is full of moral nuances. Why did

Ambedkar emphasize these moral nuances of Buddhism? He offers several reasons for this preference of universal ethics of Buddhism. The major reason he cites is to demolish the collective morality of caste society. Morality of a caste society is marked by isolation and exclusiveness as it is aimed to protect group interest and thereby becomes anti-social in nature.

Such a morality of collective interests leads to a factional and disorganized society where disharmony prevails. In such a regime of morality, the individual cannot attain a consistency of mind. Such a society that rests upon the supremacy of one group over the other, irrespective of its rational or proportionate claims inevitably leads to conflict. Ambedkar argues that the only way to put a stop to conflict is sacred universal ethics. This position of Ambedkar certainly exhibits the influence of Durkheim. As Durkheim has pointed out the element of 'sacred' in religion and its role in providing a binding force for social relationships, Ambedkar espouses the universal ethics of Buddhism to restructure society on the values of liberty, equality and fraternity (Omvedt, 2003: 260).

Understanding caste as a state of mind (Ambedkar, 1979: 75) moved Ambedkar towards embracing the universal ethics of Buddhism. Psycho-social relationships between castes had been ordered under the structure of graded inequality. Each caste acquired its selfhood within the hierarchy of the ascending scale of hatred and the descending scale of contempt towards 'other' castes. It indeed had created this predicament before any attempt of anti-caste revolution. Not only caste rivalries but even seemingly progressive anti-caste uprisings had flared a psychosis of caste hatred, which ultimately regimented the caste order. This psychosis remained a major hurdle in uniting the caste subaltern against the caste order. Buddhism, which Ambedkar identified as the lineage that fought caste by propounding universal ethics based on non-enmity, is best suited for forging unity and a sense of community amongst fragmented caste subalterns.

Another feature of Ambedkar's preference to moral Buddhism also lies in the continuum of caste struggle. The pattern that runs through the history of caste struggle is ethical and moral contestation. Stigmatized caste subalterns took the recourse to a moral disposition primarily to gain self-respect and negotiate their place in caste hierarchy. Morality remained a prime ground through which stree–shudra–atishudra contested the hegemony of caste order. Prior to Ambedkar, Laxmi Narsu has propagated a moralistic version of Buddhism. Being rooted in the anti-caste tradition of struggle Ambedkar seems convinced about the path's moral strife espousing the universal ethics of Buddhism.

Exhumation of a Buddhist past with the scientific method

Ambedkar rejected the deterministic economic canons of historical materialism. The Marxist emphasis on a material basis of history has acknowledged that only economic forces shape the course of history, which in turn denied man any role or place in the making of this history. Ambedkar categorically argued that impersonal forces (like economic, geographical etc.) are determining factors of history. However, the effect of these impersonal forces depends on man—his free will and his greatness (Ambedkar, 1989: 212). Ambedkar placed human action as central to historical causality. His commentary on Buddhist causality gives human action a major role, as important as the role of nature, in history:

> The Buddha... maintained that not only every event has a cause but the cause is the result of some human action or natural law. He rejected that man is a puppet in the hands of Time, Nature, Chance, God, Fate, and Necessity. If man is free, then every event must be the result of man's action or an act of nature.
>
> (Ambedkar, 1992: 240)

For Ambedkar, human being existed not only in the physical sense but had a spiritual super-existence through knowledge and love (Gore, 1993: 261). This freedom of reflective reasoning of human beings comprised the motive force of history.

A positivist variety of Marxism enunciates the idea of passivity of the masses before the law of history.[6] Ambedkar was challenging such fatalistic doctrines of economic determinism. He affirmed that ideas generate actions and movements of change and that man is the creator of history. He spoke of the historically determined man, that is, of a man who lives and struggles in concrete historical realities and is confronted with objective societal oppositions.

Ambedkar conceived history from the perspective of the caste subaltern. He criticized the tendency of worshiping the past and insisted that engagement with the past should not belittle the present. In his undelivered speech 'The Annihilation of Caste' he quoted Dewey in support[7] of his argument to reject the burden of history. According to it 'if the present is seen as a 'natural' outcome of the past events, it legitimatizes the present, making the present seem inevitable and 'determined.' To see the present as a 'historical given' thus discourages caste subaltern from taking up any task of changing the present. Therefore, Ambedkar admitted that life begins by leaving the past behind. He observed that the revivalist tendencies of glorifying the past enslave the present. According to him, a revivalist approach makes the past a rival of the present and the present becomes more or less a futile imitation of the past. This approach represents the present as empty and the future as remote and therefore inimical to progress. While defining the relations of past and present, he stated that the study of the past becomes significant and relevant only when the past enters into the present (Ambedkar, 1979: 79).

Ambedkar's quoting of Dewey is at times misinterpreted and misused to trivialize his historical writings. Debjani Ganguli misinterprets Ambedkar's act of quoting Dewey as Ambedkar's urge to make history dead.[8] There is a rising tendency of post-modernist scholars to treat Ambedkar's history as a self-styled imaginative account deficient in scientific history. Ganguli interprets Ambedkar's negotiation with a positivist method of history and his attempt to expand the horizon of the scientific method of history to write the history of caste subaltern as tiredness with the historical method. Picking abrupt and oblique references from Ambedkar's speeches, Ganguli termed Ambedkar's history as 'mythographic.' She cites from Ambedkar's speech of conversion at Nagpur. That traced the genealogy of Mahar community to the Naga tribes. He offered an account of the Naga struggle with Aryans and their conversion to Buddhism. He claimed that Nagas were the earliest Buddhists in Indian history. Later in the era of counter-revolution Brahmanism trampled the Naga-Buddhists under the vicious code of untouchability. Ganguli juxtaposes Ambedkar's version of Nagas with Vinaya Pitaka. According to the Vinaya Pitaka tale, Naga (snake) camouflaged his true identity and was granted full ordination in *sangh*. While he was asleep, his deception came to light and the Buddha was informed. After knowing the real nature of Naga, he commanded that 'no animal should be ordained and ordained by mistake should be expelled from the community' (Ganguli, 2005: 150).

Ganguli takes up the disparity of Ambedkar's version with Buddhist literature as an act of haste at arriving at a conclusion with the help of Benedict Anderson's theory about 'amnesias' that invariably accompany all profound changes in human consciousness. Out of such oblivion, he says spring narratives. Identity in other words, is constructed out of and through the remarkable, if paradoxical dynamic of remembering and/or forgetting. According to Ganguli, Ambedkar's invocation of the Naga tale 'is an operation of dynamic forgetting or amnesia in recasting and recreating identity'. Ganguli further connects it to Ashis Nandy's analysis.

> Nandy has also written about the principled forgetfulness in the mythic engagement of oppressed with their past and present. This feature is but flip side of the willful remembering, and together they allow the subaltern to radically define their own past—what Nandy drawing on Jürgen Habermas's phrase 'future oriented memories', calls remembering in an anticipatory fashion.
>
> (Ganguli, 2005: 151)

To treat Ambedkar's historiography as mythographic is utterly erroneous. Ambedkar's exhumation of the debris of historical evidences involved generating historical facts from mythology. Ganguli makes fashionable use of Ambedkar's term exhumation but ignores what he really meant by it.

With the help of the Buddhist canonical literature, Ambedkar categorically makes distinction between womb-born Nagas and egg-born Nagas, thereby making it clear that "the word Naga has two-fold meaning: in its original sense it stood for the name of human community" (Ambedkar, 1987: 152). According to him, Deva, Asura, Yaksha, Gana, Gandharva and Kinnara were members of the human family. Ambedkar, Phule and post-Phule Dalit activists have used myths to write history. When Phule however took myths as history, his attempt was to generate a historical account. The revolutionary moment in the history of Dalit consciousness is the rise of historical consciousness. Although the mythical world has provided space for caste contestation to Dalits, it has also justified and legitimated the given world where caste subaltern was made to accept indelibility of the hierarchical nature of caste. And contrary to it, history adept with a scientific mode of causality assured a possibility of change and thus empowered Dalits to take up the terminal fight against the caste system.

Although Ambedkar was trying to break the cage of the positivist method to write the history of the caste subaltern, he swore complete allegiance to the scientific method. His attempt was to expand the horizon of the historical method and to enlarge the terrain of historical evidences to bridge the gap of history. He did not need to undertake the operation of forgetfulness or amnesia. But he certainly took recourse to reasoned arguments. His history was not an attempt of memorializing the past, evoking either a mythical narrative or self-styled imaginative narrative of the past but a profound reasoned argument of history set in the scientific structure of the historical method.

Ambedkar's historicism[9]

Change or impermanence in history is central to Ambedkar's historical theory. He stated that 'nothing is fixed, nothing eternal, nothing sanatan; that everything changes. Change is the law of life for the individual as well as for society' (Ambedkar, 1979: 79–80). He rejected the colonial theory of stagnation in Indian history and argued vehemently in favour of historical change. Ambedkar believed that the theory of impermanence of the individual and society gives space to progress and evolution in history (Ambedkar, 1992: 241). He accepted social evolution as the governing principle of history.

Although Ambedkar conceived historical progression in evolutionary frame, he rejected the principle of inevitability in the historical progression (Ambedkar, 2007: 6). His historicism[10] is informed by Buddhism. He argued that Buddha's religion is the result of inquiry and investigation into the conditions of human life and understanding of human instincts and dispositions. For Ambedkar, historical perspectives are informed by an anthropocentric vision of reality. He wanted to study social forces of history and its impact on human instincts and dispositions. Rejecting any deterministic implications of history, he believed that social and individual freedoms are the motor forces of history (Rodrigues, 1998).

Every contemporary reality always contained constituents of historical past in it. Hence historical inquiry becomes essential for any attempt of comprehension of the reality. To understand contemporary social reality instilled by the institutionalization of caste, untouchability, women's servitude and caste-class domination, Ambedkar embarked on the project of historical inquiry. His attempt was to unravel the casual factors in the growth of institution of caste and untouchability; and to identify the patterns in the process of historical change in India. His historical inquiry was passionately engaged in building the theory of revolutionary praxis leading towards caste annihilation.

This historicist enterprise has provided Ambedkar with a theoretical vantage point of a critique of all pertinent ideologies (which relates ideas, beliefs and values) of caste-patriarchy and capitalism. His history offered a shattering critique of Brahmanism which as an ideological and cultural system enslaved the minds of caste–gender subalterns. He explained coercive and exploitative aspects of Brahmanism and condemned them as inhuman and immoral. He emphatically narrated an account of a cultural and moral battle against Brahmanism conceived under an alternative-cultural ideology of Buddhism.

History has been assigned a twofold ideological purpose: one, to conceive legitimacy for changing the present, and two, to maintain it in its existing form indefinably.[11] Ambedkar was well aware about these twofold purposes. He was against every version of a status-quoist history; he fervently rejected colonial and nationalist historiography because of their status-quoist version of the reality built on a coherent interpretation of history conveniently plotted through the continuities of the past. Colonial historians projected the history of India as monolithic 'Hindu' and 'Muslim' pasts. By rejecting monolithic portrayals of ancient Hindu and medieval Muslim pasts, Ambedkar narrated the history of India as the fearsome socio-cultural conflict between Buddhism and Brahmanism. He portrayed history not as linear and homogeneous but having ideological-cultural ruptures manifested through three stages of ancient Indian history: Brahmanism, Buddhism and Hinduism. He narrated the history of India as an endless caste struggle ranging from ancient to medieval period and thus defied the classification of the imagined homogeneity of the Muslim period.

By portraying the glorious Hindu past as being interrupted by a corrupt rule of Muslim kings, nationalist historiography placed the Vedic-Brahmanical tradition central to India and thus masked social and cultural contradictions under the picture of unity in diversity of the Indian nation. They depicted Brahmanical culture as the uniting force of the Indian nation. Ambedkar demolished this very version of nationalist historiography by unleashing a severe onslaught on every argument reflected in contemporary politics based on the dominant nationalist version of history (Gore, 1993). He argued that India has not yet achieved its nationhood; rather it is a nation in the making. Only the anti-caste revolution will bring a nationalist upsurge in India. He built his vision of alternative nationalism based on anti-caste traditions, particularly of Buddhism (Bagade, 1998). Ambedkar's historiography remains contentious. However, he has engaged in multilayered debates with a number of national and colonial nationalist historians.

Ambedkar's critical commitment to the ideologies of liberalism, socialism and Buddhism and his spirited confrontation with colonial and nationalist historiography set up a new kind of historical inquiry. His inquiries into the origin and growth of the institution of caste and untouchability have not only unfolded the structures, processes, historical changes and their continuums in contemporary caste society but has also brought out conflicting social forces that shaped these institutions. His historicist venture offers the most profound critique of caste, patriarchy and untouchability by arguing that caste and untouchability are against reason, humanity and its progress. Thus, his history sets up the revolutionary transformative agenda of caste annihilation which Omvedt has characterized as a democratic revolution.

Ambedkar affirmed that caste was not created by preaching so it cannot be abolished by preaching, his exercise was to prove the falsity of the caste system (Ambedkar, 1979: 78). His project of history writing had a direct bearing on steering the struggle against caste. His quest was to employ history as an ideological tool allowing subaltern castes to actualize new possibilities to fight against caste. A range of material and cultural struggles emerged from the insights drawn from his history pivoting the organization and politicization of the caste-subaltern. His investigations revealed ideological foundations of anti-caste struggles which helped the caste subaltern to acquire their insurgent subject position. His search for new possibilities of social existence which will lead to a reign of freedom away from caste, class exploitation and domination was based on a historical analysis. This indeed convinced him that the eradication of caste required repudiation of Hindu religion and the adoption of an alternative religion of Buddhism.

Ambedkar launched a struggle against caste, class and patriarchy. He wanted an alliance of all subaltern castes and classes. He declared war against Brahmanism and capitalism. Caste exploitation and oppression was giving scope to struggles based on caste identities. Ambedkar was aware of the fact that caste identities are opposed to the lower caste solidarity; he organized anti-caste struggle caste-groups as a unit of organization like Dalits, non-Brahmins etc. He rejected the narrative of caste histories and wrote history as the history of untouchables and shudras. He rejected the racial basis of caste and untouchability and invoked the unity within oppressed castes as economically exploited, socially oppressed and politically dominated caste groups who share a common history and culture in fighting a relentless battle against caste. In an anti-caste democratic revolution, he conceived that Dalits will work as a vanguard caste-group and other oppressed shudra and atishudra castes, peasant castes and working class will assist in the revolution. His depiction of Indian history as a history of caste struggle provided the thread of cultural and social unity to all caste-subalterns. His history assigned emancipatory identities invoked from the anti-caste traditions like Buddhism which provided universal ethics of liberty, equality and fraternity.

Notes

1 Marxists first of all made a distinction between the basic economic structure of any society, constituted by the condition of production, taken as a whole and the superstructure of laws, institution, religion and ideas. The primacy to economic structures of (imagined) class relations of production claimed that the motor for the historical progression is provided by the 'class struggle.' The emphasis on economic structure has created a variation of Marxism, which offered a mechanical interpretation of history, conforming economic determinism. Ambedkar stood against this Marxist variety subscribing itself to rigid economism.

2 Ambedkar has brought to notice that cultural boundaries of nation proved stronger than the notion of economic unity of proletariat class (Khairmode, 1998: 92).

3

> The Buddha looked upon the suffering of his age as a sickness, a disease. In suggesting remedy, he even wanted to proceed according to the principle of medical science of his times. However, he announced himself as tathagata, we do not expect him to have diagnosed the real social roots of the disease, i.e. to have analyzed the tremendous historic transformations going on before his eyes: why this stupendous progress in the productive technique was bringing with it the most awful human miseries and moral degradations. Historically speaking, what was left for him was to transform the real problem into an ideal one, to interpret objective phenomenon in subjective terms; in short to produce 'a reversed world consciousness'. The result was the transformation of the mass misery of the age into metaphysics of misery. Early Buddhism thus, became the most perfect illusion of the epoch .....Every epoch has its false consciousness which, in fact, becomes the major illusion of the epoch. The false consciousness underlying early Buddhism became the ideology—the illusion par excellence—of the age of Buddha. It is this point of view, that we propose to review the four Arya Satya as well as pratitya samutpad.
>
> (Chattopadhyaya, 1992: 500)

4 Ambedkar as quoted in (Omvedt, 1994: 228).

5 Ambedkar categorically marked out the social servitude of untouchables inbuilt in baluta relations. Untouchability as a condition of existence doomed Mahars to be dependent on baluta watan. The subservience of the Mahar caste was structured by three ways: (1) by placing patronizing authority to (Savarna) castes who gave remuneration to Mahars for their labour and Mahars had to accept it as obligation, (2) by giving insufficient, meager Baluta payment far

below than needed for survival, (3) by not allowing them to take up alternative sources of livelihood. He points out that untouchable is dependent upon the touchable for earning his livelihood as well as for the purchases of the necessities of life. The total dependence of untouchable made Mahars subservient to the village community (Ambedkar, 1989: 266–7).

6 The positivist variety of Marxism is seen in the dominant notion of economic determinism reflected in the writings of Marxist thinkers like Bukharin who argued that men's will is not free. However, men supposedly enjoy choices that are produced under the material conditions constituting them.

7 Dewey says:

> An individual can live only in the present. The present is not just something, which comes after the past: much less something produced by it. It is what life is leaving the past behind it. The study of past products will not help us to understand the present a knowledge of past and its heritage is of great significance when it enters into the present but not otherwise. And the mistake of making the records and remains of the past the main material of education is that if tends to make the past rival of present and the present a more or less futile imitation of past.
>
> (Ambedkar, 1979: 79)

8 Ganguli writes that in his speech on the *Annihilation of Caste*, Ambedkar 'donned the mantle of classic revolutionary who wanted the past as well and truly dead. He desired nothing more than disjunction between the past and Hindu Brahmanical India and the present India as a democratic republic. This was the Ambedkar who was the student of John Dewey endorsed the objectivity and empiricism of social science analysis of caste and undertook not a few such analysis himself' (Ganguli, 2005: 141–42).

9 Historicism seems to have three meanings: for most historians it is a primary historical act of perceiving historical periods in their own terms rather than imposed by historian; second and relatedly, it means accepting that every historical period has its own standards through which it determined what was trustworthy knowledge and warranted truth; third that there are inclusive, demonstrable, and determining patterns in the process of historical change. (Munslow, 2000: 130). According to Karl Popper, historicism is a dangerous belief in historical determinism and the existence of a universal pattern in the historical process. And now in a postmodern or hermeneutic fashion, it is understood by reorganizing that the-past-is-history and is used to understand the present (Munslow, 2000: 130–2).

10 Historicism is a dangerous belief in historical determinism and the existence of a universal pattern in the historical process. And now in a postmodern or hermeneutic fashion it is understood as by reorganizing that the-past-is-history and is used to understand the present. Ambedkar takes departure from these notions of historicism.

11 Hayden White writes,

> The very claim to have discerned some kind of formal coherence in the historical record brings with it theories of the nature of historical world and of historical knowledge itself which have ideological implications for attempt to understand the present however 'the present' is defined. To put it another way, the very claim to have distinguished a past from the present world of social thought and praxis, and to have determined the formal coherence of the past world, implies a conception of the form of the knowledge of the present world.
>
> (Quoted in Guha, 1989: 215)

References

Ambedkar Babasaheb in Moon Vasant (ed) (1979), *Dr. Babasaheb Ambedkar Writing and Speeches*, Vol. 1, Education department Maharashtra Govt., Mumbai.

Ambedkar Babasaheb in Moon Vasant (ed) (1987), *Dr. Babasaheb Ambedkar Writing and Speeches*, Vol. 3, Education department Maharashtra Govt., Mumbai.

Ambedkar Babasaheb in Moon Vasant (ed) (1989), *Dr. Babasaheb Ambedkar Writing and Speeches*, Vol. 5, Education department Maharashtra Govt., Mumbai.

Ambedkar Babasaheb in Moon Vasant (ed) (1992), *Dr. Babasaheb Ambedkar Writings and Speeches*, Vol. 11, Education department Maharashtra Govt., Mumbai.

Bagade Umesh (1998), *Phule-Ambedkarāncā Raṣṭravāda*, Nana Patil Academy, Ahamadnagar.

Bagade Umesh (2006), *Mahārāshtratīla Prabodhana āṇi Vargajātiprabhutwa*, Sugava, Pune.

Bapat P. V. (1997), *2500 Years of Buddhism*, Publication division Govt. of India, Delhi.

Chattopadhyaya D. (1992), *Lokayat*, People's Publishing House, Delhi.

Ganachari Arwind (2016), *Gopal Ganesh Agarakar: Buddhiprāmāṇyavādī Vicāravanta āṇi Thora Samājasudhāraka*, Popular, Mumbai.

Ganguli Debjani (2005), *Caste and Dalit Life Worlds Postcolonial Perspectives*, Orient Longmon, New Delhi.

Gore M. S. (1993), *The Social Context of an Ideology*, Sage Publications, New Delhi.

Ingale Devendra (2006), *Discourse on the Origin: Essays on Dr. Babasaheb Ambedkar and Aryan Debate*, Koushyalya prakashan, Aurangabad.

Kearney's Richard F. (2004), *On Paul Ricour: The Owl of Minerva*, Tylor Francis limited, Aldershot.

Khairmode Changdeo B. (1998), *Dr. Bhimrao Ramaji Ambedkar*, Vol. 7, Sugava, Pune.

Munslow, Alun (2000), *The Routledge Companion to Historical Studies*, Routledge, London.

Omvedt Gail (1994), *Dalits and Democratic Revolution*, Sage, Delhi.

Omvedt Gail (2003), *Buddhism in India*, Sage, Delhi.

Patil Sharad (1993), *Maraxwād-Phule Ambedkarwād*, Sugava, Pune.

Patil Sharad (1999), *Buddha*, Krantisinha Nana Patil Academi, Yeola.

Phadke Y. D. (1985), *Vyakti āṇi Vicār*, Shrividya Prakashan, Pune.

Ranade, M. G. (1992), *Miscellaneous Writings*, Sahitya Academy, Delhi.

Rao Anupama (2009), *The Caste Question*, Permanent Black, Ranikhet.

Rodrigues Valerian (1998), unpublished paper submitted in the International Seminar organized by Political Science Department Pune University on *Reconstructing the World: B. R. Ambedkar and Buddhism in India*.

Thapar Romila (1993), *Interpreting Early India*, Oxford University Press, Delhi.

10

GANDHI AND AMBEDKAR ON CASTE

Valerian Rodrigues

Ambedkar wrote extensively on caste and on issues closely bound with the caste question. The same can be said about Mahatma Gandhi too. This interest to engage with concerns related to the caste question and keeping it in the forefront of the struggle for a free India is one of the bonds they shared in common among others. This chapter argues that while there were basic differences between them on this issue, they should not occlude the shared concern. For both of them the right understanding of the caste question was central to the struggle for equality and swaraj, while other significant thinkers of the nationalist lore tended to lay priority on class relations or colonial domination or national oppression as key concerns of political freedom.[1] By drawing attention to the problematics of caste, both of them turned their gaze inward, and argued that the nationalist project would be still-born without national self-reflectivity and internal reforms.

Ambedkar's earliest major essay, "Caste in India" (Ambedkar 1978a) attempts to directly engage with the anthropological discourse on caste. The later writings on caste related it to his central political concerns such as his ideas of equality, nation, democracy, marginalization, discrimination, rights, ethical basis of public life, and so on, that propose an alternative vision of politics in a post-colonial society. While the former raise puzzles in the existing body of literature, the latter interrogate the unfolding politics in India. *The Annihilation of Caste* is the inaugural moment of this new road map. In this great text he reads the implications of caste for the national project in India and makes a case to do away with it. There are however certain concerns common across this shift: There is an understated political position in *Castes in India* linking it to caste patriarchy, and *Annihilation* develops the argument that a democratic republic is not feasible in India without annihilating caste and its encompassing principle, varna. Ambedkar returns to this argument again and again in subsequent texts to demonstrate that caste and varna are antithetical to the idea of democracy and even nationalism. His last major work *The Buddha and His Dhamma* is a call to found the republic on the basis of *Dhamma* rather than *Dharma*, the latter being inevitably caught, according to him, in claims and practices of caste.[2]

The paradoxical nature of the caste system: social closures within cultural homogeneity

The essay "*Castes in India*" basically dwelt on what Ambedkar construed to be the paradox between the shared culture of India on one hand and social closure embodied in the caste system on the other. On reviewing the work of other scholars on the issue, he hypothesizes that in India numerous ethnic groups came to be commingled and there were no distinct races as in the USA.[3] The different ethnic groups in India "through constant contact and mutual intercourse....evolved a common culture that superseded their distinctive cultures"(Ambedkar 1978a, 6). Ambedkar makes this argument exactly at a point of time when colonial ethnology was working overtime to demonstrate the fragmentariness of India, particularly highlighting caste.[4] Asserting the cultural homogeneity of India, Ambedkar states, "I venture to say that there is no country that can rival the Indian Peninsula with respect to the unity of its culture"(Ambedkar 1978a, 6). He argues that, unlike the commonly held beliefs regarding caste and endogamy, exogamy is a universal feature in India and therefore not merely marriage within 'sapindas' (blood kins) is forbidden but even among 'sagotras' (common lineage). The puzzle is the compartmentalization of thick cultural affinities "into fixed and definite units" of castes, characterized by endogamy. He conjectures that caste must have arisen in India long after the diverse races had commingled.[5] According to him, the existing theories of caste[6] offer inadequate and deeply unsatisfactory explanation to this paradox: What we find in India is the superimposition of endogamy over exogamy. Through endogamy a homogeneous culture is parcelled out into tightly bound social units called castes.

According to him, endogamy to be viable requires 'numerical equality' between the sexes within a group and a large disparity between them is likely to make the system non-viable. The problem that such groups confront is how to solve the problem of numerical disparity 'between marriageable units of the two sexes', i.e., the problem of the 'surplus man' and 'surplus woman'. The problem of the surplus woman in India was sought to be taken care of by sati, i.e. burning a woman 'on the funeral pyre of her deceased husband' and thus getting rid of her, although resort to such stratagem is extremely difficult and could not be universally enforced. But if a widow is left free in the group, she might prove dangerous to the very name of the group or prove a challenge to other women. Therefore, she is cordoned off by compulsory widowhood, while degrading her at the same time to offset her potential allure. Sati, bar on widow remarriage, and demeaning confinement of a widow are all related to endogamy and consequently to caste.

However, men cannot be handled in this particular way, due to their social dominance and physical prowess. Burning him is not a solution 'because he is a man' and, if it is done, a 'sturdy soul will be lost to the group'. Many a widower may not cherish the prospect of remaining single, and if such a surplus man remains within the group, he might prove a danger to the morals of the group. It is therefore in the interest of the group to keep him *'Grahasta'*. In this case the surplus man can be provided a wife only by recruiting one from lower age-groups. Child-marriage is its inevitable outcome. Such an institutionalization of gender relations demanded that a man or woman should not feel affection for anyone other than the one with whom he or she is united. Affections were impersonally disposed. It is the system that guards and directs affections and feelings. It is marriage that begets love rather than vice-versa.

But how did a social practice such as endogamy come to be institutionalized through the caste system? For the purpose Ambedkar assumes that division of labour in a society begets classes beyond the early stages of evolution of mankind. However, the basis of such classes could differ: It could be economic, intellectual or social. In India, the division of labour assumed the caste form. Caste and class are closely entwined: *'A Caste is an Enclosed Class'* (Ambedkar 1978a, 1, 15). Social norms assigned division of labour to a system made of classes. The class that raised the enclosure around itself first could be Brahmins, since most customs related to gender relations in India were prevalent among them. But since Brahmins held the highest place in the social hierarchy the others imitated them: 'their prevalence in non-Brahmin castes is derivative of their observance (and) is neither strict nor complete' (Ibid). Brahmins therefore could be said as 'the originators of this 'unnatural institution' (Ibid).

Ambedkar does not think that any lawgiver could have created the institution of caste and, given its atrocious character, if he was to do so he 'would not have outlived this law' (Ibid, 16). Similarly imposing the caste system on non-Brahmins by Brahmins would have been impossible. Manu merely philosophized about it, codified existing caste rules and preached caste Dharma. In other words, Manu provided the rule-book, introducing his own caste-prejudices, for widely prevalent social practices.

The earliest known classes among Hindus were Brahmins, the priestly class; Kshatriyas, the military class; Vaishyas or the merchant class; and Shudras, the artisan and menial class. But this class system was essentially open-ended, classes changing their personnel, depending upon their attributes.[7] From such classes the transition to caste took place in a specific way: *"Some closed the door: Others found it closed to them"* (Ibid, 18). Once it was adopted by Brahmins, others also tended to imitate it due to the prestige the former commanded among the rest. "It is the 'the infection of imitation' that caught all these sub-divisions on their onward march of differentiation and turned them into castes"(Ibid, 18).[8] Ambedkar uses Gabriel Tarde's laws of imitation to illustrate it (Ibid, 19)[9] Brahmins as superior were the sources of imitation and they influenced 'numerous and daily relations with other members. Those members who were nearest to the Brahmins imitated most of the aspects; however, those at a distance were not sufficiently influenced by them, even though they could not remain immune to such influence.

Caste is not an autonomous unit. Castes are bound in a system and its inexorable logic: "*Caste in the singular number is an unreality. Castes exist only in the plural number.* There is no such a thing as caste: There are always *castes*" (Ibid, 20). Once a group encloses itself, others have no chance but to enclose themselves. Any innovation that violates caste norms is likely to be spurned and such castes members would be thrown out from a caste to become another caste.

Ambedkar thought that caste operates in a milieu where there is a basic agreement across the society regarding a set of social codes. He repeats this argument in *Annihilation* where he writes that there is "similarity in habits and customs, beliefs and thoughts' (Ambedkar 1978b, 51) across India and the functioning of the caste system would not have been possible without it. At this stage, it is important to note the distinction that Ambedkar makes between endogamy among the upper castes and the lower castes. The injunctions of caste call for compliance among Brahmins and castes closest to them, while they are much more derivative/imitative as we go down the ladder. The second distinction is with respect to a social practice and a norm that links itself to the practice. Manu constructs a practice into a norm and arrests the possibility of the practice and severely limits the incidence of rebellion against the practice. The norm universalizes what was a spatially and temporarily confined practice. It is in this context that we need to understand Ambedkar's sustained vehemence against Manu and what he regards as the ideology of the varna–dharma system.[10]

It is important to stress the political significance that this understanding of caste had on Ambedkar. For the purpose we need to bear in mind the dominant concerns of the early two decades of the 20th century with its divisions on 'consent bill', social reforms and prioritization of political movement over social reforms. Against social reformers, who stressed the need for social reforms alongside political reforms, Ambedkar argued that it is not enough to strive after the abolition of sati, widow-marriage and ban on child marriage. All these social evils were closely bound with caste. Caste itself therefore has to be targeted. However, social reformers generally hailing from Brahmins showed little reflectivity on this count. Further, there was little that is of a religious character in caste although it is legitimized by attributing to it such religious resources. Against the extremists, who stressed on political reforms at the exclusion of social reforms, he argued that by attacking the caste system, pursuit of the national cause was not going to be weakened but would become stronger and beget the retrieval/rediscovery of a shared culture. Against colonial ethnology[11] he suggested that caste is neither basic nor central to the organization of wider social relations in India but a positive hindrance. Against the arrogance of the Brahmin elite leading the national movement, his advice was physician heal thyself—the divisive markers are much more their doing rather than that of the common people. By making caste a 'derivative' institution among the non-Brahmin masses, he alludes to a strong shared bond across them compared with that between non-Brahmins and Brahmins, an observation central to Jyotirao Phule's oeuvre. Caste as endogamy subjects a woman to a twofold marginality vis-à-vis a man: On the one hand a woman confronts constantly the threat of sati or widowhood, and the elimination and degradation they imply, and secondly even a young girl is constantly faced with the prospect of marrying a much older man, with little possibility of intimacy between them. While caste patriarchy bears heavily on women of upper castes, its import and significance among lower castes is a matter of inquiry rather than a simple attribution. 'The infection of imitation' in a caste-bound society binds a woman into subjection while men are given dominion over them.

The caste system and democratic political community

Ambedkar wrote *Annihilation of Caste* 20 years after 'Castes in India' and wanted to 'recast' the former by incorporating the latter in a subsequent edition, but did not do so due to paucity of time.[12] Ambedkar's central argument in this text is that social reforms in India have not gone far enough. Hinduism cannot be reformed without annihilating caste. However, annihilation of caste cannot be done unless the principles justifying caste are rejected. The sacred scriptures themselves justify caste practices widespread in the name of Hinduism. These principles have been embodied in the scriptures and Hindus believe that their caste practices have religious sanction justifying them. Therefore, the sacred scriptures themselves have to be rejected. It is not justified to separate scriptures from social practices.

According to Ambedkar, there were two political strands pursuing the national-democratic project in India: political reformers and socialists. The former, had effectively marginalized, and ignored the concerns of the social reformers,[13] and were spearheading the cause of freedom from colonial domination. It was done by trivializing the concerns of the social reform platform, accompanied by much sloganeering and slanderous attacks. Taking his own stance on the issue he underscored the continued validity of social reforms in India, if it has to strive to be an independent political community and illustrated it by citing the condition of untouchables and the continued caste atrocities in different parts of the country. How can India justifiably seek independence when large masses were subject to the thraldom of the caste system? Even if India succeeded in securing independence from Britain, the subjection of people to caste authority would persist. If this is the case why did the social reformers simply cave in? Ambedkar thought that social reformers who primarily hailed from upper castes had a limited agenda such as the abolition of child marriage, sati and widow remarriage issues pertaining to high caste Hindu families. They did not call for the 'reform of Hindu society,' in the sense of the 'break-up of the caste system', by "agitating for the abolition of caste or had the courage to agitate for it" (Ambedkar 1978b, 42). They advanced highly confined and superficial demands. They did not include the large masses caught in the thraldom of the caste system in their political imagination.

How about the socialists?[14] Ambedkar felt that they tend to emphasize on economic factors as the only or decisive source of power. They downplay or ignore the significance of status and religion in pursuing or restraining choices, and thereby the nature and range of freedom available to a person. This was demonstrably true in India. In India bonding on class-lines can hardly be contemplated without social reform. "Men will not join in a revolution for the equalization of property unless they know that after the revolution is achieved, they will be treated equally and there would be no discrimination of caste and creed" (Ambedkar 1978b, 46). In fact, the proletariat cannot even 'present a united front' for the purpose of revolutionary transformation unless the differential markers of class are taken into account. Caste is the 'monster' to be handled.[15]

Anatomy of caste and human dignity

How does caste affect social relations? Why is it deplorable so as to deserve 'annihilation'? Ambedkar thought that the caste system is not merely a division of labour but a division of labourers (ascribed occupations). Further, such divisions are graded, one over the other and vice-versa. While division of labour is unavoidable, division of labourers into watertight compartments militates against natural aptitude, violates the principle of fostering social and individual efficiency by nurturing individual capacities, and ignores the choice of the persons concerned. Caste displays an insensitivity to change and transformation and the economic and livelihood consequences that flow therefrom. It reduces human beings to callings that do not hold any appeal to them. It begets a sense of degradation and aversion on account of the slight and stigma associated with certain occupations. In the latter case, there is little engagement of the labourer with the kind of work that he does, his heart and soul is not in it and his natural capacities and powers are not in tune with social rules. 'Such callings constantly provoke one to aversion, ill-will and the desire to evade.....because of the blighting effect which they produce upon those who follow them owing to the slight and stigma cast upon them' (Ambedkar 1978b, 48). If men's hearts and minds are not in their work how can such a system be efficient? Economically caste is harmful because it subordinates "man's natural powers and inclinations to the exigencies of social rules" (Ibid).

Ambedkar did not think that the caste system had any racial basis, and even if it did, it did not explain why inter-caste marriages were forbidden. He felt that racial theories talked a lot of nonsense in the name of heredity and eugenics. He repeats his argument made in "Castes in India": "Caste system does not demarcate racial division. Caste system is a social division of people of the same race" (Ibid, 49). The eugenics argument did not apply to caste divide; if caste divisions were racial divisions, then how to explain prohibition to marry across sub-castes? If it is race then why prevent inter-dining? If it is eugenic, then how to explain the poor quality of Hindus, in a physical sense? To quote him, "To hold that distinctions of castes are really distinctions of race and to treat different castes as though they were so many different races is a gross perversion of facts" (Ibid, 48). Therefore, the bar against inter marrying and inter dining for reasons of purity of race or blood had little scientific basis. Through a process of elimination, he was suggesting an explanation that he had advanced in "Castes in India."

Impact of caste on Hindus

Ambedkar thought that the caste system has done great harm to Hinduism. On account of it, there was nothing such as a Hindu community as an encompassing bond. Caste is a self-conscious unit and often does not even recognize that it is integrally bound with other castes. Therefore, there is no consciousness 'of kind' among Hindus. Hindu consciousness is primarily consciousness of caste. From the fact that certain ways of life are shared among Hindus one cannot conclude that they constitute a society. The mere presence of certain habits and customs, beliefs and thoughts are not enough to constitute men into society. According to Ambedkar, "Men constitute a society because they have things which they possess in common...and the only way by which they can come to possess things in common with one another, is by being in communication with one another" (Ibid, 51). It is in the appreciation and acknowledgement of the shared-common and participation in common activity that gives rise to unity. Through associated activity a man feels his success as the success of his associates and his failure as the failure of his associates. The conclusion for him was obvious, "the caste system prevents common activity, and by preventing common activity, it has prevented the Hindus from becoming a society with a unified life and a consciousness of its own being" (Ibid). Unlike in 'Castes in India,' there is much less confidence in him now that a shared culture can be retrieved without consciously forging such bonding.

Caste system breeds an antisocial spirit and hatred is inbuilt into it. One's own caste is given a noble birth and others are ascribed an ignoble origin. A caste attempts to reproduce its interest and pits those interests in opposition to other castes as if they are different nations. It makes Hindus 'many warring groups each living for itself and its selfish ideal.' He also thinks that castes treasure strong memories of caste oppression, thereby preventing solidarity and bonding.[16] The obsession of the Hindus with caste does not make them extend even humanitarian considerations to others as demonstrated by their inability to reach out to the aborigines, and they entertain no remorse or repentance in this regard. Leaving them in their primitive conditions, he felt, Hindus had harboured in their midst a potential time-bomb that could spell doom. Higher-caste Hindus have also done precious little to enable lower castes to rise to their cultural level. He felt that generally Hindus have refused to share their intellectual and social inheritance with those who were ready and willing to participate in it and it expressed a meanness that was worse than cruelty.

Ambedkar thought that conversion was impossible within Hinduism because the convert did not find a place in the social life of the community. Membership of caste is not open; it is a closed corporation. Therefore, "*Shuddi* will be both a folly and a futility" (Ambedkar 1978b, 55). The attempt of the Arya Samaj at *Sanghatan* did not have any impact because the *Sanghatan* invariably would be very weak and thin. Hindus will not come to the help of other Hindus qua Hindus. The associated mode of life of the Hindus, he felt, did not produce a fellow feeling as it did among Sikhs and Muslims. Such an associated feeling is a social cement. The celebrated tolerance of the Hindus was debunked by Ambedkar in no uncertain words,

> The Hindus claim to be very tolerant people. In my opinion this is a mistake. On many occasions they can be intolerant and if on some occasions they are tolerant, that is because they are too weak to oppose or too indifferent to oppose.
>
> (Ibid, 55)

The indifference that Hindus show towards the wronged and the oppressed, he felt, was primarily an outcome of the caste system. A good cause did not bring them together.

He felt that reform and self-evaluation became possible if the group one belonged to is deferential towards such initiatives. Caste acts as the authority of excommunication and individual Hindus have no courage to violate caste injunctions. This is because an individual member cannot do without society and caste, which indicates society has sought his complete conformity to its code in letter and spirit. A caste can therefore make the life of a reformer hell. Caste shuns reform.

With caste, Hindus cannot think of forging a cohesive public domain with which they would identify themselves against odds. Ambedkar recites a litany of factors that come in the way:

> Caste has killed the public spirit. Caste has destroyed the sense of public charity. Caste has made public opinion impossible. There is no sympathy to the deserving. There is no appreciation of the meritorious. There is no charity to the needy. Suffering as such calls for no response....there is no appreciation of virtue but only when the man is a fellow caste man...my caste man, right or wrong; my caste man, good or bad.
>
> (Ibid, 56–57)

Due to the prevalence of caste, the national-democratic project in India is either going to be still-born or there is going to be a disjuncture between claims and practices. The tall claims made by different political actors have little to commend for them unless they dared to take caste head-on.

Irreconcilability between caste and democracy

A democratic ideal is in contradiction to a caste society. Ambedkar states this ideal as follows:

> An ideal society should be mobile, should be full of channels for conveying a change taking place in part to other parts. In an ideal society, there should be many interests consciously communicated and shared. There should be varied and free points or contacts with other modes of association. In other words there must be social endosmosis. This is fraternity, which is only another name for democracy....It is primarily a mode of associated living, of conjoint communicated experience.
>
> (Ibid, 57)[17]

Against such an ideal caste society fixes people into slots, laying boundaries for their outreach. Prohibitions, commands and taboos ensure that one casts his vision, if there is one possible, to the limits of one's own caste. The possibility of interacting and learning from others comes to be highly confined. The ideal of democracy or fraternity—a concept that he employs interchangeably—is informed by liberty and equality. Liberty is not merely the absence of restraint but "an effective and competent use of a person's powers" (Ibid). The latter would invariably involve freedom to choose one's profession. But a caste society is like a slave society, where human beings are "forced to accept from others the purposes which control their conduct" (Ibid). He feels that equality values a person's worth, his endeavour and exercise of his agency, rather than mere birth. In this sense equality marks off a human being from the non-human world. It instils a sense of responsibility and accountability. It is also conducive to utility, since it is "good for the social body to get the most out of its members by making them equal as far as possible at the very start of the race" (Ibid, 58). Fairness also demands that people be regarded as equal and "those individuals in whose favour there is also birth, education, family, business connections and inherited wealth" do not corner the social produce. Only by being equally considered one can give "as much incentive as possible to the full development of everyone's powers" (Ibid).

Ambedkar thought that certain attempt at shoring up Hindu identity may not enhance fraternal ties. He critiques that the Arya Samaj attempts to forge a Hindu identity by taking recourse to *Shuddi* (purificatory rituals) while upholding the doctrine of *Chaturvarnya*. If *Chaturvarnya* is based upon worth, there is no need to ascribe labels to people such as brahmin, kshatriya, vaishya and shudra. Naming in a cultural context is not an innocent activity but begets processes that are constitutive.[18] He feels that the continuation of the labels will invariably reproduce the structures of meanings associated with it.

Apart from meanings associated, he feels that *Chaturvarnya*, as employed by the Arya Samaj or by Gandhi, is impracticable, harmful and has turned out to be a miserable failure. One of the big difficulties is reducing innumerable castes into the system of *Chaturvarnya*. How to make people occupying a status vacate it for worth? How to compel people to recognize the worth of someone of a lower status? He feels that the *Chaturvarnya* scheme is close to that of Plato's *Republic* and the criticism to which Plato's doctrines of social classes is subject to is also the criticism that must apply to the system of *Chaturvarnya*. Such a system lumps together people into sharply marked off classes without conceding, "the uniqueness of every individual, of his incommensurability with others, of each individual forming a class of his own, of the infinite diversity of active tendencies and combination of tendencies of which an individual is capable" (Ibid, 60). It is not possible to pigeonhole people into classes of the kind that the *Chaturvarnya* doctrine has proposed. It is not possible to reproduce the *Chaturvarnya* system as people are free and the system has to be enforced by a law. Without a penal sanction the system is unlikely to endure for long. The *Chaturvarnya* system has no place for women. If women are classified according to the status of their husbands then, the principle of worth is violated. If it is a nominal categorization, then women are not taken seriously.

Even if it is practicable, *chaturavarnya* is a vicious system. Although it is defended on grounds of mutual support, it does not have built-in-accountability when other people fail to pursue their side of division of labour. Who then will defend the category left out? "Why make one person depend upon another in the matter of his vital needs?" Such a system came down heavily on the lowest rung; the Shudra bore all the brunt. One of the main reasons why there has been no revolution in India has been on account of the disarming of the shudra. In India the weak have been made helpless against exploitation. Although in the West there was widespread social violence, the poor were not wholly deprived of physical, political and moral claims. This has not been the case in India. The *Chaturvarnya* system 'deadens, paralyses and cripples the people' (Ibid, 63). There is little evidence to suggest that the system does away or contains strife. There is enough in the literature to suggest that rivalry and enmity between the different varnas was endemic to the system: there was incessant fight between the brahmins and the kshatriyas.[19]

Ambedkar thought that Hindus cannot take comfort by citing the continued existence of caste among Muslims, Sikhs and Christians. In his view caste among non-Hindus is fundamentally different form caste among Hindus. Among non-Hindus there are several organic filaments that unite them. What is to be noted in this context is not merely the existence of groups among communities, which would always be there. The question to be asked is,

> How numerous and varied are the interests which are consciously shared by the groups? How full and free is the interplay with other forms of associations? Are the forces that separate groups and classes more numerous than the forces that unite? What social significance is attached to the group life? Is exclusiveness a matter of custom and convenience or is it a matter of religion?
>
> (Ambedkar 1978b, 64)

Among other communities there are the 'organic filaments' that bind groups together but there is no integrating force among Hindus. The social significance of caste among non-Hindus is different from that among Hindus. Among the former caste is not the primary identity. This is not so among the Hindus. Besides, caste among non-Hindus has no religious sanction. It is not a sacred institution. Hindus consider caste institution as sacred. They regard it as religion. The survival of Hindus cannot be an argument for the perpetuation of caste. The question is not whether a community lives or dies: the questions are on what plane does it live and what is the quality of its survival. There is a big difference 'between merely living and living worthily' (Ibid, 66).

Ambedkar's magisterial answer from such a moral standpoint is, "You cannot build anything on the foundations of caste. You cannot build up a nation, you cannot build up a morality. Anything that you will build on the foundations of caste will crack and will never be a whole" (Ibid).

Rescuing Hinduism from caste

If caste is deplorable and led to the degeneration of Hinduism, how to rescue the latter from the former? Should it abolish sub-castes? (as Arya Samaj did). Such a position assumes that there is a great deal of commonality across sub-castes to forge a common unity. This is not the case. Ambedkar feels that the destruction of caste is difficult because of the internal gradation. The scaling of caste makes it impossible to organize a common front against the caste system. "All are slaves of the caste system but all the slaves are not equal in status" (Ibid, 72). Therefore there cannot be a general mobilization of Hindus. Besides, the abolition of sub-castes does not necessarily lead to the abolition of caste system. Inter-dining, even where it has been pursued as a social practice to forge unity, has not solved the problem of caste. How about inter-caste marriage? But Hindus have been vehemently opposed to it. According to Ambedkar, the known resistance to these social practices arises because they are an affront to certain deeply held beliefs:

> inter-dining and inter-marriage are repugnant to the beliefs and dogmas which the Hindus regard as sacred... Caste is not a physical object like a wall of bricks or a line of barbed wire....Caste is a notion, it is a state of the mind. The destruction of caste does not therefore mean the destruction of a physical barrier. It means a notional change.
>
> (Ibid, 68)

Hindus do not regard caste and its practices as deplorable. They 'observe caste because they are deeply religious" (Ibid).

If Hinduism is to be rescued from caste then those sources which engender the belief that it is religious have to be destroyed. For Ambedkar, it is the *shastras*, the texts and the tradition that they sustain, which are the sources that inculcate the belief that caste is a deserving ideal. "If this is correct, then obviously the enemy, that you must grapple with, is not the people who observe caste, but the *shastras* which teach them this religion of caste" (Ibid). 'The real remedy' for the caste ailment lies in the destruction of the sanctity of the shastras.

> Make every man and woman free from the thraldom of the shastras, cleanse their minds of the pernicious notions founded on the shastras, and he or she will inter dine or intermarry. It is not merely that shastras be discarded but their authority should be denied. What is wrong with the Hindus is their religion.
>
> (Ibid, 68–69)

Ambedkar thinks that caste is the natural outcome of certain religious beliefs that have the sanction of the shastras and therefore any attack on caste is an attack on fundamental religious notions. It makes an assault on caste a very difficult task. Brahmins do not entertain annihilation of caste even though they are in the forefront of political reforms. They are unlikely to be social reformers involving caste since their very authority springs from the latter. In Ambedkar's view, there is not much of a difference between secular brahmins and priestly brahmins in this regard. You cannot argue the case against caste, or rally against it through social movements. The scriptures do not uphold reason as authority. They uphold the three-fold authority; *shruti*, *smritis*, *sadachar/sistachar*, and dharma to conform to them.

The *shastras* "have smothered reflective thought" and have recommended compromise when caste injunctions cannot be followed. By depriving the reformer from reason and morality as his weapons, he lies protection-less at the mercy of the scriptures. Therefore, there is no alternative but to "destroy the religion of the *shrutis* and *smritis*. Nothing else will avail" (Ibid, 75). Further, Hindu religion does not distinguish between principles and rules. It is a multitude of commands and prohibitions. A principle is an appeal to reason suggesting a course of action deserving compliance freely given. A principle respects free and responsible agency. Rules prescribe a specific course of action. They are invested with finality and fixity. Hinduism is not a set of spiritual principles universal and applicable to all set of peoples. Under it there is no loyalty to ideals but only conformity to commands. It does not take into consideration conditions and circumstances. It is important to unmask Hinduism and demonstrate that it is not a religion but a set of rules under the mask of religion. People would be prepared to tear off the mask of law, 'old and archaic', if they are told that Hinduism is such. Hitherto it has sustained itself in the name of religion, arrogating to itself the sacrality associated with it.

Instituting an alternative to the regime of caste

While rejecting caste and calling for the destruction of its very basis, Ambedkar, at the same time, underscores the need for religion. Quoting Burke, he says true religion is the foundation of society. He thinks that it is important to reconstruct Hinduism on the foundations of liberty, equality and fraternity, or what he terms as democracy. For such reconstitution it might be important to draw in elements 'from foreign sources' or 'draw such principles from the Upanishads'. It might involve a lot of scrapping and chipping and remoulding of those resources. But it should result in, "a complete change in the fundamental notions of life....in the values of life. It means a complete change in outlook and in attitude to men and things... it means new life" (Ibid, 78). But such a new life demands that the old should cease to exist. In other words, he seeks an entire metamorphosis of Hinduism.

He feels that Hindus should not take an anthropologist's view of religion and say dispassionately that there are "different beliefs, habits, morals and outlooks on life" (Ibid). The latter are enabling resources, subject to approval and disapproval on grounds of reason for the sustenance of life. It is important to separate the chaff from the grain and decide what is to be conserved and what is to be discarded. The basis of such a judgement can only be the deliberated reasoning of the present rather than the weight of the past. The past can inform the present but it cannot be its norm. Ambedkar backs his argument in this regard by drawing extensively from John Dewey. He thinks that the perspective that should govern such approach is,

> that there is nothing fixed, nothing eternal, nothing *sanatan;* that everything is changing, that change is the law of life for individuals as well as for society...if there must be standards to measure the acts of men there must also be a readiness to revive those standards.
> (Ibid, 79)

Ambedkar addresses these concerns in the *Draft of the Indian Constitution* and particularly in the Hindu Code Bill.[20] The resistance the constitutional regime engendered led Ambedkar to write another text called *The Buddha and His Dhamma* 20 years after *Annihilation.* The Buddha rejects caste-based social callings, and reaches out to everyone irrespective of his/her station in life. In many ways it was the standard book for Hinduism that he proposed in *Annihilation.* It was not merely to be the *Gospel of the Buddha.* In this text all major protagonists of the traditions of Brahmanism and their systems of philosophy are shown as either being refuted by the Buddha, or endorse his path.

Gandhi's approach to caste and varna

While Gandhi's rejoinder to Ambedkar's exposition on caste is important, it may be worthwhile to reconstruct his position on the issue independently of this engagement. Gandhi generally made a sharp distinction between caste and varna on one hand and caste, varna and untouchability on the other. His position on these issues also underwent significant changes overtime, particularly after his encounter with Ambedkar. While Gandhi saw caste as a social institution to be valued and assessed as per the ends it is meant to serve, he considered the *varnashramadharma* as an essential feature of Hinduism. Even as early as 1920 we see him arguing, "I consider the four divisions alone to be fundamental, natural and essential. The innumerable sub-castes are sometimes a convenience, often a hindrance. The sooner there is fusion, the better" (Gandhi 1920, 67). He considered untouchability as a social evil that has no sanction within Hinduism, and associated it primarily with the social feeling of high and low. He did not think that it is an integral component of the caste system either, but its obnoxious and evil outgrowth. The caste system itself is an associated social division of labour built around skills, competences, social cooperation and a distinctive mode of reproduction of itself, little to do with social gradation and ranking. He felt that if untouchability is removed, then the caste system itself will lose its association with considerations of high and low.

> Untouchability is the product, therefore, not of the caste system, but of the distinction of high and low that has crept into Hinduism and is corroding it. The attack on untouchability is thus an attack upon this "high-and-low"-ness. The moment untouchability goes, the caste system itself will be purified, that is to say.....it will resolve itself into the true *varnadharma*, the four divisions of society, each complimentary of the other and none inferior or superior to any other.
>
> (Gandhi 1933c, 228)

Initially, Gandhi defended the caste system and wrote a small booklet called *Varnavyavastha* in Gujarati in 1922 in this regard. His arguments in defence of the system were by then familiar: It has helped Hindu society survive over time; it has protected life relatively stably in spite of changing political fortunes; it has extended support and care; it has limited worldly aspirations; it has sustained skills and competences at a relatively decent pace; it has prevented social fragmentation etc. However, by the second half of that decade he had come to criticize caste:

> Caste I hold to be an obstacle to our progress and an arrogant assumption of superiority by one group over another. And untouchability is its extreme bad example. It is really high time that we got rid of the taint of untouchability and the taint of caste. Let us not degrade varnashrama by mixing it up with untouchability or caste.[21]

Writing in 1932, he states,

> Caste distinctions are not respected in the ashram because they are not a part of dharma. They have no connection with the Hindu dharma. It is sinful to regard anybody as higher or lower. All of us are equal. We are polluted by sin, never by human beings. One who wishes to serve cannot look up on anybody as higher or lower. The belief in such distinctions is a blot on Hinduism. We should remove it.
>
> (Iyer 1986, 556)

The Satyagraha Ashram Trust deed formulated on February 2, 1926 stated, "The ashram does not believe in caste, which it considers, has injured Hinduism, because its implications of superior and inferior status and of pollution by contact are contrary to the law of love" (Ibid, 538). However, his ambiguity with regard to caste persisted, and he took few initiatives to mount collective action for its abolition.

How come then he defended the *varna* system? Unlike the prevailing belief he felt that the *varna* system upheld "absolute equality; although in the way it is presently expressed it is a monstrous parody of the original" (Iyer 500). *Varna* is not ranking of status based on inherited division of labour nor is it the division of labour in accordance with innate abilities. For him, "Varna is nothing more than an indication of the duty that has been handed down to each one of us by our forefathers" (Ibid, 502). This duty is handed down and transmitted akin to natural abilities. "Just as everyone inherits a particular form so does he inherit the particular characteristics and qualities of his progenitors" (Ibid, 500). He formulated the argument afresh as follows:

> The law of varna means that everyone shall follow as a matter of dharma, duty, the heredity calling of his forefathers in so far as it is not inconsistent with fundamental ethics. He will earn his livelihood by following that calling
>
> (Ibid, 563)

The authentic culture for man is to free oneself to spiritual pursuits. Gandhi thought that this was the great discovery of Hinduism. Varna helped one to conserve one's energy by making him expend little in the cultivation and pursuit of his occupation for his livelihood from generation to generation, thereby freeing man for higher pursuits. Varna sets human beings free, "for extending the field of spiritual research and spiritual evolution" (Ibid, 500). It limits material ambitions and frees man to pursue goals appropriate to his nature. It curbs competition, and apart from saving man from being bogged down with material pursuits and all the deleterious consequences arising therefrom, prevents the growth of inequality and class conflict arising on that ground. He found that the law of varna is "the basis of all the religions of the world." It is the law of conservation of energy in the human sphere.[22] As far as the higher self is concerned, there is no difference between one man and another. Being born in a varna does not place one advantageously over the others as far as higher pursuits are concerned. Therefore, the saints and spiritual savants have hailed from all castes and communities and are seen as equally deserving of respect by one and all.

Gandhi considered varna binding as far as the mode of acquiring one's livelihood is concerned. One earns one's material sustenance by following "as a matter of duty the hereditary calling of his forefathers." It does not prevent anyone from acquiring knowledge and skills one might wish to pursue. Therefore, "A Shudra has as much right to knowledge as a Brahmana but he falls from his estate if he tries to gain his livelihood through teaching" (Gandhi 1927c, 482). Through such distinctions Gandhi wanted to snap the link between the pursuit of a profession on one hand and access to material wealth and status that it affords on the other. Varna would save a lot of energy, which is presently expended in the name of learning. It passes on skills and talents from generation to another. Therefore, when one gives up one's varna to undertake other pursuits he sells his "soul for a mess of pottage" (Ibid). The varna system, for Gandhi, does not uphold inequality. To the contrary, by reducing competition and keeping material wants low, it is a curb on inequality. In much of his disputations and public addresses he attempted to denounce the attitude of low and high built into the varna system while at the same time persuading people to carry on their traditional callings. At the same time, he recognized that some of the callings such as *Bhangi, Chamar* etc., which were despised required mobilization of enormous moral resources to make them acceptable as equally worthy by the concerned.

Gandhi, however, felt that in the existing conditions in India both "*varnadharma* and *ashramadharma* are in abeyance" (Geetha 2004, 264). Only Shudra varna prevails, and other three varnas that were meant for spiritual and social advance have disappeared. *Varnashramadharma* as a central tenet of Hinduism has to be rediscovered afresh. He suggested that out of shudra dharma, i.e. spirit of service, "it is possible to revive spiritual knowledge, the power to defend it and the wealth to sustain it" (Ibid, 265), their correlatives being, the hallowed preoccupations of brahmins, kshatriyas and vaisyas respectively. Constitution of varnadharma thereby became an end to be pursued rather than a manifest social reality.

The social evil of untouchability

A large bulk of Gandhi's writings on caste dwelt on the issue of untouchability, a concern that he encompassed within the canvass of Hinduism, rather than Indian nationalism, as was done by Ambedkar. Gandhi argued that the responsibility of doing away with untouchability rests with the Hindus rather than the Indian nation as such. He saw untouchability as un-Hindu. It has no sanction in the Hindu tradition.[23] In fact it was the greatest "blot on Hinduism." He uses various terms to denounce it. It is 'an excrescence', 'a bar sinister', 'a sin', 'untruth' etc. He felt that 'pollution' is the essence of untouchability and was in agreement with Ambedkar on it. He speculates on the reasons for its emergence without however being definitive about them: "When cow-protection became an article of faith with our ancestors, those who persisted on eating beef were excommunicated.... Social boycott was applied not only to the recalcitrant but their sins were visited upon their children also" (Gandhi 1921e, 375). Sometimes he advanced other reasons: "Untouchability is the product, not of the caste system but of the distinction of high and low that has crept into Hinduism and is corroding it" (Gandhi 1933a, 228).

He saw the untouchable throttled by ages through despicable treatment. He found that an untouchable not merely suffers from a complex of initial inequality, but there were few resources at his disposal to enable him to self-regulate his life:

> He has no mind or business he can call his own. Has a beast any mind or business but that of his masters? Has a Panchama a place he can call his own? He may not walk on the very roads he cleans and pays for by the sweat of his brow.
>
> (Gandhi 1924, 137)

Caste Hindus for no fault of the untouchable have taken away his honour, dignity and selfhood. He has been banished to the margins of society. His work has been considered degrading and so is he. He is outside the pale of the community. He argued that untouchables cannot be blamed for their condition: "The evils are a result, and not a cause, of untouchability" (Gandhi 1933b, 70). Reparation should come from the perpetrators of the crime.[24]

He felt that untouchability has poisoned Hinduism and is slowly undermining its very existence. A religion such as Hinduism could not have nurtured such a horrendous institution within its fold. Therefore, there is no sanction for untouchability in Hinduism; 'it is a device of Satan'. Untouchables are made to suffer for reasons of religion which are not the reasons of religion. Therefore, the struggle for the incorporation of untouchables into the Hindu fold as equals is also a struggle to reconstruct Hinduism. He thought that the practice of untouchability has been one of the major reasons for the degeneration of Hinduism and India as a whole. Therefore, if Hinduism has to redeem itself and a national bond to be forged, getting rid of untouchability was a sine qua non. He felt that existing institutions of Hinduism particularly Brahmanism and priest craft have played a major role in its perpetuation and they have done precious little to eradicate this evil.

> Let me if my voice will reach them, carry my voice to the Brahman priests who are opposing this belated reform. It is a painful fact, but it is a historical truth that priests who should have been the real custodians of religion have been instrumental in destroying the religion of which they have been custodians.

Hinduism has to be washed off from such Brahmanism. "Brahmanism that can tolerate untouchability, virgin widowhood, spoliation of virgins, stinks in my nostrils. It is a parody of Brahmanism" (Gandhi 1927a, 48). After the initial enthusiasm of removing this evil quickly, he frankly admits its widespread prevalence and agreed with Ambedkar that a large number of Hindus practiced untouchability on religious grounds: "Millions of Hindus still consider present day institution of untouchability as a God-made institution as old as the human race itself." Gandhi felt that Hinduism can survive only if Hindus succeed in removing this taint. "If Hinduism is to live, the work has to be done, however difficult and even hopeless it may appear to be" (Gandhi 1940, 283). Further, in his estimate, only if untouchability is removed can Hinduism become "a faith to live for and, if need be, to die for" (Ibid).

Gandhi felt that the prevailing filth and squalor in India is on account of ignoring and despising the Bhangi:

> Our villages have today become seats of dirt and insanitation and the villagers come to an early and untimely death. If only we had given due recognition to the status of the Bhangi as equal to that of the Brahmana as in fact and justice he deserves our village today no less than the inhabitants would have looked a picture of cleanliness and order.
>
> (Gandhi 1936b, 127)

The respect that society pays to the Bhangi is in consonant with the respect in which they hold his work. He is regarded as dirt and his work is regarded as dirty and everyone would like to live the furthest from him. There is no regard for him, nor for his work. Sanitation, therefore, remains one of the least attended activities. Early in his campaign he felt that if higher castes

> persist in suppressing them (untouchables) time must come when the untouchables will rebel against us, and may have recourse even to violent methods. I am trying my utmost to prevent such a catastrophe and so must we all do who believe untouchability to be a sin.
>
> (Gandhi 1925d, 393)

For Gandhi untouchability is such a social atrocity that he even attributes the Bihar earthquake of 1934 as a "visitation for the sin of untouchability" (Gandhi 1934, 165). When chastised by Rabindranath Tagore that his comment would exasperate the superstition already existing in India and 'God himself does not interfere' in the inexorableness of the universal law, Gandhi defended himself saying that there is an intimate link between all the elements of the cosmos and divine providence marks it all. Untouchability is an affront to such a balance. Even if his belief was ill-founded, it will have beneficial consequences.

Gandhi felt that the moral basis of India's freedom and independence from the British becomes weak when Indians treat the untouchables the way they did. He saw close parallels between European domination over colonies and upper caste domination over untouchables.

> We resent, and properly, the treatment meted out to our countrymen in South Africa. We are impatient to establish Swaraj. But we Hindus refuse to see the incongruity in treating a fifth of our co-religionists as worse than dogs.
>
> (Gandhi 1926, 399)

He sometimes felt that Indians deserve the kind of treatment meted out to them for their "crime of untouchability." He occasionally echoed the feeling that the segregation of Indians in the British empire is the retribution they paid for their segregation of the pariah. "Has not a just nemesis overtaken us for the crime of untouchability....We have segregated the pariah and we are in turn segregated in the British colonies"(Gandhi 1921a, 225). He warned his listeners that it is "the justest retribution meted out by God to us for our exploitation of a sixth of our own race and their studied degradation in the sacred name of religion." (Gandhi 1921e, 411). All the charges that Indians have against the British can easily be laid by the untouchables against the Indians (Gandhi 1921a). He rhetorically says, "Read Sahebs for Brahmins, and Indians for Panchamas, and see how you feel" (Gandhi 1921d, 44, 297). He felt that the repression that the British practised in India cannot be countered without Indians renouncing untouchability first. He felt, "What charge that we bring against Dyer and O'Dwyer may not others, and even our own people, lay at our door? We ought to purge ourselves of this pollution." (Gandhi 1921c, 44). He almost echoes Ambedkar's charge in 1940s that without redefining the place of the untouchables their lot in free India is likely to be worse than in British India:

> If we come to power with the stain of untouchability uneffaced, I am positive that the untouchables would be far worse under the swaraj than they are now, for the simple reason that our weaknesses and our failings would then be buttressed up by accession to power.
>
> (Gandhi 1954, 14)[25]

Gandhi brought his theory of varna centrally to bear on his considerations on untouchability. The untouchables are equal to everyone else, irrespective of their professions.[26] It was highly unreasonable if division of labour led to superiority and inferiority. In such a case the mother who does the work of cleaning the child should be treated a *Bhangi*:

> My mother was certainly a scavenger in as much as she cleaned me when I was a child but she did not on that account become an untouchable. Why then should a *Bhangi*, who renders similar necessary service be regarded as an untouchable?
>
> (Gandhi 1925b, 260)

In fact, such services deserve greater respect from us:

> Just as we revere our mother for the sanitary service that she renders us when we are infants and the greater her service the greater is our reverence for her, similarly, the *Bhangis* are entitled to our highest reverence for the sanitary service they perform for society.
>
> (Gandhi 1925a, 16)

Gandhi admonished that the doctrine of Karma cannot be drawn to justify the practice of untouchability:

> A man's Karma is responsible for what he is, they say. But my karma does not compel me to throw stones at a sinner. Religion is made to uplift and not to keep a man crushed under the weight of Karma.
>
> (Gandhi 1921d, 296)

Gandhi too felt that the failure of Indians to handle untouchability had wider ramifications. It had a deep bearing on the issue of forging Hindu–Muslim unity. The Muslims would naturally suspect Hindus if the latter are not prepared to treat their own coreligionists as equals. In his interview to Louis Fischer, to the latter's great surprise, he says, "The Hindu-Muslim question, in the final analysis, was an offshoot of untouchability question" (Iyer 579). Earlier he had argued that the 'touch-me-not-ism' had affected Hindu–Muslim relations (Gandhi 1940, 282–285). He told Fisher that if Hindus had succeeded in getting rid of untouchability, there would not be a communal problem. By implication, the cause for the partition of India had to be attributed to the continued prevalence of untouchability.

Gandhi felt that the continuation of untouchability among converts to non-Hindu religions can be done away with only when Hindus succeed in removing it from among themselves. "Not until untouchability is removed from Hinduism will the taint be removed from Harijans, no matter what label they adopt" (Gandhi 1936b, 214).[27] He did not think that conversion was an effective mechanism for the removal of untouchability.

Interfacing Ambedkar and Gandhi on caste

Some of Gandhi's most valiant attempts to engage in radical modes of interpretation of the shastras and religious instructions can be found in his writings related to untouchability. He felt that there are a lot of contradictions across sacred literature and particularly the smritis. There have been interpolations into the texts. Some of them are caught in the limitations of the context and times. Therefore, there cannot be a literal reading of the texts. Texts do not speak by themselves and someone who reads a sacred text must read it from within the tradition. He further argued that a tradition such as Hinduism, if it was wholly vacuous, could not have produced so many saints including those who condemned untouchability in no uncertain terms. He said "I apply the test of Truth and Ahimsa laid down by those very scriptures for interpretation. I reject what is inconsistent with that test and I appropriate all that is consistent with it" (Gandhi 1925c, 335). He felt that only reasonable deduction be drawn from the smritis since "the texts that may be contrary to known and accepted morality, more especially to the moral precepts enjoined in the smritis themselves, must be rejected as interpolations" (Gandhi 1926, 230). He further argued that "Whilst I hold that the ancients gave us a moral code which is not to be surpassed I am unable to subscribe to the doctrine of their infallibility in every detail" (Gandhi 1923, 230–231). According to him the reasonable should hold the ground against a mere assertion of authority: "We must test on the anvil of reason everything that is capable of being tested by it and reject that which does not satisfy it even though it may appear in an ancient garb" (Gandhi 1922, 231).

He admitted that the shastras are deeply mired in ritualism and the sanctions they invoke are meant to reproduce the continued subjection of untouchables. But he felt it is necessary to distinguish between the tree and its rotten branches. It is necessary that the trunk be kept intact so that it can throw up new shoots. One cannot uproot the tree itself.

> Some of the branches and leaves I admit are rotten. Let us have the pruning knife and lop-off those diseased branches, but let us not lay the axe at the root....If you keep the root intact and keep on watering it, it will some day grow into a fine big tree.
>
> (Gandhi 1927b, 298)

Gandhi's reading of varna, caste and untouchability, and their mutual relationships have been challenged by many, particularly Ambedkar: Ambedkar agreed with Gandhi that texts do not speak and all readings are informed by interpretation. But he distinguished between popular religious beliefs and practices that take overboard an embedded authority of the text, and a different reading of the same by someone which does not translate itself into appropriate beliefs and practices. While Gandhi may disown a text or a belief as interpolation, people may continue to adhere to them as authentic. This has been the case with caste which Hindus consider as religiously ordained. Ambedkar argued that Gandhi's reading of tradition in favour of equality will have little bearing on the inherited system of graded social inequality in India. He thought that the teachings of saints and holy men who proclaimed equality of the devotee before the Lord had little impact on the caste divide. According to him Gandhi's interpretation of varnadharma as earning one's livelihood by following the occupation of one's forefathers upholds the caste system frontally (Ambedkar 1991, 290). Gandhi's interpretation of varna would confine people to their inherited professions even when they are indisposed to them, and even when their talents and skills suggest a change. To maintain and reproduce a system based on varna as its foundation would call for pigeon-holing people on a scale never heard before, calling for the most extensive authoritarian rule as its inevitable outcome. The low and despised are deluded by Gandhi "into accepting their misfortunes by presenting them as the best of good fortunes" (Ibid, 291). Gandhi's attempt to morally ennoble low professions and confining their members to them was nothing but leaving them wholly at the mercy of the traditional dominant castes without a collateral binding duty.

> To preach that poverty is good for the Sudra and for none else, to preach that scavenging is good for untouchables and for none else and to make them accept these, means impositions as voluntary purposes of life........ and a cruel joke on the helpless classes which none but Mr. Gandhi can perpetuate with equanimity and impunity.
>
> (Ambedkar 1991, 293)

Gandhi, of course, rejected Ambedkar's reading of the shastras, and charged him of "picking out the texts of doubtful authenticity and value and the state of degraded Hindus who are no fit specimens of the faith they woefully misrepresent" (Gandhi 1936a, 127).

Concluding remarks

It is remarkable that in spite of the sharp disagreements between Gandhi and Ambedkar there is much in common between them with regard to the categories of analysis and the significance they assigned to them: dharma and religion, caste, varna, untouchability, the shastras, tradition etc. These categories became central in their considerations of social reforms, swaraj and the national-democratic project. This marks them off from a large number of other thinkers of the period who wanted to provide a social analysis in different and/or 'modernist' categories. Gandhi eventually came to deeply suspect caste as a mode of organizing society and thought that Hinduism has little to do with it (Gandhi 1936a). He held on to varna, but imparted to the institution, an entirely new connotation. Both Ambedkar and Gandhi reject untouchability as inhuman, and call for a sustained movement against it. Gandhi did not criticize Ambedkar for the significance that he assigned to caste. Gandhi had other objections to *Annihilation* (Ambedkar 1978b, 81–85) but was equally concerned with the implications of caste and untouchability for the conception of Hinduism, swaraj and human equality.[28]

Ambedkar draws attention to the regulatory and 'disciplining' role that caste plays in social relations, and the kind of ranked order it institutionalizes, allowing little space for human agency, creativity, and democracy to thrive. It is interesting that Gandhi too thought that caste played a similar role, although in his case in a positive sense, by limiting wants and reach and keeping human strivings and desires within limits. Gandhi did not think that prohibition of interdining, intermarriage etc. was necessarily a limiting attribute of caste. He thought that the principle of 'high and low' was not characteristic of the caste system but affected it due to the prevalence of untouchability. He argued that limiting wants and desires enhances swaraj, and leaves one free to pursue goals distinctive to human self. But the way castes mobilized themselves made him convinced that they were acting as closed corporations, aggrandizing their own interests. While there is a meeting point between Gandhi and Ambedkar on this count, they differed on their approaches to the issue. For Ambedkar wider and more expansive social interactions helped to reinforce democracy and were conducive to the pursuit of self-perfection. Gandhi thought that limiting human wants and placing excess resources and abilities to subserve common good was the true measure of swaraj.

Both Ambedkar and Gandhi agreed that it is *we* who read texts, and *interpret* them. But they advanced the distinct criteria of reading and interpreting religious texts, and Gandhi argued that Ambedkar's understanding of Hinduism and the interpretation of its hallowed texts were hermeneutically flawed, and was an attempt to judge Hinduism by employing criteria external to it. Ambedkar's rejoinder to this criticism as we have outlined above is complex (Rodrigues 2011). He sought to know from Gandhi that if he had a different Hinduism he should demonstrate it in social practice; that there were few to purchase his version of Hinduism; and why should those in the margins, degraded and low, bear the burden of *his* varna utopia. Why should the right to be human be bartered at the altar of his religious fancies? Gandhi, however, was battling on two fronts: defence of Hinduism of his conception, and a swarajist project that would not fall into the lap of a liberal–modernist trap.

Interestingly, both Gandhi and Ambedkar regard equality as a central value to be fostered although they disagree as to how this value has to be fostered. Ambedkar denies that birth should necessarily be the basis of a person's occupation. It is this principal of birth that has been the basis of caste and untouchability. The untouchable is not merely polluted but is the bearer of inherited pollution. Mothers might be doing cleaning tasks towards their children but they can wash and purify themselves. The untouchables cannot. They are born with the stigma of pollution and they will die with it. Taking human agency seriously means, the choice of occupations should be left to the concerned agents. To the contrary, Gandhi argued that birth should be the basis of the occupations one pursues. He connects it to his other concerns of keeping the material requirements to the minimum, avoiding competition and conflict on account of them and freeing man to the pursuit of higher goals. Ambedkar, however, sees such relations of labour bound up with the denial of freedom, appreciation of worth, and exploitation and domination. Gandhi asserts the dignity of all labour and, by instilling it in every kind of labour, he feels the superiority and inferiority ascribed to caste gradations can be undercut. The latter is a moral defect and it has to be rectified by reconstituting a moral agency—a new set of attitudes and values. Ambedkar emphasizes on changes in social relations and not merely in imparting new meanings to existing relations.

However, what Gandhi considered as the degeneration of Hinduism is seen by Ambedkar as its essential characteristics. For Ambedkar there cannot be an impulse for equality from within the central tenets and institutions of Hinduism. It can come only from a radical reorganization of Hinduism or from outside it. To the contrary, Gandhi argued, that the central tenets of Hinduism and its institutions uphold equality. Reforms are required to shed the dross, rather than reinvent Hinduism.

There has been an argument in recent years that under colonialism caste came to be shored up to the centre-stage, made into the anchor of the religious beliefs and practices of Hindus, and led to the exclusion of other relations that were so significant in shaping India's complex socio-religious reality. It suggests that the colonial state came to play a major role in redefining social relations in general and caste relations in particular. Thereby, India was marked off as distinct from the rest. As per this view, much of the nationalist lore in India too could not remain immune to the whipped up projection of centrality of caste in determining social relations in India, and the dynamics of Indian society that it rerouted shelving off alternative ways of perceiving and engaging with India.[29] Such an account, highly exaggerated, even if accepted as true, does not affect the concerns discussed above. These concerns explore the implications to social relations informed by caste, and to the extent informed by it. It is quite possible that someone could argue that the impact of caste on social relations was limited or uneven. In fact, Ambedkar himself suggests such a conjecture in *Castes in India*, saying that caste characterized as endogamy was derivative for non-Brahmanical social groups. If we reconstruct the picture of India from the frame of the latter, caste would acquire a very different significance!

There are those who have argued that democracy and a secular polity have sustained themselves in India due to the existence of castes, which do not lend themselves to be consolidated into a social bloc that can be pitted against minorities. The existence of castes facilitates other feasible electoral alternatives. In terms of sustaining formal and procedural democracy, Ambedkar would partly agree with such a reading. But then he would say that it is not a democracy worth cherishing in the longer run. Democracy demands a 'social endosmosis' involving a specific kind of social bonding, reach, social concerns and ways of life. It cannot merely rest on the stratagem of '*modus vivendi*.'

Notes

1 At the same time it has to be noted that the caste question was made central to the nationalist project by not only the likes of Ramaswami Naicker Periyar but a few within the Indian National Congress. See, Panikkar (1933).

2 These other writings include Ambedkar (1978c, 1991, 1994, 2014a, b, 2019).

3 Ambedkar quotes Ketkar approvingly to say,

> Whether a family is racially Aryan or Dravidian was a question which never troubled the people of India, until foreign scholars came and began to draw the line. The colour of the skin had long ceased to be a matter of importance.
> (Ketkar, 82) quoted in Ambedkar (1978a, 22)

Ambedkar repeats this argument of intermixture of races in India (see Ambedkar 1978b, 48). He refers to the work of Bhandarkar, (1911), in support.

4 For a representative writing in this regard, (see Coupland 1944).

5 Such a conjecture is repeated again in Ambedkar (1978b, 48).

6 The scholars on caste whose work Ambedkar cites are Senart, Nesfield, H. Risley,. Ketkar and Denzil Ibbetson, all well-known names during his time.

7 The nationalist ethnography is replete with such formulations from early on See Ramabai (2000, 133).

8 For the difference between such imitation, and M.N. Srinivas' concept of 'Sanskritization' see Rege (2013).

9 It is important to point out that A.A. Goldenweizer at whose seminar Ambedkar read this paper was an exponent of the cultural diffusion theory himself.

10 I feel that these two-fold distinctions are not recognized by Rege (2013). Similarly, while Ilaiah (2019) rightly recognizes an autonomous culture among Dalit Bahujans, he fails to note the impact caste patriarchy has on them.

11 See Dirks (2002)

12 See Preface to the Third Edition, *Annihilation of Caste* (Ambedkar 1978b, 26). It may be good to place this text in context. It was written for a Lahore-based body called the *Jaat-Paat Todak Sangh*, an organization of upper caste Hindu reformers who had made eradication of caste system their primary objective. Hindu consolidation was one of the principal objectives that Hindu leaders were pursuing in Punjab against the perceived threat of a Muslim majority in the province for years. Under the auspices of the Arya Samaj, they resorted to the *shuddi* practice to bring back untouchables and converts from Hinduism back to the Hindu fold. While many members of the Sangh were in favour of

social reforms or even removal of the caste system, few of them thought that their endeavour called for an attack on the foundations of Hinduism such as the Vedas and the Shastras. The *Annihilation* however stretched itself to include the latter. Given Ambedkar's refusal to confine himself to the agenda of the *Sangh*, the lecture eventually had to be called off.

13 For Ambedkar, social reformers included the likes of Justice Mahadeo Ranade and Gopalkrishna Gokhale who defended the necessity of Social Conference alongside political freedom.

14 Ambedkar uses a more inclusive category called 'socialists', rather than 'Marxists' or 'communists' for consideration. At the time this essay was written, the Communist Party of India had begun to speak about People's Front, following a resolution to that effect by the Comintern, and the Congress Socialist Party, formed in 1934, was working within the Indian National Congress. In other words, the term socialist had a broader, encompassing meaning in India.

15 While criticizing the socialists for their one-track mind, Ambedkar at the same expressed his partisanship with socialism although he thought that such a project can be pursued only by taking into account the differences that mark social classes.

16 Later on, he was to argue that nationalism called for erasing certain memories and reinforcing others. For a detailed account, see Ambedkar (2014a, 29–39).

17 This is a position closely associated with Dewey's conception of democracy.

18
> All reform consists in a change in the notions, sentiment and mental attitudes of the people towards men and things. It is common experience that certain names become associated with certain notions and sentiments, which determine a person's attitude towards men and things. The names Brahmin, Kshatriya, Vaishya and Shudra are names which are associated with a definite and fixed notion in the mind of every Hindu.... that notion is that of a hierarchy based on birth.
>
> Ibid, 59

19 This conflict is elaborated by Ambedkar in several of his other writings. See for example, Ambedkar (1946). Also see Ambedkar (1987, 3–94).

20 It met with huge protests and the measure could not be carried out, proving in a way Ambedkar's own apprehensions with regard to the limits to which a Hindu social reformer could go, however hallowed he might regard his cause.

21 This excerpt is from a speech that was given at a public meeting (Rajapalayam 1927).

22 For Gandhi, "the law of life" is "nothing but the law of conservation of energy" (Gandhi 1937, 5a).

23 Gandhi's assertion that untouchability has no sanction in the tradition was met with strong opposition from the *sanatanists*. Gandhi did not go about disproving their objections through an alternative scholarly account in the same vein. He felt that truth and non-violence are the two supreme attributes of Hinduism. Such a religion could not be a party to the inhuman suffering imposed on untouchables. Occasionally, however, he refers to events and episodes in the tradition, generally construed as practices of untouchability, but on a closer look did not seem to be so. For instance, a boatman, generally regarded as an untouchable today, took Rama across the Ganga in his boat. Gandhi argues that there is nothing to suggest that Lord Rama was defiled by the boatman. Further God is addressed among Hindus as the 'purifier of the polluted' (1921b, 43). Besides, Gandhi wondered, how a religion which

has been considerate towards the cow as to establish its worship could countenance a cruel and inhuman boycott of human beings, as reflected in the practice of untouchability (1921f, 375).

24 Gandhi is deeply suspicious of the motivations of the leaders of Muslims and Christians and the British power with respect to the untouchables. Muslim representations at this stage had suggested that untouchables cannot be included within Hindus and they had equal right to bring them to their fold. From the later part of the 19th century Christian missions succeeded in converting large number of untouchables. Gandhi, therefore, is very cautious of the concern of Christian leaders towards the Untouchables. In the Vaikom Satyagraha he asks George Joseph not to fast in favour of throwing open the road leading to the Gurvayoor temple to the untouchables. When missionary leaders met him to discuss how they can help him in getting rid of untouchability he asks them to keep off saying that untouchability is a problem within Hinduism and their intervention is likely to lead to fishing in troubled waters. It was Gandhi's intervention which removes decisively the kinds of ambivalences that existed about untouchables among Hindus. Gandhi also argued that awakened Hinduism is quite capable of abolishing the sin of untouchability from its midst.

25 In fact, this charge came to be echoed in 1950s and the Commissioner of Scheduled Castes and Scheduled Tribes had to step in to say that it was far too exaggerated. See Report 1958–59.

26 He sometimes equated the untouchables with the Shudras.

> I have asked that a *Panchama* should be regarded as a Shudra, because I hold that there is no warrant for the belief, in a fifth caste. A *Panchama* does the work of a Shudra and he is therefore naturally classified as such when he ceases to be regarded as a *Panchama*.
>
> (Gandhi 1927b, 298)

27 Gandhi overtly takes this position after Ambedkar had announced at Yeola that he had decided to leave Hinduism for good.

28 In his rejoinder to Ambedkar, Gandhi is exclusively concerned about defending Hinduism from his attack, rather than commenting on the pernicious impact that caste has on India's democratic aspirations and strivings towards nationhood.

29 One of the influential works in this regard is Dirks (2002).

References

Ambedkar, B.R. 1946 *Who Were the Shudras? How They Came to be the Fourth Varna in Indo-Aryan Society*? Bombay: Thacker & Co.

——— 1978a "Caste in India." In *Babasaheb Ambedkar, Writings and Speeches (BAWS)*, Vol. 1, edited by Vasant Moon, 3–22. Bombay: Government of Maharashtra.

——— 1978b "Annihilation of Caste." In *Babasaheb Ambedkar, Writings and Speeches (BAWS)*, Vol. 1, edited by Vasant Moon, 23–96. Bombay: Government of Maharashtra.

——— 1978c "Ranade, Jinnah and Gandhi." In *Babasaheb Ambedkar, Writings and Speeches*, Vol. 1, edited by Vasant Moon, 205–240. Bombay: Government of Maharashtra.

——— 1987 "Philosophy of Hinduism." In *Babasaheb Ambedkar, Writings and Speeches*, Vol. 3, edited by Vasant Moon 3–94. Bombay: Government of Maharashtra.
——— 1991 *Babasaheb Ambedkar Writing and Speeches*, Vol. IX, edited by Vasant Moon. New Delhi: Dr. Ambedkar Foundation.
——— 1994 *Babasaheb Ambedkar Writing and Speeches*, Vol. XIII, edited by Vasant Moon. New Delhi: Dr. Ambedkar Foundation.
——— 2014a *Babasaheb Ambedkar Writing and Speeches*, Vol. VIII, edited by Vasant Moon. New Delhi: Dr. Ambedkar Foundation.
——— 2014b *Babasaheb Ambedkar Writing and Speeches*, Vol. XI, edited by Vasant Moon. New Delhi: Dr. Ambedkar Foundation.
——— 2019 *Babasaheb Ambedkar Writing and Speeches*, Vol. VII. New Delhi: Dr. Ambedkar Foundation.
Bhandarkar, D.R. 1968 (1911) "Foreign Elements in the Hindu Population." *Journal of Ancient Indian History I*, 267–328.
Coupland, Reginald 1944 *The Indian Problem*, Vol. II, 1833–1935. London: Oxford University Press.
Dirks, Nicholas B. 2002 *Castes of Mind*. Delhi: Permanent Black.
Gandhi, M.K. 1920 *Young India* December 8, 1920. *Collected (CWMG)*, Vol. 22. https://www.gandhiashramsevagram.org/gandhi-literature/collected-works-of-mahatma-gandhi-volume -1-to-98.php.
——— 1921a *Young India* January 19, 1921, CWMG 22, 224–226.
——— 1921b *Young India* April 27, 1921, CWMG 23, 41–47.
——— 1921c *Young India* May 5, 1921, CWMG 23, 41–47.
——— 1921d *Young India* September 22, 1921, CWMG 24, 282–297.
——— 1921e *Young India* October 10, 1921, CWMG 24, 370–375, 406–412.
——— 1922 *Young India* March 23, 1922, CWMG 38, 230–231.
——— 1923 *Young India* March 23, 1923, CWMG 38, 230–231.
——— 1924 *Young India* June 12, 1924, CWMG 28, 136–138.
——— 1925a *Young India* January 22, 1925, CWMG 30, 14–18.
——— 1925b *Young India* February 26, 1925, CWMG 30, 258–261.
——— 1925c *Young India* August 27, 1925, CWMG 32, 335–340
——— 1925d *Young India* September 10, 1925, CWMG 32, 392–394
——— 1926 *Young India* September 9, 1926, CWMG 36, 230–231.
——— 1927a *Young India* September 15, 1927, CWMG 40, 44–49.
——— 1927b *Young India* November 3, 1927, CWMG 40, 294–298.
——— 1927c *Young India* November 24, 1927, CWMG 40, 478–489.
——— 1933a *Harijan* February 11, 1933, CWMG 59, 227–229.
——— 1933b *Harijan* March 18, 1933, CWMG 60, 69–71.
——— 1933c *Harijan* February 11, 1933, CWMG 59, 227–229
——— 1934 *Harijan* February 16, 1934, CWMG 63, 164–166.
——— 1936a *Harijan* July 18, 1936, CWMG 69, 226–227.
——— 1936b *Harijan* November 28, 1936, CWMG 70, 126–128.
——— 1937 *Harijan* March 6, 1937, CWMG 71, 1–5.
——— 1940 *Harijan* June 1, 1940, CWMG 78, 282–285
——— 1954 *Removal of Untouchability*. 14. Bombay: Directorate of Publicity.
Iyer, Raghavan. 1986 *The Moral and Political Writings of Mahatma Gandhi*. Vol. 2. Oxford: Clarendon.

Ketkar, Shridhar V. 1909 *The History of Caste in India*. New York: Taylor and Carpenter.
Panikkar, K.M. 1933 *Caste and Democracy*. London: Leonard and Virginia Woolf.
Rajapalayam 1927 "Speech." *The Hindu*, October 6, 1927.
Ramabai, Pandita 2000 "The High Caste Hindu Woman." In *Through Her Own Words: Selected Works*, edited by Meera Kosambi, 129–180. New Delhi: Oxford University Press.
Rege, Sharmila 2013 *Against the Madness of Manu*. Delhi: Navayana.
Report of the Commissioner for Scheduled Castes and Scheduled Tribes (RCSCST), 1958–59.
Rodrigues, Valerian. January 8, 2011 "Reading Texts and Traditions: The Ambedkar-Gandhi Debate." *Economic and Political Weekly*, Vol. XLVI, No. 2: 56–66.

Part IV

RELIGION, MODERNITY AND NAVAYĀNA BUDDHISM

11

SOCIAL SOLIDARITY OR INDIVIDUAL PERFECTION

Conceptions of religion in Ambedkar and Radhakrishnan

Kanchana Mahadevan[1]

> ...[I]t is an error to look upon religion as a matter which is individual, private and personal...The correct view is that religion like language is social...
>
> (Ambedkar 2002d, 225)

Ambedkar's transition from Hinduism to Buddhism is a prescient point to examine the potential of his philosophy of religion that emphasizes social morality. By developing his concept of religion through a critique of caste Hinduism, his critical approach contrasts with Radhakrishnan's subtle advocacy of caste Hinduism. Ambedkar's Buddhism, articulated through a critique of both Hinduism and Buddhism, can be extended to other religions (including Hinduism) in its quest for egalitarianism and tolerance. Unlike Radhakrishnan's view of religion as self-perfection (a widely held opinion), Ambedkar's notion connects religion to critique. On a Kantian note, such a critique is positive in that it examines the constructive role of religion; but such a positive critique becomes possible only when critique in its negative sense is also adopted, the latter having destroyed centuries-old inegalitarian dogmas and rituals. This chapter examines Ambedkar's "religion within the boundaries of mere reason"[2] as especially relevant in the contemporary context of the rising religious identities and conflicts.

Caste as the foundation of religion: Radhakrishnan

The popular film *Aarakshan* (Jha 2011)[3] encapsulates Ambedkar's neglect by mainstream India. Despite gesturing towards the problem of caste identity on a larger national canvas,[4] its focus is privileged caste heroism. The image of Radhakrishnan—literally as a picture in the office of a college principal—looms over its erratic depiction of Dalit struggle for recognition and justice (Sen 2011). Consequently, it glosses over Radhakrishnan's justification of caste and Ambedkar's caste criticism. In the film, the eponymous school principal, Prabhakar Anand, whose patronage towards oppressed castes is the vehicle for social transformation, represents Radhakrishnan. In a rare gesture, the film has a famous actor playing a Dalit professor Deepak Kumar, who appears to have agency. Yet, the latter comes to naught because he depends on the privileged caste principal Anand, representing the modern-day Radhakrishnan. *Aarakshan*, its title notwithstanding, does not examine the social persistence of caste hierarchy and the arduous struggles against it.[5] Moreover, the film is paternalistic in that it replaces the collective voices of oppressed castes with that of just one individual, namely Kumar, who is under the moral guidance of the upper caste principal's intuitive knowledge. With the figure of Radhakrishnan, the film is also enmeshed in patriarchal strands in projecting a man as an ideal aspiration. It, thus, reflects prevalent social attitudes to caste, gender and religion. As Sen observes, Radhakrishnan might not have a direct influence on Indians at the political or even popular level,[6] but his view of caste as division for labour that was "class by birth, but not class by heredity" (Minor 397) is still accepted at the mainstream level.[7] One might add that the sexual division of labour between men and women is also similarly endorsed. So is Radhakrishnan's related notion of religion as a solitary experience (personal or indirect) of the divine (1932, 84–126).

It might be argued that Radhakrishnan critiqued the Hindu justification of caste as a "scandal" (1967, 27) with no place in modern India.[8] He also objected to caste distinctions being based on pollution and purity (Minor 1997, 387) by reinterpreting caste. Caste for Radhakrishnan, is not determined by birth or heredity, but is rather the outcome of aptitude, effort and character (1927, 127–30). In addition, he concedes to caste mobility, whereby someone born a *Sudra* can move to a higher level through conduct (1967, 131–2). Radhakrishnan's reconstructed notion of caste hierarchy attempts to enable all human beings to develop their abilities in the modern context. He adapts the traditional Hindu notion of caste rigidity to liberal notions of class, mobility and division of labour.[9] He thus believes that caste-based work in society is not hereditary, but founded on pre-given functions in an organically knit society. The functions in turn arise from individual pre-given psychological temperaments. Thus, "The four castes represent men of thought, men (sic) of action, men of feeling, and others in whom none of these is highly developed" (Radhakrishnan 1927, 111). He notes that all four traits—or *varnas*—are needed in society, and moreover, these traits can be present in specific individuals simultaneously. Moreover, individuals can change their caste position provided they have the appropriate temperamental backing. Caste implies action that arises from specific characteristics over which individuals have no control.[10] Radhakrishnan's modern version[11] upholds that caste was not injurious when it originated, but became rigid with time (1927, 93, 106–7, 127). He justifies the notion of caste as *varna* as the basis of a graded social order united through a harmonious performance of diverse functions.

Radhakrishnan's account of caste fits in with his spiritual conception of society as an organic whole with interrelated parts each of which contribute to the unity of purpose (1927, 93–95; Minor 388). For him such a notion of spiritual society is inclusive as native caste groups absorbed those who came from outside India, each caste group had a functional role in a larger totality. He upholds the four-fold caste structure as integral to social development; he understands caste to accommodate differences of culture and race, as well as, harmonize social relations through fellowship (Radhakrishnan 1927, 104–5; Minor 395–6). He does not perceive any domination in such a social order. Moreover, Radhakrishnan maintains that each tier in the caste system is equally important for the functioning of the whole. Thus, for Radhakrishnan, caste is founded on human aptitude, which all human beings have an equal opportunity to develop into character (1927, 111–2). Each individual, on this view, had to develop his or her capacity to contribute to the progress of society as a whole. As Minor observes, Radhakrishnan integrates caste with modern ideals of equality and democracy (397), wherein he defines democracy as the right to develop one's endowment (1927, 116). He also advocates a modern conception of religion based on these ideals.

Radhakrishnan does connect religion to the social domain, critiquing the indifference of religious practitioners to vulnerability and suffering, especially in what he terms as the context of the 'East' (1967, 29). He upholds religion as an individual's inclination towards the spiritual, which is realized through human perfection (1967, 42, 50). Since it is a binding force, such a religion, according to him, can be realized on the basis of caste-based social relations. Radhakrishnan discerns contemporary Hinduism as a move in this direction, a continuous "process" (1927, 129) of renewal and change through interface between tradition and the contemporary. He names Upanishadic commentators and saint poets as diverse contributors to its ethos. There is for Radhakrishnan "a common clay of human nature" (1927, 120) that is nevertheless differentiated as wise and foolish or high and low. These differences are the outcome of varied human abilities towards self-realization. Radhakrishnan discerns caste as ideally working towards a common human purpose of social cooperation, despite admittedly degenerating into segregation and untouchability (1927, 93–130). He sees it as fulfilling social needs through the development of human nature that constraints the framework of human potential and action. For Radhakrishnan, by developing one's nature from perspectives as diverse as artist, worker or saint, one gives one's bit to society by practising unity in diversity (1927, 127). He upholds what he terms as such a Hindu[12] socio-religious order as allowing each individual to focus on realizing his or her inner temperament to spontaneously harmonize with society. It does not require its members to commune in solidarity with each other; instead its focus is on individual perfection that comes from the spiritual self of all beings as one. The social aspect of caste merely facilitates such spirituality. Radhakrishnan's notion of religion as self-realization and perfection of an individual's temperament is rooted in the culturally specific idea of caste.

The seeming flexibility in his account of caste and religion notwithstanding, Radhakrishnan's egalitarianism remains partial. His reconstruction of caste, which divides human beings by ability, is as problematic as the traditional caste system's division by birth. Moreover, it is paradoxical considering his premise of the "common clay of human nature." His idea of society as based on four pre-given graded tasks actively encourages inequality. Human beings are divided into thought, action and feeling and those with lesser capacity for the same. Radhakrishnan's social distinction is not merely pluralism, as it revers those with greater abilities and powers of self-reflection as the three privileged castes (1927, 120). Moreover, it restricts the diversity of the social to a graded hierarchy of four with demarcated boundaries. Radhakrishnan does not engage with the possibility of simultaneously occupying two or three or four social locations, whereby a thinker is also simultaneously a labourer. In addition, his notion of mobility within such a rigid caste order is predicated upon the chance factor of given human tendencies. On such a view, society does not have the responsibility of cultivating aptitudes that encourage caste mobility. Radhakrishnan's version of religion reproduces this lack of social solidarity inherent to his account of caste; individuals develop their abilities within their preordained caste order. Radhakrishnan regards perfection, rather than social solidarity as the goal of religion.

For him, religion fulfills a personal quest for spirituality in a secular scientific modern world where it does not have space in the public domain. He laments that the religious impulse was fast receding among human beings as "untenable" (1932, 50) in being subject to skepticism on a global scale. He discerns the rise of communism, divisive religious boundaries and moral ineffectiveness as contributing to suspicion over religion (1932, 13–51). In the Indian context, he identifies the prioritization of scientific temperament, freedom from material impoverishment and political tutelage as grounds for departing from religion. He proclaims that the need for religion has to be reaffirmed to restore creative sense among human beings. This requires turning to prophets, rather than priests, whose personal experience and vision can inspire the resurrection of faith in religion (1932, 89). For Radhakrishnan, the very need for religion can be seen in the various substitutes that are offered for it such as, naturalistic atheism, agnosticism, skepticism, humanism, pragmatism, modernism, authoritarianism and the lack of a spiritual note (1932, 52–83). Thus, he upholds religion as a personal experience and activity that unifies all other human activities and transcends them towards spiritual life (1932, 88). All faiths are founded on intuitive experience underlining the search for the eternal.[13]

With this individualistic approach, Radhakrishnan attempts to address the vacuum created by the neglect of religion in modern political systems such as capitalism and socialism. In the context of this vacuum, religion has entered mass culture and the public sphere with renewed vigour.[14] This persistence of religious identity reveals the need for assessing its role in social life following Ambedkar; religion cannot simply be restricted to a private pursuit of belief facilitated by a caste order in Radhakrishnan's spirit. The idea that religion is a solitary quest for personal happiness or spirituality needs to be interrogated and so does its relation to social hierarchy. As Ambedkar's critique reveals, such a view has encouraged the inegalitarianism of caste and gender in the Indian context.

Critique of caste as a foundation of religion: Ambedkar

Ambedkar questions the "...assumption that religion is a purely personal matter... It is supernatural. It has nothing to do with the social..." (2002d). This view upheld by Radhakrishnan tends to homogenize religion and locate it on a transcendent plane. Radhakrishnan's stress on the intuitive authority of prophets merely substitutes for the supremacy of the priest. The pursuit of the personal takes place in social and historical contexts of religious institutions and communities. Radhakrishnan implicitly acknowledges as much by rooting his notion of personal religion in the socio-religious context of caste. Consequently, as Ambedkar argues, religion becomes a source of power in society, through which the freedom of one group of people is controlled by the other (1990, 44). Such a conception of religion differs from ideal religion or *Dhamma*. For Ambedkar the former is theistic religion, while *Dhamma* is religion based on morality.[15] In theistic religion, one's relationship to a transcendent entity is central, rendering morality as secondary. According to Ambedkar, *Dhamma*, on the other hand, necessitates egalitarian moral relation between human beings as essential. Religion as understood by Radhakrishnan was based on the God–human relation or *jīva–Brahman* as asocial and personal; it could consequently, accommodate and endorse caste and inequality at a practical–social level. Ambedkar notes that religious freedom is not evenly accessible to all, given the internal hierarchies of power, such as caste, which afflict certain religions. Again, given religious diversity, the external strife between religions too can intrude into the personal space of spirituality.

Radhakrishnan's personal space of spirituality separates religion from morality. The lack of equality both within certain religions and between them indicates that Radhakrishnan's notion of spiritual enjoyment would become irresponsible, if the aspect of morality is not taken into account. Thus, acknowledging the social and public leads to the moral dimension of religion.[16] Hence, as Ambedkar outlines, religion is a social practice/institution that inculcates "spiritual values" (2002b, 189), which in turn are moral principles that bind human beings in a fellowship (2002b, 174–5). Thus, "*Maitri* or fellowship towards all must never be abandoned. One owes it even to one's enemy" (Ambedkar 2002b, 174). Ambedkar comprehends religion as a moral force based on the affective dimension of togetherness that unites human beings and captures its etymological root of *religare*. Thus, it is not a personal relationship between the human being and a divine force as Radhakrishnan assumes. He argues that such a quest for moral togetherness cannot be equated with material well-being. These values need not be "other-worldly" nor need they breed a complacence with injustices like poverty (2002b, 187–8).[17]

The very existence of caste in Hindu religion shows that it is neither personal nor metaphysical, but social. From its social point of view, according to Ambedkar, Hinduism is a division of people from the same race into hierarchical and watertight castes (Ambedkar 1990, 47–48). Thus, just as one needs to investigate the dynamics between different religions in the context of religious pluralism, Ambedkar upholds the need to investigate the internal divide within the fold of Hinduism. Thus, caste is not a way of accommodating or harmonizing racial difference, as Radhakrishnan claims. A social harmony that is grounded on caste suppresses conflict through forced assimilation and labour. Ambedkar's critique of the *varna* system reveals that social stability could be maintained through caste only because it bred a sense of fatalism, stagnation, rivalry and fear of reprisal against social change.[18] He concludes that the *varna* system is both impracticable and harmful (1990, 68).

In light of Ambedkar's argument, caste cannot be reconstructed through Radhakrishnan's apparently benign lens. Ambedkar points out that caste came into existence in India, much after the co-mingling of races; it cannot therefore, be understood as based on heredity and eugenics (1990, 50–51). Rather caste is a hierarchical form of an exploitative Hindu social, economic and political order (1990, 52). Ambedkar maintains that one would have to unlearn caste or *jati* relations of several centuries to reach the idealized state of *varna* by merit. Further, caste is not just division of labour, it is a division of labourers—and an exploitative and interlinked one at that (1990, 47–48). This division is not based on choice but on tasks preordained in scriptures. Caste-based tasks are not just descriptive but also normative, in that manual labour is degraded and stigmatized by Hinduism (Ambedkar 1990, 49). Therefore, political inclusiveness and economic well-being mandate abolishing the caste character of Hindu religion in the social domain.

Radhakrishnan's harmony that is based on pre-ordained social roles is critiqued by Ambedkar who argues that Hindu society for him is a collection of stratified and isolated castes (1990, 52–54). The latter he upholds have a deep-rooted "warring" and "anti-social spirit" (1990, 55). He links the awareness of caste identity to the persistence of old rivalries inhibiting social solidarity (Ambedkar 1990, 56). Since these castes do not have a common social ground, Hindu society does not exist as a cooperative endeavour that brings people together. Ambedkar is well aware that caste segregation is a socio-psychological mode of embodiment and not just a "physical object like a wall of bricks" (1990, 83) that can be simply razed to create social equality. He also notes responding to Radhakrishnan that given caste Hinduism's segregated mode, "the mere fact" (Ambedkar 2014, 19) of it persisting through centuries does not imply that it has qualitative value. One has to critique the manner in which Hinduism has survived without solidarity. One has to critique its social and psychological dimensions in a sustained way as physical proximity alone does not constitute the lived relation of cooperative quest for the spiritual. Each caste is separated from every other—and each goes about performing the rites and rituals as it deems on its own. Such parallel activity, argues Ambedkar, cannot be termed as commonly shared. "The caste system prevents common activity and by preventing common activity it has prevented the Hindus from becoming a society with unified life and a consciousness of its own being" (Ambedkar 1990, 54). He further notes that the absence of a common Hindu consciousness or lack of public spirit hinders it from participating in morality or politics. Common activity requires communication and dialogue that takes place among equals. Hence, for such communication to be possible within Hinduism and between diverse religions, the oppressive feature of caste must be eradicated.

Ambedkar observes that Hindus cannot become humanitarian as long as they adhere to caste. An individual cannot enter the Hindu fold voluntarily as though it were a club, as membership in caste is based on *shuddhi* or 'purity" of birth. One can extend this line of argument to Radhakrishnan's notion of temperaments on which he founds caste; a temperament is an accidental matter of birth. Thus, there is no possibility for an outsider to adopt the Hindu set of beliefs and practices as a convert (1990, 60). This has hindered Hindu caste groups from cooperatively associating with each other through *Sanghas*. Moreover, Hinduism is at its core a highly individualist religion, which has discouraged the "associated form of life" unlike Islam or Sikhism (61). It prevents openness and tolerance towards those who are different. Such a dialogue leads to adopting those who are different as one's own, living in their midst with a sense of fellowship and "in short loving" (57) the other. Ambedkar argues that caste has prevented Hindus from engaging in any such acts with members of other caste groups or indigenous tribes (56–57). Hence, he appeals for a fundamental change to take place at the level of social relations so that Hindus can unlearn caste (68).

Ambedkar indicts Hindu *dharma* for offering rules of segregation that are ritualistic, social, economic and political (95–96). Rules centre around groups to merely prescribe and proscribe, without offering reasons. They demand an unthinking obedience to the "law or at best legalized class-ethics" (96). Against rules, principles offer universal ideals such as justice, liberty, equality and fraternity. These are intellectually grounded and offer guides for judgement. They are grounded on critique and reason. Ambedkar turns to Buddhist tradition in his search for a "Religion of Principles" (97), rather than mere rules. His arguments for Buddhism are both reflective and emotive. Religion in the sense of principled morality or Buddhist Dhamma is social in offering a fellowship of equals to human beings in the *Sangha*. It, thus, breaks with the anti-social isolationism of Hinduism. It is compatible with the domains of science, morality and politics. It accords a central position to critical thought and is integral to the development of modernity. Thus, as Christopher Queen says "Ambedkar concluded that Buddhism was the only viable religion, not only for the untouchables of India, but for the modern world at large" (Rathore and Verma 2011, xv).

Thus, unlike Radhakrishnan, Ambedkar presents an inclusive democratic way of thinking about religion in the modern context. Moreover, he has a pan-Indian relevance although he is typically regarded as a Dalit leader and constitutionalist.[19] For it is by engaging with caste inequality that Ambedkar critiques unconditional devotion as a way of maintaining the caste system. Moreover, his thesis that social democracy is a necessary condition for its political counterpart also emerges from the reality of caste relations persisting despite constitutional prohibitions. Ambedkar relates the removal of caste to so-called wider struggles such as women's equality, tolerance, religious freedom, secularism and the like. Thus, the problem of oppressed castes must matters to all Indians, regardless of their own caste origin, whereby Ambedkar's critique of caste as an analytical category has both a pan-Indian and a global relevance. It is by problematizing difference in the specific socio-historical context of caste difference that Ambedkar opens the possibility of comprehending the so-called abstract human concerns such as religion and its place in a constitutional democracy.

His critique of caste hierarchy in Hinduism, enables Ambedkar to turn to Buddhism as a non-casteist alternative. But Ambedkar's turn to Buddhism was not uncritical, nor did he think of it as a ready-made solution to the problem of caste.[20] He expressed the need for reforming some of the problematic practical aspects of Buddhism such as the lack of a single text or its "Bible", the renewal of the *Sangha* as a socially/morally relevant association and an urgent proselytization effort for transmitting the message of Buddhism (1950). Ambedkar's text *Buddha and His Dhamma* was an attempt to provide a unified reformed Buddhist text. In his introduction to this text, he is critical of some of the doctrinal and standard views associated with classical Buddhism (xli–xlii). These include explaining Prince Siddhartha's awakening to suffering through the epiphanies of death, sickness and old age; the fetishization of suffering through the four noble truths; the adherence to the law of karma and rebirth, which presupposes the soul that is denied by Buddhism; the ambivalent status of the Bhikkhu who oscillates between a perfect person and a social activist. Ambedkar's critique of Buddhism is also directed towards bringing its commitment to the morality of principles to the forefront. It also aimed at demonstrating that the conversion to the Buddhist point of view did not entail accepting its dogmas and practices mechanically; rather it entailed a critical scrutiny of beliefs and practices. This in turn implied historicizing the Buddhist tradition and desacralizing it. Indeed, in his rethinking of the sacred, Ambedkar notes that the sacred as inviolable applies to the universal, rather than "group" morality (1957, 232). He defends such a morality as a fellowship that forms the basis of an individual's growth. Further, Buddhist doctrines that are not acceptable to reason or scientific temper, such as the law of karma or the Bhikkhu as an omniscient perfect being would have to be renounced. Ambedkar's critical relation to Buddhism opened the space for reconstructing it as a moral point of view or *Dhamma* to pave way for the identification of religion with morality in a community of equals. Thus, unlike Hinduism, Buddhism had the potential to be social and foreground the principles of liberty, equality and democracy, which were central to modernity.

There have been two sets of responses to Ambedkar's writings on Buddhism that have been overlooked for decades in the academic world (Rodrigues 1993; Gokhale 2008a,b). They have been viewed from the oppositional lens as distorting the original teachings of Buddhism, promulgating a new cult and offering an ineffective politics of identity. Buddhist clerics, for instance, saw *The Buddha and his Dhamma* as effecting a break with the Buddhist cannon to dissipate the original message of Buddhism as the quest for personal salvation by reducing it to a social system (Rodrigues 1993; Gokhale 2008a, 133). Thus, Buddhist bhikshusanghas or traditionalists critiqued Ambedkar's book *The Buddha and His Dhamma* on the pages of the very same journal of the Mahabodhi society in which he had published his "Buddha and the Future of his Religion" (Rodrigues 300–1). The clergy maintained that Ambedkar departed from the Buddhist canon with his interpretation of karma, ahimsa and nibbana. They upheld that he preached a dangerous doctrine that would 'shock any real Buddhist'. Their reaction was directed towards Ambedkar's critique of the clergy as doctrinal and rigid. Another Buddhist journal indicted Ambedkar for not giving the sources of his book *The Buddha and His Dhamma* to charge him with false sources and mere ideology. According to this view, Ambedkar advocated a religion of hate while Buddhism is a religion of love. But in contrast to these orthodox monks, Sangharakshita, the Head of the World Buddhist Order, adopted an accommodative approach to Ambedkar's Buddhism. However, despite his respect for Ambedkar's conversion, tended to underplay Ambedkar's divergences with classical Buddhism.[21] Critics with a Marxist persuasion viewed Ambedkar as neglecting the material conditions of poverty faced by the Dalit community.[22]

However, Ambedkar does not believe in turning to scriptural authority as the basis of religious experience. This is indeed why he critiqued Hinduism. Hence, scholastic preoccupations with the word of Buddha would be tantamount to a fundamentalist reading of scripture from Ambedkar's point of view. In fact, against the orthodox clerics, for him it is only a free reading of Buddha that will allow for a free religion to emerge. For Ambedkar, Buddhism is an orally transmitted tradition so that interpretation is inherent with no one orthodox literal view. The *sanghas* and their social context became the basis for his rethinking Buddhism. Further, religion is political from Ambedkar's point of view. For, an oppressive political practice where there is no recognition of freedom will give rise to a bonded religion, while a free political practice will give rise to a free religion. His linking of politics and religion is an attempt to avoid intellectualization of Buddhism—to acknowledge the oppressed situation and their need for emancipatory practice. For Ambedkar, religion is a genuine need and cannot be left to individual choice. Further, its social role cannot be reduced to politics. Yet religion is also closely related to politics—the two cannot be separated from each other.[23]

Ambedkar's followers offer a contrasting response to that of the Buddhist clergy. They focused on its continuity with the canon and as faithful to the original teachings of the Buddha. By removing the burden of clerical authority, his followers argue that Ambedkar restores its original meaning to Buddhism and also makes it relevant from the contemporary point of view (Rodrigues 301). For many of Ambedkar's neo-Buddhist followers, his work *The Buddha and his Dhamma* has the same global status as classical Buddhist canon. In fact, he is said to live up to the true spirit of Buddhism and is even viewed as a modern Bodhisattva. This attitude of iconization has shown the towering role of Ambedkar in the reenergization of Buddhism and the role he played in raising the question of human dignity with respect to the oppressed castes. Thus, as Jadhav notes there is a sense of intense "gratitude" (2013) in those who follow Ambedkar without necessarily subjecting him to critical scrutiny. As Gokhale notes, Ambedkar's neo-Buddhism is viewed as a "finished product" (2008b, 150), mitigating his spirit of critique as a process. Moreover, it overlooks that there is an ongoing struggle to realize Ambedkar's progressive ideals, including the annihilation of caste. One should instead turn to Ambedkar as someone who has opened up a direction (Gokhale 2008b, 150), which should be explored further. Moreover, such a response overlooks Ambedkar's own stress on an enlightened evaluation as its foundation. His vision can develop further only if there is a transcendence of adulation. Ambedkar's own warning is telling in this respect. As Guha himself notes, Ambedkar believed that the people of India should not "lay their liberties at the feet of even a great man, or to trust him with powers which enable him to subvert their institutions."[24]

The oppositional and sympathetic responses to Ambedkar's Buddhism reveal the difficulties that are entailed in spelling out the contribution and legacy of a larger than life leader. As Jadhav puts it succinctly, "...every leader is defeated twice once by his opponents and once by his followers" (2013). Ambedkar's opponents believed that he reduced Buddhism to a mere social system, whereas for some of his followers, Ambedkar has a completed system of emancipation. Neither take Ambedkar as offering a work in progress of critique and conversion. The very spirit of a new Buddhist practice that emerged in Maharashtra as a result of his conversion to Buddhism with 380,000 followers on October 15, 1956 was the outcome of Ambedkar's critique of caste. Moreover, both his detractors and followers see Ambedkar as turning to a new religion spurred by his interpretation of Buddhism. But none of these views focus on how he arrived at his interpretation through a critical assessment of both Hinduism and Buddhism (Gokhale 2008, 109). In this preference for Buddhism, Ambedkar does not quite adhere to the position that all religions are one; but rather privileges Buddhism in the course of a comparative assessment of all religions (Gokhale 2008b, 113).[25] This critique was framed by his social understanding of religion in the "wide sense" (110) as morality or a "Religion of Principles" or *Dhamma*. Further, his view that religion has the social role of creating a moral and compassionate fellowship among human beings from diverse backgrounds tends to be undermined by these approaches. It is from this point of view that there is an urgent relevance of Ambedkar's writings on religion today. His choice of Buddhism was governed by the absence of metaphysical entities like God and soul, rationality, egalitarianism and tolerance (Gokhale 2008b, 114). It can be adopted by those who think critically, a crucial need in a democracy. Thus, Ambedkar's contribution to religion can be summarized in Rodrigues' words as that of making tradition critical.[26] For this he takes the relations of power that prevail within them into account in his comparative study of religions. Moreover, such a comparison requires that there be an evaluation of religions, which requires taking its social relations into consideration.

However, an important question emerges in the context of Ambedkar's relevance at the national (and global) level. Is the critical function of religion to be restricted to Buddhism? Can one move beyond his disparagers and devotees to extend his secular Buddhism to all other religions?[27] At first sight a negative answer seems most appropriate. There are several reasons for such a prima facie answer. Ambedkar's own conversion to Buddhism was difficult and complex in the context of the violence of caste afflicted on Dalits and his comparative study of religions (Kamble 2003; Gokhale 2008b, 111; Zelliot 2013, 143–73). Consequently, he devoted much time to the caste problem of Hinduism (1990), spelt out the disunities between Hinduism and Buddhism (1950; 1957, 242; 2002d), upheld Buddhism over Christianity, Islam and Hinduism (1950) and exhorted the masses oppressed by caste to convert to Buddhism (2002d). Indeed, one of the conversion vows that he advocates is renouncing the worship of Hindu Gods; "I embrace today the Bauddha Dhamma discarding the Hindu Religion which is detrimental to the emancipation of human beings and which believes in inequality and regards human beings other than Brahmins as low born."[28] Further Ambedkar also proclaimed that Hindus who realize the problem of caste will adopt Buddhism (1950). This statement clearly opposes tendencies to "Hinduize" (Guru 1991a, b) Ambedkar's Buddhism, whose academic roots lie in Radhakrishnan (1923, 341–476). These instances reveal that Ambedkar's break with Hinduism seems decisive to the transition to a secular Buddhism. Does this then foreclose the possibility—at least theoretically—of envisaging a reformed Hinduism without the scourge of caste? Can the lessons of Buddhism be applied to religions such as Hinduism? A deeper look at some of his works prior to his work in 1950, "The Future of Buddhism" and the posthumous *The Buddha and His Dhamma* reveals the possibility of an affirmative answer to these questions. In his 1936 Speech "Annihilation of Caste," Ambedkar suggests that Hinduism change its beliefs and practices in keeping with a changing society, which does not uphold eternal values (1990, 103). He upholds that these changes be brought into effect through a standardized book and the subjugation of priests to the authority of the state law. The latter involves abolition of hereditary priesthood, equality between laity and priests and state regulation of priests (1990, 98). Ambedkar also suggests that Hindus introspect their traditional doctrines and practices to selectively appropriate only those that are conducive to the moral growth of the whole society, which alone allows for the growth of an individual (1990, 102). He mentions the possibility of effecting change in Hinduism through contact with Buddhism. He cites the *Bhagvad Gita* as deriving its principles of social morality such as *Nirvana*, *Maitri* and *Karuna* from Buddhism (2002c, 202–4). In his *Buddha and His Dhamma*, Ambedkar gives an account of some of the Vedic Rishis who were upheld as worthy of respect by the Buddha (1957, 58–60). He also gives a detailed account of Kapila and the Sankhya philosophy as a significant influence on the Buddha for adopting its rationalism, rejection of God and acceptance of suffering (61–63).[29] Given the reciprocal influence of Buddhism and Hinduism on each other, one cannot rule out the possibility of restricting Hinduism along the egalitarian and secular lines of Buddhism. Buddhism can then be understood as a model or metaphor for a secular religion that is founded on the principles of modern morality, whose spirit can be adopted by all other religions in their endeavour to reform.

The spirit of Buddhism informs Ambedkar's critique of Brahmanical patriarchy in the practical consequence of reforming Hinduism and introducing gender parity through his reforms on the Hindu Code Bill (Rege 2013,

101–201). He critiqued the 19th-century social reform movement—which for most part concentrated on Hinduism—that split family reform from its social counterpart (1990, 37). Thus, it worked towards the abolition of child marriage and advocated widow remarriage. However, the secondary status of women in Hindu society was never linked to caste oppression; hence, social reformers did not focus on the specific need to abolish caste as a structural phenomenon. In contrast, Ambedkar introduced reforms in the Hindu Personal Law, by paying special attention to women; he did so by abolishing birth-right to property, giving half the share to the daughter, making women's limited estate absolute, ending caste hierarchy in marriage and adoption as well as advocating the principle of monogamy and divorce (2013, 212–3). In each of these, he took the secondary status of women in Hinduism as his point of departure, which again distinguishes him from Radhakrishnan. For Radhakrishnan, women in Hinduism occupy a superior position in virtue of their domestic roles (1956, 371–8). Although he does concede to their discrimination under patriarchy and defend their ability to pursue spiritual and social vocations, he upholds the primacy of their reproductive role. Radhakrishnan fails to comprehend that reproduction—biological, social and cultural—reinforces the caste system by disciplining women. Ambedkar acknowledges this through his critique of Brahmanical patriarchy as detrimental to both women and underprivileged castes. This is precisely why the Bill faced bitter opposition from orthodox Hindu groups, government apathy, as well as, piecemeal discussion and implementation, contributing to Ambedkar's resignation as a Law Minister in 1951. As Rege observes, Ambedkar's critique of caste reveals how endogamous marriage sustains both caste and gender hierarchy (2013). By arguing that the caste system is maintained through the repression of women's rights, Ambedkar reconstructs and reforms Hinduism in a gender-inclusive manner.[30] His critique's integration of faith, reason and morality also resonates with Kant.

Ambedkar's reconciliation of reason, morality and faith: Kantian resonance

Ambedkar's social and moral interpretation of Buddhism aims at bringing about a change in social relations at the grassroots level. He defends religion against socialists as a spiritual need, and as a public practice against the liberal private faith by emphasizing the precedence of the social over the political. Against both liberals and the socialists, Ambedkar makes social change in the religious sphere the precondition for political participation (1990). The liberal view believes that one can go about the matter of democratic politics independently of the democratization of society. This is reflected in its version of secularism that separates politics and religion. However, such a separation allows caste and gender oppressions to continue, for instance by denying underprivileged castes and women entry to temples. Thus, political intervention in religious practice is sometimes necessary; but then it is not effective, if caste discrimination persists in civil society. Thus, social perspectives have to be transformed prior to political intervention. Ambedkar, therefore, connects society (of which religion is a part) with politics. Socialists believed that economic well-being alone matters so that neither social nor political reform are important. This is reflected, he believes, in the socialist thesis that religion will wither away with economic progress. However, Ambedkar did not agree with such economic determinism. He maintains that the power of the priest, who holds greater social authority than the judge, is proof of how religion controls people in India (1990, 42). He narrates how plebeians in Rome could not acquire power despite getting elected through separate electorates because patrician priests were in charge of the oracle at Delphi who would initiate people into political duty only after the goddess permitted it (1990, 43–44).

Ambedkar diagnoses the political exclusion of the oppressed castes as related to their social identity as Hindus. Hence, social change requires a change in religious identity for political participation. Thus, religious reform and egalitarian identity within civil society have implications for political participation. The sanction of law in the political sphere required that the sanction of morality be adhered to in the social sphere. The latter is enforced through religion, which has a critical role in an unjust and impoverished society. It was because Hinduism failed to humanize them that Ambedkar thought it necessary for Dalits to embrace a religion that would permit them to gain equality of status, opportunity and treatment. In his *Buddha and His Dhamma* Ambedkar distinguishes between religion as doctrine or ritual and Buddhist *dhamma* as a moral commitment to core principles of liberty, equality and fraternity (1957, 225–32).[31] Thus, instead of separating civil society and politics like liberalism, Ambedkar attempts to reinvent their relation. His philosophy of religion resonates with the spirit of Marx's call for the revolution in civil society preceding a political one (1967).[32] Ambedkar's critical approach to religion also differs from that of Radhakrishnan in its affinities with Kant's project of reconciling rationality, morality and faith within religion.

Rather than pioneer an exclusively rational approach to religion that privileges Christianity, as Skaria notes (454–5), Kant dwells on the limits of reason to make room for faith (1998, Bxxx-Bxxxi).[33] Kant does suggest that religion be made compatible with reason by eradicating its irrational elements. His kingdom of ends as a version of the kingdom of god attests to a secular philosophical translation of religious terminology (Bernstein 2009, 1046; Habermas 2008, 216). Thus, standard readings of Kant suggest that he subjugates faith to reason to which Radhakrishnan subscribes. He indicts Kant for conflating religion's difference with morality and reducing them to a broad philosophical idea (Radhakrishnan 1932, 88).

Radhakrishnan discerns the personal pursuit of perfection as religion's distinctive feature that transcends morality. Further, his discussion of Kantian morality also is in tune with conventional Kant scholarship that perceives him as a rationalist who severs morality from the domain of lived experience (1911).[34] For Radhakrishnan the personal unconditional character of religion disallows it from being a part of morality that Kant upholds as it is the "apprehension of the real and an enjoyment of it for its own sake which is absent in moral consciousness" (Radhakrishnan 1932, 88). Yet his account of Kant as upholding a rational conception of religion, which is based exclusively on his ethical writings is partial and neglects Kant's discussions of religion.[35] Moreover, he also ignores the inherent conflicts in Kant's reflections on ethics and religion, which testify to the complex relationship between religion and morality.[36] Thus, Kant (begins his discussion on religion) by claiming that morality does not rest on religion to spell out an antagonism between rational morality and historically situated faith (DiCenso 2007, 168; Kant 1996, 57).[37] However, he goes on to point out that the presence of evil reveals that individuals cannot self-sufficiently attain moral ideals, as the latter are influenced by the presence of others. Mitigating evil—so as to freely follow the moral law—requires constructive relations with others, which can be garnered for Kant from shared religious institutions (DiCenso 2007, 168). Thus, religion can play a psychological and pedagogical[38] role in making individuals morally sensitized. The hermeneutics of historical religions can contribute to ethical awareness, choice and practice, as DiCenso notes. This in turn requires adopting a critical approach to religion for Kant where elements like fanaticism are filtered.

Turning to Ambedkar, he critiques Radhakrishnan's arguments in his *Hindu View of Life* (1927) that considers Hinduism's persistence through centuries of history as its strength (1990, 79–80).[39] He notes that it wishes away the role of caste hierarchy in defining the social context in India to overlook how the social frames the opportunities that are available for individual pursuit. Moreover, Ambedkar argues that by taking refuge in Hinduism's centuries-old survival, Radhakrishnan sidesteps the distinction between surviving and doing so in a worthwhile manner (1990). For Ambedkar, Brahminical patriarchy in India that accords maximum opportunities to those with caste and gender privilege has survived but this does not attest to its worth.

One can read the Kantian spirit of critique in Ambedkar's attempt to both critique Hinduism's dogma of caste and also Buddhism (a religion of his choice). Kant's critique of priesthood as "counterfeit service of God" (1996, 6:151–6:153, 6:168) breeding rules of inegalitarian social relations, powerful priesthood and ritualism resonates with Ambedkar. Kant considers such an investment as sacrificing moral conduct through subjective approval in God. Thus, morality requires religion not as its foundation but as its consequence, where the will of the mighty nonhuman lawgiver coincides with the human will in the formation of an ethical community on earth (1996, 6:99–96:100). Ambedkar's redefinition of key Buddhist themes through the ideals of the French revolution reflect Kant's claim that human beings aspire to achieve their moral goals through a community founded on ethical religion. One can advance similar claims regarding his attempt to reform Hinduism with the Hindu Code Bill. Radhakrishnan overlooks how Kant is well aware of the limits of rationality. Kant's critique of rational theology reveals as much (1998, A568/B596-A642/B670). As Bernstein notes, his critique of reason aims at creating space for faith. Hence, he also advocates a positive role to religion with God as a postulate who motivates human beings to be moral (1999a, 5:133–5:134) and later tracing religion to be the outcome of an ethical community that is forged through faith in God (1998, 6:91–96:147). Kant views religion as a psychological and moral need, rather than a cognitive fact, but does not reduce religion to morality as Radhakrishnan assumes. Similarly, for Ambedkar, religion's foundation on morality mandates that an individual exercise his or her capacity to think independently to create harmonious social relations within the empirical world. Thus, religion need not have *nibbana* or liberation from this world as its focus.

Kant also recognizes the need for a religion compatible with science. Thus, against views such as those of Radhakrishnan, science is not a challenge to religion, since they can be reconciled. For this Kant suggests that instead of reading religious texts in a literal way as biblical theology, one adopts the approach of philosophical theology (1996, 6:9–6:10). The latter acknowledges the boundaries of reason, while engaging with religion. According to Kant, the transition from being evil to being good requires taking the moral point of view. Morality is based on the idea of a free human being who is also able to bind him/herself to laws that are unconditional. It is deontological and self-sufficient in not requiring divine sanction. Yet Kant also recognizes that human beings who honour the moral law aspire to create a world in which morality could be realized, even though such a world would require the sacrifice of personal happiness. The aspiration for the realization of morality is also a hope for its endorsement by another impartial being who recognizes the human respect of the moral law in an ethical community that fulfills the conditions of freedom and equality for moral transformation.

Kant and Ambedkar share the concept of critique in their approaches to religious traditions and practices. Kant defines critique as a way of assessing the limits of an enterprise (1998, B xxii-xxv). A critical approach does not spell out substantive doctrines or systems, it instead examines the conditions of what exists through its evaluation. It has a negative role of indicating problems, but critique also has a positive role of articulating the conditions of any given phenomenon (1998, Bxxv–xxvii). Yet the constructive role of religion as bringing about a moral social order becomes possible only when there is a destruction of immoral anti-social traditions, an aspect that is missing in Radhakrishnan. Ambedkar's philosophy of religion is based on the interdependent positive and negative functions of critique, which are founded in the human being's capacity for enlightenment. The latter's Kantian sense as thinking without external force is central to Ambedkar's analysis of religion as compatible with rationality and science.

Ambedkar's reflection on religion and modernity has relevance in the search for answers that go beyond the limited approach of attempts such as Radhakrishnan's that fail to comprehend the role of the social in the private pursuit of religion. Ambedkar understands religion within a modern world as not simply individual faith, but rather as a commitment to inclusiveness and egalitarianism in the quest for faith.

Notes

1 I am indebted to Pradeep Gokhale for a detailed discussion on this paper. I thank him, the organizers and participants of the I.C.P.R. seminar *Buddhism, NeoBuddhism and the Question of Caste* at Central University of Tibetan Studies, Sarnath (held from October 3–5, 2013) for their helpful feedback. My gratitude to Aakash Singh Rathore, Biraj Mehta and Rucha Pawar for their comments on the paper, although its weaknesses are mine.
2 This expression is derived from the title of Kant's essay (Kant 1996).
3 Its title, *Aarakshan* or 'reservation', suggested that it would engage with the theme of affirmative action for underprivileged castes in India. This film was directed by Prakash Jha.
4 This detour to the world of popular culture, through Hindi commercial cinema and Avirook Sen's blog site (2011), is in keeping with Ambedkar's own awareness of the significance of the same (Rege 2013, 194, n.5).
5 The film does not historically contextualize the reservation policy. In the 1930s Dalits, under Ambedkar's leadership, asked for a separate electorate. However, it was due to Gandhi's opposition and fast that a compromise was made with reservation for underprivileged castes and tribes in government jobs, education and parliament in the Poona Pact in 1932.
6 In this respect his appearance in a popular film is an "oddity" to use Sen's term.
7 See (Hatcher 2007) for an account of what he terms as "bourgeois" Hinduism, which tried to retain supposed time-less traditional beliefs by reconstructing them in the modern context. Hatcher discusses how reform Hinduism balanced desire and spirituality wherein spirituality could be consumed. One can also argue the same for caste. Modern versions of Hinduism have tried to underplay Hinduism's caste hierarchy by redefining it in alternate ways. They have also homogenized a discrete set of practices as a world religion termed "Hinduism." One attempt is that of Radhakrishnan who is being considered in this paper, whom Hatcher mentions (2007, 302). Others include Tilak and Aurobindo. See King (96–142) for an account of modern Hinduism as a European-influenced phenomenon. King cites Radhakrishnan, among others, as an instance (60). There is no central core of Hinduism as its modern advocates such as Radhakrishnan uphold.
8 Also see Radhakrishnan (1956, 357–62) for a critique of caste as based on heredity and its defense through aptitude.

9 Also see Kiran (1950) for a similar defense of Hindu caste system against Ambedkar.
10 Radhakrishnan terms these as *gunas* (1927, 111).
11 See for instance, Radhakrishnan (1927). Sen makes a special mention of Radhakrishnan's defence of *varna* in his blog.
12 As King notes the idea of Hinduism as a unified domain is not upheld by indigenous Indians but is the outcome of colonial definitions (98–101). Moreover, it is influenced by Brahmin scholars from whom colonial rulers took help (King 102–4).
13 Thus, for instance he upholds that "The whole scheme of Buddhism centers on Buddha's enlightenment" (1932, 90).
14 At the global level, key issues pertaining to the relationship between communities—such as Islam in Europe—have addressed the relationship between religion and politics. This is precisely why European and American philosophers have started addressing the issue of religion with greater vigour, despite neglecting it in the past. Derrida, Rorty, Rawls and Habermas have all linked the resurgence of religion to the disquietudes of secularism.
15 I am indebted to Pradeep Gokhale for this clarification.
16 See Skaria (2015) for an account of Ambedkar's notion of public religion.
17 Ambedkar uses the term "spiritual" to indicate human aspiration for social freedom and equality. His use is reminiscent of the German idealistic tradition's use of the term "Geist."
18 For his critique of the four *varnas* see Ambedkar (1990, 67–76).
19 Narendra Jadhav April 13, 2013 interview. Guha too laments that the architects of modern India have become "victims of sectarian diminution" (2010, 22). Thus, Tagore is venerated by Bengalis, Patel by Gujaratis, Nehru by the Congress party and Ambedkar by Dalits. Guha himself attempts to reconstruct Ambedkar as having national significance having played an active role in drafting the Constitution of India. He approvingly cites three key themes from Ambedkar's speech to the Constituent Assembly as relevant to India at 60 (see Ambedkar 1949). These include Ambedkar's opposition to violence in civil society and hero-worship of political figures, as well as, his view that social democracy precedes political democracy. Each of these themes emerge from Ambedkar's critique of caste violence in civil society. Hence, Ambedkar's arguments regarding caste and religion are relevant to non-Dalits as well. Ambedkar's speech to the Constituent Assembly is relevant to all Indians only because caste is relevant to all Indians.
20 Skaria rightly notes that Ambedkar did not embrace an already existing form of Buddhism (452).
21 See Gokhale (2008, 134–8).
22 Gokhale gives an assessment of Kasbe in this respect, see Gokhale (2008, 138–44). Skaria makes an attempt to reconcile Ambedkar's neo-Buddhism with Marx's critique of religion (459–61). See Ambedkar 2002a for an account of the relation between caste and class.
23 With respect to the accommodative approach of Sangharakshita, as Gokhale notes one cannot overlook the differences between classical Buddhism and that of Ambedkar (2008, 144). Conversely, one cannot reduce Ambedkar's Buddhism to Marxism (Gokhale 2008b, 144).
24 Ambedkar's last speech to the Constituent Assembly quoted in Guha (22–23).
25 Ambedkar's critical approach also contrasts with the Orientalist interpretation of Buddhism as based on canonical texts and focusing on self-perfection

through meditative practice (for a brief description of Orientalist Buddhism, see King (143–60)). Ambedkar does reflect the early Orientalist idea of considering the Buddha to be a social reformer against excesses of ritualism. However, he does not regard the Buddha as a "Hindu Protestantism" (King 145) in the manner of Orientalists or Radhakrishnan as Buddhism is not a branch of Hinduism. Nor does Ambedkar advocate "Protestant Buddhism" (King 150–51). For it is not grounded in any single canon like Protestant Christianity. Ambedkar advocates Buddhism as a process of social criticism that could lead to a transformative perspective towards hierarchical and stagnant social relations.

26 This is the title of Rodrigues's essay (1993).

27 Also see Gokhale (2008b, 111–2).

28 This is Oath 19 quoted in Zelliot (2013, 171).

29 Thanks to Prof. Gokhale for bringing this point to my attention.

30 Guha has not discussed the internationalization of Ambedkar's thought in his critique of Ambedkar's sectarian reception (2010).

31 Ambedkar's interpretation of the prospects for Buddhism differs radically from colonial writers such as Karl Bleitreu who offered a "post-Enlightenment" (Manjapra 58) notion of Buddhism. For Bleibtreu, Buddhism's value rests in its commitment to rebirth and offering a perspective that goes beyond the ideals of the French revolution. His essay entitled "Buddhism: Religion of the Future" in his 1899 book *From Robespierre to the Buddha* is discussed by Manjapra (57–58). However, the relationship between Ambedkar and Orientalism is a subject for another paper.

32 Also see Skaria (2015, 452). Yet there has been a general academic neglect of Ambedkar as a philosopher of religion.

33 "Thus, I had to deny knowledge in order to make room for faith" (Kant 1998, Bxxx). For a brief overview of the complex terrain of scholarship on Kant's religious perspective, see Davies (2017). Davies rightly notes that Kant cannot be read as a Christian defender or as rooting religion in rationality. Also, see Wood (1996) and Rossi (2009) for nuanced perspectives on Kant's relation to religion and morality.

34 Radhakrishnan attempts to distinguish his own position in this respect from the widely accepted view that both Kant and the ethics of Gita are deontological and non-hedonistic (1911, 465). But he believes that Kant cannot quite be assimilated with Hindu ethics, since he has the privilege of reason and yet commits himself to a causally deterministic phenomenal world. The latter, according to Radhakrishnan, makes Kantian freedom "empty and unreal" (470) as its noumenal position does not impact the phenomenal. For Radhakrishnan, in contrast, the Gita explores ethics through concrete dilemmas between duty and inclination. Unlike Kant, the Gita does not suggest that inclinations should be destroyed but that on the contrary, they should be sublimated to freedom and reflection (474–5). According to Radhakrishnan, the Gita is, thus, a non-hedonistic and non-rationalistic alternative to Kantian ethics (466). Kant was however well aware of the problem of empty universals. This is precisely why he supplements the first formulation of the categorical imperative as a universal principle with that of humanity as an end in itself (second formulation) and that of autonomous willing (third formulation). As DiCenso notes (following Allen Wood who he acknowledges), the second and third formulations of the categorical imperative are attempts to connect its universality with the domain of lived experience and interpersonal relations (168). Radhakrishnan, however, appears to be oblivious to this.

35 Radhakrishnan subscribes to what DiCenso terms as "A strictly idealistic ethics and a corresponding view of rational religion..." (167) with respect to Kant.
36 This notion of "tension" is DiCenso's essay (2007, 167–8).
37 As DiCenso notes, Kant's universal ethics is based on this antagonism (168) In the second part of his "Metaphysics of Morals" Kant distinguishes between formal religion, which considers duties as divine commands and its material counterpart (1999b, 561). For the latter, religion comprises duties to god.
38 DiCenso aptly distinguishes such edification from determinism (169).
39 See (Bharti 2018) for a critique of Radhakrishnan's caste hierarchy from Sankrityayan's perspective as "illiberal liberalism." Also see Sankrityayan's (1982) text in Hindi for the same critique.

References

Ambedkar, B.R. 1949. "Speech to the Constituent Assembly" http://parliamentofindia.nic.in/ls/debates/vol11p11.htm accessed on 14/9/2013.
——— 1950. "Buddha and the Future of His Religion" *Maha Bodhi Mahabodhi Society Journal* http:// www.clearviewproject.org/engagedbuddhistwriting/buddhaandthefutureof.html, accessed on 20/8/2013.
——— 1957. *The Buddha and His Dhamma*. Bombay: Siddharth Publications.
——— 1990. *Annihilation of Caste*. New Delhi: Arnold Publications.
——— 2002a. "Class, Caste and Democracy" in *The Essential Writings of B.R. Ambedkar* ed. Valerian Rodrigues, 132–48. New Delhi: Oxford University Press.
——— 2002b. "Buddha or Karl Marx" in *The Essential Writings of B.R. Ambedkar* ed. Valerian Rodrigues, 173–89. New Delhi: Oxford University Press.
——— 2002c. "Krishna and His Gita" in *The Essential Writings of B.R. Ambedkar* ed. Valerian Rodrigues, 193–204. New Delhi: Oxford University Press.
——— 2002d. "Conversion (Away from the Hindus)" in *The Essential Writings of B.R. Ambedkar* ed. Valerian Rodrigues, 219–38. New Delhi: Oxford University Press.
——— 2013. "The Hindu Code Bill" in *Against the Madness of Manu B.R. Ambedkar's Writings on Brahmanical Patriarchy* Selected and Introduced by Sharmila Rege, 203–13. New Delhi: Navayana.
——— 2014 (2003). "Dr. Ambedkar's Reply to Sir. S Radhakrishnan" in *Dr Babasaheb Ambedkar: Writings and Speeches* ed. Hari Narake, N.G. Kamble, M.L. Kasare and Ashok Godghate, vol. 17 (part 2), 19. New Delhi: Dr. Ambedkar Foundation, Government of India.
Bernstein, Richard J. 2009. "The Secular-Religious Divide: Kant's Legacy" *Social Research: An International Quarterly* 76(4): 1035–48.
Bharti, Kanwal. 2018. "Why Remember Casteist Radhakrishnan on Teacher's Day?" *Forward Press* http://www.forwardpress.in/2018/09/why-remember-casteist-radhakrishnan-on-teachers-day/#_edn14 accessed on 12/10/2019.
Davies, Stephen T. 2017. "A New Kant on Religion?" *Toronto Journal of Theology* 33(1): 63–67.
DiCenso, James. 2007. "Kant, Freud and the Ethical Critique of Religion" *International Journal for Philosophy of Religion* 61(3): 161–79.

Gokhale, Pradeep. 2008a. "Dr. Ambedkar as a Philosopher: Beyond Reductionism" in his (ed) *The Philosophy of B.R. Ambedkar*, 3–26. Pune: Sugava Prakashan and Indian Philosophical Quarterly.

——— 2008b. "Dr. Ambedkar's Interpretation of Buddhism" in his (ed) *The Philosophy of B.R. Ambedkar*, 109–52. Pune: Sugava Prakashan and Indian Philosophical Quarterly.

Guha, Ramchandra. 2010. "Ambedkar's Desiderata" Outlook February 1, 22–30.

Guru, Gopal. 1991a. "Hinduisation of Ambedkar in Maharashtra" *Economic and Political Weekly* 26(7): 339–41.

——— 1991b. "Appropriating Ambedkar" *Economic and Political Weekly* 26(27): 1697–9.

Habermas, Jürgen 2008. *Between Naturalism and Religion: Philosophical Essays*. Cambridge and Malden: Polity Press.

Hatcher, Brian A. 2007. "Bourgeois Vedānta: The Colonial Roots of Middle-class Hinduism" *Journal of the American Academy of Religion* 75(2): 298–323.

Jadhav, Narendra. 2013. "Ambedkar's role is being belittled" Interviewed by Praveen Dass *The Times of India Crest Edition* (April 13).

Jha, Prakash. 2011. *Aarakshan* (film text).

Kamble, Ramesh. 2003. "Contextualizing Ambedkarian Conversion" *Economic and Political Weekly* 4305: 4308.

Kant, Immanuel. 1996 (1793). "Religion within the Boundaries of Mere Reason" in *Religion and Rational Theology* ed. Allen Wood and George Di Giovanni, 57–215. Cambridge: Cambridge University Press.

——— 1998. *Critique of Pure Reason* trans. Paul Guyer and Allen Wood. Cambridge: Cambridge University Press.

——— 1999a. "Critique of Practical Reason" in *Practical Philosophy* trans. Mary Gregor, 133–271. Cambridge: Cambridge University Press.

——— 1999b. "The Metaphysics of Morals" in *Practical Philosophy* trans. Mary Gregor, 353–603. Cambridge: Cambridge University Press.

King, Richard. 1999. *Orientalism and Religion: Postcolonial Theory, India and the Mystic East*. London and New York: Routledge.

Kiran, Amal. 1950. "Hinduism and the Caste System" *Mother India* https://auromere.wordpress.com/2015/04/07/hinduism-and-the-caste-system/ accessed on 20/6/2019.

Manjapra, Kris. 2014. *The Age of Entanglement: German and Indian Intellectuals Across the Empire*. Cambridge, MA: Harvard University Press.

Marx, Karl. 1967. "On the Jewish Question" in *Writings of the young Marx on Philosophy and Society* ed. Loyd D. Easton and Kurt H. Guddat, 216–48. Garden City: Anchor Books, Double Day and Company Inc.

Minor, Robert N. 1997. "Radhakrishnan as an Advocate of the Class/Caste System as a Universal, Religio-Social System" *International Journal of Hindu Studies* 1(2): 386–400.

Radhakrishnan, S. 1911. "The Ethics of the Bhagavadgita and Kant" *International Journal of Ethics* 21(4): 465–75.

——— 1927. *The Hindu View of Life*. London: George Allen and Unwin.

——— 1932. *An Idealist View of Life*. London: George Allen and Unwin.

——— 1956. *Occasional Speeches and Writings October 1952-January 1956*. Delhi and Calcutta: Ministry of Information and Broadcasting, Government of India and Sree Saraswaty Press.

——— 1967. *Recovery of Faith*. New Delhi: Hind Pocket Books.

Rathore, Aakash Singh and Ajay Verma 2011. "Editors' Introduction" in *B.R. Ambedkar The Buddha and His Dhamma*, ed. Aakash Singh Rathore and Ajay Verma, ix–xxii. New Delhi: Oxford, University Press.

Rege, Sharmila. 2013. "Introduction: The Unswept and Unsung Death" in *Against the Madness of Manu B.R. Ambedkar's Writings on Brahmanical Patriarchy* Selected and Introduced by Sharmila Rege, 191–201. New Delhi: Navayana.

Rodrigues, Valerian. 1993. "Making a Traditional Critical: Ambedkar's Reading of Buddhism" in *Dalit Movements and the Meanings of Labour in India* ed. Peter Robb, 299–338. New Delhi: Oxford University Press.

Rossi, Phillip. 2009. "Kant's Philosophy of Religion" in *Stanford Encyclopedia of Philosophy* http://plato.stanford.edu.

Sankrityayan, Rahul. 1982. *Vaigyanik Bhautikwad*. Allahabad: Lokbharti.

Sen, Avirook. August 13, 2011. "The Big Picture: Araakshan and its Radhakrishnan Problem" http://www.firstpost.com/ideas/the-big-picture-aarakshan-and-its-radhakrishnan-problem-60296.html.

Skaria, Ajay. 2015. "Ambedkar, Marx and the Buddhist Question" *South Asia: Journal of South Asian Studies* 38(3): 450–65.

Wood, Allen W. 1996. "General Introduction" in *Religion and Rational Theology* ed. Allen Wood and George Di Giovanni, 39–215. Cambridge: Cambridge University Press.

Zelliot, Eleanor. 2013 (2004). *Ambedkar's World: The Making of Babasaheb and the Dalit Movement*. New Delhi: Navayana.

12

RELIGION, CASTE AND MODERNITY

Ambedkar's reconstruction of Buddhism

P. Kesava Kumar

In recent times, religion is a rallying point for many struggles all over the world. Religion becomes a part of public discourse and rights are articulated in the name of religion. Western modernity has been contested for detaching religion and community. Liberal theory is either reformulated or rejected for its atomistic individualism. Against the liberal self, the self, embedded in the social, gets its philosophical prominence. It is clear that religion is centre stage in inaugurating one's own self and as a driving force for politics. The debates of moral and political philosophy are refashioned on religion. Communitarian thinkers are not only upholding a life located in social/cultural/ religious community but also in reframing modernity. The horizon of modernity has broadened. In pursuing justice, they differentiate themselves from conservatism and making their philosophical theories much more egalitarian. The contemporary religious revivalist struggles appear to be meaningful in this context. The Islamic religious nationalist movements in the Middle East against western imperialism and Hindu nationalist movement's confrontation with the secular state in India have succeeded in religionizing politics. It appealed to the people of the respective nations against shallow modernity. Simultaneously, there are manifestations of struggles of the oppressed against structural injustice by asserting one's own social and cultural life. Indigenous traditions, beliefs and practices are used as a social protest against dominance in securing dignity, self-respect and social justice. These struggles are appropriating and defending normative modernity rather than the former. In India, struggles of untouchables have established a tradition of this kind It has its historic continuity with contemporary Dalit movements inspired by the philosophy of Ambedkar. This chapter explores the importance of religion in everyday social and political life of contemporary times by redefining the very idea of religion by Ambedkar. Ambedkar not only defines the religion from a normative and rationalist point of view but also upholds religion against the assumptions of modernity. In this connection, he reconstructs Buddhism as an egalitarian and humanistic religion and negates Hinduism as a religion for its sanctity due to the hierarchical, inhuman, immoral and oppressive caste system. This chapter highlights the primacy of the righteous social life as a source of religion by locating Ambedkar's conception of religion in general and Buddhism in particular in contemporary debates of moral and political philosophy.

Dalit modernity: a critique of colonial and Brahmanical modernity

Ambedkar's modernity has been a constructive vehicle for struggles of equality on the part of those oppressed by caste. His conception of modernity goes against the colonial mediated modernity and the modernity appropriated by Brahmanical Hindu elite. For him, religion has a different meaning. He has reconstructed the very idea of religion by making it rational, normative and democratic. In fact, he viewed religion as a basis for morality and righteous social life. He explains the function of religion is the reconstruction of society based on the principles of utility and justice. He is critical about Indian modernity (Brahmanical) for grounding in Hinduism and the caste system. He argued that both Hinduism and its caste system are essentially based on the principle of inequality and immorality, against the claims of reformation by the social elite. Moreover, Ambedkar's religion is atheistic, rationalistic, human-centric and based on the morality of the community. He reconstructs Buddhism on these lines. He identifies religion with the 'saddhamma' of Buddhism. For him religion is an emancipatory idea that has the potential in liberating the oppressed (Dalits). In other words, he provides an alternative modernity that negotiates with religion rather than negating religion.

Modernity has been connoted with many meanings. The world is living with 'multiple modernities.' Ambedkar's conception of modernity has its own characterization, which both converges and diverges from dominant Western modernity. It is much more complex and is even ambiguous. Colonial modernity is an immediate available reference point for Indian intellectuals. The concept of Indian modernity has varied with the appropriation of the respective social agency, especially Dalit modernity has its own traits and is different from the Brahmanical Hindu social elite. Interestingly, both overcome the dichotomy of tradition and modernity maintained with the interest of Western modernity. Dalit modernity has been very well articulated by Ambedkar. Dalit modernity is based on the value of human dignity and self-respect. In persuasion of this, he interrogates irrational, unjust and exploitative practices of the traditional Hindu social order by invoking rationality and ethicality. He upholds the Dalit self, nurtured in indigenous tradition by claiming the elements of humane and democratic practices. On the other hand, Brahmanical class is selective of the elements of modernity. The fruits of modernity are enjoyed and even monopolized by this class at the material level, and, at the same time, they are maintained intact within their own tradition at the spiritual/religious level. The modernity project of the Hindu Brahmanical class initially seems to provide scope for reforming the traditional order and religious life but ultimately ends up as anti-modern. As an ideal of modernity, it professed equality in the spiritual realm but not ready to extend equality in the material realm. This trajectory of modernity could be seen from the continuity of the social reform of colonial times to Hindu nationalism of post-colonial times. Dalits have been systematically excluded from the project of Brahmanical modernity. In this context, Dalits are negotiating with the ideals of modernity to overcome the social exclusion, exploitation, suffering and humiliation imposed by Hindu tradition. Dalit modernity has very much mediated the liberal, radical and communitarian philosophies in its own way, both by associating and differentiating from these political traditions on different points (Kesava Kumar 2013).

In the colonial context of India, religion has invoked as the social self of the nation. People are mobilized around religion and there are attempts to redefine the very idea of religion to suit contemporary political interests. Hinduism is depicted as a symbol of spiritualism against western materialism. The intellectuals engaged in social reform and nationalist movements were actively involved in this process. As the intellectuals mostly drew from the elite Brahmanical class and imagined a nation from their subjective position, their immediate concern was to consolidate their cultural/social identity against colonial rulers. On one hand, they tried to juxtapose Hinduism as the Indian tradition with Western tradition and on other side attempted to minimize the differences within Hinduism. In that process, they were compelled to talk about their social reality, which is caste-ridden. Moreover, they were afraid that lower castes are asserting their cultural identity by moving outside of the Hindu fold. Parallel to this, the intellectuals drawn from Dalit-Bahujans have started consolidating their social identity alternative to the dominant construction of Hinduism. The scheme of this intellectual tradition exposes the nexus between caste and religion and its oppressive character. They argued for dignity and justice. They projected their cultural tradition as indigenous, naturalistic, rationalistic and humane in nature against Brahmanical Hinduism. Ambedkar is a figure of culmination of this democratic tradition and normative modernity.

In post-independent India, from the decade of the eighties, the rise of the Dalit movement, and, on the other side, the Hindu nationalist movement, brings back the discussion on religion and its relation to caste in modern times. Against the ideals of modernity, there are attempts to defend Hindu nationalism with the logic of postmodernism. Dalits are asserting their own identity by invoking the indigenous cultural traditions and at the same time articulating their rights through the logic and language of modernity. The identification of Dalits with religion and modernity is complex and it definitely differs from both Western colonial and Brahmanical modernity. Ambedkar provides historical and philosophical inputs in understanding the religion of the untouchables against the dominant conception of religion. He finds rational/natural and democratic potential of the religion of untouchables. The social rationality he put forward through the method of philosophy of religion is central to the discourse of modernity. This chapter explores the general understanding of the very idea of religion with an emphasis on the philosophical method adopted by Ambedkar in understanding religion. This has been illustrated through Ambedkar's reading of anti-egalitarian Hinduism and his construction of humanistic, naturalistic, rationalistic and ethical religion of Buddhism.

Towards an understanding of religion

Religion has been conceptualized from the debates such as tradition versus modernity, religion versus science and reason versus faith. Historically, religion has undergone many changes. Its meaning has been derived from the social context. Religion becomes a metaphor for the identity of a social group and has an invariable relation with one's own life and social practices. Historically religion has many meanings. It has been understood as a principle of governance and also as a means of exploitation of the masses. The idea of religion has changed significantly with changing social, economic and political conditions. It has the quality of both endurance and change. There are social forces defending the religion and also opposing the religion. The origin and function of religion has been explained by various philosophical, theological, anthropological/sociological, historical and psychological theories.

Religion has been viewed critically from many fronts in modern times. It was understood as a pre-modern idea. It was considered as a hurdle for progress and development. Religious faith could not stand for reason. Modernity is interwoven with the elements of rationality, science, humanism, secularism, progress and development, whereas religion was identified with tradition, irrationality, faith, dogmatism and backwardness. Marxists propagated religion as the opium of the masses, as the sigh of an oppressed creature, soul of the soulless and heart of the heartless (Marx 1970). Freud explained religion as illusion. According to him, religion was an expression of underlying psychological neurosis and distress (Freud 1961: 14). Liberal thinkers pushed it to a private affair. Liberalism favoured freedom of religion but separated religion from state. There are many strands of liberalism and there are distinguishable attitudes towards religion. Liberalism could be hostile, indifferent, mixed, cooperative or favourable with respect to religion. One kind of liberalism is hostile to religion. It proceeds from the view that institutional religion was a disreputable record of oppression, persecution and violence. This hostile liberalism finds its themes in French enlightenment. The Enlightenment arose from an antipathy to what it perceived to be blind adherence to authority, tradition, custom, habit and faith. It valourized reason, independent thought, autonomy and scientific method. This strand of liberalism was represented by Voltaire, John Dewey, Alan Ryan and Richard Rorty.[1] Voltaire's "secular philosophy was a formidable, almost irresistible rival of Christianity. For Voltaire, the "church was the implacable enemy of progress, decency, humanity, and rationality."[2] Dewey did not object to God talk, but he rejected any concept of the supernatural. He argued for democratic religion and common faith. Conservatives or Satanists, on the other hand, upheld religion. For them, God is the only solution for worldly problems. They were opposed to any kind of change in the sacred texts/shastras. Edmund Burke is the typical representative of conservative tradition. Burke contrasted tradition and reason, and in so doing placed stability, consensus, prejudice and prescription on the side of tradition. On the side of reason, Burke placed conflict, rational reflection and revolution. He was critical of French revolution on this account. In his book *Why I am not a Christian?* Bertrand Russell regards religion as a disease born of fear and as a source of untold misery to the human race. Interestingly, he differentiates Buddhism from other historic religions. 'Of the great religions of history, I prefer Buddhism, especially in its earliest forms, because it has had the smallest element of persecution. Buddhism is a combination of both speculative and scientific philosophy. It advocates the scientific method and pursues that to a finality that may be called rationalistic. In it are to be found answers to such question of interest as 'What is mind and matter? Of them which is of great importance? Is the universe moving towards a goal?'[3] It is clear that there are strong attempts to undermine religion in the wake of modernity, reason and scientific understanding of the world. In other words, modernity is opposed to religious world views by considering these views as traditional. Tradition is considered as an uncritical acceptance of the past, which is in the form of beliefs, rituals and scriptural authority. Tradition has vested in religion and its irrational social practices and mythical authority. Modernity is considered to be breaking away from tradition. We can see that a kind of dichotomous opposition between tradition and modernity has been constructed.

Construction of religion: overcoming the dichotomy of tradition–modernity

In the Indian context, both religion and modernity have acquired different meanings. Most of the Indian intellectuals contested the dichotomous opposition between tradition and modernity. The social reformers and nationalist thinkers blurred the binary between tradition and modernity in the backdrop of colonial modernity. It is argued that the dominant construction of modernity suited colonial interests at the expense of the colonized. The dominant perspective of modernity is equated with industrialization and scientific and technological advancement, which were limited to western countries. Indian thinkers were critical about the dogmatic social practices of tradition that are often identified with religion, and at the same time, they negotiated religion with modernity through the reformation of religion. Indian intellectuals have overcome the tradition–modernity dichotomy in their own way rather than accepting readymade alternatives to tradition manufactured in the west. They engaged with 'religion' on different grounds. For instance, Indian intellectuals such as Gandhi, Ambedkar and J. Krishnamurti argued in favour of religiousness (Kesava Kumar 2015). Gandhi's *Hind Swaraj* is critical of modern western civilization and argues in favour of life based on spirituality. To fulfil this idea, he proposed a universal notion of religion, Hinduism. On the other hand, Ambedkar too proposes Buddhism as the religion that is based on righteous social life. He upholds a tradition that stands for reason and morality. J. Krishnamurti totally rejects tradition, which is the product of thought and has continuity with the past. He believed that tradition is built upon myths, dogmas, beliefs and authority. Interestingly, he too argues for religion. For him, religion means deprogramming the mind of all the systems, beliefs, dogmas, superstitions and conditionings. He considers the essence of religion as freedom. It is the feeling of love and compassion, the seeking of truth. To be religious is to be chiocelessly aware that there is freedom from the known (Kesava Kumar 2015: 164).

In India, religion is often projected as a way of life. There is a strong opinion that Indian philosophy is inseparable from religion. Religion has been used as a means to suit the political interests of intellectuals. On one hand, it has been used as a means of protest by Brahmanical and anti-Brahmanical forces from different political positions against the colonial rule. On the other hand, there have been conscious attempts to converse religion in modern, scientific and rationalistic terminology. Indian intellectual history reveals that almost all major thinkers engaged with the idea of religion. Religion seems to be central to their writings, and for social and political actions. The colonial experience provided them with an occasion to rethink about their traditions and socio-cultural practices that are intertwined with religion. The policies were articulated as a protest against colonial domination in the language of religion. In other words, Indian intellectuals set religion as a protest against domination. In the process, either they reformed their religion or dogmatically supported tradition without any critical scrutiny. They came up with a new language to articulate their social anxieties and political aspirations through religion. Religion too acquired new meanings. Social reformers and nationalists of colonial times made conscious attempts to reconstruct religion in the backdrop of colonial/Western rationality and enlightenment. The Dalit-Bahujan intellectuals too reconstructed religion as a protest and this protest was launched against both—colonial dominance and Brahmanical exploitation. It is argued by some of the scholars that the Indian intellectuals of both Brahmanical and Dalit-Bahujan camps constructed religion from the source of anglicized and orientalist's exposition of Indian religious tradition. Although Ambedkar too used material supplied by the anglicized and Orientalist scholars, we can see him developing a novel, critical and creative approach in understanding religion.

The modern construction of religion is traced back to Anglicized and Orientalist understanding and intervention of Indian cultural traditions. Anglicists considered India to be corrupt. They believed that its culture was degenerate and its population irrational, retarded, superstitious and morally depraved. The Orientalists, on the other hand, genuinely sought to understand the foreign culture. Surely, they wanted to bring reform. But they were certain that a transformation could only be successful if it resonated with the mores of the natives. In their assessment of the fundamental structure of Indian society, unerringly, both identified brahmins as the 'priests'. They both were convinced that these 'priests' had a negative influence on religion and society. Brahmins were held responsible for the creation and sanctification of the caste system, which brought social development to a halt. They held that this system consisted of a rigid social compartmentalization and that it was created to preserve religious and social privileges of the Brahmin caste. Anglicists found Indian culture and society to be intrinsically corrupt from the very beginning. Orientalists, however, saw India's culture as being based on sound principles that steadily degenerated. The cause of corruption, however, was the same in both cases, viz. 'Brahmanism' (Gelders and Derde 2003: 4611). Raf Gelders and Willem Derde (2003: 4611) proposed that both the idea of religious degeneration and the role played by the priests in this process are derived from deep-seated Christian conceptions of religion. Europeans from diverse ideological and religious backgrounds identified brahmins as priests and Brahmanism as a 'religion of the priests'. This common understanding derived its consistency from a Christian understanding of religion. They further argue (2003: 4611–17) that even the writings of Ram Mohan Roy and Babasaheb Ambedkar reveal an unconditional acceptance of Europe's conceptualization in a debate over religion that continued in the 20th century. Romila Thapar too pointed out that modern construction of Hinduism is often acclaimed as following the defence of Orientalism: "The work integrating a vast collection of myths, beliefs, rituals and laws into a coherent religion and of shaping an amorphous heritage into a rational faith known now as "Hinduism" were endeavours initiated by Orientalists."[4] As she invokes Gramsci to understand the modern Hindu identity, in Gramsci's terms, the class, which wishes to become hegemonic, has to nationalize itself and the new 'nationalist' Hinduism comes from the middle class.[5] Romila Thapar further explores the nexus between caste and religion or the sects of religion in earlier times.' She reminds us that this social dimension as well as the degree to which a religious sect had its identity in caste or alternatively was inclusive of caste, has been largely ignored in the modern interpretation of early Hinduism. With the erosion of social observances and caste identity, there is now a search for a new identity and here the creation of a new Hinduism becomes relevant.[6] Sumit Sarkar observed that on the whole the major social reform initiatives were much more related to gender injustice within the reformers' own middle class, high-caste milieu. Caste was critiqued in such circles primarily for contributing to disunion, as a hindrance to the process of gradual unification of Indian people. They thought this to be progress under a fundamentally 'providential', modernizing British rule. The social injustice argument, while not absent, remained secondary (Sarkar 1998: 365). Caste was critiqued for obstructing national unity or being a hindrance for high-caste improvement. They never bothered to take note of grievances or protests of lower castes. While at the time of the Nationalist movement, political freedom was the priority and they were not bothered about either social reform or social freedom.

At this historical juncture, the dominant religion, Hinduism has not only been redefined by the Indian intellectuals but also contested by drawing from non-Brahmin sections. They even counter-posed Hinduism with alternative religions and indigenous traditions. In restructuring or democratizing the society, they recognized the nexus between religion and social institution such as caste, and eventually fought against both. The non-Brahmin thinkers such as Jyotiba Phule and Periyar treated Hinduism as an Aryan religion. They argued that their religion is distinctive from Brahmanical Hinduism. They proposed alternatives to Hinduism that were free from Brahmanical dominance. Phule proposed *sarvajank satya dharma* and Periyar attacked Hinduism from an atheistic point by arguing for the distinctiveness of Dravidian culture from Brahmanical Aryan religion. Some of the Dalit Bahujan scholars searched their identity in Buddhism. They considered Buddhism as an egalitarian religion opposed to caste dominance. Moreover, they believed that Buddhism had an impulse of modernity and stood for reason. Iyothee Thassar and Lakshmi Narasu of Madras presidency invoked Buddhism against Hinduism (Narasu 2003). G. Aloysius observed that there were attempts even before the Ambedkar's historic conversion to Buddhism, to resuscitate the core philosophical and social ideas of the Buddha, across the subcontinent, mostly in the vernacular idiom, as a means to express the existential problems of subalternized, but also as a vehicle of their socio-political emancipation (Aloysius 2004).

In early 20th century of Madras presidency, M. Singaravelu, P. Lakshmi Narasu and Iyothee Thassar of different social backgrounds with the encouragement and support of Colonel Olcott of Theosophical Society, united in their commitment to Buddhism and tended to interpret it somewhat differently to suit their own existential needs. Singaravelu, with his inclination towards the rising communist paradigm in the west, saw Buddha as an atheistic rationalist; for Lakshmi Narasu, the Buddha was a humanist rationalist par excellence; and for Iyothee Thassar, the Buddha and his teachings were primarily embodied within Tamil-Dravidian traditions contesting the conservative-vedic cultural and historical traditions, hence to be reconstructed as a main force of socio-cultural rationality (Aloysius 2004: xiii). It may be noted that though both Lakshmi Narasu and Iyothee Thassar shared similarity in fundamentals and were distinct from others, they had also minor differences in their Buddhist vision. Narasu drew inspiration from the rationalist–humanistic and scientific writings of the Western world, while Iyothee Thassar was soaked within the Tamil tradition, literature, culture and history. Iyothee Thassar did not perceive the same level of resonance with Lakshmi Narasu, he was quick to brand Narasu's Buddhism as 'strange' and 'scientific', meaning thereby that it did not make anti-casteism the central issue (Aloysius 2004: xvi).

In constructing Buddhist identity against Brahmanical Hinduism, caste occupied the central role in modern times. The Dalit intellectuals Iyothee Thassar and Ambedkar constructed their social and cultural identity by invoking Buddhism as their native religion. Both of them embraced Buddhist religion as an emancipatory identity. They identified Buddhism as a religion of the oppressed. Further, Dalit identification with Buddhism was presented as the recovery of cultural past rather than their conversion to it. As Aloysius explained the religion of the oppressed is a self-conscious, self-differentiating and self-defining sacralized ideology, set against the dominant, unethical challenge and superiority. It is an ethically ideal world view, embodying a social order that is egalitarian and by implication, envisaging a more just share in society for themselves (Aloysius 2015: 15–18).

Religion, morality and modernity

Generally, religion is viewed as an irrational belief and a matter of faith. Religion is considered to be a pre-modern idea. Modernity has been celebrated as an expression of freedom, reason, scientific rationality, enlightenment, secularism and humanism. Modernity has undermined religion by its critical approach towards the latter. According to modern rationalism, truth about the world can be reached by way of human faculties, in particular through methods that give us access to things as they really are. Such rationalism takes human comprehension as the determiner not only of how we come to know the world, but also what constitutes legitimate knowledge. Modernity has different connotations and is experienced in different ways. Across the cultures, we may find crucial differences in the ways modernity is experienced and defined. In the west, there is an increasingly critical attitude towards the modern condition in general and Western legacy of post-enlightenment rationalism in particular. Both within west and outside the west, we may find different propositions of modernity. Some came with the idea of multiple modernities. Charles Taylor (1989) and MacIntyre (2011) are critical about dominant western notions and articulated a communitarian position against the liberal view. Radical individualism, which is centred on the self and not attached to any other society, eroded the meaningfulness of life. He argues that the dominant conception of modernity has undermined the family, citizenship and community and even eroded the conditions of freedom. Modernity is a new conception of moral order of the society. Taylor (1989: 195–7) argues that the atomistic Western modernity is narrowing our horizons and flattening our lives. He holds that the normative authority of instrumental reason and social atomism is responsible for humans not realizing the richness and fuller meaning of life. He differentiates *acultural* modernity from cultural modernity (1999: 42–43). For Taylor (2007: 61, 572) modernity is grounded in religion and MacIntyre prefers a Homeric life, which is prominently viewed as pre-modern. Both argued that the meaning of life is embedded in social life. Taylor believed that the notion of 'good' shapes and opens up our moral world thereby disclosing or establishing our identity as moral agents. He reflects on morality by inviting a philosophical conversation with diverse voices of modernity and their respective sources and traditions (Taylor 1989: 62, 122). The cultural theory of modernity understands society as a picture of plurality of human cultures, each of which has a language and set of practices that define specific understandings of personhood, social relations, state of mind/soul, good and bad, virtues and vices. Taylor seeks the reflexive and hermeneutic kind of modernity (Taylor 1989: 51, 171). He distinguishes two distinctive kinds of elements of modernity—the moral order and social imaginary. The moral order is an explicit set of ideas about how we should act and why the social world is arranged in the way that it is. The social imaginary is a more elusive set of self-understandings, background practices and horizons of common expectations that are not always explicitly articulated, but that gives people a sense of shared group life. Further Taylor argues that demand for recognition is a basic human good

Ambedkar too believes that religion safeguards the moral domain. It deploys sentiments, feelings and culture to secure the moral domain and make it universal (Rodrigues 2002: 19). He too searches for a moral order in the community. In his search, he argues that Hinduism is not qualified as community and it is anti-social in spirit. He invokes Buddhism as a religion qualified as community and social. It stands for reason and morality. His notion of religion is rational, secular and modern.

Modernity does not have different meanings in India but it has come with different versions. The Indian nationalists have an ambivalent attitude to colonial modernity. Their discourse towards modernity is philosophical and cultural but often epistemologically insensitive and inconsistent to the ideal of modernity. Viewing modernity as a significant advance over the pre-modern past, Dalit Bahujan thought upholds a distinctive version, and is markedly different from mainstream nationalism. The cultural nationalism proposed by the nationalists is viewed as oppressive by these intellectuals. Gopal Guru pointed out that the celebration of India's spiritual superiority over the material west could be understood in the context of national imagination. Invoking spiritual/cultural superiority by nationalist thinkers and leaders by implication seeks to ignore the internal forms of humiliation that emanate from the social practices based on caste, untouchability and gender discrimination. He further argues that the emergence of modern society is both enabling and constraining at the same time. However, modernity creates an awareness of the conditions of the servile class and claimable rights (Guru 2009: 4).

According to Dalit Bahujan thought, the principles of modernity are superior to the principles expressed in the existing social institutions, and can therefore, be used to interrogate both colonial modernity and the modernity that brahmins were trying to install in India. Dalit-Bahujan intellectuals uphold human reason in scrutinizing traditions and customs. For brahmins, therefore, modernity is of instrumental value, while for Dalit-Bahujans, it throws up resources for their enablement and emancipation. Ambedkar resorts to Buddha's teachings and practices rather than to customs and practices, as the very embodiment of reason. Reason is contra-posed to the ritualistic and other-worldly ways. It is available to the people without the need to depend on external resources. It is embedded in the sensuous ways of life as it is in the reflective (Rodrigues 2008: 17–18). Ambedkar's understanding of religion provides a new dimension to modernity. His religion is based on a moral theory that internalizes the principles of equality, liberty and fraternity. It ensures human dignity and self-respect. For him, religion is an ideal of emancipation.

Ambedkar: a conceptual understanding of religion

For Ambedkar, religion is a moral force in governing a society. He considers religion as a social factor that provides a feeling of community and belonging. Religion is a rational and moral ideal. For him, an ideal society is that which is governed by the moral conscience with free flow of communication. Keeping in view of this conception of religion, he is critical about Hinduism and termed it as "anti-social." He held an opinion that Hindus cannot be said to form a society or nation due to lack of 'consciousness of kind'. The consciousness that exists in Hindus is the consciousness of caste (BAWS-1: 50–51). He characterizes society as a people sharing and participating in common activity rather than living in physical proximity and having similar habits, customs and beliefs. As he says, "the caste system prevents common activity and by preventing common activity it has prevented the Hindus from becoming a society with a unified life and consciousness of its own kind" (BAWS-1: 51). He characterizes that inequality is the soul of Hinduism. It is grounded on a social system called the caste system. It kills the public spirit. Ambedkar felt that there is an immediate need to reform Hinduism in his work *Annihilation of Caste* (BAWS-1: 37–80). For a healthy society, the caste system has to be annihilated. Before initiating any change, we have to reform society. In *Philosophy of Hinduism*, he provides a methodology to understand religion. He calls this methodology as a philosophy of religion. He evaluates Hinduism and its social order by this method. He found that 'Hinduism is inimical to equality, antagonistic to liberty and opposed to fraternity (BAWS-3: 66).' He understood that reforming Hinduism using his line of thought is difficult. He interprets Indian history in religious terms. He viewed Indian history as the struggle between a revolutionary religion, Buddhism, and counterrevolutionary religion, Brahmanism, in his work *Revolution and Counter-Revolution in Ancient India* (BAWS-3: 151–429). In pursuing his moral society, he constructs Buddhism in his *Buddha and His Dhamma* (BAWS-11). He brings Buddhism parallel to Marxism in *Buddha or Karl Marx* (BAWS-3: 441–64).

Ambedkar is not against religion per se. In fact, he recognizes the primacy of religion. Religion is central to his philosophy and had implications for social and political life. He often refers to Burke in realizing the importance of religion and at the same time he maintains the critical distance from Burke's philosophical position. Ambedkar, in agreement with Burke notes that 'true religion is the foundation of society, the basis on which all true civil governments rests, and both their sanction.'(BAWS-1: 76) Further he agrees with his teacher John Dewey on the recognition of the importance of religion and the need for democratizing religion. He follows the method adopted by Dewey in evaluating religion. Like him, he is critical about supernaturalism and looks for reasoned religion. In this way Ambedkar overcomes the tradition–modernity dichotomy. We could not treat him either as traditionalist or modernist in generally known terms. He locates the individual in the social, and demands that the social has to be regulated by principles of morality. He adopts social morality, internalizing the principles of equality, liberty and fraternity as criteria in evaluating religion. He philosophizes about religion and brings about the philosophy of religion as methodology. He connects religion and politics in their capacity to govern our lives. He politicizes religion from a moral framework.

Ambedkar's conception of religion has different dimensions. He unifies diverse approaches in understanding religious–anthropological, sociological, historical, theological/religious and philosophical. His approach is anthropological in explaining the origin and evolution of religion from savage to modern religion. As Ambedkar explains, it is true that savage society practices magic, believes in taboo and worships the totem. But it is wrong to suppose that these constitute religion or form the source of religion. To take such a view is to elevate what is incidental to the position of the principal. These elemental facts of human existence are incidental and means but are not ends. *The end is life and the preservation of life.* Ambedkar comes to the conclusion that "*Life and preservation of life are the core and centre of the religion of the savage society*". (BAWS-3: 10) It is these life processes that constitute the substance and source of religion. Prof Crawley endorses this (BAWS-3: 11). In both savage and civilized religions, the central interest is in the life processes by which individuals are preserved and hence maintained. But they differ on some points. In savage society there is religion without god. In savage society there is morality but it is independent of religion. (BAWS-3: 10–11).

Ambedkar's approach to religion is historical as it is about explaining the transformation of religion. For him, religion is not eternal or static but undergoes constant change with changing conditions. He argues that Hindus must recognize that there is nothing fixed, nothing eternal, nothing sanatan, that everything is changing, that change is the law of life for individuals as well as for society. He explains how religions have undergone change with changing conditions. He argues that Hinduism is no exception to this.[7] He acknowledges that science has influenced religion and has implications for our knowledge.[8] He provides the historical interpretation of religious revolution. As he quotes Tiele, all religions of the civilized and uncivilized world, dead or living are a historical and psychological phenomenon, in all their manifestations (BAWS-3: 4). It is the history of religion that provides facts. He argues that historical facts have to be understood comprehensively. He calls it as a philosophy of religion. As he opined on the philosophy of religion, we should be able to discover in the varied manifestations a common principle to whose roots in human nature we can point, whose evolution we can trace by intelligent stages from lower to higher and more adequate forms, as well as its intimate relations with the other main factors in human civilization (BAWS-3: 4).

From the historical facts, he constructs the sociological/social theory of religion. For all his philosophical discourses, the social is central.

He regards religion as based on the principle of social solidarity. He is critical of caste and Hinduism for its anti-social tendencies. He tries to understand the social from rationalistic, moralistic and naturalistic perspectives. He prefers critical tradition that is relevant in modern times. The dead past has no meaning for him. He looks for a just social order. He is critical about Hinduism for its unjust social order and demands for reforming it. He maintains that any change or revolution is futile unless and until it brings a change in the social realm. He believes that the social precedes the political.

Ambedkar's social theory is in tune with his philosophy of religion. *Philosophy is concerned with knowing the truth. Religion is concerned with the love of truth. Philosophy is static. Religion is dynamic. These differences are merely two aspects of one and the same. Philosophy is static because it is concerned only with knowing truth. Religion is dynamic because it is concerned with the love of truth* (BAWS-3: 86). It means that Ambedkar was concerned more about living with truth rather than knowing the truth. Ambedkar points out that a Hindu is not prepared to face inquiry about religion. He either argues that religion is of no importance or he takes shelter behind the view—fostered by a study of comparative religions—that all religions are good. There is no doubt that both these views are mistaken and untenable (BAWS-3: 22).

In *Philosophy of Hinduism*, Ambedkar uses his philosophical method in understanding religion and applies it to Hinduism. Ambedkar considers philosophy of religion as having both descriptive and normative character. In so far as it deals with the teachings of a religion, philosophy of religion becomes a descriptive science. In so far as it involves the use of critical reason for passing judgement on those teachings, the philosophy of religion becomes a normative science (BAWS-3: 5). He further explains that a study of philosophy of religion involves determination of three dimensions. First, what is the definition of religion? Second, the ideal scheme for which religion stands. Third, philosophy of religion is the criterion to be adopted for judging the value of the ideal scheme of divine governance for which a given religion stands. Ambedkar too approaches religion from theological point of view. He differs with traditional theologies such as mythological, civil and revealed theologies and offers natural theology. Natural theology is the doctrine of god and divine, as an integral part of the theory of nature. Ambedkar considers *religion to mean the propounding of an ideal scheme of divine governance, the aim and object of which is to make the social order in which men live a moral order* (BAWS-3: 6). According to him, the best method to ascertain the criterion by which to judge the philosophy of religion is to study the revolutions which religion has been through. To know the philosophy of any movement or any institution, one must study the revolutions that the movement or the institution has been through. Revolution is the mother of philosophy and if it is not the mother of philosophy, it is a lamp that illuminates philosophy (BAWS-3: 8). Ambedkar illustrates the religious revolutions of India. He maintains that a religious revolution touches the nature and content of ruling conceptions of the relations of god to man, of society to man and of man to man.

Ambedkar explains the historical journey of religion from savage society to civilized society. Savage society is marked by the performance of rites and ceremonies, the practice of magic or taboo and the worship of fetish or totem. Ambedkar observes that in savage society, there is no trace of god. There is no bond between morality and religion. Morality is independent of religion. These are connected to a certain occasion that represents the crisis of human life. Although the relation between God and religion is not quite integral, the relation between religion and morality is. Both religion and morality are connected with the same elemental facts of human existence—namely life, death, birth and marriage. Religion consecrates these life processes while morality furnishes rules for their preservation (BAWS-3: 12).

In civilized society god comes in the scheme of religion and morality becomes sanctified by religion. The civilized religion has undergone further radical revolution from religion of antique society to religion of modern society (BAWS-3: 12). It may be that the idea of god had its origin in the worship of the great man in society, the hero-giving rise to theism—with the society building a faith in its living god. It may be that the philosophical speculation upon the problem as to who created life—giving rise to deism—has given rise to the society's belief in god as architect of the universe. In any case the idea of god is not integral to religion. How it got fused into religion is difficult to explain.

Ambedkar elaborately explains the evolution of religion from ancient to modern. He even acknowledges science in changing the conceptions and practices of religion. He comes to an understanding that in ancient society men and their Gods formed a social, political as well as a religious whole. Religion was founded on kinship between god and worshippers. Modern society has eliminated god from its composition. It consists only of people (BAWS-3: 14). The God of the antique society was an exclusive god. God was owned by and bound to one single community. Solidarity was found between god and community. God had become attached to community, and the community had become attached to its god. This view has its own implications. Antique society never came to conceive that god could be a universal god, the god of all. It could not conceive that there was any such thing as humanity in general. As Ambedkar note, at one end of the revolution was the antique society with its religious ideal in which the end was society. At the other end of revolution is the modern society with its religious ideal in which the end is the individual. To put the same fact in terms of norms, it can be said that the norm or the criterion, for judging right and wrong in the antique society was utility, while the norm or the criterion for judging right and wrong in modern society is justice (BAWS-3: 22). In *Philosophy of Hinduism*, Ambedkar concludes that Hinduism is not qualified to be called a religion. The philosophy of Hinduism is such that it cannot be called the religion of humanity. The philosophy of Hinduism neither satisfies the test of social utility nor does it satisfy the test of individual justice (BAWS-3: 71).

In *Annihilation of Caste*, Ambedkar looks out for the possibility of reforming Hinduism based on his conception of religion. He argues that we have to recognize that Hindu society is a myth. Caste has completely disorganized and demoralized the Hindus. Ambedkar opposes rule-based religion and favours a religion based on principles. He maintains that Hinduism is bound by rules rather than principles. Hindu religion, as contained in the *Vedas* and *Smirits*, is nothing but a mass of sacrificial, social, political and sanitary rules and regulations, all mixed up. For Hindu dharma means commands and prohibitions. The word dharma as used in the Vedas in most cases means religious ordinances or rites. Even Jaimini in Purva Mimamsa defines dharma as a desirable goal or result that is indicated by injunctive (vedic) passages. What Hindus call religion is really law or best legalized class-ethics. Ambedkar refuses to call this code of ordinances, as religion. The first evil of such a code of ordinances, misrepresented to the people as religion is that it tends to deprive moral life of freedom and spontaneity and to reduce it to a more or less anxious and servile conformity to externally imposed rules (BAWS-1: 75).

Religion and caste

Historically, we may find many interpretations of a relation between religion and caste. We find an invariable relation between Hinduism and caste. Dumont in his work *Homo Hierachicus* holds that political and economic domains of social life in India are encompassed by the 'religious life.' The religious principle becomes articulated in terms of the opposition of purity and pollution. F.G. Bailey argues that caste was not a unique moral or religious system. It was merely a more elaborate form of social stratification to be found in many other societies: the true basis of the distinction between those of low and high caste was the differential access to political and economic resources.[9] Ambedkar at length discusses in *Castes in India* the nexus between caste and religion in Indian society. He explains that the caste system is sustained by Hinduism. The caste system is considered by him as a perversion of the Chaturvarnya order ascribed by Brahmanism. According to Ambedkar, hierarchy, lack of social efficiency, social immobility, disruptive tendencies, ex-communication, and endogamy are the primary features of the caste system. The caste system opposes natural law and the spirit of human development (BAWS-1). In *Annihilation of Caste*,

Ambedkar further argues that caste is anti-social, resists the spread of civilization, kills the public spirit, and denies common culture. '*The caste system prevents common activity and by preventing common activity it has prevented the Hindus from becoming a society with a unified life and conscious of its own being*' (BAWS-1: 51).

Caste is identified with social life most often regulated/prompted by principles of religion. In other words, caste is a social function of religion. The dominant Indian philosophic thought has supported the *varnashrama dharama* as a religious principle for the good of society as a whole. This kind of thinking and practice has sustained for many generations until it got contested by the victims of this social/religious phenomenon.

Colonial modernity has significantly influenced the Western liberal educated intellectuals of elite communities in reformulating their ideas on religion and caste. The reforming of religion has implications for caste. But the religious reformers are not explicit about caste. They appeal that originally religion has nothing to do with caste. The religious literature, especially Vedic, and Upanishadic and the Gita have no sanctity for the caste system of contemporary times. Gandhi is the culmination of this kind of thinking. On the one hand he broadens the scope of Hinduism through the claim of its universal inclusiveness of every religion, and on the other supports varnashrama dharma as the age-old wisdom. The practice of untouchability and caste has nothing to do with his scheme of religion although he opposes untouchability. The ideals of modernity have not changed the core of religion and caste, and their nexus. It has only altered the language in justifying religion and its relation to caste. At the same time, there exists a counter current to the dominant construction of religion, especially to Hinduism from non-Brahmanical communities. They may be marginalized in our academic discourse but had an established intellectual tradition with sound logic among their communities. The late-medieval subaltern saints fought against caste system within the religious terms. Kabir, Ravidas, Chokamela and Veerabraham are known exemplary figures. In colonial times, Jyotiba Phule and Ramaswamy Periyar came against the Brahmanical Hinduism by claiming that their traditions have nothing to do with caste. They had an attempt to read history and culture from a non-Brahmanical perspective. Scholars such as Lakshmi Narasu and Iyothee Thassar have not only exposed the Brahmanical philosophies but also redefined religion from moral and rationalistic perspectives. They counterposed Buddhism against Hinduism in contemporary times. The argument has consolidated in Ambedkar's life and works. His understanding of religion is novel and rational. His conception of religion is both modern and ethical. He negotiates Buddhism with modern sensibilities.

Ambedkar understood that inequality is the soul of Hinduism. He felt that it is a misnomer to call it religion. Its philosophy is opposed to the very thing for which religion stands. He asserted, "Hinduism! Thy name is inequality!" (BAWS-1: 86). There is no dignity and recognition for the untouchables in Hinduism due to the caste system. He opposed Hinduism, which is based on *sruti* and *smriti* tradition. He says, if you wish to bring about a breach in the caste system then you have got to apply the dynamite to the Vedas and the Shastras, which deny any part to reason, to morality. You must destroy the religion of the shrutis and the smritis. Nothing else will avail. You must discard the authority of the shastras and destroy the religion of shastras to live in the present. Ambedkar in *Annihilation of caste* made a concluding remark that only when the Hindu society becomes a casteless society that it can hope to have strength enough to defend itself. Without such strength, *swaraj* for Hindus may turn out to be only a step towards slavery.

Buddhism as revolution

Despite Orientalist scholarship, many Indian scholars interpreted religion in their own way. The Hindu intellectuals even tried to assimilate Buddhism into the Hindu fold and even propagated that the Buddha is one of the avatars of Vishnu. The thinkers of progressive movements recognized the strength of Buddhism. Especially, the Dalit Bahujan intellectuals resisted the assimilation of Buddhism with Brahmanism. They even embraced Buddhism as their own tradition. As Aloysius observed the Dalit-subaltern intellectuals and ideologists, in the course of their self-recovery, also discovered a unified and genuinely traditional stream of thought, code of ethics and sacralized symbol system with which meaningful ideological linkages and lineages could be forged, without distorting their historical truth. This brings to the fore the epistemological and ethical superiority of their collective terms (Aloysius 2004: 16). Prior to Ambedkar or as contemporary to Ambedkar, Iyothee Thassar and Lakshmi Narasu made an attempt to shape Buddhism in modern times. Ambedkar provided the unified theory of Buddhism by internalizing the positions of Iyothee Thassar and Lakshmi Narasu.[10] According to Ambedkar, the emergence of Buddhism was more than a revolution: *Buddhism was a revolution. It was as great a Revolution as the French Revolution. Though it began as a Religious revolution, it became more than Religious revolution. It became a Social and Political Revolution* (BAWS-3: 153).

Ambedkar constructed his own version of Buddhism by making it modern, moral, natural and rational. He viewed the Buddha as an enduring philosopher of mankind. Buddhism for him was a social philosophy. The Buddha according to him has not only provided a comprehensive understanding of the world that unifies economy, society and polity, but also has stood against Brahmanism. Buddhism emerged as an egalitarian and revolutionary thought against ritualistic, fatalistic, supernaturalistic philosophies. As it is observed, many major ideas of Indian philosophy can be seen, at least in rudimentary form, in the 6th century BC. The philosophers articulated their world view through their ideas on the one hand and through the institutional practices within which they created their organizations on the other. Buddhism against fatalistic philosophies strongly believed in the power of human action. The Brahmanical emphasis on social hierarchy based on varna divisions was countered by the Buddha with the practice of equal access to the *sangha* for all. Buddhist social philosophy came in response to the social inequality and the subordination of women to the patriarchal kinship system of 6th century BC (Chakravarthy 2004: 12).

Buddhism has changed over the period of time and many sects are formed. It has spread in many countries and has become a global religion, but has declined in India. It has been appropriated by Hinduism in course of time and has acquired many tendencies of Hinduism. In modern India, when the Brahmanical intellectuals were valourizing Hinduism, Ambedkar embraced Buddhism. He constructed modern Buddhism, popularly known as *Navayana* Buddhism.

Ambedkar had strong reasons for his choice of Buddhism. Buddhism was an indigenous religion that fulfilled his ideal of religion and a vision of society. It is not a religion of rituals but a rationalistic one. Its morality is not derived from a supernatural source but it is this-worldly. One's own actions determine morality rather than being controlled by an external authority. It is not dogmatic but stands for reason. It proposes a righteous life. It is an egalitarian and humanistic religion. It is a godless and soulless religion. It is the religion of present but not of a dead past. It is a living tradition. It is the original religion of the untouchables. Hence conversion to it would amount to the recovery of a cultural past of untouchable communities. Further, the Buddhist social order is based on the principles of equality, liberty, fraternity and justice. Its ultimate aim is the end of suffering like the Marxist ideal of a classless society. Ambedkar converted to Buddhism on October 14, 1956, took oath that the converted should reject the Hindu deities as well as rituals and fight for an equal and just society. While reconstructing Buddhism, Ambedkar extensively consulted Buddhist literature. By reading the literature of Hinduism and Orientalists texts about Indian religions, he developed a critical approach.[11] His hermeneutic reading of religious texts offers new meanings with contemporary sensibility. He read these texts along with the social life that lies in these works. In *Revolution and Counter-Revolution in Ancient India*, he interprets Indian history as the history of conflict between Buddhism and Brahminism. It is the struggle between two world views. It is the contestation over value systems. He treats struggles of Buddhism as revolutionary and Brahmanism as counter revolutionary. In the Aryan society a Shudra or a low caste person could never become a Brahman. But Buddha not only preached against caste but admitted the shudras and the low caste to the rank of a Bhikkhu who held the same rank in Buddhism as the Brahman did in Brahmanism. Buddha repudiated the authority of the Vedas, and he denounced the Yajna as a form of religion. Thirdly Buddha denounced was the caste system (BAWS-3: 188. 204). The principle of inequality, which is the basis of the caste system, had become well established, and it was against this principle that Buddha carried on a determined and a bitter fight. How strongly was he opposed to the pretensions of the Brahmins on their superiority over other castes is to be found in many of his dialogues such as the Ambattha Sutta (BAWS-3: 220). Far from being spiritual and elevating, the hymns of the Rig Veda are saturated with wicked thoughts and wicked purposes. According to Ambedkar the Aryan religion never concerned itself with what is called a righteous life (BAWS-3: 176). As against this, morality was basic to Buddhism. The similarity with Taylor can be brought out. Both consider religion as a moral stance that provides a meaningful community life. In other words, self is located in moral community. For Taylor those who believe cannot do so in a naive way. They have to become critically connected to religion: This is the challenge of the secular age. In Ambedkar's case, a critical approach to religion is not a challenge of the secular age. Rather, critiquing religion and reconciling religion with modernity allows one to acquire a tradition when one has been deprived of it as an underprivileged caste. Ambedkar in *The Buddha and the Future of His Religion* considers: 'The religion of the Buddha is morality. It is imbedded in religion. Buddhist religion is nothing if not morality. It is true that in Buddhism there is no god. In place of god there is morality. What god is to other religions, morality is to Buddhism' (BAWS-17.2: 98).

While underlining the rational character of Buddhism Ambedkar with conviction maintains that

> In his (Buddha's) opinion, nothing was infallible and nothing could be final. Everything must be open to re-examination and re-consideration whenever grounds for re-examination and re-consideration arise... Believe only in those doctrines, which you have scrutinized and of which you are totally convinced.
>
> (BAWS-11: 89)

Further Ambedkar holds that the Buddha held to the doctrine of wisdom as firmly as he did to the doctrine of love. He held that moral life began with knowledge and 'ended with wisdom' (BAWS-3: 188). *Buddha and His Dhamma* provides the notes for his conception of philosophy of religion as *saddharma*. A unique amalgam of *Prajna* and *Karuna* is the Dhamma of the Buddha (Ambedkar 1974: III.V.III.2). Aishwary Kumar proposes that *maitri* is central to Ambedkar's *Buddha and His Dhamma*. For Ambedkar, *maitri* categorically refuses the foundational distinction between friendship and hostility. It is extending fellow feeling to all beings. Maitri is an anti-sovereign and non-theological principle. It is an act of adoration rather than force (Aishwary 2013). In *The Buddha and His Dhamma*, Ambedkar goes beyond love. As he says, 'Love is not enough. What is required is *maitri*.' *Maitri* is foundational for Ambedkar's conception of religion/social/democracy/spiritualism. It is the principle of governance of life, society and state.

Conclusion

Ambedkar's philosophy of religion is a breakthrough in the history of Indian philosophy. His engagement with the 'social' provides a realistic approach. He argued that philosophical ideas have to be grounded in social and cultural life. He sometimes differentiates between philosophy and religion by regarding the former as static and the latter as dynamic. That is because philosophy is concerned about knowing the truth, and religion is proclaimed to be about the love of truth. His conception of religion is moralistic, rationalistic and naturalistic. The criteria for evaluating religion are the principles of equality, liberty and fraternity. By applying his method of philosophy of religion, he felt that Hinduism could not be qualified as a religion due to its anti-social spirit. For Ambedkar, religion is righteous and social. The ideal society he considers is one that provides a sense of belongingness and community life based on morality. For him society means people participating in and sharing in a common activity. It is an act of mutual communication rather than keeping in isolation. But the Hindu social order is based on the caste system. Caste kills the public spirit. Both caste and Hinduism are anti-humanitarian in nature and consequently anti-modern in their attitude. Hinduism is a religion based on rituals and regulations and it is the religion of *shastras*. It does not stand for reason. He thought of reforming Hinduism in his line of understanding of religion in *Annihilation of Caste*. But soon he realized that it is a futile exercise and chose Buddhism as a religion. Through his reconstruction he brought to the foreground the humanistic, rationalistic and democratic essence of Buddhism. He found that Buddhism has a revolutionary zeal in transforming society. Ambedkar's Buddhism internalizes the scientific and modernistic Buddhism of Lakshmi Narasu and Iyothee Thassar's location of Buddhism in cultural traditions of untouchables (Dalits). Ambedkar overcomes the binaries of tradition and modernity as it is generally understood. His notion of modernity differs from the dominant Western notion of modernity and the modernity appropriated by the Brahmanical elite. Social rationalization is central to his modernity. The realization of a moral community is his ideal of modernity.

Ambedkar's conception of religion adds a new dimension to the liberal–communitarian debate. Like the communitarian thinker Charles Taylor, he recognized the primacy of the social. He believed that the rights of individual is embedded in social life. Ambedkar was not only concerned about values and rights but also about social solidarity. In *The Buddha and His Dhamma*, he proposed *Maitri* as adoration for others, along with *Prajna* and *Karuna*. *Maitri* is foundational for social/religious/spiritualism/democracy. In moral and political philosophy, Ambedkar's philosophy links up the individual and community, tradition and modernity, religion and science, materialism and spiritualism, liberalism and communitarianism in his own terms. In other words, Ambedkar's philosophy provides the basic foundations for an egalitarian social life.

Notes

1 Shiffrin, Steven H. (2006).
2 Quoted in Shiffrin (2012: 98).
3 Quoted in *Buddhist News* (1992).
4 Quoted by Romila Thapar (1998: 35) from D. Knopf. (1980).
5 Quoted by Romila Thapar (1998: 27).
6 Quoted by Romila Thapar (1998: 10).
7 Ambedkar quotes Max Muller's observation of Hinduism as he says that we have seen a religion growing up from stage to stage, from the simplest childish prayers to the highest metaphysical abstractions. In the majority of the hymns of the Vedas, we might recognize the childhood; in the Brahmanas and their sacrificial, domestic and moral ordinances, the busy manhood; in the Upanishads the old age of the Vedic religion. We could have well understood if, with the historical progress of the Indian mind.
8 Ambedkar observed that there was a time when religion had covered the whole field of human knowledge and claimed infallibility for what it thought. It covered astronomy, biology, geology, physiology and psychology. Bit by bit this vast empire of religion was destroyed. The Copernican revolution freed astronomy from the domination of religion. The Darwinian revolution freed biology and geology from the trammels of religion. The authority of theology in medicine is not yet completely destroyed. Psychology has not completely freed itself from its entanglements. The warfare of science is against theology for 400 years.
9 Quoted in Bayle (1999: 12).
10 Lakshmi Narasu is the author of *What is Buddhism*, *The Essence of Buddhism*, and *Religion of Modern Buddhist*. Ambedkar has written a foreword for the second edition of *Essence of Buddhism* and he was acquainted with the unpublished work of *Religion of Modern Buddhist*.
11 Ambedkar argued that ancient Indian history must be exhumed. Without its exhumation ancient India will go without history. Fortunately, with the help of the Buddhist literature, ancient Indian history can be dug out of the debris that the Brahmin writers have heaped upon in a fit of madness. The Buddhist literature helps a great deal to remove the debris and see the underlying substance quite clearly and distinctively (BAWS-3: 152).

References

Aishwary, Kumar. 2013. "Force and Adoration: Ambedkar's Maitri," *Seminar* 641 (January), 68–73.

Aloysius, G. 2004. *Dalit-Subaltern Emergence in Religio-Cultural Subjectivity-Iyothee Thassar and Emancipatory Buddhism.* New Delhi: Critical Quest

Aloysius, G. 2015. *Iyothee Thassar and Tamil Buddhist Movement.* New Delhi: Critical Quest.

Ambedkar, B. R. 1947. *The Buddha and His Dhamma* (2nd ed.). Bombay: Siddharth Publication.

Ambedkar, B. R. 2014. *Babasaheb Ambedkar Writing and Speeches* (vol. 1). New Delhi: Dr. Ambedkar Foundation.

Ambedkar, B. R. 2014. *Babasaheb Ambedkar Writing and Speeches* (vol. 3). New Delhi: Dr. Ambedkar Foundation.

Ambedkar, B. R. 2014. *Babasaheb Ambedkar Writing and Speeches* (vol. 11). New Delhi: Dr. Ambedkar Foundation.

Ambedkar, B. R. 2014. *Babasaheb Ambedkar Writing and Speeches* (vol. 17). New Delhi: Dr. Ambedkar Foundation.

Bayle, Susan. 1999. *Caste, Society and Politics in India.* Cambridge: Cambridge University Press.

Buddhist News, Vol.1 (3), March 1992, http://www.buddhisttexts.org/uploads/6/3/3/1/6331706/1992_03_all_pages.pdf

Chakravarti, Uma. 2004. *The Social Philosophy of Buddhism and the Problem of Inequality.* New Delhi: Critical Quest.

Freud, Sigmund. 1961. *The Future of an Illusion.* New York: Norton.

Gelders, Raf and Willem Derde. 2003. "Mantras of Anti-Brahmanism; Colonial Experience of Indian Intellectual History," *Economic and Political Weekly* 38, no. 43 (October): 25–31.

Guru, Gopal. 2009. "Introduction, Theorising Humiliation." In *Humiliation*, edited by Gopal Guru. New Delhi: Oxford University Press, pp. 1–19.

Kesava Kumar, P. 2013. "Against Brahminical Tradition: A Dalit Critique of Indian Modernity," *Lokayata: Journal of Positive Philosophy* 3, no. 1 (March): 4–17.

Kesava Kumar, P. 2015, *Jiddu Krishnamurti—A Critical Study of Tradition and Revolution.* 195–202. Delhi: Kalpaz.

Knopf, D. 1980. "Hermeneutics Versus History," *Journal of Asian Studies* 39, no. 3 (May): 495–505.

MacIntyre Alasdair. 2011, *After Virtue: A Study in Moral Theory.* London: Bloomsbury.

Marx, Karl. 1970. *A Critique of Hegel's "Philosophy of Right."* Translated by Annette Jolin and Joseph O'Malley. Cambridge: Cambridge University Press.

Narasu, Lakshmi, P. 2002, *Religion of the Modern Buddhist*, edited by G. Aloysius. Delhi: Wordsmiths.

Rodrigues, Valerian (ed.). 2002. *The Essential Writings of B.R. Ambedkar.* New Delhi: Oxford University Publications.

Rodrigues, Valerian. 2008. *Dalit Bahujan Discourse in Modern India.* New Delhi: Critical Quest.

Romila Thapar. 1998. *Imagined Religious Communities—Ancient History and the Modern Search for a Hindu Identity.* New Delhi: Critical Quest.

Sarkar, Sumit. 1998. "Identity and Difference: Caste in the formation of the Ideologies of Nationalism and Hindutva." In *Writing Social History*, edited by Sarkar Sumit. New Delhi: Oxford, pp. 358–390.

Shiffrin, Steven H. 2006. "Liberalism and Religion," Presentation in American Philosophical Association in Chicago Berkeley, Electronic Press Selected Works. Available at: http://works.bepress.com/steven_shiffrin/12/

Shiffrin, Steven H. 2012. *Religious Left and State Relations.* Princeton: Princeton University Press.

Taylor, Charles. 1989. *Sources of the Self: The Making of the Modern Identity.* Cambridge: Cambridge University Press.

Taylor, Charles. 1999. "A Catholic Modernity?" In *A Catholic Modernity? Charles Taylor's Marianist Award Lecture*, edited by James L. Heft. Oxford: Oxford University Press, pp. 13–37.

Taylor, Charles. 2007. *A Secular Age.* Harvard: Harvard University Press.

13

AMBEDKAR AND MODERN BUDDHISM

Continuity and discontinuity

Pradeep P. Gokhale[1]

By leading a mass conversion and by reconstructing Buddha's Dhamma, Ambedkar has made a significant contribution to the world of Buddhism. Its significance, however, needs to be understood in proper perspective. One way to understand it is to consider how Ambedkar's reconstruction is related to the Buddhist tradition: To consider how it is based on tradition and how it deviates from it. But it is not proper or is at least insufficient to consider Ambedkar's reconstruction of Buddhism as isolated from what has happened to Buddhism outside India, or to be more precise, outside Ambedkarite Buddhism, in the last century. Many orthodox followers of Ambedkarite Buddhism follow it parochially. Some of them regard *The Buddha and His Dhamma* the last word on Buddhism. They think that Ambedkar's pioneering restatement of Buddhism was complete, authentic and final. But I want to suggest that that is not true. Re-understanding Buddhism was a problem faced by many Buddhist thinkers in different parts of the world. They shared some common concerns and responses. Ambedkar's contribution needs to be understood and appreciated on this world map of shared concerns and responses.

Like followers of Ambedkar, the critics of Ambedkar's reconstruction of Buddhism also have seen him in isolation. They have compared Ambedkar's reconstruction with traditional Buddhism and highlighted Ambedkar's radical deviation from the tradition. They do not consider the fact that different Buddhist leaders in the last two centuries—particularly the last century—have reinterpreted tradition and deviated from it in different ways. Hence it is important to locate Ambedkar on the world map of the modernization of Buddhism. Some scholars have duly given him a respectable position among the engaged Buddhist leaders all over the world. The works of Christopher Queen and Sallie King are remarkable in this respect. What I am doing in this paper is partly based on their work. But there is a minute difference. Their work is focused on the notion of 'Engaged

Buddhism,' which is mainly concerned with the applied aspect of Buddhism. Here I am mainly concerned with the new understanding of Buddhism, and also the re-interpretation and reconstruction of Buddhism that the engaged Buddhist thinkers have introduced and developed.

In this regard, I have tried to see in this paper how Ambedkar's understanding of Buddhism is continuous with that of many other engaged Buddhist thinkers in different parts of the world, and when it is discontinuous, how and why it becomes discontinuous.

Continuity between Ambedkar and other engaged Buddhist thinkers can be seen in relation to many different issues or themes. I have chosen the following seven representative themes for this chapter:

1 Buddhism as a religion vis-á-vis other religions;
2 Reconciling the sectarian divisions within Buddhism;
3 Affinity to science
4 Secularism (this-worldliness)
5 Protestantism and democratization
6 Attitude to Marxism
7 Status of women.

Buddhism as a religion and its relation with other religions

'Is Buddhism a religion?' Ambedkar raised this question and answered it by saying that Buddhism is Dhamma and not a religion. The question Ambedkar was facing was not unusual, as Ambedkar himself pointed out that some European theologians refused to recognize the Buddha's Dhamma as a religion (Ambedkar, 1974: IV.I.2.5). Buddhism in the modern world had an encounter with theologians advocating a Semitic conception of religion, who denied the status of religion to Buddhism.

There was a twofold response to this problem from the Buddhist side. On the one hand the Buddhists accepted the charge but not with a sense of inferiority but with pride. Unlike Christianity or Islam, Buddhism is based not on uncritical faith, dogma, a belief in God etc., but on a rational approach and emphasis on one's own experience and there was nothing to feel inferior about. On the other hand, Buddhists acknowledged the wider conception of religion and a more rational conception of ideal religion that was more fitting to Buddhism than to other religions.

We find both these types of responses Ambedkar's writings. In his 1950 article "Buddha and the future of his religion", he showed how Buddhism fulfils the criteria of ideal religion (Ambedkar, 1980) and in *The Buddha and His Dhamma* he elucidated how the Buddha's *dhamma* radically differs from religion (Ambedkar, 1974: III.IV.2).

We can trace a similar duel approach in a few other modern Buddhist thinkers. Narada Thero (a monk scholar of Sri Lanka (1898–1983)) in his work *The Buddha and his Teachings* raised the question whether Buddhism is a religion. He said,

> Buddhism cannot ... be strictly called a religion, because it is neither a system of faith and worship nor "the outward act or form by which men indicate their recognition of the existence of a God or Gods..." ... However if by religion is meant ... a system of deliverance from the ills of life, then certainly Buddhism is a religion of religions.
>
> (Narada, 1988: 290)

Some thinkers took the negative step of identifying Buddhism as a non-religion, but at a constructive level, they took the egalitarian step of treating Buddhism and other religions on a par. Buddhadasa Bhikkhu (a Thai Buddhist ascetic thinker (1906–93)) denied the status of religion not only to Buddhism, but to all religions (Buddhadasa (1969: 6)), but at a more constructive level, he equates Buddhism with other religions by treating Dhamma and God as two expressions of the same truth (Buddhadasa, 1993*:* 48).

Similarly, Thich Nhat Hanh (a Vietnamese Zen master and engaged Buddhist leader (born 1926)) on the one hand remarks, "Many people regard Buddhism as religion, but if we say that it is a way of life, we may be closer to truth." The main reason he gives is that faith in Buddhism does not mean faith in God or a metaphysical principle the existence of which we cannot really prove (Hanh, 1993: 217). But, in a more constructive mood, he acknowledges the essential similarity of all religions, "...any genuine religious life must express reverence toward life, non-violence, communion between man and man, man and the absolute" (Hanh, 2001: 20). By using the metaphor of a fruit salad of religions, he said,

> ...religious life is life and I cannot imagine how someone could eat only one kind of fruit. Although there are kinds of fruit that one does not like, there are many kinds that one can appreciate. Besides, only authentic fruits can make fruit salad.
>
> (Hanh, 2001: 31)

Another Buddhist thinker S.N. Goenka (a leading lay teacher of Vipassanā meditation (1924–2013) expresses a similar dual attitude. He distinguishes Dhamma from sectarian religions and in this way denies the status of religion to Buddha's Dhamma. In doing so he also exhibits an egalitarian spirit by treating different sectarian religions (including Buddhism as a sect) as on a par and also acknowledging the availability of the Vipassanā type of insight in different spiritual traditions (Gokhale, 2004).

H. H. the fourteenth Dalai Lama (the Tibetan Buddhist spiritual leader (born 1935)) also presents a dual approach to Buddhism, although in a different way. He does not seem to question the status of Buddhism as a religion, but he does distinguish between spirituality and religion. He also supports equality of all religions insofar as their spiritual and moral aspects are concerned (Puri, 2006: 128–9). (Bharati Puri observes that while the 'earlier' Dalai Lama was less flexible and believed that Buddhism was the best way, the 'later' Dalai Lama finds a larger concern in serving all humanity without appealing to religious faith (Puri, 2006: 128)). While appreciating spiritual and moral aspects of religions, he treats all religions as equally good and is opposed to criticizing a religion, either one's own or that of others.

With this background, if we revisit Ambedkar, we realize that Ambedkar was not a religious egalitarian in his approach. He regards Buddhism as different from and more advanced than other religions. This view of Ambedkar has closer similarities with the views of Anagarika Dharmapala (a Sri Lankan Buddhist revivalist (1864–1933)). Dharmapala in his early part of religious career was under the influence of Colonel Henry Steel Olcott (1832–1907) and the Theosophical Society. But eventually he broke with them because of their stance on universal religion. Dharmapala stated: "Theosophy was only consolidating Krishna worship;" "To say that all religions have a common foundation only shows the ignorance of the speaker. Dhamma alone is supreme to Buddhism" (Kaweesha, 2013). Dharmapala in this way represents an exclusionist approach.

Another engaged Buddhist leader who ideologically comes close to Ambedkar is Sangharakshita (the founder of Friends of Western Buddhist Order (1925–2018). Their affinity is worth considering because they were influenced by each other. Ambedkar had high regard for Sangharakshita as an ideal bhikkhu and Sangharakshita had high regard for Ambedkar as one who demonstrated substantially the social dimension of the Buddha's Dhamma (Spanberg, 82). Both aimed at propagation of Buddhism in the modern world, and in doing that they had an exclusivist attitude towards Buddhism. Both had a tendency not to assimilate Buddhism with other religions and sought to preserve its distinctive character. But an important difference between the two also needs to be noticed. For Sangharakshita, Buddhism is a religion in the conventional sense of the term. The Buddha's dhamma as presented by Ambedkar is not a religion in its conventional sense, but in an unconventional sense: as a way of life based on rationality and sacred morality. Against this background the association between Ambedkarite Buddhism and Sangharakshita's engaged Buddhist movement raises some ideological issues. We will not go into them here, to avoid digression.

Reconciling sectarian divisions within Buddhism

After the schism of Buddhism into different sects, and particularly the twofold division into Hīnayāna and Mahāyāna, we find two approaches to this schism. The Hīnayānists, particularly the Theravādins did not acknowledge the Mahāyāna as a genuine form of Buddhism; instead they regarded it as a later development, or rather as a later distortion of Buddhism. As against this, Mahāyānists acknowledge the Hīnayāna (or the Śrāvakayāna) as a genuine form of Buddhism, but as a lower form, based on the Buddha's message that was meant for people incapable of grasping the higher truths of Mahāyāna. Tibetan Buddhism largely accepts this approach and builds on it.

Against this background in modern times we come across some Buddhist scholars and thinkers primarily initiated in one sect, but gradually exposed to different sectarian traditions and arriving at the new combinations or syntheses of different sectarian views. Many engaged Buddhist thinkers can be seen from this angle.

When on the eve of the conversion ceremony Ambedkar was asked in a press conference as to which form of Buddhism he would be adopting when he embraced Buddhism, he told the assembled reporters that his Buddhism would adhere to the tenets of the faith as taught by the Buddha himself. It would be neither Hīnayāna nor Mahāyāna, but it could be called Navayāna according to him (Sangharakshita, 1986: 130–1). In his *The Buddha and His Dhamma* Ambedkar included in great proportion the elements of Theravāda Buddhism in a demythologized and secularized form. But he also included some Mahāyāna elements by dissociating them from idealistic metaphysics. For instance, he made *pāramitā* doctrine applicable to all, which in the Theravāda had a restrictive application, and included it in the Buddha's first sermon. He criticized the schools emphasizing only *prajñā* or only *karuṇā* and asserted that *prajñā* and *karuṇā* are equally important in the Buddha's *dhamma* (Ambedkar, 1974: III. V. III.2.6–7). Thus Ambedkar tried to blur the differences between the two major sects in his construction of Navayāna.

We find comparable instances in other engaged Buddhists. *Buddhadasa Bhikkhu* was trained in the Theravāda tradition, but he incorporated the Mādhyamika ideal, namely, śūnyatā in his reconstruction of Buddhism. Thich Nath Hanh underwent a complex training in Buddhism. As Sallie King observes: "Vietnamese Buddhism has long embraced both Theravāda and Mahāyāna tradition ... Nhat Hanh's studies included both traditions with emphasis upon mindfulness, gāthā and koan" (King, 1996: 322). Sulak Sivaraksa (contemporary Thai engaged Buddhist Leader, born 1933) was trained in Theravāda tradition; but he acknowledges his indebtedness to Buddhadasa Bhikkhu, Thich Nhat Hanh and also H.H. the Dalai Lama.

Sangharakshita, "Although ordained a Theravadin, had long felt an affinity with the spiritual heights of Mahāyāna" (Sponsberg, 1996: 81). He received Vajrayāna initiation as well. He tried to synthesize different sects of Buddhism in his work *Survey of Buddhism* (1966). One can say that Sangharakshita has affinity with Ambedkar on the point of reconciliation between Hīnayāna and Mahāyāna (like he has on the point of exclusionism). However, I feel that their affinity on this point should be appreciated with some reservations. Although we find an attempt to reconcile different sects of Buddhism in the thoughts of both, the ways they tried to do that are quite different. Sangharakshita was trying to present different sects as being on par, preserving the distinct identity of each other and at the same time maintaining their common core as Buddhism. He was presenting these sects as distinct and yet overlapping religious sects. Sangharakshita's version of Buddhism has been aptly called neo-traditional Buddhism (Sponsberg, 1996: 84). As against this, Ambedkar's version of Buddhism can be called trans-traditional Buddhism. Ambedkar synthesized Hīnayāna and Mahāyāna in his reconstruction. But the two sects do not retain their own identity in the synthesis; Ambedkar extracts some of their elements, and gives them a secularized, rationalized and humanized form.

Affinity to science

In the past two centuries the growth of science has posed a challenge before all religions. The encounter between religion and science has given rise to reformist thinking in different religions, which has tended to reconcile the two. This has happened in Buddhism without much conflict between the two. Some Buddhist thinkers claimed that the rationalist and scientific temper has been present in Buddhism from its inception. The *Kālāmasutta* and a verse from *Jñānasārasamuccaya* (in which the Buddha encourages scrutiny of what he says)[2] have often been quoted in this context. Since Buddhism as a traditional religion contained many otherworldly and superstitious elements, the reformist Buddhist thinkers tried to eliminate or suppress them and tried to rationally reconstruct the Buddha's *dhamma*. In his reconstruction of the Buddha's *dhamma*, Ambedkar reduced otherworldly elements, rituals, ceremonies and miracles; he even eliminated the traditional doctrines of karma and rebirth. One of the earliest Buddhist reformers who emphasized affinity of Buddhism to science was Anagarika Dharmapala. In this context, Dharmapala emphasizes three aspects of Buddhism: one, its non-dogmatic approach; two, its emphasis on cause–effect relation and three, its psychology. To elaborate:

1 He calls Buddhism a science because it had no dogma of permanent *ātman* or a creator and no prayer is needed because everything is changing with electronic rapidity. Creator God according to Dharmapala is

the doctrine of the unscientific theological dogmatists (Dharmapala, 1965: 123).

2 Darwinian Theory of Evolution according to Dharmapala is instrumental to the growth of science in the west—which has challenged the doctrine of God accepted by theistic religions. The empirical law of causation is a corollary of Darwinian law (Dharmapala, 1965: 102). Dharmapala emphasizes that the Buddha's law of *pratītyasamutpāda* is the law of cause and effect. He correlates the doctrine of causation (and also that of *Kamma*) with the denial of God as creator.
3 Dharmapala describes Buddhism as 'biological psychical science' (Dharmapala, 1965: 123). He appreciates the moral psychology of Buddhism and also its parapsychological aspects—what he calls psychicism.

Out of the above three features, the first one, namely the Buddha's non-dogmatic or rational approach and its rejection of the doctrines of the permanent *ātman* and God as creator is appreciated by many modern Buddhist thinkers—Ambedkar, Satyanarayan Goenka and the Dalai Lama, to cite a few. But after this their appreciations of the scientific character of Buddhism go in different directions. Goenka emphasizes Buddha's investigation into Dhamma—the universal causal law—with special reference to cravings and suffering. Accordingly, when one realizes this law with the help of Vipassanā meditation, one develops detachment and becomes free from suffering. The core of Buddha's science according to Goenka is his psychology with its moral and soteriological implications. In his analysis of the mind, he also believes in the possibility of coming across subtle sensations rooted in past lives. The Dalai Lama would agree with all this, but he expects much more from Buddhism as a science. He interprets *pratītyasamutpāda*, not just as causal law but as 'interdependence of all phenomena' and draws its implications to environmental science and environmental ethics. Moreover, through his continuous dialogues with scientists, the Dalai Lama makes scientists take seriously the claims of Buddhism regarding the extraordinary powers of the mind. Although scientists participating in these dialogues do not accept all the claims, they at least take them seriously. The Dalai Lama's attitude in these dialogues seems to be dual: on one hand he is a Buddhist religious scholar and a believer; on the other hand, he is an open-minded rational being (which is again consistent with the spirit of Buddhism) leaving his questions open for scientific scrutiny.

With this background Ambedkar's affinity to science seems to be more radical. He does not make room for the queer phenomenon such as 'rebirth' (as it is popularly understood). He explains the relation between body and consciousness in materialistic terms, as that between an electric field and a magnetic field.

This brings us to another theme in modern Buddhism, namely secularism or this-worldliness.

Secularism (this-worldliness)

Ambedkar in his reconstruction of Buddhism clearly denied other worlds and also rebirth (in its traditional sense). He interpreted rebirth and karma in such a way that the basic framework of materialist ontology is preserved. Other modern Buddhists did not go to this extent; but to emphasize this world and this life and deemphasize other worlds and afterlife was more or less a common tendency among the modern Buddhists.

Though Anagarika Dharmapala as a spokesman of Buddhist religious heritage sometimes records the other-worldly views of the traditional Buddhism, his own interpretation of Buddhism emphasizes this-worldly existence. According to his interpretation of the Buddha's message, "the kingdom of Heaven is within man himself. There is no heaven or hell, but our own making" (Dharmapala, 1965: XLIX). "The Buddhist heaven is clearer than hands or breathing and is to be won in this life, not in hereafter" (Dharmapala, 1965: L). When asked straightaway whether he believed that there is nothing beyond death, he replied that he believed in pure life (Dharmapala, 1965: XLVII).

Another modern Buddhist scholar who questioned rebirth and life after death was the Thai spiritual leader Buddhadasa Bhikkhu. Buddhadasa interpreted the doctrine of *pratītyasamutpāda* as applicable to any event in this life and rejected the traditional interpretation according to which the operation of the doctrine ranges over three consecutive lives (Buddhadasa, 1992: 29). Two other engaged Buddhist leaders, the Dalai Lama and S. N. Goenka express a liberal attitude to the doctrine of rebirth. The Dalai Lama makes it open to scientific scrutiny and S. N. Goenka regards it as non-essential for Vipassanā meditation. Sulak Sivaraksa has strikingly highlighted the distinction between otherworldly-ritualistic-dogmatic form of Buddhism and this-worldly-secular-rational form as one between 'Capital B Buddhism' and 'Small b Buddhism' (Swearer, 1996: 215).

Protestantism and democratization

Modern Buddhism is sometimes described as Protestant Buddhism. Gananath Obeyesekere coined this term with reference to Anagarika Dharmapala. Dharmapala was a protestant Buddhist in two senses. One, as a Buddhist he combatted with the Christian criticism of Buddhism that the latter was too otherworldly. We have seen how Dharmapala tried to give this-worldly interpretation of Buddhism. Secondly, and more importantly, Dharmapala tried to deemphasize the centrality of the monastic order to Buddhism as religion and held that lay persons have at least as good or perhaps better chances to attain Nirvāṇa in this life. To give authority to lay followers in the religious praxis of Buddhism can be called a move towards democratization of Buddhism.

We find this spirit of Protestantism and democratization clearly and strongly carried forward by Ambedkar both in theory and practice. Dharmapala was critical about the performance of the then Bhikkhus when he said, "The Bhikkus are indolent; they have lost the spirit of heroism and altruism of their ancient examples" (Quoted by Queen, 1996: 124). Ambedkar expressed a similar critical attitude about the role of Bhikkhus in his 1950 essay and then in *The Buddha and his Dhamma*. Both of these thinkers expressed their expectation that the Bhikkhus should live the life of social service and responsibility.

On the other hand, they asserted that the lay followers can attain the religious ideal without becoming a Bhikkhu. It is customary in Buddhism to hold that lay Buddhists by practicing *Śīla*, can attain *svarga* after death, but they cannot attain *Nirvāṇa*. As against this, Ambedkar held that a person can live in *Nirvāṇa* by following the eightfold path. The Buddha of Ambedkar tells the lay follower Anāthapiṇḍaka that "The bliss of religious life is attainable by anyone who walks in the noble eightfold path" and going into homelessness is not required for that (Ambedkar, 1974: II.III.5.17–20).

This democratic understanding of Buddhism led Ambedkar to go beyond the traditional bhikkhu-centric method of ordination. Traditionally, only a Bhikkhu could give ordination to anyone even to become an upāsaka. Ambedkar in the mass conversion ceremony, when he was himself ordinated as upāsaka, gave ordination to thousands of his followers to become upāsaka. As Sangharakshita observes:

> Indeed, by demonstrating that an Upāsaka no less than a Bhikshu could administer the Refuges and Precepts Ambedkar was reminding both the old Buddhists and the new that those who lived as Bhikshus and those who lived as Upāsakas and Upāsikās was only a difference, not a division....
>
> (Sangharakshita, 1986: 139)

In Theravāda tradition the gap between upāsaka and bhikkhu was remarkable partly because the two did not seem to have a common goal. In Mahāyāna tradition the gap gets reduced because bodhisattva is the common ideal for both upāsakas and bhikkhus. It is the ideal of an extreme altruist. In Mahāyāna literature we come across Bodhisattvas who lived outwardly like upāsakas but whose spiritual status was higher than that of many senior bhikkhus. It seems to me that Ambedkar by including *pāramitā* doctrine in the first sermon of the Buddha and by making altruistic social service central to the mission of a bhikkhu synthesizes the bodhisattva ideal with that of an ideal Buddhist of Theravāda tradition and also bridges the gap between bhikkhu and upāsaka.

Engaged Buddhists and Marxism

Engaged Buddhist thinkers have been generally opposed to capitalism; and some of them have been favourable to Marxism. The Dalai Lama and Thich Nhat Hanh had to face violent actions of communist governments. But they neither developed hatred towards the governments, nor aversion towards communism as such. The Dalai Lama, as his thought matured, held that Buddhism and Marxism can be complementary. As he said, "Buddhism can take many points from Marxist, Socialist and Democratic system. Similarly, those systems can benefit from many points in Buddhist theory, especially in terms of socially beneficial attitudes" (Puri, 2006: 124).

Thich Nhat Hanh led a peace movement in Vietnam. His movement was based on Buddhist principles. It refused to side with either capitalism or communism (King, 1996: 331). At a more constructive level, Hanh assimilated Buddhist community (Sangha) life with a communist way of life. There he referred to rules that the Buddhist community follows such as sharing knowledge, reconciliation and holding common property (Hanh, 2001: 110–1).

This assimilation between Buddhist Sangha life and the communistic way of life, was anticipated by Ambedkar in his essay "Buddha or Karl Marx". In this essay Ambedkar discusses what he calls the original creed of Karl Marx and what survives of that creed. According to Ambedkar what survives of the original creed of Marx consists of four points:

1 The function of philosophy is to reconstruct the world and not to explain the origin of the world.
2 There is a conflict of interests between class and class.
3 Private ownership of property brings power to one class and sorrow to the other through exploitation.
4 In a good society private property should be abolished (Ambedkar, 1987: 444).

In his reconstruction of Buddhism Ambedkar shows how all these four points are already present in Buddhism. According to Ambedkar, Buddhism departs from Marxism mainly on the question of the means to be employed for bringing about an ideal society. Like John Dewey, the Buddha of Ambedkar accepts the principle, that the end determines the means, whereas Marx does not accept it.

Like Thich Nhat Hanh and Ambedkar, Buddhadasa Bhikkhu also tried to find a way between capitalism and communism. Buddhadasa calls his ideology dhāmmic socialism and distinguishes it from both liberal capitalism and communism. Both the latter ideologies are adhāmmic according to Buddhadasa. Liberal capitalism is adhāmmic because of extreme individualism and communism too falls into the same category because of the brutality rooted in authoritarianism (Buddhadasa, 1993: 31).

It is possible that the criticism of communism made by many engaged Buddhists was at least partly due to their (mis-)interpretation of Marxism guided by the way it was put into practice in Russia. It seems, however, that even if we accept a democratic interpretation of Marxism, some differences between Marxism and Buddhism will remain untouched. For instance though mental or cultural elements have a role to play in Marxian theory, primacy is given to the material or economic conditions whereas, the Buddha gave primacy to the mental ("*manopubbangamā dhammā*"—Dhammapada 1.1) In his reconstruction of Buddhism, Ambedkar gave a materialistic explanation of the origination of consciousness, but he retained the primacy of the mental in the context of individual and social life, as he says, "Once consciousness arises, man becomes a sentient being. Consciousness is, therefore, the chief thing in man's life" (Ambedkar, 1974: III. IV.4.55). But this is not my main point here. My simple point is that opposition to capitalism and closeness to Marx or finding a socialist way between capitalism and Marxism is a common concern to Ambedkar and many other engaged Buddhist leaders.

Status of women

Like capitalism, patriarchy has been a chief concern of many modern egalitarians. Ambedkar too, when he expressed his egalitarian concerns was keen on the equal status to be given to men and women. As a modern interpreter of Buddhism, he asserted and argued that the Buddha supported gender equality.

As a matter of fact, all religious traditions exhibit signs of patriarchy with a greater or less extent and religious reformers belonging to different religious traditions address the question in different ways. The question arises basically at two levels. Firstly, the question arises whether women have equal right or the capacity to attain liberation (or the ultimate goal of the given religion), as men. Secondly the question arises whether women have equal status as men in mundane aspects of life—physical, sexual, economic, political, social and cultural. Some modern Buddhist thinkers have acknowledged the Buddhist approach of gender equality in religious as well as mundane realm. Anagarika Dharmapala makes a blanket declaration of gender equality on behalf of Buddhism when he says—"The same rights are given to women as to men. Not the least difference is shown and perfect equality has been proclaimed" (Dharmapala, 1965: 21).

Ambedkar is keen on contrasting Buddhism with Hinduism on the issue of caste and gender equality. As he asserts in his 1950 article:

> According to Hinduism neither a shudra nor a woman could become a teacher of religion nor could they take Sannyasa (or initiation into the ascetic life) and reach God. Buddha on the other hand admitted

> shudras into the Bhikshu Sangha. He also admitted women to become Bhikshunis. Why did he do this? Few people seem to realize the importance of this step. The answer is that Buddha wanted to take concrete steps to destroy the gospel of inequality.
>
> (Ambedkar, 1980: 7)

The 14th Dalai Lama refers to the fourth class of Buddhist Tantras according to which there is no distinction between masculine and feminine; enlightenment may come about just as easily in a woman's body as in a man's (Dalai Lama, 1994: 77). Rita Gross in her work "Buddhism after Patriarchy" demonstrates that the core teachings of Buddhism promote gender equality rather than male dominance.

Barring such general claims, Buddhism has to address some specific issues before it can make a strong case for gender equality.

1 According to popular narrative, Gotama the Bodhisattva, left home and became a recluse by keeping his wife in the dark, when he should have sought her permission before leaving her.
2 Though the Buddha agreed that women are equally capable of attaining Nirvāṇa as men, he was hesitant in the formation of Bhikkhuṇī-saṅgha; and even when he allowed the formation, he suspected that this would affect the longevity of his Dhamma.
3 While allowing Mahāprajāpati Gautamī to become a Bhikkhuṇī, he enforced eight chief rules on Bhikkhuṇīs, some of which were humiliating to them.
4 As an offshoot of the number (2) above, we come across the tendency to disallow the formation of Bhikkhuṇī-saṅgha, that is, to oppose full ordination to be given to the women aspirants, in Theravāda Buddhist communities even today.

From among the above four issues Ambedkar can be said to have answered the first two issues. By rejecting the popular narrative of Gotama's renunciation, Ambedkar accepted the narrative constructed by Dharmananda Kosambi on the basis of the latter's research in Pali canons. According to this narrative Gautama left home for a social cause with full notice and permission of his wife Yaśodharā. While narrating the incidence of admitting Gautamī to enter the Sangha, Ambedkar makes the Buddha explain his initial hesitation to admit Gautamī as being based not on gender inequality, but on practical grounds (Ambedkar, 1974: II.VII.1.20). He refers to 'Eight Chief Rules', but avoids giving details and hence appears to have bypassed the issue of the humiliating character of some of the rules. It is possible that Ambedkar had reservations about the content of the rules and that was the reason for excluding the details from the narrative.

After Ambedkar we find many thinkers and leaders entering the controversy and trying to restore justice to women in Buddhism. The Dalai

Lama's efforts to consider the possibility of reform in the Buddhist Order, by bringing together the representatives of monastic communities, are an important step in this direction.

How is Ambedkar different?

One objective of this paper was to show how Ambedkar's conception of Buddhism is continuous with the conceptions of Buddhism according to other modern/engaged Buddhist thinkers. These conceptions of Buddhism are continuous partly because they are conceptions of Buddhism and partly because they are modern conceptions. Because they are conceptions of Buddhism, they promote universal love, and not violence. They promote primacy of mind, not that of material conditions. They promote moral and democratic values and not military rule or authoritarianism. And because they are modern conceptions, they promote modern values like liberty, equality, scientific temper and secularism and are critical about poverty, superstitions, ritualism and other-worldly beliefs.

In a very broad way these conceptions follow a common pattern, but they also differ from thinker to thinker, depending upon each thinker's sectarian background, his own psychological and intellectual makeup and the challenge Buddhism has to face in the regions to which he belongs. Ambedkar's conception of Buddhism becomes different for the same reasons. On this background I will mention some of the major aspects that make Ambedkar's conception different.

One important point of difference was that other engaged Buddhist thinkers were first Buddhists and then they became socially engaged and modern. In the case of Ambedkar, the order is reverse. First, he was socially engaged and modern and then he became a Buddhist. The other leaders had an advantage: the new manifestations and applications suggested by them were more deeply rooted in the tradition. But the disadvantage was that many of them could not radically transcend the traditional limitations. As against this, before deciding to embrace Buddhism, Ambedkar was thoroughly grounded in modern values. He was influenced by the values of the French Revolution, those of liberalism, pragmatism and socialism; rationalism and scientific temper. With this background he was to leave Hinduism and embrace a different religion. Naturally these values became the criteria for the choice of Buddhism as the new religion and they also became the principles of re-interpretation and reconstruction of Buddhism. Probably this is one of the reasons why Ambedkar's reconstruction of Buddhism is more radical than that of many others. It questions the traditional Karma–rebirth framework, gives a materialistic interpretation of the rise of consciousness; regards dhāmmic pursuit and achievement as essentially social and does not attach a central role to meditation.

Although Ambedkar gives a subordinate status to meditation, it is doubtful whether he was radically opposed to it. Social issues are central for Buddhism as interpreted by Ambedkar and meditation can play only an instrumental role according to him. Bhikkhu according to him is a model social worker. According to Ambedkar's analysis, the Bhikkhu should discharge both the functions: practicing self-culture and providing service and guidance to people (Ambedkar, 1974: V.II.4). 'Practicing self-culture' includes meditation. For Ambedkar self-culture is necessary, but not enough; it should be translated as social activity. This view can be compared with the views of Sulak Sivaraksa, a contemporary engaged Buddhist leader:

> Those who want to change society must understand the society as well as the dimension of the inner personal change. It is this personal transformation that true spirituality can provide.
>
> (Sivaraksa, 2005: 13)

And more precisely:

> We should not treat meditation as a form of escapism or personal salvation. Rather mental training must awaken our wisdom; so we will be able to wisely engage with society and deal with the multiple crises of greed, hatred and delusion in the present.
>
> (Sivaraksa, 2005: 72)

It is possible that the difference between Ambedkar's approach to meditation and that of other engaged Buddhist leaders is that of degree than that of kind.

What prompted Ambedkar to abandon Hinduism and embrace a different religion was his realization that Hindu society cannot annihilate the caste system and give equal and respectable status to the people of the downtrodden castes. Naturally he looked at the Buddha as giving a solution to this problem. In his image the Buddha was essentially a critic of Brahmanism in general and of the caste system in particular.

Other engaged Buddhist leaders were concerned with different problems, like those of war, violence and consumerism. They were looking at the Buddha as the messenger of peace, non-violence and a simple life. Caste was not the central problem for them[3] (except for Sangharakshita and his followers whose organization in India accommodated Ambedkarite Buddhism at its core). Since Gandhiji was an influential advocate of values like peace, non-violence and simplicity, he was looked upon as the modern symbol of Buddhism by many modern Buddhists.[4] Ambedkar could not appreciate Gandhi as symbolizing Buddhism, because Gandhi was handling the issue of caste not as a rational, egalitarian thinker, but as a Hindu apologist.

This also explains why Ambedkar's Buddhism is so exclusivist with regard to Hinduism. His inclusion of 22 vows as an essential part of the conversion ceremony clearly indicates that he wanted to avoid every possible admixture of Buddhism with Hinduism, and to keep Buddhism always at a safe distance from Hinduism.

It should be noted here that the question of inclusivism with regard to Hinduism and that with regard to other religions are not of the same type. Hinduism is a non-egalitarian religion in its practical philosophy as the varṇa–caste system is a core-aspect of the Hindu social philosophy. Comparatively, other religions are by and large egalitarian at their core. With regard to other religions, Buddhism has an issue at the metaphysical level; with regard to Hinduism, it has an issue with regard to both the metaphysical and practical levels. Apart from the metaphysical gap between Hinduism and Buddhism, the latter cannot take an inclusive stance with respect to the former for the following reasons:

1 Hinduism has already tried to appropriate Buddhism by treating the Buddha as the ninth incarnation of Vishnu. Naturally if Buddhism reconciles with Hinduism, it will have a subordinate status with regard to Hinduism, that of a sect of Hinduism and not an equal and independent status.
2 Since Hinduism is already crippled by the varṇa–jāti system, if Buddhism seeks reconciliation with Hinduism, it will have to adjust with the varṇa–jāti system, leading to a moral defeat of Buddhism.

The inclusive Buddhist thinkers who speak the language of the equality of all religions do not seem to be clearly aware of this problem. This happens because Hinduism has two faces—one external and the other internal. The external face is that of Vedānta, the face it shows to the outer world, the one through which it has dialogue with other religions. The internal face of orthodox Hinduism, which the Hindu society has not rejected in spite of many reform movements, is that of inequalities, hierarchies with which it speaks to the members of the Hindu community, with which Hindus talk and interact with one another. The inclusive Buddhist leaders highlight the external face of Hinduism and leave the internal face suppressed as the orthodox Hindu leaders would like it. As against this, Ambedkar was primarily concerned with the internal face and on this background refused to make compromises or admixtures with Hinduism.

Twenty-five hundred years ago Buddhism started a combat with Brahmanism. This task of Buddhism is still incomplete and it is to Ambedkar's credit that he re-launched the combat through the mass conversion and a rational reconstruction of Buddhism. This task of combating Brahmanism is not a matter of serious concern for most of the engaged Buddhist thinkers and hence the difference between Ambedkar and the other thinkers remains glaring.

To conclude, Ambedkar would agree with many engaged Buddhist leaders on many points, but there are some points on which he differs from many others arguably for just reasons.

Notes

1 This paper was presented as Buddha Jayanti Lecture on December 28, 2013 at the 88th session of Indian Philosophical Congress held at Madurai, India. It was subsequently published in *Indian Philosophical Quarterly*, Vol. 45, Nos. 2–3, April to September 2018, pp. 91–114, and is used here with permission.

2 In Kālāmasutta the Buddha says to Kālāmas;

> Do not accept anything on mere hearsay, ..tradition, ..rumours, …because it accords to your scriptures, ..by mere supposition, .. inference, ..appearances, …because it agrees with your preconceived notions, ..because it seems acceptable… thinking that the ascetic is respected by us. But when you know for yourself, that these things are immoral, ..blameworthy, ..conducive to ruin and sorrow.. do reject them. When you know for yourself that these things are moral, ..blameless,…conducive to wellbeing and happiness… do live and act accordingly.
>
> (Abridged from Narada (1988: 284–5))

In the verse from *Jñānasārasamuccaya*, the Buddha says: "As the wise test gold by burning, cutting and rubbing it (on a piece of a touchstone), so are you to accept my words after examining them and not merely out of regard for me." (Narada, 1988: 285)

3 I am not suggesting that other (Non-Indian) engaged Buddhist leaders were not aware of the evils of the caste system. Thich Nhat Hanh, for instance, held that the self that people of Buddha's time used to worship was the real cause of social injustice, through ignorance, through stagnation; that society was full of evils; the system of castes, the control of life by the brahmins, the treatment of the untouchables. It is not clear, however, whether Hanh was aware that this situation still persists in India and it was Ambedkar who tried to alter it through different means including the revival of Buddhism. Similarly, the Dalai Lama in one of his interviews mentions that the Buddha spoke very critically about the caste system and adds that there is no need to take a certain position on caste, racial discrimination (Puri, 2006: 167), probably meaning thereby that the Buddha's criticism of caste is valid and no justification of caste is needed. But he does not seem to show any special concern for the issue.

4 With reference to different influences on engaged Buddhism, Sallie King, in her introduction to *Socially Engaged Buddhism* says,

> The greatest influence from non-Buddhists comes from Gandhi (himself Western educated), who has exerted a great influence on the engaged Buddhist leaders, with the exception of Dr. Ambedkar (who worked with Gandhi but eventually broke with him owing to Gandhi's refusal to reject the caste system.) (Her claim that Dr. Ambedkar worked with Gandhi is questionable.)

References

Ambedkar, B. R. (1974). *The Buddha and His Dhamma* (2nd ed.). Bombay: Siddharth Publication.

Ambedkar, B. R. (1980). *Buddha and the Future of His Religion* (3rd ed.). Jullunder City: Bheem Patrika Publications.

Ambedkar, B. R. (1987). *Dr. Babasaheb Ambedkar: Writings and Speeches* (vol. 3), ed. Vasant Moon. Mumbai: The Education and Employment Department, Government of Maharashtra.

Buddhadasa-Bhikkhu. (1992). *Paticcasmuppada: Practical Dependent Origination*. Nonthaburi, Thailand: Vuddhidhamma Fund.
Buddhadasa Bhikkhu. (1993). *Dhammic Socialism*. Translated and edited by Swearer, D. K. (2nd ed.) Bangkok: Thai Inter-religious Commission for Development.
Buddhadasa-Bhikkhu. (1969). *No Religion*. Bangkok: Sublime Life Mission.
Dalai Lama. (1994). *Beyond Dogma: The Challenge of the Modern World*. Calcutta: Rupa Co.
Dharmapala, Anagarika. (1965). *Return to Righteousness*, ed. Ananda Guruge. Ceylon: The Anagarika Dharmapala Birth Centenary Committee, Ministry of Education and Cultural Affairs.
Gokhale, Pradeep. (2004). "Secularizing Buddhism: A Comparative overview of B. R. Ambedkar's and S. N. Goenka's Approaches to Buddhism," in Buddhism *In Global Perspective*. Mumbai: Somaiya Publications,
Hanh, Thich Nhat. (1993). *For a Future to be Possible: Commentaries on the Five Wonderful Precepts*, Berkeley: Parallax Press,
Hanh, Thich Nhat and Berrigan, Danial. (2001). *The Raft Is Not the Shore: Conversations towards a Buddhist Christian Awareness* (2nd ed.). New York: Orbis Books, Maryknoll.
Kaweesha, Gunathilaka. (Revised in August, 2013). "Anagarika Dharmapala," Wikipedia: The Free Encyclopedia.
King, Sallie. (1996). "Thich Nhat Hanh and the Unified Buddhist Church: Nondualism in Action," as included in Queen and King (eds.) *Engaged Buddhism: Buddhist Liberation Movements in Asia*. Albany: State University of New York Press, pp. 321–364.
Narada. (1988). *The Buddha and His Teachings* (4th ed.). Kuala Lumpur: Buddhist Missionary Society.
Puri, Bharati. (2006). *Engaged Buddhism: The Dalai Lama's Worldview*. New Delhi: Oxford University Press.
Queen, Christopher and King, Sallie (eds.). (1996). *Engaged Buddhism: Buddhist Liberation Movements in Asia*. Albany: State University of New York Press.
Sangharakshita. (1986). *Ambedkar and Buddhism*. Glasgow: Windhorse Publications.
Sivaraksa, Sulak. (2005). *Socially Engaged Buddhism*. Delhi: B. R. Publishing Corporation.
Sponsberg, Alan. (1996). "TBMSG: A Dhamma Revolution in Contemporary India," as included in Queen and King (eds.) *Engaged Buddhism: Buddhist Liberation Movements in Asia*. Albany: State University of New York Press, pp. 73–120.
Swearer, D. K. (1996). "Sulak Sivaraksa's Buddhist Vision for Renewing Society," as included in Queen and King (eds.) *Engaged Buddhism: Buddhist Liberation Movements in Asia*. Albany: State University of New York Press, pp. 195–235.

Appendix I

VAJRASŪCI

Sanghasen Singh[1]

[**Preface:** The text *Vajrasūcī* came into light in this modern age, when B. H. Hodgson translated it in 1829 and L. Wilkinson edited it for the first time in 1839. It is understood that the purpose of this work is to refute the system of four *varṇa*s based on birth. The author has stressed upon unity of the four *varṇa*s and has said that the four *varṇa*s were classified on the basis of expertise in deeds and action and not based on birth. He has emphasized the importance of conduct. However, he has accepted on the other hand the authority of the *Veda*s, *Smṛti*s and the *Mahābhārata*. He seems to be an advocate of the doctrine of soul also because he has considered the soul and body separate from each other.

Aśvaghoṣa has been regarded as the author of this work. The introduction of the work mentions the name 'Aśvaghoṣa' and the colophon mentions the name 'Siddhācārya Aśvaghoṣa.' Given this situation, there is a question whether the author of this work and the author of *Buddhacarita* may be considered as one and the same. This is a moot question. After a careful study of this work, it is clear that it is not the composition of Aśvaghoṣa, the author of *Buddhacarita*. There is a possibility that there were two or more Aśvaghoṣas. There must have been a considerable time gap between Aśvaghoṣa, the composer of *Buddhacarita* and Siddhācārya Aśvaghoṣa, the composer of *Vajrasūcī*. There is great difference between the styles of the language of both these authors. The language of *Vajrasūcī* seems to be comparatively later than the language of *Buddhacarita*. Apart from this, there are some more evidences to prove that the composition of this work has taken place after a significant time gap between both these texts. It is possibly composed in the 8th to 9th CE. To facilitate clarity in providing evidences, we divide them into two, viz external evidences and internal evidences. Firstly, let us focus on external evidences:

1 None of the scholars after Aśvaghoṣa (the author of *Buddhacarita*) has mentioned this work (*Vajrasūcī*) to be composed by him.
2 Itsing has not mentioned this work along with other compositions of Aśvaghoṣa.

3 The Chinese translation of this work, which is found in the Chinese *Tripīṭaka* catalogues as '*Vajrasūcī*' has been between 973 and 981 CE. The name of the composer has been mentioned as Dharmakīrti. As per the opinion of Sujitkumar Mukhopadhyaya, the Chinese translation or rendition of this work has been undertaken in the last lap of 10th CE.[2] Had the work been the composition of Aśvaghoṣa, the author of *Buddhacarita*, it would have been translated or rendered long before 10th CE.

4 The Tibetan sources neither mention this work along with the other works of Aśvaghoṣa nor its translation. Enthusiastic Indian scholars and Tibetan Lamas even undertook the translation or rendition of non-Buddhistic works. It is a matter of surprise as to why they had not translated this work, especially when they knew that this is the work of the noble Aśvaghoṣa?

Internal evidences appear to be stronger than external evidences. One can claim on the basis of them that this work is not the composition of Aśvaghoṣa, the author of *Buddhacarita*.

1 A careful examination of *Vajrasūcī* proves that the author of this work was not a staunch Buddhist. He was an admixture of a Buddhist and a brāhmaṇa. Some thoughts expressed by him prove him to be a Buddhist, while other thoughts prove him to be a brāhmaṇa or a supporter of the brāhmaṇa community. On the one hand the text opens with '*om namo mañjunāthāya*' and stresses on the importance of *śīla* i.e. (good) conduct. On the other hand, the verse employed in the introduction of this text has accepted the authority of *Veda*s, *Smṛti*s and 'other statements' related to *dharma* and *artha*.[3] As far as the composer of *Buddhacarita* and *Saundarananda* is concerned, one can clearly perceive Brahmanical influence on him, however, he has not dared to accept the authority of *Veda*s, *Smṛti*s etc. and '*om namo mañjunāthāya*' cannot be his opening obeisance. The author of *Vajrasūcī* has neither doubted the authoritativeness of the *Veda*s, *Bhārata* i.e. *Mahābhārata*, *Mānavadharma* i.e. *Manusmṛti* nor has he challenged them. It is natural for the Buddhist thinker to challenge the authoritativeness of these Brahmanical texts and refute the superiority of the brāhmaṇa varṇa. There has been nothing of this sort in this text.

2 Buddhist tradition has accepted the following order of varṇas—kṣatriya, brāhmaṇa, vaiśya and sūdra. But this text has retained the Brahmanical order as it is. This order has been in agreement with the *Smṛti*s and *Purāṇa*s. This proves that the present text has been a later composition, when Buddhist tradition had become weak and blurred.

3 This text has clear reference to the four *Veda*s. The tradition of three *Veda*s has been clearly forgotten. This shift (from three *Veda*s to four)

happened in the Brahmanical tradition quite late. This indicates that the text has been of a later date.

4 The author of this text has accepted the system of four varṇas based on the 'line of action and deed'. Buddhist tradition has been against the varṇa-system be it based on birth or 'line of action and deed'. This (acceptance of) the four varṇa system has been the line of thought of a later thinker and not Aśvaghoṣa, the early Buddhist thinker.

5 This text has references to *Harivaṁśa*, which has been mentioned by the author as *Bhārata* (*Mahābhārata*). It appears that by the time of the composition of this text, *Harivaṁśa* was accepted as a part of the *Mahābhārata*.[4] Historically, this situation has happened quite late. While establishing the date of this work, Sujitkumar Mukhopadhyaya has not paid attention to this internal evidence.

6 The entire text mentions neither the Buddha, nor *dharma* nor *saṅgha*. Aśvaghoṣa (the author of the *Buddhacarita*), who has eulogized the Buddha cannot be expected not to praise the Buddha or not to quote the sayings of the Buddha. The first 1,000 years of Buddhism had not shown such an anomaly, because the hold of *dharma* had been quite strong in this period and it would not have been possible to take such an audacious step. This evidence too proves that the text is a composition of a later author.

By these evidences one can say that this work is a composition of some author of 8th to 9th century CE whose name probably was Siddhācārya Aśvaghoṣa. As has been said earlier, the text was translated or rendered later in Chinese in 10th century CE.

There is one more point emerging clearly about this author. Although he quotes from the *Smṛti*s or the *Mahābhārata*, many of the quotations are not located in the respective texts. The statements made here regarding the origins (births) of the sages are not generally in consonance with the traditional account. Taking into consideration all these aspects, it seems that this work might have been composed by some later spiritual masters (*siddhas*), who had no concern of displaying their scholarship but their purpose was to present their contention in simple words so as to make it acceptable to all. For that if they required any evidences, they unhesitatingly quoted them, whether they were available or unavailable in the quoted texts.]

Vajrasūci

(English Translation)

1 Salutations to Mañjunātha

2 After having offered obeisance (salutations) to Mañjughoṣa (alias Mañjunātha), the teacher of the whole universe, with my speech, body and

mind, I Aśvaghoṣa (hereby) write in the form of concise rules *Vajrasūcī* in consonance with (śāstric) injunctions (1).[5]

3 *Veda*s are the authority (*pramāṇa*), *smṛti*s are the authority; the speech (*vacana*) related to religious merit (*dharma*) and material benefit (*artha*) is the authority. If one shall not endorse these authorities as authority, then who shall testify his/her speech as authority? (2)

4 If you accept that 'brāhmaṇa varṇa' is superior amongst all varṇas,' then we ask, who is a 'brāhmaṇa'? Is it (= the ground of brahmaṇa-hood) the soul, the birth, the body, knowledge, behaviour, deed or the Vedic scripture?

5 Now, the soul is not a brāhmaṇa, because *Veda* is authoritative (in this case), *Veda* states,

> the Sun was an animal, Soma was an animal, Indra was an animal, gods are animals. In the beginning and at the end, the same persons become animals and gods (through rebirth). Even those who eat (literally, cook) dog's flesh (the lowest in the varṇa framework) are also gods.

6 Therefore, due to the authority of the *Veda*s we consider that one does not become a 'brāhmaṇa' just because he is a soul. The *Mahābhārata* also bears testimony to this. It is said in the *Mahābhārata*:

"The seven hunters from Daśārṇa country, deer in the Kālañjara mountain, *cakravāka* birds in the Śarat island and swans in the Mānasa lake were born as brāhmaṇas endowed with the highest knowledge of the *Veda*s in the Kurukṣetra region" (3).

7 Therefore, with the testimony of the *Mahābhārata*, owing to the possibility of the observation with regard to hunters, deer, swans and *cakravāka* birds, we consider that soul is not a brāhmaṇa. This is also endorsed by the testimony of the Manu's Book of Law, where it has been stated: "A brāhmaṇa, who having studied the four *Veda*s along with its ancillary and sub ancillary texts keeping in view its essential elements, accepts monetary benefits in return from a *śūdra*, becomes a donkey". Further Manu has said: "He becomes a donkey for 12 births, hog for 60 births and dog for 70 births" (4–5).

8 One does not become a brāhmaṇa on the basis of birth. How is it so? As testified by *Smṛti*. *Smṛti* says:

"Acala was born from a female elephant, Keśapiṅgala was born from female owl, Agastya was born from the Agasti flower and Kauśika came into being from *kuśa* grass" (6).

"Kapila was born from the tawny coloured cow and Gautama was born from the cluster of weeds, Ācārya Droṇa from a container/pot and Tittirī is the son of *Tittiri* (partridge) bird" (7).

"Reṇukā gave birth to Rāma (Paraśurāma) and a doe gave birth to Rśyaśṛṅga, a fisherwoman (Satyavatī) gave birth to Vyāsa and śūdra-woman gave birth to Kuśika" (8).

"Caṇḍālī gave birth to Viśvamitra and Urvaśī (the celestial nymph) gave birth to Vasiṣṭha, thus their mothers were not brāhmaṇa but they were regarded as brāhmaṇas in the public (conventional) practice" (9).

Thus by the testimony of the *Smṛtis* we hold that one does not become a brāhmaṇa on account of birth.

9 Supposedly if you say, one's mother may not be brāhmaṇa but his[6] father were brāhmaṇa and from that one becomes a brāhmaṇa, then sons of female slaves, born from brāhmaṇas would be *brāhmaṇas*, but this is not acceptable to you.

10 Moreover, if the son of a brāhmaṇa is a brāhmaṇa, then one has to accept the non-existence of a brāhmaṇa, because there is uncertainty regarding the brāhmaṇa-gotra of the fathers of the present brāhmaṇas. This is because it is seen that female brāhmaṇas are in conjugal contact with the śūdras. Therefore brāhmaṇa is not determined on the basis of birth. This is also as per the testimony of the *Dharmaśāstra* propounded by Manu. The laws of Manu state that:

"The *brāhmaṇa* attains downfall if he trades meat, lac and salt. A brāhmaṇa selling milk becomes a *śūdra* in three days" (10).

"Brāhmaṇas travelling through air face downfall if they consume meat. Therefore after having observed the downfall of the brāhmaṇas one should avoid consuming of meat" (11).

11 Therefore, by the testimony of the law book of Manu, one does not become a brāhmaṇa by birth, if yes then how can he face downfall and become a śūdra? Can a faulty horse ever become a pig? Thus, one cannot become a brāhmaṇa by birth.

12 Body frame is not (the mark of) a brāhmaṇa. How is it so? If body frame is a brāhmaṇa then fire (which burns the dead body of a brāhmaṇa) will be (called) the one who kills a brāhmaṇa; relatives who cremate the mortal body would be accused of killing a brāhmaṇa. Moreover, kṣatriya, vaiśya and śūdra who have emerged from the body of brāhmaṇa (or those kṣatriya, vaiśya and śūdra offspring of brāhmaṇas from the women of these castes) would have been designated as brāhmaṇa, but this is not seen. If mere body frame was a brāhmaṇa, then the fruit originating from the actions viz; sacrificing, officiating a sacrifice, learning, teaching, undertaking charity and accepting charity which have accrued from the body of a brāhmaṇa would have been destroyed due to the death of the brāhmaṇa-body;

but this is not desirable. Therefore, we think that (mere) body frame is not a brāhmaṇa.

13 Knowledge is not (the mark of) a brāhmaṇa. How is it so? The reason being excess of knowledge. Those śūdras who are knowledgeable will also become brāhmaṇas. Śūdras, though rarely, are seen to have knowledge of *Veda*, Vyākaraṇa (grammar), Mīmāṁsā, Sāṁkhya, Vaiśeṣika, Jaina,[7] Ājīvaka[8] and all other knowledge systems. They would not be brāhmaṇas. Therefore, we consider that (one who possesses) knowledge is not a brāhmaṇa.

14 Conduct (that is, a person who possesses good conduct) also is not a brāhmaṇa. If (one who possesses) conduct is a brāhmaṇa, then the *śūdra*s endowed with (good) conduct would become brāhmaṇa. It is observed that actors, soldiers, fishermen, theatre persons etc. undertake variety of great actions but they do not become brāhmaṇas. Therefore, conduct is not (the mark of) a brāhmaṇa.

15 Actions (that is, occupation[9]) are also not (the mark of) a brāhmaṇa. How is it so? It is seen that kṣatriyas, vaiśyas and śūdras perform variety of actions viz; sacrificing, officiating a sacrifice, learning, teaching, undertaking charity and accepting charity. But you do not accept them (all) as brāhmaṇas. Therefore actions are also not (the mark of) a brāhmaṇa.

16 One does not become brāhmaṇa by *Veda*. How is it so? There was a *rākṣasa* named Rāvaṇa. He had studied the four *Veda*s viz; *Ṛgveda*, *Yajurveda*, *Sāmaveda* and *Atharvaveda*. Practices pertaining to the *Veda*s are prevalent in the homes of *rākṣasa*s also,[10] but (by that) they do not become brāhmaṇas. Therefore, we think that one does not become a brāhmaṇa by (learning) the *Veda*s.

17 How does brāhmaṇa-hood come into existence? It is said:

"Brāhmaṇa-hood does not come into existence by scriptures, by purificatory rites, by birth, by lineage, by Vedas or by actions" (12).

18 "Brāhmaṇa-hood, which means eradication of all sins is white (pure) like *kunda* flowers and Moon."

19 It is said that (brāhmaṇa-hood is achieved) because of vows, penance, rules, fasting, charity, control, restraint and conduct.[11] It is said in the *Veda*s:

"Gods consider that person as a brāhmaṇa, (who is) selfless, devoid of ego, without attachment, without acquisition, free from passion and envy" (13).

It is said in all scriptures:

"Truthfulness is Brahman, penance is Brahman and control of senses is Brahman, compassion towards all living beings is Brahman; these are the characteristics of a brāhmaṇa."

"Lack of truth (truthfulness), lack of penance, lack of control of senses, absence of compassion towards all living beings are the characteristics of a cāṇḍāla."

"Those who do not indulge in sex (sexual pleasures) with gods, men, women and animals, they are highly wise and brāhmaṇas" (14–16).

Śukra has also said: "Birth is not taken into consideration, virtues are beneficial. Even if a cāṇḍāla is established there (that is, in virtues), gods consider such a person as brāhmaṇa" (17).

20 Therefore (it is said that) neither birth, nor soul, nor body frame, nor knowledge, nor actions, nor livelihood, nor knowledge of the *Veda*s makes one a brāhmaṇa.

21 Moreover, you have said, "Śūdras are not supposed to go for renunciation (*pravrajyā*), their duty is servitude of the brāhmaṇas. They are the lowest as the word śūdra is uttered as the last among four varṇas."

22 If this is so, then Indra would have been the lowest. The Paninian sutra viz; "the 'va' in *śvan*, *yuvan* and *maghavan* is vocalized when there is an affix other than *taddhita* affixes" enlists *śvā* i.e. dog, *yuvā* i.e. young man and then *maghavā* i.e., Indra, the king of gods. Hence Indra should have been the lowest in comparison to a dog and a young man. But this is not seen. Besides, does fault arise because of (the order of) utterance alone? Similarly the compounds such as *umāmaheśvarau* ("Umā and Maheśvara," that is "Goddess Pārvatī and the Lord Śiva") and *dantauṣṭham* ("teeth and lips") are used amongst people. This does not mean that teeth and Umā were born earlier. Only a compound of *varṇa*s has been made namely *brāhmaṇa-kṣatra-viṭ-śūdrāḥ* ("brāhmaṇas, kṣatriyas, vaiśyas and śūdras"). Thus, your claim that only the servitude of brāhmaṇas is their duty does not hold any grounds.

23 Moreover, the case of brāhmaṇa-hood is not determinate. It is said in the Manu's Book of Law:

'That brāhmaṇa, who has sucked lip-moisture of a śūdra woman (at the time of copulation), enjoyed her breath and has procreated from her, does not get relief (from the sin)" (18).

"One (a brāhmaṇa) who consumes food from the hands of a śūdra woman continuously for a month, becomes a śūdra while alive (in this very life) and is born as dog after death" (19).

"A brāhmaṇa, surrounded with śūdra women, whose wife is a śūdra, loses any sanctification from his forefathers and gods and attains Raurava hell (one among permanent hells)" (20).

24 Following the testimony of the above statements the case of brāhmaṇa-hood is uncertain.

25 Moreover, a śūdra can become a brāhmaṇa. What is the reason? It is mentioned in the Manu's Book of Law:

"The great sage, Kaṭha by name, who was born from the sacrificial fire sticks became a brāhmaṇa by penance, therefore birth is not the reason (for being a brāhmaṇa)" (21).

"The great sage, Vyāsa by name, who was born from the womb of a fisherwoman became a brāhmaṇa by penance; therefore, birth is not the reason (for becoming a brāhmaṇa)" (22).

"The great sage Vasiṣṭha also, who was born from the womb of Urvaśī (a celestial nymph) became a brāhmaṇa by penance; therefore, birth is not the reason (for being a brāhmaṇa)" (23).

"Rśyaśṛṅga, the great sage who was born from the womb of a doe, became a brāhmaṇa by penance; therefore, birth is not the reason (for being a *brāhmaṇa*)" (24).

"Viśvāmitra the great sage, who was born from the womb of a Cāṇḍālī, became a brāhmaṇa by penance; therefore, birth is not the reason (for being a brāhmaṇa)" (25).

"Nārada, the great sage was born from the womb of a Tāṇḍalī (an outcaste woman), became a brāhmaṇa by penance; therefore birth is not the reason (for being a brāhmaṇa)" (26).

"One who has won over oneself, who has no rival, who has control over five senses, he becomes a brāhmaṇa by penance. Brāhmaṇa is one who leads the life of *Brahmacarya* (*Śramaṇacaryā*)" (27).

"They were not sons of brāhmaṇa women but were considered as brāhmaṇas in the world. Brāhmaṇa-hood is based on conduct and purity, thus family lineage is not the reason (to be a brāhmaṇa" (28).

"Conduct is prime and not family lineage, for there is no use of being born in a high-varṇa family but devoid of good conduct. Many learned people were born in low-varṇa families but they attained heaven by good conduct" (29).

26 "Who were Kaṭha, Vyāsa, Vasiṣṭha, Rśyaśṛṅga, Visvāmitra and other *brahmarṣis* (brāhmaṇa sages)? They were born in low families, but were brāhmaṇas for the world. Thus, by accepting this statement as a testimonial (towards brāhmaṇa-hood), the case of a brāhmaṇa is not determinate, for (a person born in a) śūdra family can also become a brāhmaṇa."

27 What else? In your opinion:

"Brāhmaṇa is born from the mouth, kṣatriya from the arms, vaiśya is born from the thighs and śūdra (is born) from the feet" (30).

28 Here we state that there are many brāhmaṇas and we do not know who all emerged from the mouth. (On the contrary) there are brāhmaṇas

from fisherman, washerman as well as cāṇḍāla families. Purificatory rites like tonsure, Muñjā-grass thread ceremony are being done for them, they are also designated as brāhmaṇa. Therefore, kṣatriyas and others also are like brāhmaṇas. Hence we see that there is only one varna. There are no four varṇas.

29 Besides, if they (*varṇas*) have originated from one man (*puruṣa*), how can there be four (different) varṇas? Here someone called Devadatta procreates four sons from one woman, there is not differentiation based on varṇa as this one is brāhmaṇa, this one is kṣatriya, this one is vaiśya and this one is śūdra. How is this so? Because they have one father. In that case, how can brāhmaṇas and others constitute four varṇas?

30 Here, we see different footprints of bull, elephant, horse, lion, tiger etc. as this is the hoof mark of a bull, this is the footprint of an elephant, this is the hoof mark of a horse, this is the hoof mark of a deer, this is the pugmark of a lion and this is the pug mark of a tiger. But we cannot identify the foot-print of a brāhmaṇa, the foot-print of a kṣatriya, the foot-print of a vaiśya and the foot-print of a śūdra. Thus, as there is no differentiating factor in the foot-prints, there is one varṇa and not four varṇas.

31 Here, in the case of (animals) like bull, buffalo, horse, elephant, donkey, monkey, goat and ram, we find the difference between their genital organs, colour, body constitution, stool, urine, odour, sound and so on, same is not seen in the case of brāhmaṇas, kṣatriyas etc, therefore, owing to no differentiating factor there is only one *varṇa*.

32 And also, just as swan, pigeon, parrot, cuckoo, peacock and others are identified with differentiating factors like form, colour, hair, and face, this is not the case with brāhmaṇas and others, therefore as there is not differentiating factor there is only one varṇa.

33 Just as trees like banyan, *bakula*, *palāsa*, *aśoka*, *tamāla*, *nāgakesara*, *sirīṣa* and *campaka* have a differentiating factor be it stem, leaf, flower, fruit, bark, seed, juice or odour, similar differentiating factors are not evident in the case of brāhmaṇas, kṣatriyas, vaiśyas and śūdras and there is no difference in skin, flesh, blood, bone, semen, excrement, complexion, body constitution and also in the case of delivering a child. Therefore, because of absence of differentiating factors, there is only one varṇa.

34 Moreover, O brāhmaṇa, there is no differentiating factor in the case of brāhmaṇas and others pertaining to happiness, grief, survival, intellect, behaviour, death, birth, fear and sexual behaviour.

35 You may take into cognizance the following. Just as fruits grown on one tree such as *udumbara* or jack fruit do not have varṇa-difference as fruits. Fruits of *udumbara* and jack fruit whether they grow on branches, stem, lower part of the stem and roots are identified as one and not as 'this is a brāhmaṇa fruit,' 'this is a kṣatriya fruit,' 'this is a vaiśya fruit' (and) 'this is a śūdra fruit.' That is because they grow on

one tree. In the same way there is no differentiation amongst human beings as they are born from one *puruṣa* (that is, a human male).

36 Besides, there is one more flaw. If a brāhmaṇa (male) is born from the mouth (of the great cosmic *puruṣa*), then from where has a brāhmaṇa female come into existence? If she has come into existence through the mouth then, alas! there is the problem of her being sister (of a *brāhmaṇa* male). It is not appropriate (for a brāhmaṇa) to have sexual relationship with her. It is against the norms of the society. Therefore, Brāhmaṇa-hood is indeterminate.

37 The system of four varṇas is indeed based on specific actions. When Yudhiṣṭhira asked Vaiśampāyana, he explained that the system of four varṇas is based on specific actions.

The renowned son of Pāṇḍu named Yudhiṣṭhira having approached Vaiśampāyana respectfully asked (him) (31).

"Who are brāhmaṇas and what are the characteristics of brāhmaṇas? As I am desirous of knowing this, you may please explain" (32).

Vaiśampāyana said:

> The first characteristic of a brāhmaṇa (is as follows): A brāhmaṇa is endowed with the virtues like forbearance. He is the one who gives up use of weapons; he follows the practice of meatless diet and does not injure or kill living beings (33).
>
> The second characteristic of a brāhmaṇa (is as follows): A brāhmaṇa does not accept wealth belonging to someone else, neither in full (nor in part) whether fallen in the street or in someone's home if it is not given (or offered) (34).
>
> The third characteristic of a brāhmaṇa (is as follows): A brāhmaṇa has given up cruel nature, is devoid of possessiveness, who does not receive anything (without being given), who is liberated and who wanders regularly (freely) (35).
>
> The fourth characteristic of a brāhmaṇa (is as follows): A brāhmaṇa has permanently given up sexual acts with gods, men, women, birds and animals (36).
>
> The fifth characteristic of a brāhmaṇa (is as follows): Truth is purity, compassion is purity, controlling sense organs is purity, kindness towards all living beings is purity and penance is purity (37).
>
> O Yudhiṣṭhira, I regard such a person endowed with these five characteristics as a brāhmaṇa, the remaining others are termed as śūdras (38).
>
> A person does not become a brāhmaṇa by family lineage nor by birth; (he becomes a brāhmaṇa) by actions[12] (good conduct), for O Yudhiṣṭhira, even a cāṇḍāla who has a good conduct is a brāhmaṇa (39).

Vaiśampāyana further added:

> O Yudhiṣṭhira, earlier there was only one varṇa in this world. Four varṇas were established because of expertise in deeds and actions (40).
>
> All mortals are born through the womb, all release urine and excrement, all have similar sensory organs and (cognize similar) sensory objects, therefore they become brāhmaṇas (literally twice-born ones) on account of good conduct and virtues (41).
>
> Even a śūdra endowed with good conduct and virtues becomes a brāhmaṇa and even a brāhmaṇa devoid of good conduct becomes lower than a śūdra (42).

These are the statements of Vaiśampāyana:

> O Yudhiṣṭhira, if a śūdra has crossed the abysmal ocean of five sensory organs (successfully), then limitless charity needs to be offered to him (43).
>
> O king, one does not look for birth as virtues cause well-being. Gods consider such a person as brāhmaṇa, who has dedicated his life for righteousness, (for the well-being) of others and exerts day in and day out with forbearance (44).
>
> O Yudhiṣṭhira, the Son of Kuntī, those who after having renounced household life, become desirous of attaining liberation and who are detached from desires are called brāhmaṇas (45).
>
> Non-violence, non-possessiveness, abstaining from miraculous actions, withdrawal from attachment and envy are the characteristics of a brāhmaṇa (46).
>
> Forgiveness, sympathy, subjugation (of passion), (generosity) in charity, truth, purity, mindfulness,[13] disgust,[14] learnedness, specific knowledge[15] and belief (in life after death) are the characteristics of a brāhmaṇa (47).
>
> A brāhmaṇa, who knows the *Gāyatrī mantra* only and is well controlled (in senses) is far better than a brāhmaṇa who has knowledge of the four Vedas, but is uncontrolled (in senses), and consumes everything and sells everything (48).
>
> O Yudhiṣṭhira, one does not attain the (high) position (after death) even by performing thousand sacrifices, which one attains by practicing *brahmacarya* (that is, the life of a *Śramaṇa*) just for one night (49).
>
> He is known as a brāhmaṇa, who has full knowledge of all the Vedas, who has performed consecration at all sacred places and who being liberated practices righteousness (50).
>
> One, who does not perform dreadful sins towards all living beings through body, mind and speech, attains Brahman (51).

We have said this to remove confusion amongst brāhmaṇas who have lost thinking power. May the virtuous people accept it if it is reasonable (if they agree with it) and leave it if it is unreasonable (if they disagree with it) (52).

This work is by the revered and accomplished Aśvaghoṣa.

Notes

1 This is an English translation by Madhavi Narsale of the Hindi article written by Sanghasen Singh published in *Buddhist Studies* (the journal of the Department of Buddhist Studies, University of Delhi, Delhi), Late Professor Dharmananda Kosambi Commemoration Volume, May 1977, pp. 45–69.
2 Vide Mukhopadhyaya, 1950: xii.
3 VS, verse no. (2).
4 Vide Mukhopadhyaya, 1950: xvii.
5 The numbers in parentheses refer to the numbers of the verses in the text.
6 The word used in the original text is '*teṣām*' (meaning, 'their') which should have been '*tasya*' (meaning, 'his'). It is translated accordingly.
7 The original text uses the word *nagna* (meaning naked) which probably refers to the system of the Jainas. The reference to Nigaṇṭha Nāthaputta. The historians have identified him with Mahāvīra. The two sects of Jainism must have been available at the time of the composition of this text. It appears that the author has designated both the sects by the common term, 'nagna.'
8 This probably refers to Makkhali-Gosāla.
9 Here the term *karma* (literally, action) may better be interpreted as occupation. The word *kamma* (karma, action) has a different connotation in the well-known verse from *Suttanipāta*, "*na jaccā vasalo hoti, na jaccā hoti brāhmaṇo*| *kammunā vasalo hoti, kammunā hoti brāhmaṇo*||," (One does not become a śūdra by birth; one does not become a brāhmaṇa by birth. One becomes a śūdra by *kamma* (action); one becomes a brāmaṇa by *kamma*).
10 This is not consistent with the Brahmanical tradition. One does not know on what basis the author has said this.
11 This is quite an odd definition of Brahmin-hood. Compare, *Dhammapada*, "*Brāhmaṇavagga*."
12 "*kriyābhir brāhmaṇo bhavet.*" Unless the statement is interpreted differently (as 'good conduct'), it will not be consistent with earlier statement. Sujitkumar Mukhopadhyay translates, "A man is not brāhmaṇa .....by ceremonies," which is wrong (See Mukhopadhyay, 1950: 21).
13 The word '*smṛti*' seems to be used here in the Buddhist connotation, namely, 'Mindfulness.'
14 '*ghṛṇā*' (disgust). Probably this refers to disgust towards sins.
15 '*vijñāna*' (specific knowledge). Is the word used according to Buddhist terminology?

References

Mukhopadhyaya, Sujitkumar, (1950) *The Vajrasūcī of Aśvaghoṣa, Sanskrit Text.* (Sino-Indian Studies), Santiniketan, Visva-Bharati.
VS: *Vajrasūcī* as included in Mukhopadhyay (1950).

Appendix II

VAJRASŪCI AND ITS REVERBERATIONS[1]

R. C. Dhere

History has seen a great number of rational men and women, known and unknown, who have raised their voices against determining a person's social status based on his birth. One such rational person, who is unknown to history, wrote a great book by the name *Vajrasūci* or *Vajrasūcikopaniṣad*. In it, the author has severely criticized Brāhmaṇa-hood determined by birth.

Although this Upaniṣad falls into the category of the New Upaniṣads, it dates back beyond the 9th century of the Christian Era and there is simply no way to firmly identify its author. A copy of the manuscript of this book came to the notice of B. H. Hudson in Nepal, in the year 1829. According to the information gathered by Hudson from the legends, the creator of this treatise is one Aśvaghoṣa. Later on, another copy of this manuscript made by someone in the year circa 1710, was found in Nashik, Maharashtra. In Maharashtra, however, the Upaniṣad is credited to Ādi Śaṅkarācārya.

In circa 973–981 A. D., the Upaniṣad was translated into Chinese. The Chinese consider the original author of the book to be a Buddhist scholar by the name Dharmakīrti. Some other sources even offer the names of Mañjughoṣācārya, a disciple of Aśvaghoṣa and someone by the name Mṛtyuñjayācārya.[2]

This is a very small Upaniṣad (contained in a single crown-size sheet) and is included in the collections of Upaniṣads published by various publications like Nirnaysagar (Mumbai), Khemraj Shrikrishnadas (Mumbai), Sarvahitaishi Company (Varanasi) *et al.* A detailed, annotated edition of the Upaniṣad is also available. The manuscript in the possession of this author clearly states that Aśvaghoṣa is its creator.[3]

A synopsis of *Vajrasūci*

True to the term *Vajra* in its name, meaning a very strong and indestructible club-like weapon or thunderbolt, *Vajrasūci* consists of hard-hitting thoughts. It affirms very logically that Brāhmaṇa-hood does not get established or proved by birth, body, caste, knowledge, deeds or religiousness.

The Upaniṣad strongly adheres to the ideal definition of Brāhmaṇa as 'He, who has understood *Brahma* is a Brahmin' (*Brahma jānātīti brāhmaṇaḥ*).

The rational-minded author of *Vajrasūci* says, 'Let me teach you the enlightening set of universal principles (*śāstra*) called *Vajrasūci*, which is the pride of the knowledgeable and the curse of the ignorant. There are four varṇas or classes, Brāhmaṇa, Kṣatriya, Vaiśya and Śūdra. The *śrutis* and the *smṛtis* tell us that among them, the Brāhmaṇa-varṇa is the highest or the most superior. This obviously leads one to think, who exactly is a Brāhmaṇa? What is it, among birth, body, caste, knowledge, deeds (*karma*) and religiousness that proves the Brāhmaṇa-hood of an individual?

Saying this, the author of *Vajrasūci* avers that none of these six factors determine Brāhmaṇa-hood. He further states that only a person, who rids himself of the six faults, achieves restraint of the senses and experiences selfless, detached existence—is a Brāhmaṇa.

An understanding of this manifest meaning of the *Vajrasūci* will enable us to realize the greatness of the rational thoughts it puts forward. Its author regards his laconic work to be 'the curse of the ignorant' and 'the pride of the knowledgeable'. Saint Jñāneśvara says: "Knowledge is the eye of deed and it ought to be impeccable" and his contemporaries or the saints that followed him, belong to this same tradition.

Bhaviṣyapurāṇa and *Vajrasūci*

While the *purāṇas* have sung paeans for the Brāhmaṇas on one hand, on the other hand they have also set forth the ideals of Brāhmaṇa-hood and have severely condemned those Brāhmaṇas who are found wanting against those ideals.

The Bhaviṣyapurāṇa in particular has practically uprooted the concept of Brāhmaṇa-hood by birth in an elaborate manner, just like the *Vajrasūci*.[4] This Purāṇa says,

śūdra-brāhmaṇayor bhedo mṛgymāṇo'pi yatnataḥ|
nekṣyate sarvadharmeṣu saṁhatais tridaśair api||

(Even all the gods, if they come together and search diligently, they will not be able to discriminate between a Śūdra and a Brāhmaṇa.)

Like *Vajrasūci*, the Bhaviṣyapurāṇa too, says: "there is no rule whatsoever that a Brāhmaṇa's colour is white, that of a Kṣatriya is yellow and that of a Śūdra is black." This call for equality among the humans by the Bhaviṣyapurāṇa is a great and laudable attempt to revive the legacy of *Vajrasūci*.

Vajrasūci and the Mahānubhāva sect

The process of researching the tenets of the Mahānubhāva Sect with the object of pure pursuit of knowledge in an objective and unbiased manner is yet to begin in Maharashtra. Unless that happens, several enigmas of the cultural history of this state over the past seven centuries will remain unresolved. There is a room to believe that the Sect accorded importance to *Vajrasūci*. It is quite natural that the followers of Cakradharasvāmī, who has condemned Brāhmaṇa-hood in such terms as '*Sarvādhamatva Brāhmaṇatva*' (Brāhmaṇa-hood is the vilest) or '*Ācārya-naraka*' (hell of the teachers), should have a particular affinity towards *Vajrasūci*, which is a scathing criticism on Brāhmaṇa-hood by birth. Frankly, I have not been able to follow the ancient literature of the Mahānubhāvas in this respect. However, the list of Mahānubhāva literature given on the back page of a book published by Mahant Dattaraj in Peshawar (now in Pakistan) in the year 1908 mentions '*Vajrasūcikopaniṣad*'. Similarly, a modern publication of this Sect, 'Viṭṭhala-Darśana arthāt Satyaśaṅkā Prakāśa' (authored by Shindewadikar),[5] though it does not cite *Vajrasūci* manifestly, puts forth the Marathi translation of thoughts in it in the form of Marathi ślokas.

Vajrasūci and the Warkari saints

The saints belonging to the Bhāgavata Sampradāya who, setting forth the criteria of a high caste, says: "*Uttama tyā jāti, deva śaraṇa ananyagati*" (Those castes, who surrender to God are the high castes), were the proponents of the rational thought of equality of all humans, not unlike the author of *Vajrasūci*.

However, the similarity found between the thought promoted by *Vajrasūci* and that of the saints does not establish a direct relationship between them. Yet, there is person among the hallowed list of Marathi saints, in the nurturing of whose thoughts *Vajrasūci* has actually played a role and that person is Saint Bahiṇābāī, an influential disciple of Saint Tukārām.

In her life there was an extraordinary situation developed at the time when she was in search of her guru. While she was staying at Kolhapur (Maharashtra), she had an opportunity to listen to Saint Tukārām's verses (*abhaṅgas*) in a devotional sermon (*kīrtana*) by Jairamsvāmī Wadgaonkar and she yearned for more of the saint's thoughts. She also saw in a dream that Saint Tukārām himself enlightened her. However, her orthodox husband refuted the idea as he could not imagine a Brāhmaṇa lady making a lower caste person, her guru. Bahiṇābāī was born in a Brahmin family whereas Saint Tukārām belonged to the Kuṇabī caste by birth. Bahiṇābāī's husband did not just oppose her; he even tortured her.

It was during that period of oppression that Bahiṇābāī began thinking about who a Brahmin is. In this contemplative phase of her life, *Vajrasūci* gave her the ideological support. Perhaps she received a copy of the Upaniṣad from Jayarāmasvāmī. Thereafter, she wrote a poetic (*abhaṅga*) commentary on *Vajrasūci*.[6] In a small set of mere 18 *abhangas*, she presented a detailed, lucid explanation of the thoughts of *Vajrasūci* and affirmed that, 'He, who has realized Brahma, is a Brahmin.' She said,

Bahiṇī mhaṇe, brahmī nānde to brāhmaṇa /
yātiśī pramāṇa, nase tethe //

(Bahiṇā says, he, who dwells in the realm of Brahma is a Brahmin. Caste has nothing to do with it.)

This couplet is the concluding part of the eighteenth and final *abhaṅga* of Bahiṇābāī, contained in her poetic commentary on *Vajrasūci*. The commentary no doubt has a special place in her spiritual life, but one must say that it is an expression of the rational outlook of the Maharashtrian saint tradition. The literature of the Marathi saint-poets is a literature replete with the ideology of equality. While in the traditional Indian society, Brahmins have been regarded as the most superior by birth, most saints have tried from time to time, to make the Brahmins whose behaviour was not exactly in keeping with their high position in the society aware of the standards or ideals of Brāhmaṇa-hood. They have also sternly refuted the principle of social superiority or inferiority based on one's birth.

They reviled the pseudo *gurus*. They accorded a great importance to the institution of Gurus, yet they stood up against the corrupt and imposter *gurus* and declared unequivocally that any virtuous devotee, irrespective of his caste can be initiated into spirituality by a *guru*. *Vajrasūci* appears to have been influenced by the thought-movement that assumed the expression of Gautama Buddha's view of equality, which said, "No one is a Brāhmaṇa or a Cāṇḍāla based on his birth; his Brāhmaṇa or his Cāṇḍāla status is determined by his karma or deeds that he does." And the speech and actions of the Marathi saints seem to reverberate the core of the thoughts contained in *Vajrasūci*, indirectly if not directly. Bahiṇābai's commentary on the Upaniṣad provides a strong evidence of it.

Poetic translation by Shyamraj

When looked at from the social point of view, the acceptance of *Vajrasūci* by the saint tradition is quite significant. Besides Bahiṇābāī, Saint Gopālanāth and his younger brother as well as disciple Śyāmarāj alias Nānā Mahārāj have also translated *Vajrasūci* in the form of *abhaṅgas*.[7] Both these saints were born at a place that had enormous influence of Bahiṇābāī's thoughts and belonged to the liberal tradition of Saint Ekanāth. Fellow disciples of Shri Śyāmarāj belonged to various castes. Even a Muslim by the name Shaikh Sultan was among them. The *guru* of Shri Śyāmarāj's *guru* belonged to the caste of goldsmiths (Sonar). The biographer of Gopalnath has explained this phenomenon of a Brahmin accepting a Sonar as a guru in the language of *Vajrasūci*. "A person is not a Brahmin if he has no knowledge of Brahma and a person who has realized Brahma is a great Brahmin, whatever may be his caste."

Even more obvious proof of *Vajrasūci*'s influence than this indirect evidence is the translation of *Vajrasūci* done by Shri Śyāmarāj in just seven *abhaṅgas*.[8] Shri Śyāmarāj has taken a review of the entire saint tradition in these seven *abhaṅgas* and has suggested in the eighth *abhaṅga* that the reader should look at the Marathi saint tradition in light of the earlier seven because the saints are from all castes and they are Brahma in themselves because they have experienced the Brahma.

Nāthalīlāmṛta of Ādinātha-Bhairava

Ādinātha-Bhairava was a saint-poet from the Nātha sect in the first half of the 19th century. He wrote a book named '*Nāthalīlāmṛta*' in 1836 that consisted of the legends of the accomplished men in the Nātha tradition.[9]

The book is a testimony to Ādinātha's erudition. Evidently, *Vajrasūcikopaniṣad* was very much in the range of his knowledge. While narrating the life of Śaṅkarācārya, in the 27th chapter of the book, he has included a translation of *Vajrasūcikopaniṣad*. Ādinātha has described a meeting between Śaṅkarācārya and Bhairava, the guardian spirit (Kṣetrapāla) of Kashi (Varanasi). At that time, Bhairava had assumed the persona of a Cāṇḍāla and unaware of his true identity, Śaṅkarācārya had refused to talk to him. At that time, Bhairava preached him not to be proud of the greatness of being a Brahmin. This entire discourse is nothing but a translation of the core message of *Vajrasūci*.

Vajrasūci and some social reformers of the 19th and 20th century

The beginning of the 19th century marked a period of rapid development in hard self-evaluation and cultural analysis in Maharashtra, under the early British Raj. The thinkers and social reformers of that era were of the opinion that outdated and rubbish concepts ought to be discarded resolutely; however, while establishing new thoughts in their place, it would be great if they can get some justification from the tradition.

Accordingly, the ancient piece of literature that offered a strong support to reformers like Raja Rammohan Roy in their endeavours to eradicate social disparity was none other than *Vajrasūci*. The principle 'The high or low status of a person does not depend on the caste in which he is born but on his individual qualities or lack of them' was pursued by him with the help of *Vajrasūci*. Raja Rammohan Roy wrote a commentary on *Vajrasūci* in Bengali language and began publishing it in the form of a series of articles. Unfortunately, he could not complete it.[10]

In Maharashtra, the various movements for social reforms have been associated with *Vajrasūci* right since the beginning. A person going by the name Subaji Bapu had published *Vajrasūci* along with its English and Marathi translations in the year 1839. 'Jātibheda -vivekasāra' an article written by Tukaramtatya Padwal under the name 'One Hindu' was from the same school of thought. Its second edition was published by Mahatma Phule.

The wellspring from which the famous Prārthanā Samāj movement originated was Paramahamsa Sabhā and its chief protagonist Dadoba Pandurang had written a book 'Dharma Vivecana' for his brainchild. The book was published in 1868 and the sixth chapter in it is titled 'All humans belong to one caste.' This chapter is in fact, an excellent commentary on *Vajrasūci.* This fact becomes clearly evident if one undertakes a comparative study of the two books.[11]

Another reformist leader of the masses in Maharashtra, who was greatly influenced by *Vajrasūci* was Svatantrya Veer V. D. Savarkar. Savarkar had published an elaborate article introducing *Vajrasūci* and celebrating the rational thoughts in it, in the monthly magazine *Kirloskar.*[12] It is quite unfortunate that his thoughts were neglected in the movement for social equality. However, Savarkar has described *Vajrasūci* as 'A book discussing pros and cons of casteism in stark words.' He has also very clearly advocated the book.

Notes

1 Editor's note: This is a summary of the chapter, "*vajrasūcīce āghāta*" (pp. 92–121) of the Marathi work authored by the late R. C. Dhere (1930–2016): *Santasāhitya āṇi Lokasāhitya: Kāhī Anubandha,* 1st edn (Pune: Shrividya Prakashan, 1978); the chapter has been summarized by Aruna Dhere in Marathi and the summary is translated into English by Prashant Talnikar. The works titled *Vajrasūcī* and *Vajrasūcikopaniṣad*, though similar in content, are two different works, not composed by one and the same author. The *Vajrasūcī* is ascribed to Aśvaghoṣa, although he may not be the same as the well-known author of the *Buddhacarita.* The other work, *Vajrasūcikopaniṣad*, probably modelled after the first one, is listed among late Upaniṣads. R. C. Dhere in this article is talking about both the works without distinguishing between them. Dhere here deals with the influence of *Vajrasūcī/ Vajrasūcikopaniṣad* on the saints and social reformers/thinkers.

2 See Mukhopadhyaya (1960).

3 Two manuscripts in the personal collection of R. C. Dhere.

4 *Bhaviṣyapurāṇa, Brahmaparva*, Chapters 41–42.

5 Editor's note: Reference to the book (Shindewadikar, Mahant-Govind-Charudatta-Teerthankar-Sadhu, Viṭṭhala-Darśana arthāt Satyaśaṅkā Prakāśa, Mahatma Govind Pathurkar, Solapur) is found in Dhere's original chapter without mention of the year of publication.

6 Dere (1976, 93–121) Appendix, pp. 190–203.

7 See Dhere (1973).

8 See Dhere (1973).

9 See Dhere (1972).

10 Keskar (1915, 74).
11 Priyolkar (1966, 63–122) (Reprint of '*Dharmavivechan*' written by Dadoba Pandurang at the end of this book) (First print of the book, 1868, record of coming to Mumbai).
12 Savarkar (1993, 130).

References

Bhaviṣyapurāṇa, Gitapress, Gorakhpur, 1992.

Dhere, R. C. (Ed.) (1972) *Śrī Ādinathbhairava Virahita Nāthalīlāmṛta*, Shri Samartha Granth Bhavan, Mumbai, (Fourth Edition).

Dhere, R. C. (Ed.) (1973) *Śrī Śyāmraja yāncā Gāthā*, Triputi Math, Dist. Satara, (First Edition).

Dhere, Dr. R. C. (1976) "Shri Bahinabai Virachit Vajraūocikopaniṣad Bhāṣya", in *Santsahitya Ani Loksahitya: Kahi Anubandha*, Dr. R. C. Dhere, (First Edition), pp. 93–121.

Keskar, B. B. (1915) *Raja Rammohan Roy*, Manoranjan Press, Mumbai, (First Edition).

Mukhopadhyaya, Sujitkumar (Ed.) (1960) *The Vajrasūci of Aśvaghoṣa*, Visvabharati Santiniketan.

Priyolkar, A. K. (1966) *Paramhaṁsasabhā va Tice Adhyakṣa Ram Balkrishna*, Mumbai Marathi Granthsangrahalaya, Mumbai (Reprint).

Savarkar, Shantaram (Balarao) Shivram (Ed.) (1993) *Samagra Sāvarkar Vāṅmay*, Volume IX, Published by Shantaram (Balarao) Shivram Savarkar, Mumbai.

INDEX

Note: Page numbers followed by "n" denote endnotes.

abrāhmaṇa 41–2
Advaita-Vedānta 7
Agarkar, G. G. 162
age-mismatched marriages 128–9
alianation, concept of 120–1
All India Women's Conference (AIWC) 137
Aloysius, G. 240
Ambedkar and Radhakrishnan on caste 17–18; pre-ordained social roles 216–17; reconstruction of caste 216–17; *religare* 216; religion and morality 215–16, 224; social harmony 216; temperament 217
Ambedkar, historicism 176n9
Ambedkar on caste: alternative to the regime of caste 190–1; anatomy of caste and human dignity 183–4; ancestral calling 96; *Annihilation of Caste* 87, 96, 99–103, 107–8; anti-caste struggles 174–5; authority of *śāstras* 104; binding organic filaments among Hindus 188; Brahmanism over Buddhism 100; Brahmins 97–9, 109n13; "The Buddhist Society of India" 106; caste as self-conscious unit 184; caste-based society features 97; caste hierarchy 218; caste definition 95; caste impact on Hindus 184–6; *Castes in India: Their Mechanism, Genesis and Development* 87; caste question 178, 203n1; *Chaturvarnya* 102–3, 187–8; child-marriage 97, 180; class system 180–1; cohesive public domain 186; commands and prohibitions in Hinduism 190; compulsory widowhood 179; conversion within Hinduism 185; democratic ideal 186–7; *Dhamma* 105–6, 178; division of labour 96, 180; division of labourers 183–4; doctrine of karma 106, 108; *Draft of the Indian Constitution* 191; "enclosed class" 95; endogamous marriage 223; endogamy 95, 97, 107, 179; equality and swaraj 178; evils of the caste system 99–101; exogamy 179; fairness 187; gender parity 222–3; genesis, mechanism, and spread of caste 97–9; graded inequality 100–1; *Grahasta* 179–80; Hindu Code Bill 191; Hindu identity and *Shuddi* 187, 204n18; Hindu society survival 102, 110n15; ideal society 101–2; imitation 180–2, 203n8; imitation and excommunication 98; institution of caste 180; inter-dining and inter-caste marriage 189; intermarriage and inter-dining 98, 103; irreconcilability between caste and democracy 186–8; liberty and equality 105, 106, 108, 109, 186–7; Manu Dharma 180; memories of caste oppression 185, 204n16; men in society 184; need for religion 190; notions of caste 103; paradoxical nature of caste system 179–82; political exclusion of the oppressed castes

224; political participation 223–4; political reformers 182; political revolution 101; principle of eugenics 96; principles from the Upanishads 190; racial division 184; racial purity 96; reason and morality 104; recusing Hinduism from caste 189–90; refutation of caste 101–3; religion of rules and religion of principles 104–5; remedy for abolition of caste 103–9; sacred scriptures 182; *saddhamma* (ideal religion) 105; *saṁsāra* (transmigration of soul) 106; sanctity of the *shastras* 189–90; *śāstra*s sanctity 103–4; sati 97, 179; scriptures for interpretation 199; shared culture of India 179, 181–2; social closure in caste system 179; social codes 181; socialists 182–3, 204n14; social practice and norms 181; social reforms 181–3, 203n12; status and occupation of a person 96, 98; sub-castes abolition 103, 189; thesis stages 87; understanding caste 95–7; unpublished work 87; varnadharma 200; varṇa *vs. jāti* 96–7; Vedic conception of varṇa 95–6; woman to twofold marginality 182; *see also Castes in India, Their Mechanism, Genesis and Development; Manusmṛti; The Buddha and His Dhamma*

Ambedkar on Marxism and Buddhism: alienation concept 120–1; binary in exclusivism 113–14; capitalism and Brahmanism 120–2; caste annihilation 119–20; caste hierarchy 118; caste question 116; critique of caste 118–19; Dalit Marxism 111; Dalit Panthers 114–15; dialectics 115; epistemic pluralism 113, 114; Indian Left and caste question 115–20; individualisation of thought 113; intellectual tradition 113, 114; leftist scholars 114; liberal institutions 119; liberalism 115; manual and mental labour 119; ontological wounds 112–13; proletariat and untouchable 120–4; "*Purnachi Poli*" 115; radicalism 111; respective qualities and discursive power 113; social and intellectual activism among Dalits 118; *Social Scientist* 114, 125n6, 125n7; spectre conception 121–4; stage theory of history 115; transcendence of caste 120; untouchability 118–21

Ambedkar on religion: *Annihilation of Caste* 244, 248; anthropological approach 245; caste system 244; *Bhagvad Gita* 222; civilized society 247; code of ordinances 248; dharma 248; evolution of religion 247–8; healthy society 244; Hinduism as "anti-social" 243–4; historical approach 245, 254n7; natural theology 246; philosophy method 246–7; *Philosophy of Hinduism* 244, 246; primacy of religion 244–5; religion and politics 220; religion based on principles 248; savage society 245, 247; scriptural authority 220; social morality 244–5; social solidarity 246; sociological/social theory 245–6, 254n8; spiritual values 216, 228n17; theological approach 246; tradition–modernity dichotomy 244

Anāgārika Dharmapāla 35, 152, 260, 262–5, 267

Anantmurthy, U. R. 121

Anāthapiṇḍaka 265

ancestral calling 89, 96

ancient societies women 133

Anderson, B. 171

Annihilation of Caste xviii, 87, 96, 99–103, 107–8

anuloma: (along the stream) marriages 2; (hypergamy) 129, 130

Aryan decadence 165–6

Aśokāvadāna 57–8

Assalāyanasutta 89, 91

Aṣṭādhyāyī *aphorism*: "alpāctaram" 42–3, 58n3; "*jāterastrīviṣayād ayopadhāt*" 44, 59n5; "nañ" 41–2, 58n2; "*puṃyogād ākhyāyām*" 43, 58n4

Aśvaghoṣa 11, 18, 151, 275

authority of the *Vedas* 158, 252, 275, 276, 278

Avantiputta 32

Bagade, U. 13, 21

Bahenabai xvi, xvii, 12, 158, 289

Bahulkar, S. 9, 12, 21
Bailey, F. G. 248
Bansode, T. 142
Bapu, S. 292
Basaveshvar 7, 14
Base–superstructure 112, 124
Bauddho-Vaishnavas 155–7
begetting of progeny 143–4
Bhāgavata Purāṇa 153, 157, 159n1
Bhagvad Gita 222
Bhagwan Kassapa 34
Bhakti movement 152, 157–9
Bhandarkar, R. G. 152
Bhangi 196, 198
Bhāṭṭa-Mīmāṃsā 9, 40, 49, 53, 54
bhikkhu-centric method of ordination 265
Bilgrami, A. 71
Bimbisāra, King 88, 95
Bodhisattvayāna 8–9
brāhmaṇa (brahmin) 1, 3, 4, 5, 9, 29, 30, 31, 32, 33, 40, 41, 42–4, 46, 47n1, 57, 62, 77, 79, 80, 81, 83n10, 92, 103, 194, 196, 276, 278, 279, 280, 281–5, 286n5, 286n12, 287–90
Brahmanical culture 131–4, 173–4
Brahmanism 7, 13, 21, 91, 92, 166–7; *see also* Hindu society
Brahminhood 54, 91, 92, 97–9, 104, 109n13, 278–82; Aṣṭādhyāyī 41–4, 58n2, 58n3, 58n4, 59n5; genesis and strengthening of 97–9, 109n13; Jaina critique of brahminhood 52–4; Jayanta Bhaṭṭa on 48; Prābhākara Mīmāṃsakas 54–6; *see also* classical Indian philosophy, universals
Buddha 7–14, 19–21, 24n21, 29–37, 62, 66, 73, 74, 75, 77, 78, 80, 87–110, 112–15, 124, 132, 133, 151–9, 161, 162, 165, 166, 168, 171, 172, 175, 178, 191, 218, 219, 220, 222, 224, 229n25, 240, 241, 243, 250, 251, 252, 253, 254, 257–72, 275, 277, 290
The Buddha and His Dhamma 87, 97, 105, 108, 178, 191, 203n2, 219–20, 222, 252–3
Buddhacarita 151, 275
Buddhism 66–7; as false consciousness 164, 175n3; as non-casteist alternative 218–19, 228n20; Bodhisattvayāna/Mahāyāna 8, 9; Brahmanism and 7, 13, 21; caste and gender 11; caste critique 13–19; Dharmakīrti 9; early-Buddhist and Ambedkarian approaches 10; forms of 8, 24n21; *vs.* Jainism 5–6; metaphysical entities 221; as religion 7–8, 258–60; as revolution 165–6, 250–3; Saṅgha 8, 9; Sautrāntika and Yogācāra 9; schools of Buddhism 7–10, 21; secular Buddhism 221–2; Śrāvakayāna/Hīnayāna 8, 9; Tantrayāna 8–10; *see also* Buddhism and Hindu Society; Classical Buddhism, Modern Buddhism, Neo-Buddhism
Buddhism as revolution 250–3
Buddhism and Hindu Society: authority of the Vedas 158; Bauddho-Vaishnavas 155–7; Bhāgavata Purāṇa 153, 157, 159n1; Bhakti movement 152, 157–9; Bhakt Vijay 155, 156; Buddhacarita 151; *Buddhism in India* 157; Buddhist monastic universities 158; decline of Buddhism 151; European scholars on Indian Buddhism 152; Gītagovinda 153; Jñāneśvar 158; Mahānubhāva cult 152; *Mahāvaṃso* 156; *Mānasollāsa* of Someśvara Cālukya 153–4, 159n3; medieval India 11–12; medieval religious cults 152–4, 157; *Merutantra* 154; *Puṇḍalīka Caritra* of the *Pāṇḍuranga Māhātmya* 154; Śaṅkarācārya 158; *Śāṅkaradigvijaya* of Mādhava Vidyāraṇya 158; Saundarananda 151; *Śrīrāmasahasranāma* 155; Tukārām 154–6; "Tukaram: A Study of Hinduism" 156; Vaiṣṇavism 151; Vārakarī Sampradāya 157; *Varṇāśramadharma* 158; Viṣṇu Purāṇa 153, 159n1; Viṭṭhal/Viṭhobā 153–5
Buddhist monastic universities 158
Buddhist past as cultural conflict: Ambedkar historicism 172–5, 176n9; Aryan decadence 165–6; Brahmanism 166–7; counter-revolution by Brahminism 166–7; cultural analytics 168; economic and non-economic power plots 163–4; economic class 163, 175n2; existence of material

soul 161; Hindu inheritance 161; historical materialism 169–70; human action 170; legal sanctions and caste system 163; Marxist economism 162–3, 175n1; nationalist movement 162; positivist variety of Marxism 170, 176n6; power source and authority 163–4; principled forgetfulness in mythic engagement 171–2; psychosis of caste hatred 169; religion and sociality 163–4; socio-religious revolution 165; *see also* History, Religion
Buddhist revolution 165–6
Buddhist Text Society 152
Burke, E. 237

Caṇḍālas 34–5, 37n36
capitalism and Brahmanism 120–2
caste 127; class mechanism in exploitation and domination 163; hierarchy and patriarchy 166–7; struggle 169; subaltern 170–2
caste-based costumes and customs 138–40
caste-class discrimination 78–9
caste identity 1, 3, 65–75, 174–5
caste *panchayat* 135–6
caste question 116; *see also* Ambedkar Marxism and Buddhism
Castes in India: Their Mechanism, Genesis and Development 87, 248
caste system 8, 10, 20, 29–37, 248–50; *see also Kālacakratantra* (KC)
"*Catu-parisā*" 29
cause–effect relation 263
Chakravarty, Uma36
characteristics of a brāhmaṇa 47–8, 59n13–59n20, 284–5
Chaturvarnya 40, 102–3, 187–8
Chaudhari, J. 142
child marriage 97, 141, 180
classical Buddhism 8, 219–20; *Vimalaprabhā* and *Kālacakra* tantra 77–83
classical Indian philosophy: 40–62; authority of the vedic sentence 46–7, 59n9; Avadāna texts 56–8, 61n44, 61n49; Bhāṭṭa Mīmāṃsā 48–9; Brahminical schools 40; Buddhist views on universals 48–51; Dharmakīrti 51; *dravyatva* and *guṇatva* 55; Jaina critique of brahminhood 52–4; Nyāya and Vaiśeṣika schools 48–51; *Nyāyamañjarī* 48; Prābhākara Mīmāṃsakas on brahminhood 54–6, 61n42; *Pramāṇavārttika* 51, 60n24; *Pratyakṣasūtra* 45; *Ślokavārttika* 45–6; *Tantravārttika* 46–7; *see also* Brahminhood, universals
classless and casteless society 10–11
communism 267
communitarianism 254
compulsory widowhood 179
conduct 6, 32, 41, 42, 43, 46, 47, 78, 186, 212, 225, 275, 276, 280, 284
construction of religion 237–41
conversion within Hinduism 185
corrupt words 79
counter-revolution by Brahmanism 166–7
critiques of caste: Ambedkar on Marxism and Buddhism 118–19; dogma of authenticity 17; Gandhi and Ambedkar approaches 15–17; Hindu nationalism 18–19; inter-caste marriage 16; non-vedic reformer 14; religious texts 16–17; truth and non-violence 17; varṇa and caste distinction model 15–17; V. D. Savarkar's model 18–19; vedāntic/spiritual/saintly model 14–15, 24n23; vedic reformer 13; *see also* Ambedkar and Radhakrishnan
Cunningham, A. 152

Dalai Lama 260, 263, 266, 268
Dalit-Bahujan 203n10, 235, 239, 240, 243, 250
Dalit identity 139, 141
Dalit Mahila Federation 138, 140–1
Dalit Marxism 111, 112
Dalit modernity: *see* Modernity
Dalit Panthers 114–15
Dalit women 11, 130, 131, 138–43
Darwinian Theory of Evolution 263
Dasa-Shudra Slavery(Patil) 133
Das, S. C. 152
Dayanand Saraswati, Swami 15–17, 96
democracy birth 96
democratic ideal 186–7
democratic principles 95
democratization 264–5

Deokar, M. A. 10, 15, 21
dependent origination 166
Derde, W. 239
devdasi 130, 142–3, 146n3, 146n8
Dewey, J. 96, 171, 191, 237, 244
dhamma 18–19, 32, 105–6, 142, 178, 215, 219, 252–3, 259–60
Dharmakīrti 9, 49, 51, 74, 276, 287
Dhere, R. C. 12, 21, 154
Diñnāga 9, 49, 74
divine origin of four varṇas 80–1, 83n9, 90
division of labour 96, 183–4
doctrine of wisdom 252–3
doctrines of Vedas 80–2, 83n11
dogma of authenticity 17
Dongre, S. 140
dowry 141
Draft of the Indian Constitution 191
Dumont, L. 248
Durkheim, E. 163

early Buddhism on caste: *Ambaṭṭha sutta* 34; Anagarika Dharmapala 35; ancestral calling 89; *arhathood* 34; *ārya* and *dāsa* 33; *Assalāyanasutta* 89, 91; *Assalāyanasutta* of the *Majjhimanikāya* 32–3; Brāhmanas 29; Caṇḍālas 34–5, 37n36; *Citta-Sambhūta Jātaka* 35; *Dhamma*/righteousness 32; *Dīghanikāya* 29, 36n5; discrepancies 34–5; discrimination 30–1; *Esukārīsutta* 89, 92; evils of the caste system 90–1; "Four-Fold Assembly"/"*Catu-parisā*" 29; Gahapatis 29; genesis, mechanism and spread of caste 89–90; *gotra* 88, 109n8; graded inequality 90; guiding principles of life 93, 109n10; institution of caste 91; intellectual class of society 93; inter-caste marriages 95; *jāti* 31; **kamma** 30, 31; Khattiyas 29; later degenerations 34–5; *Lohiccasutta* 89, 92; *Madhurasutta* 92; *Mahāpadāna sutta* 34, 37n25; *Mahāparinibbānasutta* 29; *Majjhima-Nikāya* 35; mind 93; monks and nuns 34; morality and knowledge 33–4, 37n24; Pāli *Tipiṭaka* 87; P. L. Narasu 35; refutation of caste 91–3; remedy for abolition of caste 93–5; right to education 90; right to knowledge 89, 90, 92; safeguards and healthy practices against discrimination 94; Saṅgha to all 35, 93–4, 109n11; *śāstras* and divine authority 93; self-esteem 91; social justice 29–30; social order 29; superiority of Brahmins 32–3; *Suttanipāta* xv, 34, 37n26; Swami Vivekananda 35; *Tipiṭaka* 29; varnas 29, 36n1; varṇa and *jāti* 88, 109n1; *Vāseṭṭhasutta* 91; *Vāseṭṭha sutta* of the *Sutta Nipāta* 31
economic and non-economic power plots 163–4
education for girls 144
Ekanath 12, 154, 290
Emperor Aśoka 57, 58
endogamy 89, 95, 97, 107, 127, 179
enforced celibacy 128
enforced widowhood 128
engaged Buddhism 7, 257–8, 266–7
Engels, F. 114
epistemic: pluralism 113, 114; *pramāṇas* 71, 73
equality 92
equality and freedom 129, 226, 228n17
essence of castes 127
essentialism 9, 21, 66, 68, 72, 74, 75
Esukārī 89, 97
Esukārīsutta 89, 92
existence 70–2, 74
exogamy 179

"Four-Fold Assembly"/"*Catu-parisā*" 29

Gandhi, M. K. 15–17, 96, 104, 187; and Ambedkar approaches 15–17
Gandhi, M. R. 114, 118
Gandhi on caste: hereditary/traditional calling 193–4; law of conservation of energy 193–4, 204n22; moral code 199; reading of the shastras 200; Satyagraha Ashram Trust 192–3; scriptures for interpretation 199; shastras 199; shudra dharma 194; untouchability 192, 194–8; *varnashramadharma* 191, 194; *varna* system 193–4, 199–200; *Varnavyavastha* 192; *see also* Ambedkar on caste
Ganguli, D. 171
Gargi-Maitreyi 133

gatis 4–5, 5
Gavali, N. 139
Gelders, R. 239
gender, caste and 11
gender equality 267–8
gender injustice 240
Gītagovinda 153
Goenka, S. N. 259, 263, 264
Gokhale, P. 74, 220
Goldenweizer, A. A. 87
Gombrich, R. F. 35
Goreh, N. 156
Gore, M. S. 167
gotra 88, 109n8
graded inequality 2–3, 22n6, 90, 100–1
Grahasta 179–80
Grant, A. 156
Gross, R. 268
Guha, R. 220
Guhyasamājatantra 77
guiding principles of life 93, 109n10
guṇa 3–4, 23n9
Guru, G. 10, 11, 21

Habermas, J. 65, 67, 171
Hegel 114
hereditary/traditional calling 193–4
Hewavitame, D. 152
Hindu–Muslim unity 198
Hīnayāna 8–9, 261
Hind Swaraj 238
Hindu Code Bill 134–8, 191, 222–3
Hindu *dharma* 217–18
Hindu inheritance 161
Hinduism 235, 249–50; Hindu *dharma* as rules of segregation 217–18; Hinduism without solidarity 217; as spiritualism 235
Hindu nationalism 18–19
Hindu Personal Law 223
Hindu society: Advaita-Vedānta 7; *Bhagavadgītā* 3; Buddhism 5–7; *dharma* 6; divine origination of caste order 3; *gatis* 4–5, 5; God and karma faith 3–5, 5; "graded inequality" 2–3, 22n6; *guṇa* 3–4, 23n9; inequalities 1–2; Jainism 5–6; Lokāyata 5; Manu categorisation of species 4–5, 5; non-egalitarian and egalitarian tradition 6–7; non-vedic tradition 5; occupation 1; *Puruṣasūkta* of *Ṛgveda* 3; qualities and actions division of varnas 3–4, 23n8; *rajoguṇa* 3; *sahaja-karma* 3–4; saint tradition 6–7, 24n20; *sattvaguṇa* 3; socio-religious obligations 6; survival 102, 110n15; *tamoguṇa* 3; varṇa-caste system 1–2, 22n3
Hindu View of Life (1927) 225
history: homogenization of Indian 162; status-quoist 173; mythographic 171–2; positivist method 171, 176n8; socio-historical analysis 168
historicism 176n9
historiography 161, 173–4; colonial 161; nationalist school 161
homogenization of Indian history 162
Hudson, B. H. 287
human dignity and self-respect 234, 235
humane and democratic practices 234–5

ideal religion 105, 251, 258
ideal society 101–2
identity 70–3, 235; ascriptions 70
imposed property 48, 54; *see also* universals
incarnation 12, 78, 111, 151–8, 271
Indian Left and caste question: caste annihilation and political agenda 117, 119; caste hierarchy 118; class category 120; communalism 116–17, 125n11; critique of caste 118–19; Dalit agenda 116–17; independent theoretical status 117–18; leftist historians 118; liberalism 115; material exploitation 117; political power limits 118; regional response to caste question 116; social and intellectual activism among Dalits 118; working-class solidarity 116–17
individual perfection: *see* Radhakrishnan on caste
Indrabhūti 78
institution of caste 91
intellectual tradition 235
inter-caste marriage 2, 16, 95
intermarriage and inter-dining 98, 103
Islamic religious nationalist movements 233

Jadhav, N. 220, 221
Jahaksulabha 133
Jaina 9, 23n17, 52, 53, 54, 75n5, 153, 280n13, 286n7
Janābāi 154
jāti 31
jātibādhakas 50, 60n23
"*Jatyucchedaka Nibandha*" (*Caste-eradicating Essays,* Savarkar) 18
Jayanta-Bhaṭṭa 48, 58
Jñānasārasamuccaya 262, 272n2
Jñāneśvar 158

Kabir 10, 12
Kālacakratantra (KC) 10, 21, 90; Abridged Tantra 78; Concise *Kālacakratantra (laghukālacakratantra)* 78–9; Kalkin 78; King Sucandra 78; last Buddhist Tantric works 77; *Paramādibuddha* 78; path of enlightenment 77; Tantric ritual 77; Vajra-family initiation 78; varṇas in Kali age 80, 82n7; *see also Vimalaprabhā* (VP)
Kalicharan, M. 139
Kalkin 78
Kamble, S. J. 139
kamma 13, 30, 31
Kant, I. 20, 224–6
Kant: Kantian resonance 224–7; Kantian morality 224–5; priesthood 225–6; rational theology 226
karma 3, 5–6, 90, 106, 108; Buddhism 5–6; doctrine 4, 198; *gatis* 4; hierarchical social order 4; Jainism 5–6; Manu categorisation of species 4–5, 5; mechanism 4; *Sāṅkhya* categories 4
Keluskar, K. A. 10, 152
Ketkar, S. V. 162
Keune, J. M. 157
Kierkegaard, S. 113, 114
Kishwar, M. 137
Kosambi, D. 35, 92, 95, 152, 162, 167, 268
Kotangale, R. 142
Krishan, Y. 73
kṣatriya 1, 5, 7, 9, 29, 30, 40, 41, 43, 44, 46, 47, 57, 61n45, 62, 83n7, 88, 92, 95, 103, 276, 279, 282, 283, 288
Kumar, A. 252
Kumar, B. 8, 20, 73
Kumārila-Bhaṭṭa 9, 45–8, 53
Kumar, P. K. 14, 20, 21

Lakṣmīṅkarā 78
language 71, 72, 77, 79–80, 82n5; essentialism 68–9; features 67; fixed designations 71; immutable structure 72; issue of 69; knowledge and language 65; particulars 68; permanence 68; stability 68
law of conservation of energy 193–4, 204n22
law of imitation 180–2, 203n8
leftist scholars 114; *see also* Indian Left and caste question
liberal capitalism 266
liberalism 115, 174; secularism 223
liberal view 223–4
liberty and equality 186–7; and fraternity 105, 106, 108, 109
Locke, J. 70
Lohicca 89, 92
Lokāyata 5
Lokhande, N. M. 139

MacIntyre, A. 242
Maha Bodhi Society 152
Mahadevan, K. 17, 19, 21
Mahākaccāna 32, 33
Mahākaccāyana 92
Mahānubhāva 22, 152, 288–9
Maharaj, S. 114, 139
Mahāyāna 8–9, 77, 261
Mahāyāna Buddhism 9, 11, 66–7
Maitreyi 133
Mantrayāna 77, 82n1
manual and mental labour 119
Manu Dharma 180
Manusmriti 133–4; a legal code 98–100
Marxism 111, 266–7; *see also* Ambedkar on Marxism and Buddhism
Marxist economism 162–3, 175n1
Marx, K. 266
medieval religious cults 152–4, 157
meditation 270
men in society 184
mind 93
Mitra, R. 152
mixed marriages 129–30
Mleccha Dharma 82

modern Buddhism 13, 19–20, 251, 257–72; affinity to science 262–3; bhikkhu-centric method of ordination 265; Buddhism as a religion 258–60; caste 270, 272n3; combat with Brahmanism 271; communism 267; Darwinian Theory of Evolution 263; democratization 264–5; Dhamma and God 259–60; engaged Buddhism 257–8, 266–7; gender equality 267–8; Hīnayāna 261; *vs.* Hinduism 271; ideal religion 258; inclusion of 22; vows 270–1; inclusivism 271; liberal capitalism 266; Mahāyāna 261; Marxism 266–7; mass conversion to Buddhism 257; meditation 270; metaphysical and practical levels 271; moral and democratic values 269; neo-traditional Buddhism 262; *Nirvāṇa* 265; non-dogmatic approach 262–3; *partātyasamutpàda* 263, 264; peace, non-violence and simplicity 270, 272n4; *prajñā* and *karuṇā* 261; primacy of mind 269; Protestantism 264–5; psychology of Buddhism 263; rational approach 258, 262–3; reconstruction of Buddhism 257; sectarian divisions within Buddhism 261–2; sectarian religions 259–60; secularism (this-worldliness) 264; Semitic conception of religion 258; social activity 270; status of women 267–9; śūnyatā 261; theologians 258; Theravāda tradition 261, 262; trans-traditional Buddhism 262; universal love 269; upāsaka 265
modernity 19, 20, 21, 120, 218, 219, 227, 233–54
morality 18, 19, 20, 34, 100, 104, 105, 107, 108, 129, 156, 166, 169, 188, 190, 199, 211, 215, 217, 218, 219, 221, 222, 223–7, 229n33, 234, 238, 241–5, 247, 250, 251, 252, 253, 260
moral nuances of Buddhism 168–9
More, R. B. 117
Mukhopadhyay, S. 11
mythographic history 171–2

Nāgrjuna 69
Nanak, Guru 7, 12, 14, 104
nañ-tatpuruṣa 41–2, 58n2
NaradaThero 259
Narasu, P. L. 14, 35, 152, 169, 240, 241, 249, 250, 253
Narayanaguru 7, 14
Nāthacult/sect 22, 291
natural theology 246
Navayāna xvii, 7, 13, 19, 20, 21, 251, 261
Navayana Buddhism 251
Neo-Buddhism 10–11, 13, 19–21; Buddhism and Marxism 111; classless and casteless society 10–11, 22; Vows 142, 270–1; *see also* Ambedkar on Marxism and Buddhism; Navayāna
neo-traditional Buddhism 262
Nhat Hanh 261
Nirvāṇa 265
*nirvasitaśūdra*s 40
non-dogmatic approach 262–3
non-vedic reformer 14
notions of caste 103
Nyāyamañjarī 48
Nyāya system 67, 69
Nyāya-Vaiśeṣika 40, 49, 55

Obeyesekere, G. 264
Olcott, H. 152
Omvedt, G. 129, 130, 157, 168
ontological nature of society 65
ontological status to universals 9
ontological wounds 112–13
order of society 65
Orientalism 239–40
orthodoxy and orthopraxy 66, 75n1; Other71

Padwal, T. T. 12, 292
Pali Text Society 152
Pande, G. C. 36
Pāṇinian system of grammar 79
paradoxical nature of caste system 179–82
Paramādibuddha 78
Pāramitānaya 77
Pardeshi, P. 11, 21
"Parivraja" 132–3
partītyasamutpāda 263, 264; *see also* Dependent origination
Pasendi Kosala 95
Patañjali 41, 43, 44, 79
path of enlightenment 77
Patil, I. 140

Patil, S. 114, 168; *Dasa-Shudra Slavery* 133
patriarchy: age-mismatched marriages 128–9; All India Women's Conference (AIWC) 137; Ambedkar opposition to atrocity against women 142–3; ancient societies women 133; *anuloma* (hypergamy) 129, 130; begetting of progeny 143–4; birth of daughter as sorrow 131–2; Brahmanical culture 131–4; Brahmanical patriarchy 222–3; Buddha approach 132–4; caste-based costumes and customs 138–40; caste identity 138; caste *panchayat* 135–6; caste system and subordination of women 130–1; child marriage 141; Dalit and Adivasi women exploitation 131; Dalit identity 139, 141; Dalit Mahila Federation 138, 140–1; *Dasa-Shudra Slavery* 133; devdasi 130, 142–3, 146n3, 146n8; Dhamma 142; dowry 141; economic freedom 137; education for girls 144; endogamous marriage 223; endogamy 127; enforced celibacy 128; enforced widowhood 128; free and compulsory primary education 142; gender parity 222–3; The Hindu Code Bill 222–3, 134–8; Hindu Personal Law 223; identities 138–9; Mahad Satyagraha 138; Mahatma Phule legacy 143–4; *Manusmriti* 133–4; mixed marriages 129–30; non-Brahmanical path of women liberation 144–5; orphaned children and unwed mothers 143; "Parivraja" 132–3; Phule-Ambedkarism 130; practice of endogamy 127–9; *pratiloma* (hypogamy) 129–30; rights to divorce 135; right to freedom 133; right to knowledge 132–4; right to property 134–5; *The Rise and Fall of Hindu Women* 131, 143; *sati* 128; self-respect of Dalits 142; sex ratio 128; spiritual knowledge 132; temple entry 139, 141; untouchable women consciousness 138–42; women as gateways to caste system 127–30
peace, non-violence and simplicity 270, 272n4
Periyar, R. N. 14, 240, 249
Phule, J. 10, 14, 114, 139, 143, 182, 240, 249
positivist method of history 171, 176n8
positivist variety of Marxism 170, 176n6
postmodernism 235–6
Prabhācandrasūri 9
Prābhākara Mīmāṃsakas 48, 54–6
prajñā and *karuṇā* 261
Prakrit languages 80, 82n5
pratiloma (hypogamy) 2, 129–30
pre-ordained social roles 216–17
'priests'239
primacy of mind 269
principle of eugenics 96
principle of inevitability 172
principles from the Upanishads 190
Prinsep, J. 152
proletariat and untouchable 120–4
Protestantism 264–5
psychology of Buddhism 263
puṃyogād ākhyāyām 43, 58n4
Puṇḍalīka Caritra of the *Pāṇḍuranga Māhātmya* 154
Puṇḍarīka 78, 79
puruṣa 283, 284
Puṣkarasārin 56

racial purity 96
Radhakrishnan on caste: caste-based social relations 213; division for labour 212; egalitarianism 214; Hindu socio-religious order 213–14, 228n12; human perfection and aptitude 213, 214; individualistic approach 215; notion of caste hierarchy 212–13, 227n7; patriarchal strands 212; privileged caste heroism 211–12; temperament 217; women in Hinduism 223
Radhakrishnan on religion: Hindu socio-religious order 213–14, 228n12; human perfection and aptitude 213, 214; individualistic approach 215; morality and religion 215–16; notion of religion 212; patriarchal strands 212; religion as self-realization 213–14; religion *vs.* politics 215, 228n14; spiritual conception of society 213; women in Hinduism 223

Radhakrishnan, S. 17–19, 21, 222, 223, 225–7; model of 17–18
radicalism 111
Rai, R. R. 12
rajoguṇa 3
Ranade, M. G. 162
rational approach 258, 262–3
realism 65–75
reconstruction of Buddhism 257; alternative religions for Hinduism 240; Anglicists 239; assimilation of Buddhism with Brahmanism 250; caste system 248–50; Conservatives 237; Dalit identification with Buddhism 241; Dhamma of Buddha 252–3; doctrine of wisdom 252–3; gender injustice 240; human dignity and self-respect 234, 235; humane and democratic practices 234–5; ideal of religion 251; indigenous traditions 233, 236; institutional religion 237; intellectual tradition 235; liberalism 233, 236–7; moral order and social imaginary 242–3; principles of utility and justice 234; radical individualism 242; reasons for choice of Buddhism 251–2; righteous social life 238; 'saddhamma' of Buddhism 234; *sangha* for all 251; social life and religious life 248, 249; social rationality 236; society 244; socio-cultural rationality 241; speculative and scientific philosophy 237; structural injustice 233; tradition 237, 238; tradition–modernity dichotomy 237–41; understanding of religion 236–7; *see also* Hinduism, Religion, Modern Buddhism, Modernity
reconstruction of caste 216–17
reformers 3, 8, 10, 12, 13–16, 19, 22, 23n16, 104, 139, 152, 162, 166, 181, 182, 183, 185, 190, 203n12, 204n13, 223, 229n25, 238, 239, 240, 249, 262, 267, 291–2
religion 224–7, 230n37, 237–41; Ambedkar understanding of religion 243–8; economic order 162–3; of endurance and change 236; ethical religion 225, 226; faith 236; ideal religion 105; and morality 215–16, 224; morality and righteous social life 234; and sociality 163–4; as personal and caste as social 17–18; of principles 104–5; as protest against colonial domination 238–9; religious (socio-cultural) power plot of history 164; religious sanctions and caste system 163; religious slavery 164–5; religiousness 238; socio-cultural analysis 167–8 ; religious reform 164, 224, 249, 267; religious slavery 164–5; religious texts 16–17
Rhys David, T. W. 152, 161
Ricœur, P. 164
Righteousness *see* Dhamma
right to divorce 135
right to education 90
right to freedom 133
right to knowledge 89, 90, 92, 132–4
right to property 134–5
The Rise and Fall of Hindu Women(Ambedkar) 131, 143
Rodrigues, V. 15, 16, 21
Root-tantra *(mūlatantra)* 78
Rorty, R. 237
Roy, R. R. 291
Russell, B. 237
Ryan, A. 237

sahaja-karma 3–4
sāmānyalakṣaṇa vs. svalakṣaṇa 69–70, 75n3
saṁsāra (transmigration of soul) 106
saṃvṛti-satya and *paramārthataḥsatya* 73
Saṅgha 8–9, 93–4, 109n11
Ṣangharakshita 260, 262, 265
Śaṅkarācārya 133, 158
Śāṅkaradigvijaya of Mādhava Vidyāraṇya 158
Sanskrit 77, 79–80
Sarahapāda 77
Ṣarao, K. T. S. 36
Śārdūlakarṇāvadāna 56–7
Sarkar, S. 240
śāstras 93, 103–4, 189–90, 199
Sastri, H. P. 152
satī 97, 128, 179
sattvaguṇa 3
Satyagraha Ashram Trust 192–3
Saundarananda 151
Sautrāntika 9
Savarkar, V. D. 12, 18–19, 162, 292
Savitribai 143
schools of Buddhism 7–10

science 20, 21, 96, 113, 175n3, 176n8, 218, 226, 227, 236, 244, 245, 246, 247, 254, 258, 262–3
scriptural authority 220
sectarian divisions within Buddhism 261–2
sectarian religions 259–60
secular Buddhism 221–2
secularism (this-worldliness) 264
Sen, P. K. 9, 21, 71
sex ratio 128
shared culture of India 179, 181–2
Sharma, R. S. 36
Shastras Sectarian division 261–2
Shinde, T. 114
Shinde, V. R. 114, 139
Shuddi 187, 204n18
shudra dharma 194
Siddhācārya Aśvaghoṣa 11, 275, 277
Singaravelu, M. 241
Singh, S. 11, 21
Sivaraksa, S. 270
Skaria, A. 224
Ślokavārttika 45–6
smṛtis 46, 278, 286n13
social collectivities 70–1
social democracy 218, 228n19
socialism 174; economic well-being 224
socialist reform 101, 102
socialists 182–3, 204n14, 224
social rationality 236
Social Scientist 114, 125n6, 125n7
socio-cultural analysis 167–8
spectre conception 121–4
spiritual values 216, 228n17
Śrāvakayāna 8–9
Śrīrāmasahasranāma 155
stage theory of history 115
status and occupation of a person 96, 98
status of women 133, 223, 258, 267–9
Stevenson, J. 155–7
sub-castes abolition 103, 189
subordination of women 127, 130, 131–2, 135, 137, 138, 144, 145, 251
Sucandra, King 78
Śuddhodana 95
śūdra 40, 281–2; *see also* Shudra
Sulak Sivaraksa 261
Sundarikabhāradvāja 88
Śūnyatā 261
Śūnyavāda philosophy 72–5
surplus man 11, 128, 129, 179, 180
surplus woman 11, 128, 179

tamoguṇa 3
Tantravārttika 46–7
Tantrayāna 8–10
Tantric Buddhism 77, 79
Tantric masters 77–8
Tantric ritual 77
Tarde, G. 180
Taylor, C. 242, 254
temperament 217
temple entry 139, 141
Thakur, R. 136, 137
Thakur, V. K. 36
Thapar, R. 239, 240
Thassar, I. 14, 240, 241, 249, 250, 253
theistic religion 18
theory of change/impermanence 172
Theravāda tradition 261, 262
Thich Nhat Hanh 259, 261, 266
Tipiṭaka 29
Tisgāvkar, D. S. 154
traditional Hindu social order 234
trans-traditional Buddhism 262
Trevor Ling 35
Triśaṅku 56
truth and non-violence 17
Tukārām 154–6

universal ethics of Buddhism 169
universal love 269
universals 40–1, 44–52, 54, 55, 59n8, 60n29, 68–9; *aupādhika* 54; Buddhist views on 48–51; common properties and abstract properties 50, 55; configuration (*ākṛti*) 55; "cross-division" (*sāṅkarya*) 50; Kumārila Bhaṭṭa on universals and 45–8; natural properties 40; Nyāya-Vaiśeṣika and Buddhist views on universals 48–51; ontological status to universals 9
untouchability 2, 118–21, 167, 175n5; Bhangi 196, 198; conversion to non-Hindu religions 198; despicable treatment 195; free India 197; Hinduism 192, 195–6; Indian segregation in the British empire 197; reparation 195, 205n24; as un-Hindu 194, 204n23
unwed mothers 143
upādhi 48, 50, 51, 54, 55
Upāli 30, 35
upāsaka 265

Vaiṣṇavism 151
vaiśya 1, 3, 4, 6, 23n18, 29, 30, 36n4, 40, 43, 44, 47, 58, 62, 80, 82n7, 83n7, 88, 92, 95, 103, 109n12, 194, 276, 279, 280, 281, 283, 288
Vajra-family initiation 78
Vajrasūcī xvi, 11–12, 21–2; actions are brāhmaṇa 280, 286n9; Ādinātha-Bhairava 291; Aśvaghoṣa 287; author 275–7; authority of the *Vedas* 278; *Bhaviṣyapurāṇa* and 288; *cāṇḍāla* 281; Dadoba Pandurang 292; external evidences 275–6; internal evidences 276–7; Mahānubhāva Sect 288–9; meaning 287; *Nāthalīlāmṛta* 291; New Upaniṣads 287; *puruṣa* 283, 284; Raja Rammohan Roy 291; Shri Shyamraj 290–1; Siddhācārya Aśvaghoṣa 275, 277; and social reformers 291–2; Subaji Bapu 292; *śūdra* 281–2; synopsis 287–8; Tukaramtatya Padwal 292; V. D. Savarkar 292; and Warkari saints 289–90
Vajrasūcikopaniṣat 22
Vajrayāna 77
Valangekar, G. 139
Vārakarī Sampradāya 157
varṇas 80–1, 82n7, 83n9, 275, 283–4; *Bhagavadgītā* 3; Brahmanism and priest craft 195–6; and caste distinction model 15–17; *dharma* 6; divine origination of caste order 3; graded inequality 2–3; *guṇa* 3–4; inequalities 1–2, 22n3; and *jāti* 88, 109n1; Manu categorisation of species 4–5, 5; *Puruṣasūkta* of *Ṛgveda* 3; qualities and actions division of varnas 3–4, 23n8; theory 197–8, 205n26
varnashramadharma 158, 191, 194
vedāntic/spiritual/saintly model 14–15, 24n23
Vedas 5, 10, 11, 12, 13, 14, 15, 18, 22n2, 23n19, 24n25, 31, 41, 43, 51, 54, 56, 71, 77, 79, 80, 81–2, 83n11, 104, 132, 133, 154, 158, 166, 204n12, 248, 250, 252, 254n7, 275, 276, 278, 280, 281, 283–5
Vedic Dharma 81–2, 83n12
vedic reformer 13
Verma, A. 9, 21
Vimalaprabhā (VP) 9–10; caste-class discrimination 78–9; King Yaśas 78–9; Mleccha Dharma 82; prophesy of the Buddha 78; Puṇḍarīka 79; right to education deprivation 90
Viṣṇu Purāṇa 153, 159n1
Viṭṭhal/Viṭhobā 153–5
Vivekananda, Swami 14, 35
Voltaire 237
vrātya 54, 61n38
Vudyabhushan, S. C. 152

Wheel of Law 77
Wilhelm, J. 114
Winternitz, M. 33

Yajnavalkya 133
Yaśas, King 78, 79
Yogācāra 8, 9

Printed in the United States
By Bookmasters